Calling the Station Home

Calling the Station Home

Place and Identity in New Zealand's High Country

Michèle D. Dominy

ROWMAN & LITTLEFIELD PUBLISHERS, INC.
Lanham • Boulder • New York • Oxford

ROWMAN & LITTLEFIELD PUBLISHERS, INC.

Published in the United States of America
by Rowman & Littlefield Publishers, Inc.
4720 Boston Way, Lanham, Maryland 20706
http://www.rowmanlittlefield.com

12 Hid's Copse Road, Cumnor Hill, Oxford OX2 9JJ, England

British Library Cataloguing in Publication Information Available

Library of Congress Cataloging-in-Publication Data

Dominy, Michèle D., 1953–
    Calling the station home : place and identity in New Zealand's high country /
Michèle D. Dominy.
        p. cm.
    Includes bibliographical references and index.
    ISBN 0-7425-0951-6 (cloth : alk. paper) — ISBN 0-7425-0952-4 (pbk. : alk. paper)
    1. South Island (N.Z.)—Rural conditions. 2. Sheep ranches—Social aspects—New
Zealand—South Island. 3. Spatial behavior—New Zealand—South Island. 4. Group
identity—New Zealand—South Island. 5. Human geography—New Zealand—South
Island. I. Title.

HN930.5.S68 D65 2001
307.72'09937—dc21

                                                                    00-062639
Printed in the United States of America

To Marty

Contents

Illustrations

Figures

Tables

Maps

Photographs

Acknowledgments

Gratefully, I acknowledge support from the Wenner-Gren Foundation for Anthropological Research (Grant 5128); from Bard College for Professional Development Grants, Faculty Research and Travel Grants, an Asher Edelman Release-Time Grant, and a Bard Council Research Grant; and from the University of Canberra for residency as a research scholar at the Cultural Heritage Research Centre in 1995. The University of Canterbury Library, Canterbury Public Library, Canterbury Museum, United States Library of Congress, and National Library of Australia provided generous access to their collections. I thank Jane Dougall and Jane Hryshko of the Stevenson Libraries of Bard College for resourcefully addressing my reference requests. I appreciate the rich responses of many remarkable anthropology undergraduates in class, but especially Suzin Hagar, Jonathan Hearn, Marriam Leve, Joan Mielke, and Janice Sandwick, who have transcribed field notes and tapes, proofread, and tracked down references. Carol Brener copyedited the manuscript with a characteristically sharp eye for detail.

Some of this material has been discussed in seminars or presented in lectures at various universities and academic conferences, including the Australian National University, Cornell University, Lincoln University, the University of Canberra, the University of Canterbury, the Association for Social Anthropology in Oceania, the American Anthropological Association, the American Ethnological Society, the East Asia Pacific Mountain Lands Conference, and the Western Social Science Association. The following organizers, participants, discussants, colleagues, and editors provided productive commentary: Terri Cundy Aihoshi, Mark Auslander, Sanjib Baruah, Claudia Bell, David Beriss, Mario Bick, Don Brenneis, Caroline Brettell, Diana deG. Brown, Laurence Carucci, Ann Chowning, Nicholas Dirks, Hastings Donnan, Michael Donovan, Brian Egloff, John Fout, Roger Good, F. Allan Hanson, Laurie Hart, Terry Hays, James Hess, Eric Hirsch, Jeannette Hope, Alan Howard, Thomas Isern, Margaret Jolly, Robert Kaplan, Nancy Leonard, Michael Lieber, Christopher Lindner, Lamont Lindstrom, Jocelyn Linnekin, Cluny Macpherson, Mac Marshall, Judith Modell, Fred Myers, Laurie Patton, Nicolas Peterson, Lin Poyer, Jan Rensel, Miles Richardson, William Renwick, Margaret Rodman, Steven

Sangren, Karen Sinclair, Karen Sullivan, Nicholas Thomas, Robert Tonkinson, Geoffrey White, and Elie Yarden. Elvin Hatch thoughtfully read and commented on a full draft of the manuscript. I alone am responsible for all deficiencies.

I thank New Zealand scholars—Garth Cant, John Fairweather, Bob Hall, John Hayward, I. G. Chris Kerr, Alison Kuiper, Kon Kuiper, Rosemary du Plessis, Kevin O'Connor, Simon Swaffield, Nick Taylor, and Bill Willmott—for their advice and interest in my work. The Kuiper family has provided friendship, insight, and hospitality since I first began my work in Aotearoa/New Zealand in 1979. Jocelyn Armstrong kindly led me to Brian Lill of New Zealand Federated Farmers who directed me "up the gorge."

Guy Gallo calmly interrupted his own writing to take "Word for Windows to the edge" in skillfully creating macros and adapting the illustrations and tables for me. I thank Jeannine Dominy for her perceptivity. I thank Marty Gearhart for her constancy.

The Rakaia gorge families are as stunning with their generosity as their country is stunning in its expanse. Fieldworkers exist by the grace of the people with whom they work, and to the Redcliffs, Glenrock, Glenaan, Glenariffe, Double Hill, Glenfalloch, and Manuka Point families and their extended families, as well as many other South Island high-country families from Marlborough to Southland, I owe the possibility of this work. Hamish and Belinda Ensor have sustained me in every way, respecting my intentions, trusting my interpretations, and understanding that anthropology is to me as animal husbandry and stewardship of the land is to them.

Permissions

by permission of Reed Publishing New Zealand Ltd.; "Glenmark" by Basil Dowling from *The Unreturning Native and Other Poems*. Copyright © 1973. Reprinted by permission of Nag's Head Press; *A State of Siege* by Janet Frame. Copyright © 1966, 1980 Janet Frame. Reprinted by permission of George Braziller Inc. as U.S. publisher and Curtis Brown (Australia) Pty. Ltd. Sydney for the rest of the world; *Down from the Tussock Ranges* by David McLeod. Copyright © 1980 by David McLeod. Reprinted by permission of Penguin Books New Zealand; *Died in the Wool* by Ngaio Marsh. Copyright © 1973. Reprinted by permission of Little, Brown and Company; N*gai Tahu Claim Report 1991* by the Waitangi Tribunal. Copyright © 1991 Crown. Reprinted by permission of the New Zealand Waitangi Tribunal.

The author acknowledges previous publication of these articles: "'Lives Were Always Here': The Inhabited Landscape of the New Zealand High Country," extracts in introduction and chapter 2 reprinted by permission from *Anthropological Forum* vol. 6, no. 4, 567-585, special issue on "Custom Today." Copyright © 1993 Department of Anthropology, University of Western Australia; "Photojournalism, Anthropology, and Ethnographic Authority," extracts in chapters 1 and 2 reprinted by permission from *Cultural Anthropology* vol. 8, no. 3, 317-337. Copyright © 1993 American Anthropological Association; "Toponymy: Positionality and Containment on New Zealand High Country Stations," extracts in chapter 5 reprinted by permission from *Landscape Review: An Asia-Pacific Review of Landscape Architecture* vol. 2, no. 2, 16-29. Copyright © 1995 Michèle Dominy; "White Assertions of Native Status," revised version in chapter 7 reprinted by permission from *American Ethnologist* vol. 22, no. 2, 359-375. Copyright © 1995 American Anthropological Association; "Transformations in the Domestic Landscape of New Zealand Homesteads," in *Home in the Islands: Housing and Social Change in the Pacific*, eds. Jan Rensel and Margaret Rodman, 103-131. Copyright © 1997 University of Hawai'i Press. Revised version reprinted with permission in chapter 3; "The Bonding of Pastoral Peoples and Mountain Lands: The Language of Topography on New Zealand Sheep Stations," in *Mountains of East Asia and the Pacific*, eds. Mary Ralston, Ken Hughey, and Kevin O'Connor, 12-17. Copyright © 1996 Centre for Mountain Studies, Lincoln University. Extracts reprinted with permission in chapter 5; "Legislating a Sustainable Land Ethic in New Zealand," revised version reprinted in chapter 8 by permission from *Pacific Studies* 22, no. 3, special issue on "Sustainability in the Small Island States of the Pacific." Copyright © 2000 Brigham Young University—Hawai'i.

Introduction

Up the Gorge

The river-bed was here about a mile and a half broad and entirely covered with shingle over which the river ran in many winding channels, looking, when seen from above, like a tangled skein of ribbon, and glistening in the sun. . . . Behind us rose the lowest spurs of the second range, leading abruptly to the range itself; and at a distance of half a mile began the gorge, where the river narrowed and became boisterous and terrible. The beauty of the scene cannot be conveyed in language. The one side of the valley was blue with evening shadow, through which loomed forest and precipice, hillside and mountain-top; and the other was still brilliant with the sunset gold. The wide and wasteful river with its ceaseless rushing—the ineffable purity of the air—the solemn peacefulness of the untrodden region.
—Samuel Butler, *Erewhon or Over the Range* (1987[1872]:28-29)[1]

Halfway across the riverbed I saw it, the dreaded Wilberforce. It was split into two streams, each about fifty yards wide. I had hardly time to wonder how deep they would be before the leaders pulled down into the first of them and I was pleasantly surprised to see that the water barely came up to their knees

The waters of the Wilberforce were locked up for the winter in the heavy matrices of snow and ice that rested on the mountains. Months later I was to see it with the spring thaw on its back—brown ugly and raging, a killer river that no man in his senses would cross. Now it was a gentle murmuring stream.

On the other side the road climbed gradually uphill in a series of twists and bends, following the course of the Rakaia above where it forked with the Wilberforce. There was a primitive beauty in this country. Everywhere I looked there were glistening, snow-covered mountains rising at angles not quite credible to eyes more used to the plains. Their whiteness was harshly slashed here and there by rivers which wound round their feet and seemed to slither through deep gorges as if the steep rock might try to deny them passage. A wild, unfettered quality in my surroundings combined with my excitement about a new and different life to sharpen my vision and perceptions.

As the waggon grumbled its way slowly nearer the mountains, the sun dipped behind their jagged outlines and dark shadows blotted the lower hills. The cold, which I had hardly noticed before, became intense.

—Mona Anderson, *A River Rules My Life* (1963:13)[2]

With large Crown leaseholdings and its pastoral heritage, South Island high-country sheep-station cultural practices, processes and forms—both romanticized and stigmatized in the national imagination—give the impression of being the last preserve of a colonial legacy of New Zealand pioneer-derived rurality to confront radical change. Since the beginning of Anglo-Celtic settler activity in the 1850s, high-country sheep stations have imposed a continuously responsive and yet constant sociocultural order on the land. Because sheep-station life captures and condenses the particularity of the New Zealand mountain landscape and its cultural heritage—its remoteness and containment, sparse settlement and vast expanse, seeming cultural homogeneity and tight social interconnectedness, short history, and pastoral and utopian self-conceptions[3]—it enables us to explore some of the specific ways in which a particular geographic and cultural landscape is mutually constituted with social and cultural identity. It serves also as a metonym for the countryside and its multiple contested refractions—as simultaneous wilderness and postfrontier—as a fluid environment that must be understood in terms of social, affective and cultural, as well as ecological, economic and political components.

Transnationally, cultural elaborations of the distinctions between countryside and city, and wilderness and frontier contribute in complex ways to ecological and economic conflicts. Analysis of cultural hierarchies between these distinctions, expressed ethnographically and textually, provides insight into the relationship between cultural, social, political, and economic dimensions of the rural experience. My analysis calls more generally for a theoretical and comparative perspective on the sociopolitical construction of place, on rurality's increasing peripheralization, erasure and commodification, and more specifically on the ambivalent sentiments and varying meanings attached to public lands by competing constituencies. While remaining mindful of place as physical ecosystem,[4] we must shift our attention from place as locale to place as conceptual category and site for cultural-identity negotiation. Parallel comparative processes of the sociopolitical construction of place deserve study in other British-diaspora settler-descendant mountain rangeland environments from Australia to Canada,[5] from Chile to South Africa[6]; here I draw from comparative theoretical materials in the ethnography of rural life and pastoralism in Great Britain, the United States, and Alpine regions,[7] as well as in Western European agrarian history and rural patterns of inheritance,[8] and environmental/ecological history.[9]

Especially ignored as "marginal places," as "peripheral sites and regions," these "hinterlands and frontiers are defined and ranked relative to the 'center' through processes of social spatialization" (Shields 1991:3). Gerald Creed and

Barbara Ching (1997:3) argue that a focus on identity politics has eclipsed this rural/urban axis by race, class and gender, neglecting to focus on the ways in which rural people "concretely live the distinction between the country and the city" created by "hegemonic urbanity" (1997:5); they ask us to examine the "analytic possibilities opened up by attention to life at the rustic margin." As New Zealand high-country pastoralists have moved to the nation's economic and political fringes, they have begun to elaborate the cultural dimension of their lives as part of a process of contestation over whose rights to, and conceptions of, land prevail. Theirs is a contest for habitation, a localized version of identity construction in the nation-state context; it is also a contest for pastoral land definition, preservation, and management. In addition, both the image and the yarns (folklore or actual) of high-country runholders[10] remain a significant part of New Zealand cultural heritage and continue to occupy a place in the national imagination.[11] Their existence and perpetuation provide a challenge to modernity. Modernity has led to a "decline in [their] areal diversity, to standardized landscapes and to social homogeneity through urbanization, the mass media, and increased mobility" that has erased the rural (Entrikin 1989:34). Such processes of modernization and capitalist transformation are not monolithic, however, unless one insists on working the analysis from the top down rather than the bottom up. By pointing to the dynamic persistence of traditional aspects of settlement culture embedded in the constancy of change and the strategic value of primordial attachments, we—and they—restore to them agency within the nation state.

Examining social spatialization in particular enables me to explore what it means to come to belong to a place. By social spatialization I mean the sociocultural construction of the spatial at the level of what Rob Shields in *Places on the Margin* calls "the social imaginary (collective mythologies, presuppositions) as well as interventions in the landscape (for example, the built environment)." Shields invites studying the "cultural logic of the spatial" and "its expressions and elaboration in language, and more concrete action, constructions and institutional arrangements."[12] I examine place not as setting, but as what high-country folk call "country," a physical space invested with cultural meaning, a site of intense cultural activity and imagination—of memory, of affectivity, of work, of sociality, of identity. I examine place as it is conceptualized endogenously not merely as scenery or panorama, but as habitat, as an inhabited and deeply culturalized landscape. This requires looking at the processes by which a settler-descendant population "settles in," at the processes of what Robert Netting (1981) terms "environmental incorporation." I ask, What forms does Anglo-Celtic settler-descendant indigeneity take? as I seek to examine the mutuality of spatiality and cultural identity.

In sticking with "ethnography through thick and thin," George Marcus (1998:16) argues, "If there is anything left to discover by ethnography it is relationships, connections, and indeed cultures of connection, association, and circulation that are completely missed through the use and naming of the object of study in terms of categories 'natural' to subjects' preexisting discourses about them." Like Marcus in articulating the new ethnography in an age of contact zones, Lila Abu-Lughod (1993) writes "against culture" and "ethnographic typi-fication," and Akhil Gupta and James Ferguson write "beyond culture" to dis-mantle the "assumed isomorphism of space, place and culture" (1992:7). Conse-quently, the kinds of "native constructions of particular localities" that I represent here (Feld and Basso 1996:6), some of which explicitly naturalize at-tachment, are not only suspect, but also unfashionable in critical ethnography. But what if such isomorphism is deployed as an indigenous trope in a contested, postpioneer place? What if isomorphic configurations are localized, practically mediated, and historicized expressions?[13] And what if such a trope in a "discur-sively constructed" setting signals "particular social modalities" (Appadurai cited in Feld and Basso 1996:5)? To address this, we still need to focus on the "detailed cultural processes and practices through which places are rendered meaningful" (Feld and Basso 1996:7) because, as Geertz notes, senses of place are "barely diminished in the postmodern world" (1996:261). These theorists call on us to explore, as I do here with settler descendants, "forms of local knowledge and localized forms of expression" (1996:7).

My analytic unit is the station, or "run," a sociocultural environment, de-fined by and in turn defining the physical and conceptual landscape of high-altitude tussock grasslands and mountain lands. Its residents articulate their sense of "social and spatial distinctiveness"[14] in response to persistent external economic challenges, as well as globally recognizable and shifting ideological and political pressures from those with an interest in resource management and the public estate. My fieldwork was done in a time of radical transition in gov-ernment economic policy, in environmental and land-tenure reform, and during the mediation of indigenous land claims. My research participants represent one category of social actors participating in those encompassing processes of post-colonial cultural-identity construction currently characterizing nation-state evo-lution in the South Pacific.

I concentrated on fifteen properties in the Mid Canterbury high country, but my field research took me to eleven other progressive properties, politically engaged and generationally uniform in similar ways, and linked through politi-cal, social and kin networks extending down the backbone of the Southern Alps from Marlborough to Canterbury and the Mackenzie country to Otago to the Lakes.[15] I was to focus most intensively and systematically in the upper reaches of the Rakaia river valley, known as "the gorge" (map I.1).[16] On the southern bank I worked on the five Ensor properties comprising the original nineteenth-century Double Hill station (Double Hill, Glenrock, Glenariffe, Glenaan, and Redcliffs), and I spent time on two adjacent Todhunter properties—Glenfalloch and Cleardale—and on Manuka Point across the river (map I.1). Brothers have subdivided these estates over four generations, sons and wives (at Glenrock and Glenariffe) and a daughter and husband (at Double Hill) have taken over leases and property, and pairs of sisters have married in (a generation ago at Double Hill and Glenrock and later again at Glenrock and Glenfalloch). These proper-ties range in size from 7,300 to 15,400 hectares, stock units number from 3,400 to 13,000, and the resident population in my initial 1987 ethnographic present included twenty-six adults and seventeen children, with departed daughters, sisters, sons and brothers, and retired parents interviewed throughout New Zealand and Australia numbering sixteen.

Based at Glenaan for much of my stay in the valley, first in the unoccupied hired-man's hut, and later in the homestead, I traced the daily routine and the station's farming cycle of late summer, autumn, winter, and spring by witnessing livestock sales, sheep-dipping, back-country and rotational grazing, autumn musters, breeding, winter feeding, shearing, lambing, marking, tailing, and silage-making.[17] I engaged in "localized long-term, close-in vernacular field research" (Geertz 1998:69) in a field site that, though seemingly bounded and remote, is a contact zone as Clifford (1998:56, 68) has imagined it, simultaneously a nexus of relationships as well as a site produced by local, national and transnational forces. I also attended seasonal social and civic activities such as agricultural and pastoral shows, farming field days, the South Island High Country Federated Farmers' Conference and High Country Committee meetings and annual tour, as well as the biannual church services, school sports events, dog trials, and rugby matches that frame social action and its meanings. Interviews with former teachers and governesses, stock and station agents, Catchment Board officers, Land Settlement Board members, employees of the Department of Conservation, and scholars at the University of Canterbury, Lincoln College, and the former Tussock Grasslands and Mountain Lands Institute provided the complementary perspective of informed outsiders.

Getting There

My way into the high country was convoluted and fortuitous, as fieldwork paths often are. An anthropologist friend, born in New Zealand, gave me the name of her husband's distant cousin, and I took the bus in June 1986 from Christchurch to Ashburton to meet with him for the day. A retired farmer, he was past president of the Mid Canterbury branch of Federated Farmers. Although not a high-country person, he was captivated by high-country life and admired "the families who survived up in the hills." He warned me of the closedness of the community and of the need for an entrée into it; he told me that once there and accepted my relations could snowball with people passing me up and down the Alps. He thought immediately of one particular individual who might be willing to help— Hamish Ensor, a third-generation Rakaia gorge farmer in his early forties, who was active both in farming and high-country politics. He agreed to telephone him on my behalf.

That same week I took the Road Services bus across the Banks Peninsula to Akaroa to visit a woman, active in local politics, whose work on rural women I had read. We had met briefly for coffee in Christchurch the previous week, and she was excited at the prospect of having an anthropologist study the changing role of women in her community, a farming community under stress from the economic downturn and the development pressures of tourism. She told me that she had a high-country background and initially discouraged my interests up there as not especially useful—"it's very traditional" she said, "nothing ever

Map 1.1 Upper Rakaia Valley
(New Zealand Department of Survey and Land Information 1999a) Scale 4.5cm=5km.
Sourced from Land Information New Zealand data. Crown Copyright Reserved.

changes." I spent several winter days by the homestead fire on their beautiful property in a remote bay in the Banks Peninsula hill country reading through boxes of her materials. As I read, I found a clipping about her marriage citing her maiden name and childhood home in the Rakaia; she was, it turned out, the eldest sister of the farmer who was expecting to hear from me. So she too put in a call to Hamish, introducing me as a friend.

The following month I drove my borrowed Suzuki lawnmower of a car up into the Rakaia valley. My instructions were quite specific: drive south on the main road,[18] cross the bridge over the river and at the crest of the hill turn right and follow the nonmetalled road on the south side of the river. Be prepared to ford eight streams, which run down off the slopes across the road and down to the river. After about twenty miles pass a small schoolhouse, the Double Hill School, on the left and a property named Glenrock to the right. Go two more miles and look for a large mailbox with Glenaan on it; the homestead is modern, up on a hill with three dormer windows. In midafternoon as I pulled into the teardrop driveway, it was still drizzling. Hamish's wife, Belinda, came out to the garden gate to meet me. "You made it" were her first words. I felt as if unwittingly I had passed a test.

She had to move a "break fence" temporarily dividing one of the paddocks to give the two-tooths access to a new patch of choumoellier, and I asked if I could walk with her. She supplied me with gumboots and off we went; I started to ask questions about feeding regimes, sheep terminology, and property boundaries; she answered openly, and eventually she and Hamish became not only key interlocutors and guides, but like siblings to me. I spent several days at Glenaan and met with seven other wives up the valley, including the schoolmaster's wife; at the time I was considering a study of gender roles, but all the women discouraged me: "we work as families up here," "my husband is my best friend," "it wouldn't make sense to view us separately." Only later did I understand that this surface ideology signaled the equal value of male and female station labor where "families" are strongly nuclear with cohesive husband/wife working partnerships, and yet masked the gendered practices that were very much an issue to daughters and sisters who depart, and the cultural logic of gender that spatializes labor. On the last day as I was getting into the Suzuki, Hamish stuck his head in the passenger window and said he would like to show me their shepherd's hut on a rise in a paddock not far from the homestead. It was a modular unit he had put together: "If you decide you want to do your study up here," he said, "you could stay in the hut." I had passed the initial test for "getting there."

Glenaan is in many senses "ideal" in terms of how most high-country people would define it. It is at high altitude (ranging from 460 meters to 2,330 meters), remote and isolated, with difficulty of access off the tar-seal (macadam) on a no-exit road. Parts of the property are above the snow line, but its topography protects it from the worst of the southerly snows; on average there is eighteen inches yearly with six falls of usually a few inches, and "a real dollop every now and then." It faces north with sunny faces where snow melts fast, but which can suffer from "ferocious spring nor'west winds" and summer droughts. With a mix of flat and fan paddocks, hill faces, open tussock grassland "back country," and dramatic shingle screes and high peaks, it was both freehold (private) land, pastoral leasehold (government-owned or public) land, and retired "unoccupied Crown land," that is, land now free of stock. One high-country farmer told me that of all high-country properties in the South Island, this one is among the best both for farming and in terms of remote scenic beauty, while others noted that the valley is visually the most arresting in the South Island. Such a run is well situated for farming with lots of "sweet" (as opposed to "strong") country, and yet it also meets certain aesthetic and lifestyle conditions that match a public's often romanticized perception of high-country life in the Alps.[19]

Almost a year later after six continuous months of field research in the valley, my place in the community and my passing a test were again marked for me. The yearly dog trials were being held at Redcliffs and one of the two judges was Peter Hall, a young photographer/shepherd, who had worked across the Rakaia at Mount Algidus and was launching his book *A Shepherd's Year* (1987). Usually the wife of the judge awards the prizes after the trials, but since Peter was unmarried, I was asked to award them; I was to stand on the shearing board in the woolshed, shake hands and offer a kiss. Charlie Ensor, the pastoral lessee at Glenrock who coordinated the event with his wife Judy, announced the winners and that I would be handing out the cups and checks and tray on which the winner's name would be inscribed. He said that I had been living in their community and had become a part of their lives; then he announced that I had taken two top beats on his muster in April when the sheep were brought in from the distant back country. Jim Morris from Manuka Point across the river, whose resistance to my inclusion in some events had been explicit, added that I had come as a credentialed professional and that I had become (more acceptably) a friend. He reiterated these words again in July at the combined annual midwinter and farewell dinner for me when he, as initially the most doubtful of my work, was asked by Hamish to make the toast.

Other more subtle reminders of scrutiny and markers of some acceptance contribute to my claims of ethnographic authority: a comment from one woman when I went to stay that they would talk openly with me since they had watched to know that the information people gave to me was not circulated; a comment from another that she was relieved after I went there and was happy to rake and burn leaves showing that I was interested in the mundane tasks as well as the exciting outdoor farming activities such as sheep-dipping. Being and seeming interested in everything was vital. I had been warned by outsiders—other farmers, academics, urban friends—that the high-country community is not known for its openness, and I never knew the precise conditions I was supposed to meet to gain acceptance. In each instance, acceptance rode on my ability to pitch in and help in varied tasks from routine household tasks such as slicing string beans to strenuous but more novel activities such as shearing and mustering. The willingness to take on a challenge is valued, as is a willingness to fit in. My acceptability rode on my capacity to work hard on whatever task presented itself, always "putting one's mind to it," or "getting on with it," despite obstacles and discomforts including, and perhaps most especially, my own fieldwork. One always has "to do one's best."

My hosts' role as my social guide in correcting mistakes was crucial. When I was talking with all of the boarding-school children during the May holidays, I was slow to arrange to meet with the children from one station because I had hoped that they would agree, as they eventually did, to guide me around their schools during term time. Their mother wondered when she heard that other children had been interviewed why I had not yet spoken to hers. My most unthinking mistake, not told to me until the end of my stay, was in sending a short, technically dense version of a research proposal before my arrival. As a result some families initially did not quite understand what I was doing or were unsure of my goals and so did not anticipate when or if to include me in their activities. I was eventually told in a predeparture discussion with one family that my reticent but engaged pose worked as much for me as against me in this reserved community. My not being married "got in your way since people didn't know how to relate to you as unmarried—you couldn't click into their lives on their terms," but then if I had been married "leaving a husband behind would have been incomprehensible." Throughout, the Glenaans[20] defined a structural place for me in a valley where I had no recognized social slot, and skillfully guided me through multifarious—physical, experiential, social, and conceptual—high countries. My account is reserved as I have sought to honor in ethnographic style and focus the cultural reserve of a community that is not mine. To protect privacy and to preserve trust, I have followed their laconic conventions in not writing about the personal tragedies and losses, deaths and illnesses, tensions and disagreements, which are reminders that high-country lives, despite the security of routine and heritage, are not uniformly secure.

The Road

Driving into the valley that first time, I was surprised. Across the plains from the coast, one can see the white irregular backdrop of the Southern Alps—cold and dense and impenetrable and yet at the same time serene and magnetic and very light, much as in a John Gully original.[21] I had imagined life "up there" as very high in elevation, with a closed-in feeling, dark, tucked away from the world. But the Rakaia valley is not at all like that. The river is broad, between two and three miles wide even up above the gorge where the river narrows and the main road crosses. Driving along and above its shore imperceptibly higher into the valley, it opens up more and more until you can see on the horizon beyond the bends in the road the peaks and glaciers of Mount Arrowsmith, and the depths of the Alps with the widely braided river and all the gently sloping tussock grasslands on both sides. The clarity of the air and the openness of the landscape distort distance. I could see for a seeming infinitude of miles and yet not realize the distances involved. Such clarity and visibility make the land's expanse omnipresent, highlighting its contours and formations.

Photo 1 Glenfalloch driveway and the end of the road, with alluvial fans, front paddocks, and the back country beyond

Photo 2 Glenaan homestead with ha-ha in front and shelterbelt behind

Eight adjacent homesteads, linked physically by the shared road, are built on alluvial fans above the river with the hills leading to saddles into the back country behind, and with the verandas facing the Rakaia River and northern opposite-shore hills (see map I.1). Within reach of the road, the homesteads are seldom more than two miles away in the instance of the older homesteads, and much closer in the case of the newer homesteads. The cost of power lines in the present and location of water and shelter from the wind in the past determine location. The Rakaia River sounds everywhere as it breaks over rocks; after floods the sounds of rushing water are inescapable. To me the beauty of the country lies in its smoothly undulating surfaces and raw topography; because these are tussock grasslands and paddocks, one can see the curvature of the land. To those who love forests and native bush this kind of pastoral land seems naked, stripped, vulnerable, but it reminds me of England's Cotswold Hills where I lived as a child. As many women who live in this valley told me, people either love or hate the high country. Some of them had met contractors who could not leave fast enough despite the hospitality of generous meals, overnight accommodation, and sociability. At Avenel Station in Otago the runholder told me that he sees the physical hesitation of visitors at the expanse of landscape as they huddle together.

All residents, except for those born to the properties, can tell "arrival stories" of the conventional sort anthropologists are wont to tell; while our stories insert the authority of personal experience as I have done here (Pratt 1986) and evoke the privileged perspective of cultural dislocation, theirs affirm the remote, but attractive, inaccessibility of the high country and the difficulty of travel in earlier years. The discursive conventions used in opening narrative self-portraits "come straight out of the tropology of travel writing" specific to an ethnographic area (Pratt 1986:42),[22] but the image of a high-country pastoral utopia embedded in the remote austerity of its rugged landscape is the discursive convention characterizing not only New Zealand's tropology of such travel writing but also indigenous descriptions of place and people in documentaries, photojournalism, settlement narratives and national literature.

Peter Ensor writes of his mother's first trip up the valley to Double Hill station in his unpublished memoir, "Many Good Years, Some Not So Good: A History of Double Hill Station":

> Pop and Mother spent a week here in the winter of 1917, her first visit. Quite a journey from Rakahuri [the property in North Canterbury where Peter was born] in an open car then probably another two and a half-hours on a hack. . . . She was here again in 1921 and I must have been on that trip . . . my only recollection was the long and tedious trip over the river in a spring cart—I was cold and tired and thought the journey would never end.[23] (Ensor 1990:9)

At this time there was no road on the Double Hill side of the Rakaia, rather it was on the Peak Hill side, and the river had to be crossed roughly where Glenrock station is now in an area then called "Gunn's Paddocks." Work on the new road on the south side of the river was started about 1923 and was probably finished by late 1925. Even so there would have been no bridges fording the main creeks—Little River, Hutt Stream, Terrible Gully and Redcliffe Creek—between Blackford, just off the main road, and Double Hill, a distance of about twenty-five miles (see map I.1). Similarly across the Rakaia to the north and within sight of Double Hill is Mount Algidus, whose access was (and still is) also across a river, the "dreaded Wilberforce," as described by Mona Anderson in this chapter's epigraph.

Peter's wife Louise's recollections cluster around significant markers of boundaries linked to arrival. She talks about her first trip into the valley in the local idiom of "up the gorge":

> First time up here, oh yes, well . . . Peter's mother and father picked me up in this old truck, that's all they had, in Christchurch where we were living and then we went to Ashburton because he had a meeting there, [turns to Peter] didn't he? It was one of those hot summer Ashburton days. Terrible. I remember Mrs. Ensor and I we'd done Ashburton and we sat on the green between the railway line and the street waiting for him. And then we headed home. We got to the, what we call, the Boundary Gate; there's no gate there now. [Peter: Terrible Gully.]. . . . Where all that shingle is now, the bank of it. And Mr. Ensor said don't worry, this is our front gate. Of course in those days it was nearly an hour's drive. [Peter: Nineteen miles.] It took a long, long time. He didn't drive fast. I was hot sitting in between them, and I was carsick. I'll never forget that. It was 1930, I think. First trip to Double Hill. [Peter: Later than that.] Are you sure? No, it was 1930. Funny old boy, that was his pet joke, don't worry, we're there nearly, this is the front gate.

Lou stresses the distance traveled and the inaccessibility of the road as measured by the slowness of the trip, and she implies that with altitude ("up the gorge") both distance and containment—or separation from Ashburton—are reinforced. That Mr. Ensor's joke consisted of defining the first or boundary gate to the station as the front gate reveals his expansive, and perhaps ironic, sense of possession. It is indeed the entry point to the valley, but it would not have been the entry point to Double Hill, but rather to all three properties (including Glenariffe and Glenrock), the leasehold for only one of which he would have "owned" at the time. It does suggest that Mr. Ensor recognized how unusual it was to have properties of such size. It also suggests that the entry to the gorge was the front of the property; the station was gated like the garden in front of the homestead. Today the road is segmented with cattle stops or grids (and attached gates which can be closed across the stops to allow the cattle access between paddocks), but in the 1930s (and until 1957) the sixteen gates had to be opened and closed with every trip.

The road was very unreliable. It prevented visitors from coming up during the Ensors' early years of marriage in the 1930s and during the war when petrol was scarce. Only in later years with improved roads, more cash, and Peter's airplane was access easier. Access involved the difficulty of receiving mail delivery, transporting stores in and bales of wool out, being able to get out in an emergency when a child swallowed washing soda, and of getting the cream out to be sold.

David McLeod, author of several books on life at Grasmere Station in the neighboring Waimakariri gorge, and his wife Mary came to Double Hill in 1951 for two nights. Lou told me how different they found the Rakaia from their gorge: "Well, they started up the shingle road and then it all opened out. I'll never forget—it was autumn, and all the poplars had dropped their leaves on the lawn; I was so busy cleaning the house for them that I didn't have time to go up and rake those leaves. They said don't touch those leaves—they are so beautiful." Although qualifying his knowledge of the Rakaia because he had "never mustered there" McLeod told me that the Rakaia country is different from Waimakariri country because it is very fertile, which he thinks explains the continuity—"people have stuck there better than most." The fertility has implications for social organization since the Rakaia has a social community where all know and cooperate with each other. At Grasmere, "our neighbors were not congenial in the same way," and the thirteen gates separating them from friends at Craigieburn were said to discourage visits.

Some of the qualities defining the high country make the gorge distinctive. Peter and Lou imply that the gorge is "real" high country, more so than two neighboring valleys—the Waimakariri to the north and the Rangitata to the south—one with a paved road and the other with a small town as a community center. Lou says, "We were just an isolated spot and there you were." Other valleys are perceived as different because of ease of access, a road going through, the train line, and Lou stresses that those are not a community as in this valley. She and Peter romanticize their notion of community attributing it not to kinship but rather to the shared experience of physical situation, location, and activity.

For those living across unbridgeable rivers, such as the Manuka Point family on the north side of the Rakaia, the sense of remoteness is still equally acute and also romanticized through the expression of distance from urbanites as reflected in neighbor Jim Morris's poem "Different Worlds" (1996a:4).[24] The local poet takes a dangerous tumble as his horse hits a soft spot in deep water while "Riding the river/Looking for a ford":

> Looking skyward
> Way above,
> See jumbo jet
> Sydney bound.
>
> Silken businessman
> Orders a gin.
> Monogrammed handkerchief
> Wipes caviar from chin.
> Away it winged
> Like some great silver dart;
> I rolled a wet smoke—
> We're worlds apart.

Only several years later when flying from Sydney to Christchurch did I realize how exactly these jets trace the Rakaia; I glanced down expecting to see an unknown high-country landscape and recognized through the autumn air with startling clarity the shapes of homesteads and shelterbelts I knew. The visual violation of the isolation felt acute and my own illusions of remoteness unveiled, as I realized how exposed we were to those daily flyers.

More significant now than arrival stories are "thwarted access" stories of "the road going out," as it is blocked by slips and slides especially at Terrible Gully and Black Hill. Rocks and shingle loosened by the rain slip down the streams onto the road. Sometimes the obstacle is less apparent, such as when the fords turn to porridge under the water and driving an ordinary vehicle into it brings trouble. In the Rakaia, floods from the river and creeks have been an ongoing threat through the years and, like snow years, are chronological mileposts. For example, Roderick Ensor's terse and informative entries from the Glenariffe diaries document: in April 1951, "Easterly rain, high floods all over Canterbury, roads blocked and all flood gates washed out"; in June 1954, "Road washed out this side of Stony Creek [Glenrock Stream]"; then in February 1955, "High flood in river took away road this side of Stony Creek and round Black Hill and also the head of the groin"; on 6 May, "Big flood again. Black Hill road washed away as I walked girls from Craighead home, leaving land rover on the flat"; two days later, "Groin completely disappeared mainly due to Wilberforce [river] changing course towards Black Hill"; in September, "Road meeting at Black Hill with Council and Catchment Board. Decided to try to keep road open rather than make new road via Lake Heron"; in February 1965, "Creeks from Whiskey to Little River in worst mess ever, bridge gone"; in August 1970 "High flood in river and creeks. Road impassable"; two weeks later on 13 September, "Highest flood in Rakaia for 13 years"; then twelve days later, "Floods again, stores and mail in by jet boat." Loss of access heightens isolation as it disappoints expectations of trips home or away and cuts off supplies and contact; the road, as a humanly constructed scratch on the landscape, condenses the consequences of weather, preserves remoteness, and stabilizes challenge. Similarly, Peter Ensor's Double Hill history documents every troublesome arrival and departure over a forty-one-year period. The two most significant stories concern the time the road went out for eight months in 1956, and the time the road became inaccessible shortly before a Double Hill daughter's wedding.

Lodged in the memories of the children who grew up in the valley in the 1950s was the closing of the road in April 1956 after a year of uncertain conditions on the cutting around Black Hill between Redcliffs and Glenrock. Many recall that the army transported the cars and trucks on a pontoon to the other side of the slip so that there were vehicles on both sides of Black Hill. They tied ropes around the children so they could walk across the slip on a "goat like track" to the other side—for those in boarding school it was "pretty exciting"; they would get in the car and "on we'd go to town."

Peter arranged for an air service with the chief instructor of the Aero Club, John Neave. For the next eight months, a plane would come up every Friday

Photo 3 Slip over Black Hill cutting closing the road above the Rakaia, 1956. Pauline Ensor of Glenariffe on the right. (Courtesy of Roderick Ensor.)

Photo 4 Double Hill mailbox and the road heading west toward Glenfalloch, Manuka Point, and the Arrowsmith Range

with stores and mail to supply the five stations past Black Hill—Glenrock, Glenariffe, Double Hill, Glenfalloch and Manuka Point. Peter writes in his history that in some weeks three or four trips would be necessary.

> In June a rough track from Donald's Hill was constructed down to the river, whilst the river was fairly low, the Army brought up some big vehicles and ferried seven cars out to the end of Black Hill. This meant that we now had decent transport after walking the mile round the bluff. A fixed road was later erected to make walking easier.
>
> At the same time, the Army also brought in about sixteen tons of badly needed heavy goods. . . . The aerial topdressing [pioneered in New Zealand] was carried out using the Algidus road on the other side of the Wilberforce as a runway. It made the operation somewhat more expensive.
>
> Finally in late August, a decision was made to try and reopen and renew the original cutting round Black Hill that was constructed in the nineteen twenties and was abandoned a few years later owing to rock and shingle slides.
>
> A contractor, Doug Hood, was engaged, and he started to work on September 4 with an estimated time of two months. The actual time was ten weeks to finish the job, and in the meantime, he tipped the 'dozer over the edge one day finishing up in the river three hundred feet below. With skillful driving he managed to slew the machine round and drive it forward down to the bottom. Another day a shingle slide from above buried the machine and it took half a day to dig it out again. On November 14 the job was finished. (Ensor 1990:100)

In February 1965, Lou and Peter's second-born daughter Nicola was to be married at Double Hill. The worst ever flood, according to Peter's diary and confirmed in Roderick's, was recorded at Little River on 31 January; the approach on the south side of the bridge was wiped out, Whiskey Creek was washed out, and Terrible Gully brought down "a terrific amount of shingle." A week later the road was still impassable and Terrible Gully was too soft for any machine to work on. The family car, a Rambler, was on the non-Double Hill side of the slips and so for the next twelve days Peter was able to use his airplane to ferry his youngest daughter Clare out to school, himself to Wellington for a meeting, and his other three daughters home. By the time of the wedding the road was clear.

Now with better maintenance because of the presence of the "Fish Trap," a salmon research station run by the Ministry of Agriculture and Fisheries (MAF), the road is kept in better repair—it is shingled more often and bulldozed quickly after slips, averaging six a year. Even so the Rakaia can always pose a threat to the road's course. In 1997, I learned from Roderick's granddaughter, Fiona, that:

> The Rakaia has finally decided it's time to move over to this side of the valley and burst its banks, flooding around Little Double Hill [a roche moutonnée] and the Fish Trap. It has subsided now, but the general feeling is that this is only temporary, so Dad [Hamish], AH

> [his brother, Alastair of Glenariffe] and Ben [Hutchinson from Dou-
> ble Hill Station] are a little perplexed about what to do. Long term it
> could mean the end of the flat for grazing and a change of the road to
> right in front of our house. (E-mail to author, 24 December 1997)
> (See map I.1)

The distances and time involved to get to the main road and to major cities such
as Christchurch are significant (ninety miles) and the wear and tear on tires and
cars are factored into the farm expenses, calculated at NZ$150 per trip.[25] Some
women in such valleys have a place in town and leave the valleys more often
than in the past to visit children at school, or family, or the shops, and to attend
garden club or play golf, but their husbands note the expense, and their neighbors note their absence. With binoculars at hand, people in all valleys watch and
listen to see who is "going up and down the road" as a substitute for the social
knowledge lost with the end of the communal radiotelephone.

Not only is the road a channel into and out of the valley, but it is a panoptic
site, a shared point of orientation, providing a narrative on a collective past and
present. In early May 1995 Hamish, his son Paul, and I drove "down the road"
to meet a busload of visitors who were coming up for the day "to see the valley"
and for whom Hamish would serve as docent. An unrelenting nor'wester poured
through the night, into the morning, and still on into the evening. It was one of
those days when the weather paints an invisible landscape. Known in varying
degrees of detail to each of us, what I superficially knew to be behind the mist
and low hanging clouds disappointed our visitors in its absence. Hamish was
challenged to verbally construct the visual and primarily physical landscape that
they thought eluded them, as well as a social and historical landscape that he and
his siblings and cousins and children all see in it.

Hamish's narrative led the bus sequentially up the valley property by property to construct a valley, punctuated by unstable creeks, as both physical, social
and memory site. He began with sitings of diversification—deer-farming operations, one owned by an Indonesian group, and a safari shooting exercise, to be
followed up the valley with additional instances of progressive diversification in
salmon farming and merino wool production. Boundary lines were mapped in as
Blackford Station was differentiated from Mount Hutt (map I.1). En route to
Cleardale, Hamish sketched out a settlement history that began in the 1850s and
was completed by the late 1860s by which time Joseph Palmer had purchased all
the leases to hold them for ten years before selling to William Gerard who "also
farmed all the country on the other side of the river." Prior to the division of the
"great estates" at the turn of the century, six of these stations were farmed by
Gerard who held twenty-one runs (then incorporated into Double Hill, Manuka
Point and Snowdon) totaling over 134,868 acres and running 54,000 sheep
(Scotter 1965:87). The original Double Hill Station, once comprising the entire
valley and falling between Terrible Gully to the east and Lake Stream to the
west, was cut up in 1911 and 1912. Double Hill is still "the core of [Hamish's]
heritage" with the other properties as "spin offs." Today the eight properties are
linked by kinship ties, and residents are "all collected up" (like sheep), as
Hamish puts it, in what I would gloss as a "gorge kindred"; they are related

through consanguineal and affinal ties, and linked through social interaction and cooperation, material and knowledge exchange, and shared histories. Hamish's family whose members I interviewed lineally and laterally over three generations, began their tenure in the valley in 1916 when their apical ancestor Hugh Ensor, grandfather to five of the current runholders, purchased the Double Hill leasehold of 37,300 acres and with his brothers-in-law also purchased the leases of two neighboring stations, Glenrock and Glenariffe. He took over active management of the runs when he came from North Canterbury to live in the valley in 1929.[26] The three properties passed to his three sons, and two of the properties, Glenrock and Glenariffe, are now divided between his four grandsons with the additional names respectively, of Redcliffs and Glenaan (map I.1).

Hamish's next cues were geographic: an active fan with the worrisome and endlessly shifting buildup of shingle in the creek bed at Little River, the fresh spring at Whiskey Creek where musterers once stopped for a whiskey, the exposure of earthquakes in a clay cliff over on the Acheron Bank, the irony of needing the generator in the creek bed at Redcliffs within sight of the Coleridge Power Station one-half mile across the river, signs of the old road in the riverbed, the variations in tussocks that provide cozy shelter from the wind for lambs, the spectacular twist in the road as it rounds Black Hill through the Black Hill cutting, marked by the constancy of its rock falls.

Hamish told his guests about the valley's two families—the Todhunters and the Ensors—and noted that none of the land has changed families since their arrival although there were "odd shuffles within families" in this landscape of marked family continuity. Like Peter Gow's Piro of Western Amazonia (in Hirsch 1995:9) who "see" kinship when they look at land and for whom "kinship and land are mutually implicated," Hamish spoke of belonging inextricably to family and to country, and in reminding the visitors of "a constantly changing landscape," he used the ongoing demand to cope with the road to metaphorically show how community works—"what it's all about [in the high country] is people helping each other." The potential primacy of the visual landscape for the visitors in scenic vistas was countered through different narratives for constructing a sociocultural environment, narratives that convey an intimacy "achieved through cultural constructions of the environment based on close observations accumulated through time" (Rose 1988:384).

Hamish's narrative makes it clear that two crucial aspects of identity signal high-country families' cultural distinctiveness in social and geographical space: (1) their relationship to a shifting physical geography, to a land they call "country"—encompassing altitudinal, edaphic and climatic factors—as it simultaneously shapes and is shaped by the social and conceptual order in an extreme and seemingly remote environment; and (2) the significance of kinship networks and property-transfer practices for preserving intergenerational continuity and naturalizing place attachment—tending toward genealogical depth, and partible inheritance, patrilocal residence, and marital links between properties and families. My ethnographic explorations examine the inextricability of country and kinship, that is, of farm and family, and the mechanisms by which they are linked, and the mutuality of their meanings for station families.[27] Their attachment to the high country is, I argue, physical and material, conceptual and emotional. These modes of attachment are expressed in a complex interplay of affectivity, cognition and practice.[28]

Through an ethnographic portrayal of everyday processes of high-country farm life in the South Island,[29] I focus on ways in which contemporary high-country families claim, sustain, and reimagine remarkable connections to the land; I point to some of the elements constituting high-country discourses of authenticity as these families' affinity to land is voiced in the complex interplay of social practices, and linguistic and symbolic forms. These include the semiotic qualities of narratives (chapter 2); the social cartography of the homestead and station layout (chapter 3); gendered patterns of property transfer and land tenure (chapter 4); discursive practices of naming and systems of land classification, and vernacular topographic idioms and ways of talking about country (chapter 5); farming practices, philosophies of stock, and knowledge of land (chapter 6); Maori land claims (chapters 7); and the emergence of discourses of sustainability (chapter 8). I respond to Feld and Basso's call for us to focus on the "detailed cultural processes and practices through which places are rendered meaningful" (1996:7).

Notes

1. Samuel Butler (1835-1902) came to New Zealand in 1860 and established and lived at Mesopotamia station in the Rangitata gorge for four years before returning to England. The first five descriptive chapters of *Erewhon* are modeled on Mesopotamia, but the "real focus of the *Erewhon* chapters is not New Zealand, but the England Butler is satirizing" (Jones 1991:115). Butler's prose fits the mold of "literature as legal way of lying" according to Patrick Evans (1990:21) in his discussion of the poetical pastoralism of Victorian New Zealand fiction.

2. Described as "homely" in terms of its literary merit by Dennis McEldowney (1991:580), *A River Rules My Life* sold 48,000 copies in its first three years of publication; by 1968 it was in its tenth edition. Mona Anderson lived in the Rakaia gorge on Mount Algidus, between the Mathias and the Wilberforce Rivers, for thirty-four years until 1974. I met with her in Darfield in 1986. See also Anderson (1965).

3. Work in the comparative social history of New Zealand, Australia and the United States debates the atomization of colonial society. See Fairburn (1975, 1982, 1989). For contrasting views see Olssen (1981), Griffen (1991) and Hirst (1991).

4. Many ethnographies, both European and American, provide illustrations of the importance of land in studying rural peoples, especially farmers, and emphasize the ways in which those who rear sheep work within the constraints of the "total environment"—comprised of the geographical landscape and the macro-structures of society—through both Barthian choices and applications in technology and social organization (see for example Berg 1973, Pinson 1973, and Orlove 1980). Mountain environments as particular ecological types impose certain constraining conditions, and David Pitt (1978:3) characterizes the worldwide "montane problem" as comprising deteriorating watersheds, loss of vegetation cover, accelerated erosion, turbid streams leading to floods and landslides, and a general decline in resource potential. Mountain populations, he notes, have become accustomed to responding to sharply fluctuating environments and "sudden, widespread or intensive changes in land use."

5. For a comparative Western U.S. perspective, see Donald Worster's (1992:37) presentation of "cowboy history" and its focus on an evolving human ecology of pastoral farmers (ranchers, graziers) as people adapt to the limits and possibilities of a region behaviorally, affectively, and conceptually.

6. Detailed studies of localities over limited periods of time in the New World are necessary for productive comparisons. Brooking (1986:48) sees the dominance of family farmers in rural society in the American Midwest and the Canadian prairie provinces as most like New Zealand.

7. For example, Bradley and Lowe, eds. (1984), Chibnik (1987), Cohen, ed. (1982, 1986), Cohen (1987), Cole and Wolf (1974), Guthrie-Smith (1999[1921]), Ingold (1980), Netting (1981), Rhoades and Thompson (1975), Shanklin (1976, 1985), Strathern (1981).

8. For example, Goody, Thirsk and Thompson, eds. (1976), Le Roy Ladurie (1978), Newby, Bell, Rose and Saunders, eds. (1978), Rogers and Salamon (1983), and Salamon (1992).

9. For example, see especially Axtell (1985), Clark (1955), Cronon (1983, 1991, 1993), Crosby (1986), Cumberland (1981), White (1985, 1991), and Worster (1977, 1992).

10. "Runholder," "lessee," "woolgrower," "farmer," are used self-ascriptively and almost interchangeably to refer to those who practice high-country pastoralism. Exclusively high-country ascriptors, "runholder" is a traditional term derived from land units called "runs," and "lessee" stresses the runholder's occupation of land through a pastoral lease with the Crown. Egalitarian-minded New Zealanders most commonly use the more generic term "farmer," but Australians distinguish "graziers" from farmers, the latter being those "who drive a tractor." My use of the terms is somewhat contextually sensitive, but at times random, as is their use.

11. My chapter epigraphs provide a literary reminder of the ways in which mythologizing the high country is perpetuated by and for the nation, revealing a landscape that metonymically embodies the nation, and reinforcing the cultural elaboration of hierarchies between center and periphery textually.

12. See also Kathleen Stewart (1996:137) whose social imaginary is "a fabulation of place contingent on precise modes of sociality and on tense, shifting social deployments of local discourses that give place a tactile, sensate force."

13. See Thomas's call for such an ethnographic investigation of colonialism (1994:172).

14. See Nadel-Klein (1991:501).

15. In Mid Canterbury these include Mount Algidus, Lake Heron, Manuka Point, Glenfalloch, Double Hill, Glenariffe, Glenaan, Glenrock, Redcliffs, Cleardale, and Snowdon in the Rakaia catchment; Mount Peel, Mesopotamia, Inverary, Glenthorne, and Castle Hill were in adjacent catchments. Other properties include Mount Gladstone, Snowdale, Castle Hill, Acheron Bank, Ben Avon, Birchwood, Glenmore, Glen Dene, Clayton, Avenel, and Cadrona.

16. Initially during my first Rakaia visit in 1986 I spent two months on hill-country farming properties in North Canterbury and the Banks Peninsula, which serve as a comparative backdrop for the high country.

17. I follow the cycle for wool production, although some properties have diversified with cattle and deer. The research was conducted over a four-year period—June and July 1986, January-July 1987 (summer to winter), August 1988, and September-December 1990 (antipodal spring) with additional visits in May 1993 and 1995. To compensate for those breaks in the continuity of an agricultural year I recorded and examined entries in the farm diary for each of the years (1986-1990) in their entirety. While the overall routine of the agricultural cycle remains relatively constant, changes especially in breeding programs and in the acquisition of new lines of stock such as fine-wooled meri-

nos affect the constancy of dates such as taking the ewes to the ram, or shearing before lambing.

18. Route 72 although never referred to as such.

19. A run which is good for farming and yet has the homestead located on a main highway would not be considered ideal despite the ease of access. A run where the homestead is difficult to access and the country is hard would also not be considered ideal although some farmers would value the challenge.

20. Families are often referred to by the station name, as I will discuss in chapter 5.

21. See John Sidney Gully (1984).

22. For example, in "Fieldwork in Common Places," Mary Louise Pratt (1986) contrasts the romantic arrival scenes invoked by the use of familiar utopian travel images in Bronislaw Malinowski's description of his arrival in the Trobriand Islands and Raymond Firth's in Tikopia with the more miserable arrival scenes invoked by the use of familiar anti-utopian travel images by E. E. Evans-Pritchard and David Mayberry-Lewis in describing their arrival encounters with the Nuer and Shavante respectively.

23. Stevan Eldred-Grigg's (1980:162) only mention of the Ensor family in his *A Southern Gentry: New Zealanders Who Inherited the Earth* refers to Hugh Ensor's Talbot car, which ran visitors the thirty-nine miles from Rakahuri into Christchurch in an hour and a half. He notes that by 1910 every second landowner seems to have owned a car.

24. Jim Morris published his collected poems as *Different Worlds: Backcountry Yarns* (1996a) in memory of his wife Juliet who died in April 1993. As of early 2000 the proceeds to the Cancer Society Support Services had reached close to NZ$80,000.

25. All currency is written in New Zealand pounds and dollars, unless otherwise indicated.

26. Hugh Ensor's children had grown up at Rakahuri, purchased in 1903.

27. European ethnographers will recognize these categories. The European alpine ethnographic tradition tends to elaborate the significance of land as a resource, rather than as a symbol of or template for cultural identity, but in his historical ethnography of Torbel, a Swiss mountain community, Robert Netting (1981:3) hints at the ways in which a landscape is an extension of a people who belong. Also central to the European ethnographic tradition, but not salient in the sparsely settled New Zealand high country, are the concepts of community and village. Anthropologists of the Pacific will also recognize the familiar and overarching categories of kinship (relatedness)/inheritance and place/land in the literature of their geographical and cultural areas both as the analytic categories of the anthropologist and meaningful constructs for our participants (see Howard 1990:266-267).

28. See Low and Altman (1992:5) who define cognition as "thought, knowledge, and belief," and practice as "action and behavior."

29. Theoretical literature in rural New Zealand social history (for example, Brooking 1986, Fairweather 1985), sociology (Bedford 1979, Hall 1987, O'Connor 1978, Somerset 1974 [1938], Willmott 1985), and anthropology (Hatch 1992, Mahar n.d.) is sparse.

PART I
MYTHS

Photo 5 Peter Ensor speaking at a field day in the Double Hill yards, 1987.
Homestead is in the background, right

Chapter One

High-Country Mystiques

> When I am very earnestly digging
> I lift my head sometimes, and look at the mountains,
> And muse upon them, muscles relaxing.
> —Ursula Bethell, "Pause" in O'Sullivan (1997:2)[1]

Often in fieldwork, our interlocutors hand us those understandings that help to shape our analyses of their lives. This happened on a wintry June evening while I was eating a fireside dinner with pastoral farmer John Chapman at Inverary station in the Rangitata valley, to the south of the Rakaia. Thoughtful and well-read, he sketched his theory that a sense of "visual ownership" of the high country is felt by many urban New Zealanders who oppose its occupation and who deny the strength of farming families' affinity for the mountains. Words painted on the pelmet over an expanse of living room window read—"I shall lift up mine eyes to the hills." This farmer clearly believes the mountains are his spiritual home. He referred me to M. H. Holcroft's *The Waiting Hills*, a work of 1940s pakeha[2] autochthonous philosophy in which the author points to New Zealand's primeval landscape as a source of religiosity and emerging cultural identity.

A year before during a pilot study, I had heard the contrasting views of a slightly eccentric Anglican vicar whose congregation included high-country families. He had told me that high-country people do not have a spiritual affinity for the land, although it can be found in the Scottish and Celtic literary tradition of some of the people who settled. This, he said, is "country where people should not live." The vicar's view is typical of many urban people, environmental activists, and Maoris who perceive those in the mountains as not having the right to live in what should be the "wilderness," to "own" a national resource, or to have a monopoly on a national symbol. Because many New Zealanders assume that white symbolic constructs and beliefs are weak and that rural pakeha ideology is materialistic, they imagine only an uninhabited high-country world as mystical and assert different kinds of attachment as salient, thus replicating the binaries of "secular mundanity" and "spectral mystery" against which John and Jean Comaroff write (1992:4).[3]

This contrived tension between pakeha notions of spiritual and material attachment to country is clear in the juxtaposition of passages from two nineteenth-century New Zealand texts by Samuel Butler. The first "monarch-of-all-I-survey"[4] scene from *Erewhon*, his often cited allegorical novel of New Zealand's Canterbury back country, is simultaneously a parody of the Machine Age and of Victorian England:

> The country was the grandest that can be imagined. How often have I sat on the mountain-side and watched the waving downs, with the two white specks of huts in the distance, and the little square of garden behind them; the paddock with a patch of bright green oats above the huts, and the yards and wool-sheds down on the flat below; all seen as through the wrong end of a telescope, so clear and brilliant was the air, or as upon a colossal model or map spread out beneath me. (Butler 1987[1872]:20)

Of equal significance is Butler's *A First Year in Canterbury Settlement*, based on his letters and journals as sources for a guide to taking up settlement on a New Zealand run. Here Butler catches himself admiring Mount Cook:

> I am forgetting myself into admiring a mountain which is of no use for sheep. This is wrong. A mountain here is only beautiful if it has good grass on it. Scenery is not scenery—it is "country", *subaudita voce* "sheep". If it is good for sheep, it is beautiful, magnificent, and all the rest of it; if not, it is not worth looking at. I am cultivating this tone of mind with considerable success, but you must pardon me for an occasional outbreak of the old Adam. (Butler 1964[1863]:63)

Substituting a nineteenth-century functional rhetoric of utility (Ritvo 1987:79), he squelches Edenic lyricism and provides an insight into how settlers (unlike travelers) viewed the landscape, that is, in terms of sheep; that man's relationship to the land is mediated through stock is a constant discovery in my fieldwork and contributes to my own understanding of the ways in which today's runholders conceptualize the land they inhabit as pastoral, but not solely reducible to commodity.

John Robert Godley and Edward Gibbon Wakefield, committed to the idea of systematic colonization, planned a Church of England settlement in Canterbury in 1847. Godley was motivated by "an almost morbid consciousness of evil and destructive forces at work in Church and [western] society" (Webb 1957:137). He blamed manufacturing industries for destroying the *gemeinschaft* of agricultural society and for co-opting the landed gentry and the farmers. Wakefield, acutely aware of the inadequacies of British colonization elsewhere, was committed to colonial reform in which the "sufficient" price of land would regulate the social life of the colony (Webb 1957:138, 143-144).[5] Certainly paradise stood to be regained in New Zealand, but utopia in the antipodes was meant to be distinct.

From the 1970s on paradise has stood again to be regained in New Zealand in our (western) images not only of land but also of indigenous mysticism. If the "open vistas" provided an escape from industrialism into pastoral ideology in the nineteenth century, then our "visions of primitivity" provide an escape from modernity and its ecological consequences into "pastoral myths of [Pacific] primitivity . . . infused with Western idealizations of communal life" in the late twentieth (Keesing 1989:30). So for example, Keesing (1989:35) can assert that "the cosmic philosophy of the Maori, the mystical worldview, is as much a European as a Polynesian creation."[6] Once again antipodean pastoralism, like the notion of the reinvention of culture in anthropology, is in fashion.

As pakeha New Zealanders try on words such as "indigenous," "authentic," and "autochthonous," they, along with anthropologists[7] and Pacific peoples, are simultaneously exploring what it means to have a Pacific identity. As Renwick (1987:205) writes:

> Our consciousness of ourselves as New Zealanders is changing and continues to change. We are caught up in a fascinating process of interaction. The more we reflect on our experience in these islands, the more do we appreciate its uniqueness: the more we know and the more deeply we feel about what it is that constitutes that uniqueness, the clearer and more coherent do our views about ourselves and our identity as New Zealanders become.

In the South Island, the encounter in the nineteenth century with the colonized turned out not to be significant for most colonizers of the back country—the encounter was essentially with the land and not with the indigenous other. In 1988, however, the Waitangi Tribunal was hearing the claim of Henare Rikiihia Tau and the Ngai Tahu Maori Trust Board against the New Zealand Crown, and the complex significance of the encounter with the indigenous other is more apparent to many pakehas. The Ngai Tahu tribe claimed remedies for past violations of the 1840 Treaty of Waitangi. The compensation they sought includes high-country land held under Crown pastoral-lease tenure by 360 sheep-farming families of European descent (see map 1.1). Ngai Tahu land claims, and radical changes in national economic policy, as well as ideological and political pressures from conservation and recreation constituencies, from a worldwide economic downturn in farming, and from urban and overseas developers, have prompted high-country station families to actively seek to understand and proclaim their cultural authenticity in an oppositional context where rights to land based on colonial dispossession of precolonial peoples and their participation in the postcolonial enterprise are being challenged. Selectively invoking the past in the present through tradition or reconstituting traditional epistemologies simply may be ways in which individuals continue to engage in a process of rendering their lives meaningful, but it can also suggest engagement in a relatively unselfconscious discourse about culture, in custom (as Linnekin defines it)[8] or *kastom* (as does Donner [1993] for Melanesia) that can validate and objectify "culture" in the present.[9] Here culture as "an interested representation" bridging the cultural and the political is potentially instrumental (Linnekin, personal communication).

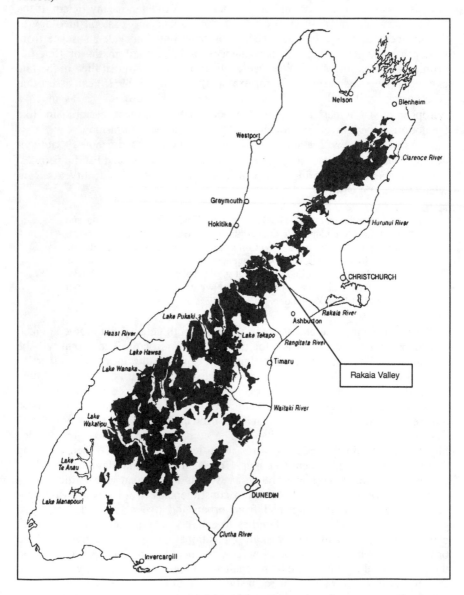

Map 1.1 South Island Pastoral Lease Land
(South Island Working Party on Sustainable Land Management 1994:85)
Sourced from Land Information New Zealand data. Crown Copyright Reserved.

The mystique the high country carries therefore evokes ambivalent senti- ments and reflects varying meanings attached to landscape. Its geographical distinctiveness, which Holcroft (1943) calls a primeval landscape, has made it central to the national imagining, carrying multiple meanings within a shared dialogic space, something belonging to all New Zealanders, a focal point for fusing Pacific and European identities for pakehas.[10] Even those who challenge the rights of pastoral lessees adhere to the logic of the romance the landscape holds:

> The "land in question" is 2.7 million hectares, or 10 percent of New Zealand's land area: South Island pastoral lease land, a tawny tussock outback long celebrated by poets and painters. A dramatic landscape, the high country arouses equally dramatic emotions. Sandwiched be- tween native forests and alpine herbfields and spreading a mantle across the South Island's eastern ranges, its tussocklands rival the world's other famous natural grasslands such as the prairies of North America, the pampas of Argentina and the steppes of Russia. (Hutch- ing 1986:14-15)

But runholding families and station hands whose relationship to that land is his- torically specific and whose cultural identity is experientially linked to it also inhabit the high country. The antipathy between these two constituencies—those who do not inhabit the high country and those who do—is deep, and my concern is with exploring its significance for those who do inhabit the high country; its history is complexly layered, and its implications for shaping political activity in New Zealand, and beyond, are far-reaching.

Much romanticized as place and as lifestyle in documentary films and nar- ratives, television specials, newspaper feature articles, and photojournalistic essays, the high country is both positively and negatively stereotyped, simpli- fied, and misunderstood. Within the high-country farming community such mis- understandings—about its history of expansive settlement, its patterns of pro- ductive land use, and its perpetuation of a "southern gentry"—are believed to threaten its continuity. As we attend to the ways in which particular categories of humans "trace patterns on the landscape" (Cronon 1993:19), we must exam- ine the subtle complexity and diversity of these pastoral populations whose ac- tivities, beliefs and values are often misapprehended and sometimes criticized in the metanarratives of contemporary ideological activisms.

Expansive Settlement

If one looks to public and popular history in New Zealand, the ownership and stocking histories of the high-country runs are well-documented,[11] and the names of properties such as Mount Algidus, Mesopotamia, and Molesworth are familiar to most urban New Zealanders. A prolific high-country documentary tradition is partly responsible for this: Mona Anderson's *A River Rules My Life* (1963), on life on Mount Algidus in the 1940s, 1950s, and 1960s, is probably the best-known book on the New Zealand high country; Samuel Butler's utopian novel *Erewhon or Over the Range* (1987[1872]) was set at Mesopotamia in the Upper Rangitata River valley, where he lived as a young runholder in the 1860s before returning to England; Molesworth, documented by L. W. McCaskill, is now managed by Landcorp (a state-owned enterprise) and is the largest pastoral leasehold run in the South Island. Both the tremendous size of pastoral leasehold properties and their placement in the Southern Alps render them valuable to all New Zealanders as an emblem of a settler nation. The Rakaia valley's stations hold a particularly important place in that history.

In early settlement days when the plains had been taken up (often in large blocks by notable founding families such as the Deans and the Griggs), pioneering folk headed for the high country and claimed large tracts of land.[12] In the Rakaia, the original Double Hill block in 1858 was taken up by Colonel Alexander Lean and stretched from Terrible Gully to the boundary with Upper Lake Heron; today this would include the properties extending from Redcliffs to Glenfalloch along the south side of the Rakaia (see map I.1). By 1866 Joseph Palmer, a banker, held the leases to all of the upper Rakaia properties including the Turton and Barnard runs, which later became part of Double Hill (and are today included in Glenaan), part of the Redcliffs block, and Manuka Point. Double Hill was offered for sale by auction in January 1874 but did not reach its reserve price of £26,000, and so Palmer sold Double Hill privately to William Gerard of Snowdon with 30,000 sheep and 114,500 acres for £20,000 (see map I.1). He also sold Manuka Point to Gerard, who burned the manuka-scrub-covered Mathias country and first stocked the property with sheep. An unpublished Manuka Point station history indicates that Gerard purchased 20 acres freehold from the Crown and set up station buildings at the Point.

Jim McAloon's (1996:54) analysis of the origins of the "southern gentry" reveals that powerful Canterbury names could belong to lower-middle-class individuals who, like many pastoralists, moved up in the colonies "with more talent than means." McAloon's investigations reveal that Joseph Palmer was born in Britain in obscure circumstances, emigrated to Australia in 1851 as a bank clerk, married well and became a bank manager; William Gerard was the son of a small farmer who managed a property before taking up Snowdon (the parent property to Double Hill). McAloon's evidence differs from the "MacDonald Dictionary" (P:44), which suggests that Joseph Palmer (1829-1910) was born in London of a well-known Bedfordshire family, rather than in obscure circumstances. He was educated in London and sent to Sydney in 1850 as a clerk, having entered service of the main branch of the Bank of Australia in London. He transferred to Adelaide and did a good deal of buying there; he married Emily Anne Fisher in Adelaide, daughter of Sir James Hurtle Fisher who probably helped Palmer to buy Double Hill. In 1856 he was transferred to the Canterbury branch, situated in Lyttelton; he soon opened an office in Christchurch and used to ride over the Bridle Path twice a week to attend to it; after two years he was transferred to Christchurch. At the young age of thirty-two Palmer was for a time, MacDonald says, the most important man in Canterbury. In 1861 when the Provincial Treasury was empty, people went to Palmer to honor his drafts. William Gerard (1822-1898), according to MacDonald (G:113) and McAloon (1996:52), managed Cheviot Hills, and his home was the first real home to be built there—part cob and part wattle and daub, ten rooms and a veranda on three sides; Mrs. Gerard kept three maids and many passers-through had to be attended to.[13] Despite manager beginnings, Gerard's landholdings were extraordinary beginning with Snowdon in 1866 and eventually encompassing almost all of the Rakaia's north and south banks.

Although the practicalities of settlement were socially leveling and everyone sought to possess land (Graham 1981:138), vast estates followed the runholding phase (1852-1870) for many hill and lowland properties as capital investment was channeled from stock into land, and production was intensified between 1870 and 1890 (Fairweather 1985); but high-country farming was "a hazardous enterprise" from the 1860s on (Acland 1975[1930]:29). Fairweather argues that at this time estate owners and urban capitalists lacked the class conflict characterizing other settlement societies as many men were both pastoralists and businessmen; such links are apparent in the station histories of current residents whose families moved into the high country later, in the second decade of the twentieth century. Opposition to them—emerging in the depression of the 1880s and 1890s when land was scarce and privilege resented—was based on notions of New Zealand as an experimental egalitarian country where extremes of wealth were unacceptable. But resisting the homogenization of colonial white settlement societies through space and historical conditions,[14] Fairweather notes that relationships between land and capital shift and "during each period of investment, there are distinctive production, social, and economic relationships" (1985:253).

Eventually in the 1890s legislation was passed to limit the extent of runholdings and to limit the number of leases that a given individual could have. In 1889 the leasehold runs were rearranged and new numbers were given to them. Double Hill was offered as two runs totaling 64,00 acres and 49,500 acres respectively and retained by Gerard despite a considerable increase in rental and "keen competition" (Scotter 1972:351). Gerard died in 1897 with ownership going to his son who held the Double Hill country in its entirety until 1911 and 1912 during which time it was cut up into four runs. Neither Palmer nor Gerard lived on the property, which was run by a series of managers with George Leslie Nell as Gerard's last manager of the combined Double Hill country from 1908 to 1912.

In 1911 the government responded to pressure that the larger runs should be leased by ballot, and the Double Hill runs, although asking comparatively higher rentals, attracted from twenty-six to twenty-eight applications each; "these were large numbers considering that there were not many people with the necessary experience and with the financial backing required by the department—sufficient funds to cover seven years' rent" (Scotter 1972:175; Scotter 1965:221).[15] The diaries of Mary Nell, who was married to George Leslie Nell, portray the comings and goings of prospective buyers and land valuers in the years immediately preceding the 1912 breakup of the Double Hill country. Mrs. Nell wrote that Angus McLeod came to Double Hill from Methven twice in November 1911 to locate the freehold fence line on the Gunn's paddocks. The Glenrock freehold was called Gunn's paddocks in the Nell diaries. McLeod was to buy Double Hill from Gerard, who lost the lease when it came up for ballot in 1912. On 6 February 1912, Mrs. Nell documented 29,716 sheep shorn at Double Hill. Fencing was being packed out to the Gunn's paddocks and Redcliffe [*sic*] and the fence line was laid out in January and February. She also documented the comings and goings of the Robertsons, who purchased neighboring Glenfalloch from Gerard in 1912. On 30 January, Mr. Gallagher, who was to purchase Glenariffe from Gerard (and who could have named the properties after the Glens of Antrim in Northern Ireland), arrived from Snowdon and went into the back country as far as Comyns Hut. In February, Mrs. Nell wrote: "Valuators went over flat fences," and "Mr. Hay is piloted across the river to 'value.'" At this time, there was no road along the south side of the Rakaia to the Double Hill properties; instead access was across the Rakaia from Peak Hill via Mount Algidus to Glenrock (see map I.1).

When McLeod left for war in 1916, Hugh Ensor bought Double Hill, now a run of 37,300 acres, and John D. McCracken, brother of Ensor's wife Kathleen, bought the lease from Gallagher to neighboring Glenariffe, a run of almost 27,000 acres. Gerard retained the Glenrock lease of 22,475 acres and its adjoining freehold at auction and worked both until 1917 when he sold the leasehold land for £800 per annum to Peter McCracken, John and Kathleen's brother, and the freehold to John D. McCracken and Hugh Ensor. Gerard also bought the lease of Redcliffs for £800 in 1911. Hugh Ensor and his two brothers-in-law were able to consolidate the three contiguous leases—Double Hill, Glenrock and Glenariffe and the freehold—back under the management of one family in an illustration of the ways runholders had of dodging rules through "aggressive land purchasing tactics" (Fairweather 1985:246), and through practices of land consolidation known as grid-ironing, spotting and dummying (see Burdon 1938:123, Scotter 1965:109). Until 1930 when he took over active management of all the Double Hill properties and left his eldest son, James, to manage his North Canterbury family property, Hugh Ensor appointed William Pollack as manager. The Double Hill diaries, with the exception of Mrs. Nell's 1908-1912 diaries, begin from this date.[16] Despite the distinction between lowland freehold estates and high-country leasehold runs, and the transition from stations to family farms documented above—where, as Peter Ensor said, "farmers worked their own land and never amassed wealth on the same scale as the fertile estates on lower country"—an external perception of elitism has persisted. On this level, opposition to high-country farmers is rooted in a historical legacy where distinctions between runholders on leasehold land and estate owners on freehold land are mistakenly collapsed.

Part of the urban sentiment is a resentment both of privilege, evidenced at Double Hill by continuity of family residence and ownership indicated in the surnames notably inherited from early Canterbury settlers, and coincident large-scale land management of leasehold lands. Since the 1930s high-country farmers have maintained this pattern of continuous leaseholding within the family, rather than owning freehold land. This kind of continuous permanence preserves wealth and suggests that place fixity, as with any estate, works as "an extra-somatic substance shared by family members within and across generations" (cf. Handler and Segal 1990:48-49).

Double Hill Ownership, 1930-1970

Double Hill station from settlement until the present illustrates the evolution and continuity of inheritance patterns in station life and reveals how intergenerational continuity of family ownership and connection to place can be perpetuated—continuity upset in other cases only by the exclusion of daughters who have brothers. Today Double Hill is both a station with some freehold land and a Crown pastoral leasehold property whose history of ownership recounts more than three-quarters of a century of management across three, almost four, generations of the same family. But the boundaries of Double Hill country have shifted over time with amoeba-like consistency. They have been defined with geographical and cultural boundaries, respectively, marked for example by natural features and land legislation, sometimes coincident, sometimes not; in addition, different kinds of cultural boundaries—legal versus nuclear-family farm units—are also sometimes coincident, but sometimes not. The use of the indigenous term "country" does not presuppose either a geographic or cultural boundary, but is a multivocal term allowing for the imposition of different definitions over time.

Double Hill "country" once comprised the current "stations" of Redcliffs, Glenrock, Glenaan, Glenariffe, Double Hill, Glenfalloch, and Manuka Point (see map I.1) as described above. Hugh Ensor's purchase of Double Hill in 1916, and his McCracken brothers-in law's purchase of neighboring Glenrock station (including part of the present Redcliffs) and Glenariffe station (including the present Glenaan) reconsolidated the properties under the management of a single extended family. Early in the Depression in 1930 Hugh Ensor took up residence at Double Hill and began active management of these properties in what Peter Ensor describes as a "new era at Double Hill." By 1934 twelve permanent men were on Glenrock and Double Hill including two of Hugh Ensor's five sons, Peter and Duncan, and by 1936 Roderick too was a permanent member of the gang. Shortly after, Hugh Ensor's wife Kathleen exchanged her one-third share in the McCracken estate, Hayland, with her brother John in exchange for his share in Glenariffe (with Hayland and Glenariffe shares being equal). Peter McCracken's share of the estate was left as a mortgage on Glenrock. In paraphrasing extracts from Hugh Ensor's diaries between June and August of 1937, Peter Ensor details the transactions and illustrates the way diaries can help in reconstructing property transactions and patterns of transfer (1990: 22):

> 22 June 1937: Pop and Mother [Hugh and Kathleen] arranged with Wanklyn (Solicitor of Lane, Neave & Wanklyn) to offer the mortgages on three places [Double Hill, Glenrock and Glenariffe] $4,000 reduction and to get mortgages extended for 5 years @ 4-½%.[17] Mrs.

> Turton's trustees to be asked to accept $800 less than their proposi-
> tions of the above, as I am compelled to put that amount into build-
> ings on the Freehold to comply with government regulations. This
> amount increasing their security, but the $800 not to be deducted
> from their mortgages.

> 16 July: J. D. McCracken also intimated his desire to exchange his
> shares in these runs to Kathie [Hugh's wife] for her share in Hayland.
> On values there will not be much difference. Kathie willing to do so.
> We think advisable not to do anything until the P. McCracken Estate
> share paid out. [Uncle Peter McCracken died earlier on.]

> 21 August: Resolved—Proposed that the P. McCracken share shall be
> left as a mortgage on Glenrock Run. Estimated amount $1,000 and
> any monies owing to J. D. McCracken be paid off.

Given lease restrictions, however, Hugh Ensor could not hold onto more than
one pastoral licence and so the lease of Glenariffe run was passed to his son
Roderick Ensor; that of Glenrock was passed to Duncan Ensor, and Hugh and
Kathleen Ensor retained Double Hill and its freehold in partnership. There were
two halves to the freehold. Duncan and Roderick worked Glenrock and Glenariffe in partnership, with Glenrock subleasing the freehold east of Stony Creek,
called the Glenrock paddocks, and Double Hill retaining half of the freehold
west of Stony Creek to the Glenariffe boundary, called the Double Hill paddocks, not to be confused with the Double Hill homestead paddocks. Effectively
this second block was divorced physically from Double Hill.
    During 1938, 1939 and 1940 the Glenrock and Glenariffe diaries were kept
jointly, and the Double Hill diaries were kept separately. Coincident with routine station activities noted in the combined Glenrock/Glenariffe diaries for
these years are those concerning the separation from Double Hill. These ex-
cerpted entries are typical of the first months after separation: Stock had to be
drafted and divided and land made ready for them,

> Drafted wethers off Broad Spurs to get Glenrock and Glenariffe
> sheep to be transferred from Double Hill. (7.vii.38)

> Changed earmarks on all the above sheep. (9.vii.38)

> Big burn on face of Donald's Hill. (10.ix.38)

The fencing is ongoing,

> Duncan packing fencing out to fence between Donald's and Black
> Hill. . . . Duncan and Roderick put in new fence on slip between
> Donald's and Black Hill. . . . Duncan mending fence between Top
> and Front Redcliffs. Roderick packing fencing out to MacIntosh's
> and camped there. . . . Roderick fencing from MacIntosh's. (1-
> 8.xi.38) (See map I.1)

Two transport lorries up with fencing material, posts, strainers, stays
and wires. (25.vii.39)

Such activities contribute to the construction of a station as a bounded entity—
earmarking sheep to denote belonging of stock to a particular property; fencing
boundaries between properties, blocks, and paddocks, usually, but not necessarily, to coincide with natural features; planting trees both as windbreaks for shelter for stock and for humans. Boldfacing the functional and symbolic imprint of
culture on the landscape, trees lend definition to the homestead block as well as
integrating homesteads into the landscape. The process repeats itself with each
generation in the valley as Glenariffe and Glenrock each began to subdivide
between brothers again a generation later in the 1970s and 1980s.

In June 1943, Hugh Ensor died at Rakahuri during a heavy Canterbury
snowstorm, and news of his death was dropped to Double Hill by airplane on
July 4. His estate comprising Rakahuri in North Canterbury, Double Hill and the
Double Hill freehold was left to his six children—James, Ann, Peter, Duncan,
Roderick and Michael with James, Peter and Duncan appointed as trustees of the
estate. In his history of these post-Depression years, Peter noted that the liabili-
ties on the estate exceeded the assets with heavy mortgages on Rakahuri and the
Double Hill properties. In August 1943 L. G. D. Acland came to Double Hill to
examine the property and its value. Peter Ensor's diary of August 20 reads:

> With Mr. Acland's assistance and after valuing all the places we have
> come to the conclusion that Rakahuri, Double Hill and Turton's free-
> hold will have to be run as an estate for some years. There will be no
> alteration in the present working position as Duncan and Rod will
> continue to sublease portions of Turton's freehold to work with their
> leases. As there is no equity in Glenrock and Glenariffe both Duncan
> and Rod to retain their full 1/6 share in the [Double Hill] estate. Self
> to manage Double Hill for the estate and James the same at Rakahuri.

Another plan that could have been made, but was not, was for the Double Hill
lease to have been left to Peter and the freehold to his siblings Ann and Michael;
that his father's will did not provide for this shaped Peter's decisions at Double
Hill throughout his farming days. Birth order determined that James, Duncan
and Roderick would farm Rakahuri, Glenrock and Glenariffe respectively.

The following year James sold Rakahuri and its mortgage, and he used rehabilitation assistance to buy his own property on the coast near Cheviot. Rakahuri's contents and the family furniture, except for that retained by Katherine
Ensor, were sold in a clearance sale. Two years later, Duncan and Peter met with
a legal adviser about the estate paying off the mortgage on the freehold, and
their offer was accepted. After two more years, Dalgety and Company "with-
drew their joint securities over the three properties leaving Double Hill independent of the other two."

From 1943 until 1969, Peter worked to make Double Hill his own. During
the early years of the wool boom in 1951, he bought James's interest in the estate thus increasing his own holding to a one-third interest in the entire estate.

Three years later in 1954 the Hugh Ensor estate was wound up, and Peter bought out Roderick and Duncan's interests in the estate giving him a larger share of the partnership than Ann and Michael. In 1966, members of the Lands Department and the North and South Canterbury Catchment Boards began to pay a series of visits to Double Hill in preparation for the renewal of the lease.

Peter's Double Hill history and his inclusion of the diary entries shows how he continued to try to settle the estate so that he could become the owner of the lease, rather than the manager, of Double Hill. The diary on 26 September 1968 reads: "I received official advice from other partners that they are not pre-pared to make any concessions to effect a settlement of the partnership, will settle only for the full value of 1965 valuation." And on 18 November: "Another meeting with [the family attorney] and the other partners who agreed that my salary should be raised to a reasonable level; more renovations on the woolshed, finished shearing on 14 December, 8,800 sheep shorn, 241 bales of wool" (En-sor 1990:149-150). The meetings continued with much back and forth between the partners and Peter concerning the valuation throughout 1969 with "basic agreement for the dissolution of the partnership and arrangements to enable me to carry on with the Double Hill lease" being reached in 1970. Finally in June 1970 with the partnership ending, Peter got title to the Double Hill homestead and the following year acquired the new pastoral lease when the old one expired. The Double Hill freehold was sold to Glenariffe and Glenrock for $75 per acre enabling Peter to buy out Ann's and Michael's remaining shares of Double Hill with $69,000 being the price for the Double Hill leasehold land, buildings and plant.

Tracing patterns of property transfer specifically suggests that for both Hugh Ensor's generation and the generation of his sons—Peter, Duncan and Roderick—partible inheritance of the leasehold land, freehold land, and assets without regard to gender was the norm at a time when land was more available. Hugh's wife, Kathleen, exchanged her shares in her family estate for those of her brother in Glenariffe. Also, Peter's sister, Ann, inherited her share in Double Hill in equal proportion with her male siblings. Had either woman wanted to farm in her own right, the privileging of men to actually farm the land would probably have prevailed. Partible inheritance suggests then that the value of the entire estate may be equally divided between siblings with the opportunity to farm the land (leasehold or freehold) going to boys before girls.

Peter and I had many discussions about inheritance issues as they con-cerned Double Hill, and both in conversation and in the history he constructed, he emphasized his concern with gaining ownership of the property and alleviat-ing the financial hardship he felt he endured. For him to be a sole owner of the lease was far preferable to managing the property on a fixed income for the Hugh Ensor Estate and partnership. This kind of arrangement, where a son man-ages a property for siblings who are shareholders, often creates tension in sibling relationships that parents today strive to avoid. One of Peter's nephews noted the inequity for Peter: "he spent his whole life working for his brother and sis-ter." The indigenous rule has become a high-country cliché—often described as "one [sibling] can't buy out two." Peter's life's goal was to be able to dissolve the partnership with his siblings by buying their shares even at the cost of selling the Double Hill freehold to two of his brothers in order to make the property his. It is inevitable, given the usual productive potential of freehold land, that people will speculate about whether, if a farmer had farmed differently, he could have avoided selling the freehold. For Peter, it took most of his working years for Double Hill to become his. In 1971 he had a stroke, and his son-in-law stepped in for an initial few years as manager.

One well-known Canterbury high-country station was sold out of the family for precisely "the one can't buy out two" reason. The estate originally was inherited by a daughter from her father; she had three children—a daughter and two sons; although initially she planned to leave the land to the sons and assets to the daughter, she changed her will at a time when farming was booming and left the estate in equal shares to her children. One brother went overseas and the other remained to farm the property. Their sister decided that she wanted her money out of the estate, but her farming brother could not afford to buy out her one-third share. Within Canterbury circles, there was a verbal backlash against the daughter for wanting her money out of the property and for causing it to be sold out of the family. Her self-interested actions were at the expense of family continuity and estate integrity.

W. J. Gardner's *A Pastoral Kingdom Divided: Cheviot, 1889-1894* (1992) traces the consequence of William Robinson's decision to place partible inheritance before the interests of his Cheviot Hills estate. Gardner provides a gripping account of an inheritance drama of family tension and strife that documents the resulting breakup of one of the largest nineteenth-century farming estates. Gardner documents Robinson's attempt to reconcile his desire to hold the estate together "while ensuring that it was run for the benefit of his daughters," as five equal beneficiaries, each entitled to one-fifth income from the estate (1992:16). In serving his daughters' interests Robinson created administrative mechanisms based on a complicated trustee system that treated the estate as a single capital asset. As Gardner notes, Robinson "counted on the collective family spirit of his daughters, and their devotion to him and to his great achievement, to safeguard Cheviot Hills" (1992:18). Not only a contribution to land-settlement history in the South Island, *A Pastoral Kingdom Divided* also reveals a private world in which structural tensions between the interests of individual heirs and the interests of estate integrity and continuity compete. It is a world to which I will return in chapter 4.

Productive Land Use

History holds the image of high-country farming static from the 1850s, as people generalize about farmers' attitudes to land. Early settlers subdued the vegetation with fire, built shelter and subdivided and cultivated the land around their station homes (McLeod 1980:16). Early runholders abused the land, viewing it solely as an economic commodity with no regard for conservation values—and a few still do—burning off excessively, monopolizing huge tracts, and overgrazing the tops. Soil conservator Lance McCaskill in his introduction to *Molesworth*, a history of New Zealand's largest pastoral run, outlines the early story of conflict between different cultural impulses:[18]

> This is a story of land, of tussock grasslands and mountain lands; it is also a story of people. It is the story of how the vegetation was damaged so that it became but a tattered umbrella; of how burning provided an environment more attractive to sheep and how they in turn helped make an environment attractive and suited to rabbits; of how the country was laid bare over vast areas, to allow the frost and wind and rain to dissipate the soil and leave the mountains groaning to the movement of scree and shingle-fans.
>
> It is no purpose of this story to allocate blame. Much has been said and written in vilification and in defense of the runholders who occupied these runs. They made mistakes; so did their managers and their men; so did the Lands Department. . . . There is no real evidence that the heritage due to posterity was thoughtlessly squandered; reversion to the Crown was a chain of fortuitous events, not the consequence of rapacious exploitation of the land by irresponsible and conscienceless runholders. (1969:14)

McCaskill's reference to reversion to the Crown is the Land Act of 1948, a crucial piece of legislation that figures heavily in runholders' claims to security of tenure. The sequence of events to which McCaskill alludes invites summary; it is the history with and against which contemporary discourses of sustainable land management are written (see chapter 8).

The role of early European farming practices in accelerating erosion in the South Island high country is the source of constant debate in the literature and in practice. Geomorphologist Ian E. Whitehouse (1984), in an overview, concludes that erosion rates in the geologically recent Southern Alps may be "naturally" quite high, especially during high intensity storms and earthquakes, and that the distinction between "accelerated" and "normal" erosion is awkward; he points to the longevity and antiquity of many scree slopes formerly attributed to European mismanagement, and indicates that some erosion features attributed to vegetation depletion following early European pastoral management cannot be linked to it (1984:18). And yet according to Douglas and McRae (1992:122) ecosystems have been destroyed in the high country, and "the preservation of fauna and flora of the tussock grasslands has suffered 130 years of neglect"; runholders told me that "none of us know" really, and that ignorance rather than neglect would better describe what had happened. While land degradation is attributed primarily to monocultural grazing of tussock grasslands by stock and rabbits, much of it is the consequence of invasion by introduced species, noxious weeds and pests (South Island Working Party on Sustainable Land Management 1994:v). But as Bell and Douglas (1992:93) point out and many runholders agree, the invasion of rabbits into tussock grasslands did not occur until these habitats had been severely modified by grazing and burning; on the other hand runholders note that rabbits came in the 1880s and took hold better in degraded land, but took hold nonetheless. We must take into account how changes since the Land Act of 1948 characterize farming, and how the current generation of progressive young farmers behaves. The act, in guaranteeing continuity of tenure, tried to redefine the interaction of pastoral lessees with the land to control use and guarantee sustainability. The 1994 Report of the South Island Working Party on Sustainable Land Management resists definitive statements but unequivocally states that even the current system of pastoral tenure is incompatible with sustainability (1994:28).

At issue in current discourses of place in New Zealand is the definition of what a "natural landscape" or a sustainable ecosystem might be.[19] Like cultural identity, the high country as a landscape is not static, nor "original" in its autochthonous sense; it is quite transformed, a landscape, modified by Polynesian and European populations, and subject to the consequences of shifting and conflicting definitions. Those with a stake in this landscape are often described in opposition to a predominantly urban New Zealand, and yet they all seek some kind of sustainability, characterized by agricultural historian Thomas Isern as a "potentially stable and beneficent state of ecological climax," which, he argues, cannot exist (personal communication). Isern continues,

> The grasslands of New Zealand have been hopelessly altered by human intervention. This would be the case if there were no sheep and no pastoralists in the country. The introduction of exotic species changes everything. Rabbits, conifers, and hawkweeds are, it seems to me, usurping and assertive species in the New Zealand setting. Land taken out of pastoral production will not revert to some happy state of nature. It will, instead, be plunged into ecological chaos. (Letter to author, 23 August 1994)

The discourse revolves around the rhetorical (and overly simplified) dichotomies of production versus conservation, which often are highlighted in the environmental regulatory arena. Conservative pastoralists who depend upon ecological stability for their livelihood and way of life could fuse production and conservation in a form of active curatorship of a changing ecology that is informed by observation, skill and experience.

For two decades, and especially throughout the period of my fieldwork, the high country has been a highly contested zone in a rapidly changing New Zealand political arena. The land at stake is vast with few inhabitants. Total Crown land is 5.5 million hectares or 22 percent of New Zealand's land area—tussock grasslands, peaks, glaciers, rivers, lakes and some native forests. Of this, in 1983 2.7 million hectares of land or 10 percent of the land surface were held as Crown pastoral leases in the South Island, administered by the then Land Settlement Board (New Zealand Department of Statistics 1984:335); of the 369 pastoral leases held, 83 percent were high-country runs (Centre for Resource Management 1983:7-9) with an average run size of 6,850 hectares (McSweeney and Molloy 1984:5).[20] The pastoral high country can be held under pastoral lease, pastoral occupation licence,[21] university endowment, lease in perpetuity, and as freehold land. The balance of Crown land consists of unalienated Crown Land, mostly mountain crests in the South Island, land development blocks and a variety of leased Crown land (for farm, urban and industrial purposes) (McSweeney and Molloy 1984:5).

My initial fieldwork in 1986, 1987 and 1988 overlapped with the period of radical reorganization by the Labour government in the management of pastoral lands;[22] new institutional arrangements were part of a radical approach in economic and environmental policy, and public sector restructuring (Hayward 1987a:41). Key players include government departments in the Ministry for the Environment and the Ministry of Agriculture, the Public Lands Coalition of conservationists lobbying to retire leasehold land, and recreationists urging open access; the South Island Ngai Tahu Maori who brought claims before the Waitangi Tribunal against the Crown for compensation in pastoral leasehold lands; and the runholders who lease the pastoral high country from the Crown. Other processes included ongoing land-legislation reform, the privatization of state-owned enterprises begun in 1987 under the Labour government,[23] an economic downturn in agriculture, and the pervasive exercise of urban-based negative stereotypes of high-country families as a southern, that is antipodal, "gentry" (Eldred-Grigg 1980).

"A Southern Gentry"?

Urban populations increased and runholders' prosperity declined beginning in the 1960s (Hatch 1992:37-43), but outsiders read wealth as they see private planes, jetboats, and Range Rovers; attractive homesteads and gardens, swimming pools, tennis courts, and pleasure horses; the private boarding-school education provided to many high-country and rural children; fashionable city clothes. In some senses they are right; some properties I studied were valued at over two million dollars.[24] However, the cash is seldom liquid because, although a property may be worth a certain amount on the books, the farmer may be in debt to parents from whom he is gradually buying out the property, or, in cases of joint inheritance, to his/her siblings or a family corporation. Many runholders blame former agricultural subsidies for their distorted image and urged Federated Farmers to oppose such policies. Given the current economic downturn in New Zealand and the pressures on farmers as a consequence of late 1980s Rogernomics, the fourth Labour party's radical policy of 1980s economic reform (Easton 1987), such perceptions may be heightened because the high country so far has been the most secure financially. There are several reasons. Partly it is a result of low debt overhead: those high-country farmers born to this land (those who "bought in" would be a notable exception) often did not borrow to diversify or develop; with small mortgages to parents or siblings they were able to diversify without borrowing at excessive interest rates. World wool markets have remained strong for the fine-wooled merino sheep that are adapted to high-altitude grasslands. The pastoral farmers have been able to capitalize on both the meat and wool markets by breeding dual-purpose Corriedale sheep that do well on their type of country. And many Corriedale farmers are carefully increasing their merino flocks in some cases with sophisticated breeding plans to create "elite" very fine-wooled flocks. Other runholders have cushioned themselves by diversification into deer farming, salmon hatching, farm holidays, rafting and heli-skiing. Most of the farmers with whom I worked were smart businessmen, entrepreneurs who did their homework, sought expert advice, took carefully considered risks, and ventured into new territory. As a result, high-country farmers, although adapting to the economy and cutting back their stock, are not going bankrupt as often as many down-country or smaller farmers. Antielitism may be further exacerbated by the purchases of some of these smaller down-country farms by high-country farmers for use for cropping or winter grazing;[25] some properties resist buying available land specifically in order to unseat such perceptions.

In the Rakaia valley six sons and two daughters of an initial five stations returned in the 1970s after boarding school, agricultural college or overseas travel and service to tend, develop and preserve what have become—through expansion, development and retirement or surrender of land—eight properties. All of their sons speak of returning to the high country to farm, although most at the beginning of my research were still in school. I spoke about the aspirations of these children with the headmasters and masters of the private separate-sex boarding schools in Christchurch attended by many high-country boys and girls. Many masters said of high-country boarders, "they can't get back there quickly enough." All agree that "the pattern to farm in these families is strong," and many characterize it as a consequence of strong intergenerational lineal traditions in inheritance, in schooling, in social networks and in political ideology. Characterized positively, loyalty and attraction to a way of life prevail; characterized negatively, narrowness of vision and material acquisitiveness for family wealth prevail. One runholder put it directly: "It's a good life, why wouldn't people want to return?"

Inheriting the opportunity to farm by purchasing a lease from parents is a central practice in high-country life, and family continuity in property transfer is essential for maintaining high-country identity and its link to the past. High-country families are rooted to a particular property, not just to farming, and those families are born into place and try to remain in place. It is important to differentiate the pull of a particular high-country property—the attachment of a family name to a station and the land and heritage it represents—from the pull of the occupation—attachment to being a high-country pastoral farmer. Many runholders acknowledge a greater attachment to place in the high country as a consequence of its scale, altitude and topography. One runholder echoed others in saying: "The challenge of getting to know your patch, trying to understand it all once you've learned it—it's something you can pass on, can hold on to and not let go unless you want to. By comparison, a thousand acres on the plains and the hill country is the same as the one next to it. Information is not so vital and so it's not so precious to hold onto it." As I will illustrate, attachment is accentuated in the high country because scale is synonymous with knowledge; but the attachment also illustrates a generalized pattern, an exaggeration of feelings that may hold true in the down country too, in which identity is linked to place.

People say that high-country runs tend to change hands less frequently than hill-country or down-country properties although measuring this is difficult because there are fewer runs. In discussion, a High Country Committee member noted that five properties recently had been put up for sale. Runholders hold the correlation between size and financial stability partly accountable for continuity of ownership. Certainly inheritance patterns reveal the ways in which each generation of fathers and mothers creates opportunities for their children, usually sons, to continue pastoral farming, and as sons seek to return. Runholders link continuity to the need for stability and security on Crown pastoral leasehold lands that were guaranteed by the Land Act of 1948—the meaning of rent on pastoral lease properties is not simply a monetary exchange, a payment, but rather a symbolic exchange that establishes a relationship with the Crown in which the runholder must tend the land with concern for soil and water values— and to production advantages in continuous stewardship; they also stress the need for expertise to maintain the balance between production and conservation for future generations on a particular property. Runholders say that this knowledge of a property's weather patterns, terrain, geological history, wetlands, vegetation, and stock movement is passed from generation to generation because high-country runholders have to know the country and are trained from childhood for this. Families who do sell and move on do so usually as a consequence of financial exigency.

Continuity of land ownership and the ascribed nature of high-country ownership are paralleled by the ascribed nature of high-country identity. While such identity may come from owning a station, that is not really sufficient; pastoral farmers who bought into the high country by purchasing leases were marked as newcomers; identities were negotiated in terms of the nature of one's lease, one's altitude, one's snow risk, the degree of one's isolation, and especially one's skill. A high-country farmer who purchased geographical high country that is not leasehold told me that he was regarded warily by the high-country section of Federated Farmers because he is considered "not really high-country."

The identity is not easily claimed or acquired because it also depends upon being firmly rooted within high-country networks; such relationships may be inscribed in place.[26] Those social networks are reinforced in a number of ways. Indeed the folk concept of social circles has applicability here; often these circles lead people to each other and do not link into other circles. In Canterbury the most significant are formed by the private boarding schools. Teachers note the tremendous loyalty of the "old boys" to the school and the unbroken lineal tradition of sending their sons not only to the same school but demanding in some cases the assignment of their sons and daughters to the same school house,[27] such that "family ties determine children's friends" as sons and daughters bond with the children of their own parents' school age-mates despite the masters' attempt to encourage the cultivation of friendships with nonboarders (usually city children). A city-born high-country farmer who was a day boy at Christ's College described high-country boarders as "stuck together like glue." The schools provide a forum in which rural children with boarding allowances and well-off urban children get to know each other for a concentrated six-to-ten-year period. Children initially make same-sex friends and eventually, through siblings and cousins, opposite-sex friends at counterpart schools, and given the tightness of networks, daughters often marry into the families of their friends. Even children under twelve who attend Selwyn House (for girls) and Medbury (for boys) in Christchurch share coordinated social activities such as folk dancing. Sports provide an arena also for siblings and friends to meet opposite-sex friends, and rugby and cricket matches, for instance, are large and well-attended social occasions. Not only are the private schools an arena for children to meet, but also for adults of the parental and grandparental generations. As their children begin to attend school, mothers and fathers find themselves associating with other "old girls" and "old boys" at the school events that define their social lives—dramatic productions, rugby, cricket, and rowing matches; one elderly woman after her granddaughter's performance in the Selwyn House school play told me that she had great fun seeing "all of her granny friends," as it put her in touch with her old mates from her school days at Rangi Ruru in Christchurch. Given the small population of the South Island and the paucity of private secondary schools with quality boarding facilities, social interaction is concentrated for girls around three schools, St. Margaret's College, Rangi Ruru, and the former Craighead school, and for boys around two schools, St. Andrew's and Christ's College; less often attended until recently, state boarding schools include Christchurch Girls' High and Christchurch Boys' High.

Other social networks are salient in reinforcing high-country identity and keeping the circles tight. Virtually all social activity other than school-related activity is concerned with pastoral farming. Such activities include agricultural and pastoral shows, dog trials, stock sales, agricultural field days, the regional High Country Federated Farmers meetings, and the more exclusive High Country Committee Meetings and Annual Tour. The social networks are defined by the conditions and circumstances of the way of life, inextricably bound with a way of earning a livelihood. Individuals who manage properties for runholders do not seem to be integrated into the social networks in the same way as pastoral lessees, but managers today are few with most on corporate farms.

The closed circles sustain an image of high-country elitism and cliquishness. Women told me that when they go to town (their nearest rural center) people seem to see them as private and set apart and tend not to interact with them, and at many rural events, such as the local agricultural and pastoral show, I observed high-country families clustering together, talking mainly to each other, a consequence in part of circumstance, dictated by what one knows, and who one knows from school days, from field days, from the High Country Committee, from one's own geographic region, and dictated also by lack of practice in talking to others.[28] Even Federated Farmers has a high-country division that further serves to separate down-country farmers from high-country pastoral lessees. Some refer to the tightness of the networks and the resistance to social change as provinciality—"they are circumscribed and don't see enough other alternatives to recognize their own unique values." Other outsiders, such as schoolmasters, similarly noticed a social conservatism. Although some boys and their parents question the future of farming, and although the schools encourage boys to consider a range of career options, one headmaster noted that the boys often have a "narrow vision of what is possible." The masters told me, "the boys are very set in their views and inherit them from the high country, bringing them with them—they don't change their positions during their time at boarding school";[29] in listening to their discussions one prefect noted that "high-country boys just don't hear the counterarguments." And yet another master balanced the slightly negative cast by saying "everybody likes high-country people, they're good people, likeable people, and they care about their children"; another noted how trusting the parents are and commented positively on the children's sense of community in their willingness to have more input into the school than city children.

Visual Ownership

Negative feelings toward pastoral lessees also stem from a sense that this land is national land and should "belong" to no one.[30] Admittedly Crown pastoral lease land is not owned by the runholders although the leases they hold give them certain rights and obligations. Providing the horizon beyond Memorial Avenue in Christchurch—a high-country daughter at boarding school in Christchurch told me how homesick she was to see the Alps through the bathroom window as she brushed her teeth—and the characteristic dragon-tail silhouette en route to the Banks Peninsula,[31] the Southern Alps are not only a visual reminder across the Canterbury plains, but also a symbol of New Zealand nationhood and, more particularly, South Island identity. Tourists to New Zealand no doubt are drawn by the attraction of the much-touted beauty of the mountains. Runholders too recognize their commercial value: "The mountain image gives us a marketing advantage other sectors envy" (South Island High Country Committee of Federated Farmers 1992:2). The environmental and recreation lobby, including groups such as Royal Forest and Bird Protection Society, Federated Mountain Clubs, Acclimatisation Societies, and National Forest Action League, share sentiments that public lands are national lands and should not be owned or privately controlled but rather should belong to the nation. These have been moved out into the legal sphere. The idea of open space being public space is prevalent in urban perceptions of rural people and of land,[32] and those who live in the mountains are often perceived as not having the right to live on a national resource. Not only political-action and public-interest groups, but also academics as well as down-country farmers voiced explicit urban antipathy toward station families. For example, a former Catchment Board officer told me early on that high-country people wear tweeds and brogues rather than gum boots and that the road up the Rakaia was smooth enough for driving a Jaguar XJ7, implying that access is no longer a challenge. (Neither statement was really accurate: tweeds and brogues are from another era; and high-country folk don't complain about access, instead seeing it as character building.) Both a hill-country farmer, and an agricultural scholar at Lincoln University told me that high-country farmers don't have much to do except move sheep from paddock to paddock; unlike dairy farming, whose practitioners do wear gum boots, high-country farming is seen as less demanding. Such negative sentiment toward station families and the mystique their habitation embodies emerges over issues of public access and pastoral land use, of Crown ownership and private control, of definitional power and the privilege of habitation.

In other ways, high-country life and landscape are romanticized positively for related reasons—their pastoral tradition, their pioneer heritage and links to the first settlers who explored the wilderness, their continuity of landownership, their beauty and self-containment, their distinctiveness, their *Erewhon* sense of isolation. Here skill—my interlocutors mean innate stockmanship as well as intimate cultural knowledge of country—is "the ultimate leveler" and smoothes away materially based differences in prestige. Elvin Hatch has suggested to me that nonfarmers and nonhigh-country farmers are proud of the existence of a New Zealand social elite that enables them to stand beside other countries such as Great Britain and the United States. As he points out, the plethora of high-country station and local histories and their popularity gives common people access to the lives of the rich while simultaneously relegating social hierarchy to the past.[33] Social historian Stevan Eldred-Grigg (1980) asserts that because the station owners were the symbolic equivalent of an elite they have been disproportionately written about compared to other classes that settled New Zealand.

By examining colonial probate records for data on the value of assets, Jim McAloon provides findings on the "colonial wealthy"—defined as those who employed a workforce rather than using family labor or their own—that suggest that Eldred-Grigg overestimated this aristocratic gentry tradition: "If there was a transplanted upper middle class with aristocratic pretensions, it was not a rural one, as Eldred-Grigg maintains, but an urban mercantile elite" (McAloon 1996:53). Early arrival in New Zealand and access to capital through patronage, family networks, luck and hard work were crucial elements in upward mobility in this settlement outpost of the British world system where "wealth was accumulated not for the individual but for the family," and where partible inheritance prevailed over primogeniture with little emulation of the British landed gentry for whom land was a basis of dynastic power (1996:59). Despite public perceptions, high-country families are not simply "an old elite interested in retaining [their] primacy in the face of socioeconomic change" (Wylie 1987:185) nor a self-interested marginal population for whom tradition as an "ideological resource" has both "pragmatic" and "intrinsic" value as an assertion of localism in the face of modernity (Cohen 1982:5), nor a people for whom localism is merely a response to "the logic of the modern political economy" (Nadel-Klein 1991:502). Instead, people are an extension of country and country an extension of people to such an extent that the inscriptive processes linking people to land and land to people seem ineluctable, unremarkable and generic to them. Only recent political pressures have forced them to voice their "spirit of the high country."[34]

In *A Destiny Apart: New Zealand's Search for National Identity*, Keith Sinclair (1986:6-7) explores the idea of New Zealand nationalism by looking at the creative works of indigenous pakeha New Zealanders and finds the expression of similar sentiments of belonging. Citing Victorian romantic novelist Edith Searle Grossmann's "The Growth of a Colonial Sentiment," he writes: "It is as though we have been imprinted by images of our land"; and turning to poet Charles Brasch, he writes, "Our personal experiences are stronger than inherited traditions," and "the country . . . [became] an interior landscape of my mind . . . the shapes, textures, scents, sounds of all its landscapes grew into me and grew with me" (1905; Brasch 1980:20 in Sinclair 1986:6-7). The kind of *tangata whenua* spirituality to which Brasch gives voice evokes Morgan Holcroft's (1943:77) conception of spiritual existence by which he means "the discovery of values that seem to postulate a larger existence than we know within temporal and spatial limits." For him "the physical suggestions" of the mountains must be included "in the framework of our lives." [35]

Leonard Wilcox in writing of the quintessential New Zealand myth of the lonely struggle to transform a wild and remote country into a pastoral utopia, pinpoints the shared basis for high-country romanticism in New Zealand as resistance to the iconography of raping the land:

> an ideal of harmony between man and nature suggests a profound re-
> sistance to modernism, an effort to preserve a virgin land and virgin
> moral order in spite of the penetration of modernism into nearly
> every part of the globe. . . . New Zealanders define themselves in
> terms of their geographical separation and pastoral isolation from the
> conflicts of modernism. (1985:67-68)

And so within the context of contemporary nationalism, urban New Zealanders too look to an idealized countryside and to uninterrupted expanses of tussock grasslands and the stark ruggedness of the alpine landscape for an image of nationhood and an image of resistance to modernism. In spite of New Zealand's distance, the world began to "impinge on New Zealand's pastoral innocence" in the 1960s (Wilcox 1985:69). New meanings and significance have begun to emerge as New Zealand has engaged in a "quiet revolution" (James 1986). Rogernomics has splintered town and country; at the same time "the European century of ascendancy is ending" (James 1986:197) as late-capitalist New Zealand struggles to define itself as an Asia-Pacific nation: "We are suddenly sharply individualistic, forced into more personal independence with too little security, made more Pacific and nationally independent than many are ready for" (see also Sinclair 1986; Vowles 1987).

Notes

1. Born in England, Mary Ursula Bethell (1874-1945) grew up in Rangiora, Canterbury, and began writing poetry at the age of 50. Jackson and Caffin (1991:369) write that "the rugged and vast landscape [Canterbury plains and Southern Alps] and seascape that she surveys from her small cultivated space [her garden in the Cashmere Hills] is a constant reminder of human impermanence." If a poetics (and philosophy) resides in Bethell's juxtaposition of "the earnestness of close attention" with "the relaxation of musing on what is distant" in the three initial lines of "Pause," as Vincent O'Sullivan

(1997:xxi) suggests, so too does an anthropological poetics endeavor to bring "experience near" and "experience far" simultaneously into view. Similarly, Bethell's Englishness provides her, in Stuart Murray's words (1998:84), with an "intellectual distance" from Canterbury that I would claim is also anthropological. In the simultaneity of her indigeneity and exogeneity and in her reliance on the soil of the land, she encapsulates the fraught condition of the settler-descendant, whom she characterizes as the "foreign tribes, (even ours, ours the invaders)" in "Levavi Oculos" (in O'Sullivan 1997:33-34). For these reasons, I cite Bethell's poetry at the beginning of chapters 1, 3, 6, 8, and the epilogue.

2. Although many New Zealanders of European descent use the appellation "pakeha" self-ascriptively, many do not and some resist the use of the term. James Urry notes that pakeha is a "trendy" term and "an empty category as it does not represent an identity but merely means non-Maori" (1990:20). For convenience I use the term "pakeha" to refer to New Zealanders of European descent as distinct from Maori New Zealanders. Most of the high-country people with whom I worked actively rejected the label for themselves, arguing that it originated as an insult by Maoris toward whites. They refer to themselves as New Zealanders. I refer to them as high-country people.

3. They gloss the former as "European modernism," the latter as "African [or Polynesian] primitivism."

4. Pratt's (1992:205) term for the rhetoric of presence characterizing Victorian discovery literature.

5. Historians Carrington (1950:398-401), Sinclair (1959) and Stuart (1971), in analyzing the ways in which the Wakefield plan failed, have had to ask if the Canterbury settlement was an "imagined" community gone awry. Neither frontier expansion nor the class structure could be controlled by land price because, as Godley quickly realized, resources were primarily pastoral rather than agricultural.

6. See Hanson (1989:894) who argues that inventions of Maori tradition reject objectionable elements of pakeha culture such as its pollution of the environment and presumed lack of connection to the land.

7. The development of the anthropology of place and identity is well illustrated by Pacific, especially Melanesian, research. See, for example, Rodman (1992, especially 647-650), Jolly (1992), Kahn (1990), Lindstrom (1990) and Weiner (1991).

8. Similarly, for example, Hawaiian nationalism involves a selective and self-conscious creation and objectification of self that elaborates otherness and generates social categories simultaneously engaging in the politicization and commoditization of culture (Linnekin 1983:247).

9. Elsewhere Linnekin (1985:241) examines tradition as an ever changing system of meanings, which is reinterpreted with each generation and which uses a model of the past to define it. Thus she writes: "authenticity is always contextualized, defined in the present."

10. Renwick (1987:206) writes, "We are at once the remotest extension of Western and Polynesian culture. That dual heritage is not to be found anywhere else."

11. See for example, Acland's *The Early Canterbury Runs* (1975) and Pinney's *Early South Canterbury Runs* (1971).

12. Barbara Harper's *The Kettle on the Fuchsia*, which tells the story of Orari gorge and the Tripp and Acland families in the nineteenth century, and Samuel Butler's *A First Year in Canterbury Settlement* suggest that these early settlers often had family backing in England or a sufficient fortune to buy the lease and to stock it initially.

13. Many of the early homesteads were built of cob, consisting of a dampened mixture of earth, a proportion of clay, chopped straw or tussock grass, and cow dung (Thornton 1986:15; Salmond 1986:38).

14. For instance, in his consideration of wealth, Elvin Hatch suggests that Canterbury and California farmers give it different definitions such that they would not recog-

nize the same social hierarchies. In asserting that he needs to know the "cultural code" to "read" the local hierarchy of wealth, Hatch (1992:107) reminds us not to equate their cultural codes with ours and implicitly challenges assumptions of western cultural uniformity.

15. Scotter also notes parenthetically: As against this restriction the department bought all improvements and allowed the new runholders to pay for them by installments.

16. Gerard kept the Double Hill diaries through 1916, but they were burned in the Snowdon fire of 1929.

17. Throughout his history, Ensor has converted New Zealand pounds to their 1990 equivalent New Zealand dollars.

18. Rangelands scientist Kevin O'Connor's (1989) memorial lecture, "The Conservation of Culture and Nature in New Zealand Mountains" was in honor of McCaskill.

19. See especially Grant Anderson *The Land Our Future: Essays on Land Use and Conservation in New Zealand* (1980) on the wise use of land. Contributor Kevin O'Connor focuses on historical forces at work in the use of mountains, and the interaction of these forces with natural phenomena.

20. As of 1994 2.45 million hectares of South Island high country contained 341 pastoral leases stretching from Marlborough to Southland (South Island Working Party on Sustainable Land Management 1994:84) (see map 1.1).

21. Pastoral occupation licences grant grazing rights for a limited time, without right of renewal, and confer occupancy rights giving the licensee full powers of the Trespass Act. They are a transition measure in the surrender of land from pastoral lease and were administered by the Land Settlement Board (Barr 1986:18-24).

22. For discussions of recent changes in land administration (pastoral land and administrative reforms), see New Zealand Mountain Lands Institute (1989), Tussock Grasslands and Mountain Lands Institute (1987), and chapter 8.

23. See especially *The Fourth Labour Government: Radical Politics in New Zealand*, edited by Boston and Holland (1987).

24. One property on the market in the 1980s asked a half-million dollars, and this on harsh and difficult country, hard to access and farm but with significant development and fencing having taken place and extensions and renovations done to the homestead.

25. From one valley two such farms were purchased while I was in the field.

26. See for example, Riley (1992).

27. New Zealand boarding schools follow the British convention of assigning students to residence houses, with their own matron and internal system of organization, for example, a prefecture system.

28. Jill Conway explains how such social circumscription can be seen as snobbish when she describes her experience of going to an Australian urban school as an outback child. "I had no idea how to behave or what the rules were for managing social boundaries"; later in a school with many country boarders she saw that she and they had "to overcome their shyness and become social beings" (1989:94); "at breaks between classes they understood my tongue-tied silence" (1989:98). On one remote station, across an unbridged river, the runholder began to make the difficult and costly (in time and vehicle wear and tear) trip out each Saturday morning to take his seven-year-old son to rugby in town, not only for sport, but also to develop his social skills.

29. In the Rakaia valley in particular the entire lives of the current generation of farmers have been defined by this world—their families, their social networks, their work lives. This is an integrated life where even the boundaries between the world of work and the domestic world are indistinct.

30. For a presentation of this argument in the media see Hutching (1986, 1987) in the *New Zealand Listener*.

31. This was my first sighting of the Alps in 1979 as I drove south from Christchurch; their visual allure drew me back for high-country fieldwork seven years later. Even now, on first sighting, I pull the car off the road to stop and look.

32. See Brooks (1987) for a comparative American study on the ethnography of trespassing.

33. While most high-country libraries include such books, I do not know to what extent urban or other rural people read them.

34. Jonathan Wylie analyzes the survival of traditional Faroese culture as an ideological resource (1987:177). Anthony Cohen's *Belonging: Identity and Social Organisation in British Rural Cultures* illustrates that "local experience mediates national identity" (1982:13); as Nadel-Klein (1991:502) suggests, his work places localism together with class in Britain as the ethnographic equivalent of honor-and-shame discourse for the Mediterranean. See South Island High Country Committee of Federated Farmers (1992).

35. Morgan Holcroft (1940:29) in *The Deepening Stream*, his philosophical essay on the conditions necessary for the emergence of a New Zealand national soul, writes, "the spirit of a country . . . is a kind of collective definition undertaken by a line of creative writers." In *The Waiting Hills* he makes a similar point—if New Zealanders are "to make themselves a spiritual home they must find it . . . in the affirmations of literature" (1943:42). It is not surprising that Keith Sinclair begins *A Destiny Apart* with the words of Grossmann and Brasch among others. Charles Orwell Brasch (1909-1973) was born in Dunedin, Otago "an area which remained important to him all his life" (McNaughton 1986:359). Abroad in London and Egypt, he returned to New Zealand in 1947 and founded *Landfall*, which he edited for twenty years. Brasch's work illustrates the adaptation of poetic language to a new environment (Jackson and Caffin 1991:342). By extension, Allan Hanson (1989:894), in an article, "The Making of the Maori," refers to Samuel Marsden's recognition of the capacity of men like James K. Baxter with the "soul of a poet" to "enter into the existential [and mystical] dimension of Maori life." Holcroft in *The Waiting Hills* suggests that authentic poets "are never far removed from the kind of mysticism" which reaches after the "unknown, or dimly apprehended, forces of their environment" (1943:65). He envisions a parallel mysticism for Europeans.

Chapter Two

Compositions of Country

This page or half page of our history
Is precious to me, human history;
The sort one finds, outside the history books,
In gossip, and yarns around campfires,
And precious even more because my father
Served here his hard apprenticeship with sheep.
     —Basil Dowling (1973), "Glenmark"[1]
      in McNaughton (1986:259)

In examining the imagined worlds of the British empire, John Comaroff criti-cally explores the colonizers' images of empire in the wake of the industrial revolution, one being the notion of "idyllic countryside" that "stood for the pos-sibility of paradise regained, a Utopian rhapsody for the future. . . . In practice, these dreams could not be realized in a greatly changed England. However, the open vistas of the non-European world seemed to offer limitless possibilities" for the remaking of British society (1989:668), especially in New Zealand as the sole white-settler colony established after the industrial revolution (Brooking 1986:49). These idealizations qualify as Renato Rosaldo's (1989:120) "imperial-ist nostalgia" or Donna Haraway's (1989:267) "colonial-nostalgic aesthetic."[2] Rosaldo "dismantles" the "ideology of imperialist nostalgia" examining the "process of yearning for what one has destroyed"; he suggests, provocatively and disturbingly, that anthropologists "inhabit partially overlapping ideological spaces" with colonizers and missionaries in "mourning the passing of traditional society" (1989:115-116, 120). One could implicate postcolonials and photojour-nalists in sharing this "conventional trope" of yearning for a pastoral past. As Raymond Williams reminds us, the persistence of these images of pastoralism accompanying agrarian capitalism is matched only by their historicity and by variable and powerful meanings "in feeling and activity; in region and time" (1973:289, 4). Although such images were constant, "in most places, at most times, colonialism did (and does) not exist in the singular, but in a plurality of forms and forces" (Comaroff 1989:680).[3]

Idyllic representations of New Zealand high-country life proliferate in a variety of genres, authored indigenously and exogenously. For indigenous authors who sparsely inhabit this country of tussock grasslands—runholders, and station hands such as shepherds and shearers—high-country pastoralism is taken for granted as a way of life.[4] Exogenous authors do not inhabit the mountain lands but have contact with them—urban and down-country people may be recreationists (hikers, skiers, fishermen), conservationists, farm advisers, service people, journalists, writers, artists, or sometimes tourists. Representative genres include imaginative writing—detective fiction,[5] novels,[6] poetry,[7] and cartoons;[8] indigenous nonfiction—station correspondence, scrapbooks, farm diaries, station and family histories,[9] autobiographies, and descriptive accounts of high-country pastoral life, usually in the form of vignettes and yarns; and exogenous nonfiction—documentary films and television features, photojournalistic pieces in magazines and picture books, and magazine feature articles.[10] For the ethnographer, these materials taken as forms of cultural production provide a way of examining the varying representations of high-country life within a national and historical context as well as of examining representations and constructions of knowledge in indigenous narrative.

I limit myself in this chapter first to an indigenous station history, that of a senior-generation couple, Louise and Peter Ensor of Double Hill station, which recollects their experience of locality, and then to an illustrative analysis of non-indigenous nonfiction, specifically photojournalism of the genre that Donna Haraway (1989:139) has described as "the adventure travelogue of seemingly participatory, popular, democratic science characterizing the *National Geographic.*"[11] Postmodernist attention to the pluralities of discourse—Haraway's "contested narrative fields" as situated knowledge—provides us with a trope that can be appropriated to understand how the ethnographer's representations might be distinguished from that of the inhabitant and of the photojournalist. Anthropology's use becomes especially paramount in its explorations of examples of photojournalism as the discourses of a western science for the people—showing that meaning sought within the self-contained object is illusory, at least in so far as western cultures are concerned. Only by exploring difference, by searching out the object of study both from within and from without, and assessing these different perceptions, can an understanding of latency be achieved. What we seek to represent in our ethnographies is not a singular description of overt aspects of culture, but a reflexively qualified cultural interpretation and understanding of the multiply latent;[12] this I shall attempt in the following pages. We should, however, be wary of postmodernist polemicism that assumes a homogeneity of so-called Western hegemonic discourse, for such assumptions may lead us in looking at postcolonial white-settlement societies to imagine their cultural codes as ours. Herein lies a danger of "imperialist nostalgia."

Indigenous Representations

Although the precious human history of which Basil Dowling writes in "Glenmark" is that of his manager-father's engagement with the high country, Dowling's nostalgia for the slopes of tussock, for the shadow of magnificence, and for historical memory measured by tall trees mirrors the nostalgia shared by an older generation of station-owners in the South Island high country. This sort of endogenous historicity linked to place and family and embedded in literature, oral narratives and documented in written records and histories can be examined anthropologically as an indigenous high-country discursive practice that contributes to an understanding and construction of identity and spatiality in which the high country is conceptualized as habitat. The act of production—of engaging in custom as a discourse of writing and speaking about culture—is as important as the product, as a people construct the past through recording routine life, inscribe themselves on the landscape, and signal local epistemologies about place as constitutive of identity.[13]

Station, regional and provincial histories proliferate in the archives and libraries of New Zealand rural homesteads, of local historical societies and museums, and of national archives.[14] Sometimes histories are prepared for family reunions, or celebrations of the family's arrival in New Zealand. Families collect such books to maintain complete collections; one family asked me to remember the location of out-of-print copies for their library. Station guests are provided with histories on their bedside tables, and runholders and their families freely narrate the history of the station as they take visitors through their properties.

In a critical way, Elvin Hatch has argued that this genre of local and station history outlines the principles of regional social order, establishes family credentials, provides name recognition (of family and property) and levels social difference by providing information to all about notable rural families. He writes that published regional histories in an area of southern Canterbury "memorialize" the great estates of the past (1992:53). Similarly Thomas Isern (1992:4) suggests that the genre is suspect, because authors are kin, and provides a microscopic history, highly localized and "patriarchal, seeking to fashion an epic past for particular pastoralists and agriculturists."

Family archival materials available to me included station records, farm diaries, airplane logs, pastoral leases, run plans, correspondence, wills, farm accounts, bookkeeping ledgers, wage statements, scrapbooks, family photograph albums and genealogies.[15] As the oldest station on the south side of the Rakaia, Double Hill provided access to continuous extant station records dating from 1908, including the diary of Mrs. Nell from 1908 to 1912. Peter wrote a station history based on the Double Hill diaries while I was in the field, which we supplemented with taped narrative sessions with Peter and his wife, Lou. His brother Roderick completed a station history for Glenariffe before his death in 1991, and their brother Duncan at Glenrock similarly left a complete run of the station diaries. In providing lineal depth, such extensive documentation is pragmatic agriculturally but also indicates pride in the evolution of local community and heritage, as well as commitment to documentary preservation of the past.

That station families value such records points to the importance of documentation for creating an impression of historical depth in a context where
European settlement has a shallow history.[16] The diaries create a physical link
with the past that supplements spatially chronological measures of time: important sites—a homestead, a mustering hut, woolshed, mustering beat, the road,
any named place such as a paddock or saddle—are described in terms of use and
transformation, such as an addition to the house, a fallen tree on the sunroom, a
new fireplace after an earthquake, a hut destroyed by avalanche. The history
equates the station with family and signifies a relationship with place by documenting sociocultural continuity and solidarity. It simultaneously creates and
reinforces a sense of local belonging for this settler-descendant population. In
both Lou's and Peter's narratives a pioneering spirit emphasizing physical and
financial hardship in a dangerous landscape is cultivated and revered.

After initially describing his grandfather's and father's runs in terms of
name, size, location, stock bred, buyers and sellers, Peter Ensor brings his father
to Double Hill on the first day of March 1930. Peter reconstructs that history by
noting the lines of the old fencing "because of their construction which gives an
indication as to date," probably around 1890. He is able to determine dates by
describing the materials used, and perhaps even more significantly, he is able to
extrapolate the kind of labor and effort required; for example, "my estimate is
that it would entail about thirty pack horse loads per mile to transport" the snow
fence out. He writes "I have spent some time on fencing, in particular on the
snow fence, because it became an integral part of stock management, being able
to divide the summer country from the winter." Such physical divisions define
the country in terms of ownership and distance from the homestead, but also
functionally in separating sheep bloodlines and rationing their food.

In a middle stanza of his poem, "Rewards," local poet and neighboring
runholder from Manuka Point, Jim Morris, in echoing Peter's focus on fencing,
articulates a presence:

> But man intrudes to run his stock
> And "make a go" of this rough block;
> With puny efforts—some say in vain
> Where he has tried this land to tame.
> Though cash rewards are not immense
> And there was need of many a fence;
> And profits few and far between
> You now can see where he has been. (1996a:5)

The tracing of fence lines enables Peter to identify by name the key topographic
features of old Double Hill station as well as the transformation of boundaries
between the properties that have evolved. Fences like landforms create enclosures. Paul Carter (1989:137) has examined the process for Australians of settling the country as also symbolic and linguistic in character. "Enclosure is essential, not only to the act of settling, but also to the *description* of settling.
Where there is no enclosure, no desolate spot, it must be invented" (1989:152).
The process can be expressed grammatically, in which "to name a space, to turn

it into a negotiable place, was like constructing a sentence." Through naming, symbolic boundaries were created, and accounts of early days of settlement, according to Carter, are about the multiplication of such symbolic boundaries. Identifying features by name enables Peter to locate himself in the landscape; names, like physical boundaries, serve a definitional function, placing individuals in space relative to other places and serving to render the high country vast and yet known in all of its diversity and complexity.[17]

While Peter's narratives are not specifically high-country focused in terms of describing the landscape adjectivally, he describes the back country in terms of activities—the musters to bring sheep in from the back country for winter, fencing endeavors and retirement programs. He takes the reader along the traditional six-day mustering line through Double Hill, Glenariffe and Glenrock in order to identify saddles, peaks, streams, valleys and huts, and to describe the character and topography of the land in terms of the effort taken to traverse it. The specificity of place is important in his narratives, for example, mustering up Petticoat Lane down to Comyns Hut or situating a particular gate such as the Boundary Gate at Terrible Gully (see map I.1). The "country" is never an unnamed expanse. The narrative suggests attentiveness to a particular kind of detail, and suggests that it matters to know the country in all its size. Recognizing a place would depend upon knowing in detail its natural features, usually from experience. Having it all named means that it can be talked about. Carter (1989:153) notes the frequency with which wall, doorstep, gate and fence serve as "spatial metaphors through which [one's own] history can be told."

According to Peter, a crucial shift in the gorge history was from manager-occupied properties to owner-occupied properties. Simultaneous with properties becoming owner-occupied in the 1930s, a downturn in economic conditions lasted until World War II[18] followed by a significant postwar boom during the 1950s when current perceptions of high-country elitism were shaped. An adviser to the Meat and Wool Board in sketching this perceptual history for me noted that farmers were marked in town by their smart vehicles and fashionable clothes, and still are today, but their wealth "is insignificant compared with urban wealth." He told me that high-country farmers, as were many similarly positioned, are the last to face economic pressures because "they are savvy farmers on top of the issues." The current boom began in the late 1970s.

Hugh Ensor, "Pop," was the first owner to live up the gorge. With his and Mrs. Ensor's arrival in 1930, the homestead was improved and the garden planted. Lou talks with respect about her mother-in-law's first coming to a neglected homestead, noting her elegance, her propriety, and her efforts to beautify Double Hill; she sees this in terms of "never letting the flag down," and of creating beauty and fineness in particularly "primitive" conditions. Lou contrasts the challenge of the "gorge" with the gracious down-country life her in-laws had left.[19]

> I'd been to Rakahuri; I'd been there. Had a lovely week up there once before you [Peter] came up the gorge, wasn't it, before I came up the gorge. We played tennis and [went] picnicking. It was just before the rot set in [1930], wasn't it, or it had set in and it was not noticeable.

There was still a bit of gracious living. Very gracious living. Mrs.
Ensor came up here [to Double Hill] and every night you'd think she
was going to a cocktail party in a most lovely gown, and old Mr. Ensor would be in his velvet smoking jacket and his tie, and they never
let the flag down did they, Peter? [P: No.] [I used to] change—it's
only since we've been coming up [from their retirement home in
town] and down [from the station cottage] I've got lazy enough not to
change every night and make myself respectable in later years. It was
just amazing how she lived. I can still see her. At six o'clock or half
past six the cook would go out, and they've still got it [at the home-
stead], he would bang on the gong with a bit of iron. It would mean
dinner was ready. And Gran would pick up the silver candelabra and
there was a procession down the cold, cold, cold veranda and [we
would] sit down and have our dinner. There was no back passage or
anything. I've never been so cold in my life as when I was first married, as I was that first winter. (Ensor 1990:26)

Lou noted that Mrs. Ensor put in French doors and a garden—"this was
just a shack more or less when Gran came up and put her French doors in and
made it civilized, and made it just beautiful." Both acts have to do with the incorporation of landscape into a gradually beautified domestic world, the French
doors like verandas opening the inside up to the outside or bringing the outside
inside. The garden is part of that civilizing, neatening process.[20] She finds the
symbols of cultivation beautiful, as well as what she calls the natural surroundings. Lou's world, and those of other women of her generation, was clearly con-
fined by the garden fence, not the property fence, and they specifically note occasions of going beyond that fence. In contrast, Peter never talks in terms of
beauty but of the activity of men and stock in "country."

Significantly opposed to a memory of pioneer life is an encroaching civilized life. This opposition is essential for understanding how Peter and Lou see
the past contrasting with the present. They see themselves as part of that transitional process, and civilization in the sense of modernism is spoken of particularly with reference to the "young." Lou attaches a mystical quality to that pioneering life, but not to the civilized life. She struggles to find opposed terms,
clustering "civilized" around a complex of attributes such as tidy, fenced, acces-
sible, comfortable in terms of living conditions with inside passageways, convenient kitchens, gardens and the like. Lou stresses the challenge of the earlier
days when things were rough and hard, and Mrs. Ensor scrubbed verandas and
kitchens on her knees. She speaks often in terms of the quality of time, the quality of a life lived as well as the hardship. Her perspective is echoed in Jim
Morris's nostalgic poem "Rewards" (1996a:5) where he explains that each day's
satisfaction working in the "rugged grip" of the mountains far exceeds the
pleasure of money and it conveniences, and that a mountain storm feels safer
than a suburban lawn. His closing line is "His recompense—the love of it."

Lou is nostalgic for the vibrant and diverse internal community that defined gorge life before 1971 when a new generation began to farm the properties. Mustering and shearing times were exciting to her, the dogs barking, the
men coming and going "—[Today] it's not the activity that I remembered and

loved. Mustering time was a thrilling time, I thought." And "shearing time was an event." Given the need for greater manpower the population density was greater. Almost there is a subconscious yearning for *gemeinschaft*; the circles were tighter even within the valley when stations were more interconnected and tied through shared radiotelephone contact, and not as autonomous, private and nucleated as they now are.

Of the loss of mystique, Lou says "But there's something, it's lost, it's gone for me that feeling when I was first married and when I used to come up, that mystery. It was down at heel, would you say down at heel, the surroundings. There was a mystery about it, it's all been cut down, tidied up and fenced." Planted trees play a part in Lou's perception of change, the growth of trees and their felling serving, like fence lines, as a measure of time. She told me this the winter before her son-in-law cut out the long plantation of pines that were planted the year she and Peter were married. Trees are a way of marking time, of locating events, of reading the history of habitation, of marking and measuring attachment.

The sense of "mystery" is the clearest reference to Lou's feeling of connection to place. The essence of this is remoteness, and boundedness but not wildness. I asked her directly: "When you say it had a mystery then—it seemed wilder? Less tame?" She replied, "No. It just seemed remote and, you see we've altered the homestead and, oh I don't know what it was about it, but it's gone for me. The only way I get it now, and I'm too lazy to do it, is to go for a walk, you know, around up the cutting up here [she points behind the cottage]. It's . . . civilized [Peter provides her with the word], that's what it is. It was mysterious before to me." Here she makes reference to being beyond the garden fence, that to be "up the cutting" brings back that sense of mystery, of remoteness, which must encompass a notion of inaccessibility, of making do, of struggling, of being an adventurer, set apart, special in being different. The loss of mystery correlates with the homogenization of high-country culture with New Zealand culture. Peter claims to have never had a feeling of mystery, and Lou instantly agrees that he would not have, but he does pinpoint it as a "life of being in places like that, a pioneering sort of thing."

Peter had a list of stories that he wanted me to tape and transcribe and work into the Double Hill history for him when I returned for a winter visit in August 1988. He and Lou knew both sets of stories (his "mustering stories" and her "cookshop stories") but told them separately while often helping or correcting the other as we sipped our noontime sherry. One of the reasons that lengthy interviews with Peter and Lou were possible is that they had an investment in the Double Hill (their) history being told.[21] Our visits too were social events.

Usually the stories were about an unusual event within a routine aspect of life, such as going mustering, or having the shearers up, or the girls going horseback riding; a medical emergency, a fall, a broken arm, a runaway packhorse, disrupt such routines. But as often the story is about those cyclical yearly routine events that punctuate life, particular Christmases, a wedding, the gymkhana, the yearly cricket match, or the High Country Tour. What defines an event is inevitably a break or twist in routine, a mishap, or a joke. Lou cued me in with the

mantra that is part of the settler romance "I'll always remember . . ." or "I'll
never forget . . ." to memories of daughter Clare looking horrified at the egg she
thought she had laid under her chair, or the moment of embarrassment before
her in-laws when she and Peter forgot to bring the mail the nineteen miles up the
valley from the box at the corner by the old Creamery.

Lou knows the details of people's lives, such as where they went after they
left the valley, how they dressed, whom they married, if they were still alive.
Her "assigned" stories are those about the family, especially the children. She
discusses family members, her daughters and her daughters' current lives, "the
young" up the gorge today, her grandchildren and their cousins, the workers
immediately around the homestead such as the cowman/gardener, the cook, occasional child-care helpers and the like. Family history is her domain including
Peter's family history; when I asked Peter questions about his family, he de-
ferred to Lou to provide information about origins, and how the family money
was made. Peter does know in detail all aspects of the inheritance issues concerning Double Hill and he and I had many lunchtime discussions about them;
his narrative in conversation and his written history is dominated by his concern
for maintaining his connection to the property. His life's mission was to be able
to dissolve the estate partnership with his siblings by buying their shares in order
to make the Crown lease his.

Historian Jill Conway (1989:30) in her autobiography *The Road from Coorain*, writes of her childhood in the Australian outback, "our world revolved
around the land and its creatures, the weather and our parents." In Conway's
narrative, in "Glenmark," in Peter and Lou's reminiscences, and in Morris's
ballads, the centrality of narrative is inseparable from attempts to document routine activities, and to inscribe a settler-descendant population on the landscape,
denoting the physical place as a sociocultural space, underscoring a settler insight that the pastoral myth/utopia is neither singular in its expressions nor simply a British derivative. Conway writes of her honors dissertation on the evolution of an Australian merchant family:

> by telling their story I was also tracing the way their prose changed
> from the conventions of early romanticism to a crisper, clearer sense
> of Australia as a place not just to be conquered and made to yield
> wealth, but a piece of earth where one sinks one's roots and learns to
> live as a native rather than an exile. (1989:190)

Such ways of "contriving and manipulating" boundaries of identity and diversity
are often symbolic as people make "ordinary and unremarkable aspects of their
behavior eloquent statements of their identity," as part of a process that Cohen
(1986:viii) defines as consisting of "sectional explosions." In the high country, a
sectional explosion is occurring, which is the process also occurring in peripheral, rural British cultures threatened by "the diminution of structural boundaries, such that geographical distance is bridged . . . cultural distance is attacked"
(Cohen 1986:viii). In this South Island valley, distance has been metaphorically
bridged with improvements in communications and in access, and yet also unbridged with the increasing peripheralization of rural culture. On the one hand

modernization is embraced, and yet on the other a distinctive identity selectively enmeshed in the past is being asserted; that identity is not a static identity constructed out of remnants of history but a blended identity in which an urban upmarket world is selectively integrated with rural life of an immediate past. More is going on than sustaining or reinventing tradition.

Keesing (1989:31) speaks of two processes characterizing the fetishization of culture, both of which are occurring simultaneously in the New Zealand high country: the celebration of "fossilized" or "fetishized" cultures, and the destruction of cultures as ways of life or thought. The senior generation in the high country seems to be evoking visions of the past within their lifetime in their discursive practices, but while aspects of that past are idealized by them, the younger generation sets itself against the fossilization of the colonial past, noting the different ways in which they farm and imagine their relationship with the land. They see themselves not only as stewards of the land but also as conservationists to whom environmental issues are central; changes in farming practice and philosophy support a countercolonial stance. The meanings of their pastoral myth reflect an idea of integration and oneness with the environment rather than of transformation and opposition to the environment. The changing valences of meaning attached to "country" suggest that we must historicize custom (cf. Schwartz 1993).

Keesing (1989) has spoken of the pastoral myth as a Western obsession, but the content of its meaning is changing and variable across generation and gender, and between pakehas. The memory and meaning of the past through reminiscences are shaped by the contingencies of the present. As a colonial past is condemned by Maoris and liberal and egalitarian-minded New Zealanders for whom high-country life, as its legacy, symbolizes elitism, its evocation as a symbol of nationhood is problematic for pakehas. Constructing nationhood in New Zealand today means in part turning away from symbols of that colonial past and turning to the particularities of a cultural (Maori) and geographic (high-country) landscape (which not surprisingly excludes its inhabitants) to construct an identity. Ironically too, descendants of a settler people who came to New Zealand to start a nation anew need to reject and leave the past behind, not to perpetuate it. If "genuinely" indigenous peoples throughout the Pacific and elsewhere stress the symbolic in the absence of continuity of cultural content, high-country station families stress the content of daily life and its perceived continuities with a past. Their "culture" is at an earlier stage of endangerment.

Exogenous Representations

During a return trip to the valley in 1988,[22] I found two photojournalists on a two-week assignment for *Equinox*, a *National-Geographic*-type magazine, who came to research a photo-essay on a runholding family (see Momatiuk and Eastcott 1989). I had read their high-country pictorial book (1987 [1980]) and an earlier magazine article (1978) and thought both exemplified quality photojournalism, not only for the photography and descriptive lyricism, but also for their sensitivity to the central categories of behavior and thought shaping high-country life. Noting that they were "asking us the same kinds of questions you do," families referred the team, Yva Momatiuk and John Eastcott, to me to answer questions about genealogy and history.

In response to my research participants' inquiries into the differences between photojournalism and anthropology, I found myself struggling to articulate for them the distinctions between the tasks involved in each. The event provides an opportunity to explore the theoretical implications of those differences. I focus on this case study as a moment in cultural production, and drawing on preceding and subsequent photojournalistic representations of this particular valley and others, explore some of the distinctions between exogenous media and anthropological representations of the pastoral lessees. As I juxtapose a photojournalistic representation against the context of my own fieldwork, analysis and ethnography, I delineate the uniformity in elements comprising an ongoing high-country mystique.[23] Anthony Cohen urges such an exercise when he discusses the empirical mission of anthropology:

> The anthropologist anxious to avoid the fallacies of cultural reductionism has to distinguish between the locality's voice to the outside world, and its much more complicated message to its own members. Indeed, he must try to make the public message intelligible in terms of the private conversations—and not the other way around. His account must therefore differ from, and seek to enlighten, the gross simplifications of the politician, the bureaucrat, the journalist. (1982:8)

The anthropologist, unlike the journalist, must penetrate the "conventional trope" of high-country nostalgia by contextualizing self-presentation and must explore the motivations surrounding the construction and perpetuation of nostalgia by others.

The *Equinox* team was invited to profile Glenariffe in their story and lived, as I was doing at neighboring Glenaan, in the home of a valley family whom they knew. John had attended Christ's College with Alastair who ran Glenariffe with his wife, Prue. The story they were writing was a portrait of a high-country family, but they ventured beyond this to include other properties because, as Yva and John told me, it was important to be thorough. Some folks were surprised at the choice of locale, which was not typical but certainly special. When Hamish and Alastair divided the family station into two properties of equal carrying capacity, 10,000 hectares including the back country went to Glenaan, and 800 hectares went to Glenariffe. Therefore in size, intensity of cultivation, altitude and topography, Glenariffe does not fit some definitions of "high country"; in terms of its isolation, the social and physical community within which it is embedded, and the placement of the homestead it *is* "high country." Visually the property is splendid and Glenariffe's location in this valley is especially picturesque. The extent of Glenariffe's energetic diversification renders it fascinating to outsiders. Alastair, his brother and their wives systematically implemented innovative breeding schemes for a very fine-wooled merino and also a freshwater fish farm. Prue raises angora rabbits for their fleeces and grows and dries flowers. She was educating the children at home on New Zealand Correspondence School.

To see journalists at work intrigued me. The team asked questions, conducted taped interviews, borrowed reading materials on high-country life, looked at station diaries, and took photographs of station activities. They were sensitive in eliciting native categories and themes and in following the suggestions of their hosts about whom to interview and what activities to observe. I was curious to know about the interaction between photojournalists and informants. How did their presence affect behavior? What were they told and not told? What vision of high-country life would they see and be given? The family must have found it difficult to be onstage over a two-week period, and neighbors sympathized with the strain of constant smiling and posing. Other families recognized that they had to be into their "high-country roles," suggesting to some degree that such non-quotidian roles were familiar to all as well as consciously constructed for outsiders. Because they engineer composition, the team explained to me that their work is not merely documentary. Sometimes a shooting was contrived, such as in a photograph (not used) of a daughter formally dressed holding family heirlooms of cut glass in front of a window.

Despite my curiosity I became mildly frustrated and yet amused as I found that wherever I went, like good ethnographers they too were there. My sense of isolation as a lone fieldworker heightened as I watched the team complement each other in research skills. An essential difference between us is the relatively slight inconvenience of hosting journalists for two weeks and the tangible product to offer hosts in return—hundreds of professional photographs and an article in a popular magazine—in contrast to the perpetual presence of the anomalous participant-observer and her less immediately tangible product. I was concerned that our differently positioned joint presence might create tensions in the community. The presence of Yva and John at Glenariffe and me at Glenaan, two functionally separate properties dyadically linked through brothers and sisters-in-law, could have provided strain (but did not). We might have altered family dynamics in a farming context where economic cooperation and competition is structurally inherent, and in this valley socially and culturally managed and contained.

I spent time with Yva and John.[24] Yva interviewed me about my research, read my proposal, and was eager to know my findings. Their avowedly central challenge in any assignment is to win trust and elicit cooperation, an explicit part of which involves telling people about who they are at home, and making friends. On two occasions they asked me how to approach particular individuals in a way that would not offend. Here, as anthropologist, I was asked to play a role in delineating community dynamics in order to facilitate entrée and ensure fluidity of movement. In their interaction with "my" family, Hamish and Belinda asked to include me and directed the team to me for certain information, such as the name of the ship on which Hamish's great-grandfather came to New Zealand. My interlocutors called on me as an expert on their lives; but perhaps more significantly, they protected me at times by acknowledging my prior claims to specialized knowledge. For example, Peter and Lou had given Yva access to the station diaries, but when I stopped by, I was told that Yva "hadn't got as much out of us as you do." While extended fieldwork might contribute to claims to ethnographic authority as does my preceding sentence (cf. Clifford 1983), it also contributes to our interlocutors' sense of our ethnographic legitimacy, especially in a context where effort is valued above all.

Longitudinal fieldwork obviously enables anthropologists to read roles connotatively rather than denotatively, and in so doing we examine them as manifestations of structural conditions rather than personality alone. The journalists treated me primarily as an outsider in a structurally parallel position whose perspective might be helpful in understanding the dynamics of the valley; although their presence is part of my story, understandably my presence there was not part of their story. Journalists do not share with the anthropologist a "theory of praxis" in which anthropology is perceived as "an activity which is part of what it studies" (Fabian 1983:157) and the process of the production of knowledge is politicized and documented as participants involved are seen as coeval with the anthropologist rather than allochronic (Fabian 1983:30). Responses to the article echo high-country residents' continuing contestations about identity, which are not apparent in the article: Who is truly high-country? Which properties are more high-country than others are? Being born to the high country, "knowing one's geography," traveling by foot or jeep rather than motorbike, holding a pastoral lease or a certain acreage or altitude or remoteness are some of the variables used to negotiate belonging. Some high-country folk who read the *Equinox* article saw it as a portrait of the personality of the particular family and its members, not as a comparative statement about high-country life even though in the end the title suggests that the article was about contemporary high-country life in a more general sense. The photographs reflected not only attention to the daily activities defining high-country life, but also the visual world of high-country inhabitants and the importance of the past.

Yva and John were attuned to composition, aesthetics, and narrative in framing their shots. They had creative control over that part of the process, but in constructing the article they were mindful of the editors' power to determine which photographs would be published. One cannot know from the article how their choice of subjects to photograph comprised a sense of the place; they had to preselect in such a way as to ensure the selection of certain photographs— photographs that were visually powerful or photographs that they thought would please their subjects. Because one family went to considerable effort to stage a correspondence-school session, the team chose to include one of those photographs for their editors even though they had taken better shots of another family, but the photograph was not published. John shot at least nine rolls per day. He explained that of several hundred shots that might go to the editor for selection twenty to twenty-five might make it into the article. He and Yva mark their own preferences.

Twelve photographs define the story: a cover photograph, a double-page photograph, three full-page, four half-page and three less-than-half-page photographs. On the front cover, Alastair carries a pregnant ewe in a rainy setting, working dogs by his side. A double spread again portrays Alastair and his dogs working against mountain, river, and tussock-grassland backdrop. Three full photographs illustrate stock guiding the viewer toward a backdrop of river and hills, a neighboring high-country farmer with his rams against a setting of rolling tussock, and an interior portrait of the same farmer with his young daughter.

A simple content count reveals an emphasis on pastoral activity: sheep (7 instances), tussock and male lessees (5 each), working dogs and hills (4), the river and children (3), stationhands (2), and women (1). The vast scale of the landscape is stressed with tussock grass, the mountains, and the wide rocky, braided South Island river as its central features. Significantly, there are no photographs of the homesteads, but one photograph is set (unidentifiably) in a kitchen, two in the woolshed, and one in the rabbit shed. Working dogs and children are well represented; women are not, nor is the domestic domain, with the exception of one father-and-daughter photograph. Implicitly in the photographs and explicitly in the text, men are equated with their dogs, both love their life "scrambling over the hills" (32).[25] No interaction between people is seen, but Alastair's words in the text emphasize that he cherishes both the land and "the people in this valley" (45). Rather than presenting Rakaia life as a whole, the work of farming, especially stock management, is stressed. This focus on a world of working men, of attractive children and picturesque vistas, reflects *Equinox's* editorial decisions—decisions shaped perhaps by its Canadian audience with its own parallel pioneer heritage and Western grasslands—and distorts Yva and John's sensitivity to the centrality of the family as a work unit where women and men creatively redefine their roles. These published images reinforce old stereotypes of a pioneer world of maleness and traditional gender roles.[26] The dominant static pictorial narrative of the article is reinforced by its misleading descriptor "New Zealand's high-country farmers prepare for modern times" as if change were new to this well-established progressive generation of young farmers; the first title Yva submitted, "Oh what a life! But sheep farmers of New Zealand's high country meet worrisome times" is far more balanced. Despite the centrality of the pictorial, here Yva and John's authorial voices are silenced.

The magazine's front cover reads "High-Country Chronicles." Using a chronological organizational trope, the text effectively follows an August day with diversions to the yearly agricultural cycle, the history of settlement in the valley, and the current political and economic climate. It weaves around the photographs and includes anecdotes and vivid descriptions of the physical place, the people, and the activities and farming details that define their lives. Alastair moves an electric break fence to give the Corriedales more feed, checks on pregnant ewes, and returns to lunch at the homestead where correspondence lessons supervised by Prue are photographed. He locates Glenariffe in the valley, tracing out the links between families and properties; he takes phone calls; in the afternoon, he goes to the sheepyards with the hired man to drench sheep against intestinal worms. The reader is reminded of the juxtaposition of traditional methods with modern drugs (35). The yearly agricultural cycle is explained, as is the price of modernization for this generation of farmers, as mountain "tops" were retired from farming and lower pasture was improved with new grasses (37). The theme of continuity and change shifts the reader back from electric fences and machinery syndicates to the arrival of Alastair's grandfather 130 years ago. The 19-year-old son of an Anglican rector was "hell-bent on investing in the fabled Pacific utopia" (39). The narrative moves quickly through 130 years of farming prosperity and debt. High-country resilience emerges in the words of Alastair's mother—recalling the discovery at marriage that the Glenariffe homestead was a rabbiter's hut, she said as she had said to me "so I had to get on with it" (39).

"The old country's customs endured" during the Depression and World War II as the family "kept their gardens beautiful, updated home libraries and shipped pianos upriver" (39); the river "that once controlled access to the outside world" is less formidable in the age of jetboats. The day's routine moves to the woolshed and a description of shearers and their lives. Some are Ngai Tahu, and Yva takes the opportunity to discuss Ngai Tahu claims against the Crown for restitution of high-country lands (41).[27] The seemingly uncomplicated trajectory of Maori and pioneer pakeha over the landscape is summarized, echoing the pastoral lessees' telling of history (42). Other adversarial forces—the demands of hikers, fishermen and skiers for greater access to land, conservationists' demands to limit grazing and burning and to retire more land, and the omnipresent threat of the weather—are mentioned. The reader is taken by Toyota Landcruiser further into the Southern Alps to a station across the river where one hears "the steady drone of the engine in low gear and the rush of the river" (43). Here, at this run, is Butler's *Erewhon*-equivalent, at the remotest remove from civilization.[28] The fascination for the past is underscored by the authors' use of terminology—the old-fashioned term "runholder" is preferred to pastoral lessee in the narrative; some self-conscious traditionalists use the term self-ascriptively, but many younger high-country farmers do not.

The textual narrative argues that high-country farmers' attachment to the land echoes a spiritual affinity for place. Yva writes: "Runholders seldom talk about the land in spiritual terms as if words could not live up to anything so important" (42). The "as if" is speculative; equally speculative is her assertion that the farmer "may say" (but does not?), "It's loving it [the land], rather than owning it" (33). The anthropologist's presence may have primed informants to present themselves in a particular way.[29] Our central narratives are shared; my own research proposal posited a distinctive sense of place as constitutive of high-country identity. Seldom did runholders convey their feeling directly in language or response to my questions, although they have begun to articulate the affinity in testimony before the Waitangi Tribunal (see chapter 7). For the most part, I have had to read the meanings embedded in the land in farming practices, kinship patterns, architectural design, toponymy and symbolic inscriptions. That is not to say, however, that the high country is not under particular pressure that evokes an active and more explicit process of identity formation.

To document spiritual affinity, the journalists essentialize and naturalize the farmers' link with an opening story about a sheepdog's love of his shared life with the farmer (32). Yva writes that "like the dogs, Alastair was born into steepness and he moves agilely across it." His genetic connection seems unassailable, and my study of inheritance reveals that social patterns ensure the transmission of the particularity of knowledge of a given property from generation to generation in ways that similarly naturalize attachment. The narrative progresses—people farm here "being *part of* a very special country" where "ties have long roots" and "affinity for the high country . . . is now being tested by more than just flooding rains, scorching droughts and windshield shattering freezes" as "unfriendly forces rock New Zealand runholders" (35, emphasis added).

The key image constructed in photograph and text is of pastorality characterized by the integral link between people and the physical place. The essence of the article can best be conveyed with a quote from Alastair: "Everybody who visits this valley says, 'Here you are in your own little world, cut off from reality' while we know everything that touches us. We farm land some believe cannot be farmed at all. It is true for all of us; you have to love it to want this life" (45). Through Yva's textual voice, Alastair simultaneously breaks the Edenic view of a remote utopia that his audience might expect and perpetuates and reconstructs a different pastoral view for that same audience, one idyllicized through the challenges it provides.[30] Even so in the final product the pastoral image seemingly shared by the runholders is homogenized for a homogenized audience. But I would argue that urban people, or even all other high- and non-high-country farming people do not share it. And yet, in the immediacy of its portrayal, the article is remarkable.

Two contemporaneous articles in the *New Zealand Listener* (Ansley 1989a, 1989b) and a segment of New Zealand Television's *Country Calendar* on one of the valley's properties parallel one another especially in conveying a sense of deep almost genetic affinity for the land and place. *Country Calendar* weaves its story around the pastoral lessee as a combination of romance and reserve, and it asserts that "this country holds a grip on its high-country men that is hard to shake off." The 15 July 1989 issue of the *Listener* ran photographs of a husband/wife farming team with text reading "the high country is bred into them, like the eye in a good dog" (1989b). Yva, as I have mentioned, writes of Alastair that like the dogs he was "born into steepness." Each of these articles reflects the runholders' uncertainty over their tenure as pastoral lessees, that "it would only take the stroke of a pen from some politician" to end it. The words were echoed in Yva and John's interview with Hamish: "everything touches us here." People assume an isolation that is false, as government decisions have always affected their lives. Since I began to study the stations in the valley, there have been two Australian magazine articles, two agricultural on-site field days, and a third television film.[31]

This sort of attention to the high country is not unusual.[32] Its mystique is renowned, its literature extensive (in fact almost synonymous with New Zealand literature). One runholder said she was "tired of being an attraction," and that "things have got out of hand up here." Another farmer told his wife and me that he would not maneuver his horse across the river for the photojournalists—"one gets bloody sick and tired of it all." Finally he did, many times for many shots, "for Mum's sake." They wonder what is so interesting about their lives. A property toward the end of the valley does not mind the attention, because it is good promotion for their tourist ventures. While their shepherd shyly takes the long way home to avoid the cameras of Japanese and American skiers, the lessee willingly "poses between two birds" and jokes about the holes in his work jersey. The attention has heightened as runholders have sought to protect their land against the claims of Ngai Tahu and environmentalists and market their sense of self to tourists, Maoris, and urban people by engaging in diversification schemes such as running heli-skiing operations and farm holidays. But such contextualized attention gives runholders a complicitous voice.

Photojournalistic representations reflect captivation by the received and perceived romance of pastoral life. Inhabitants and photojournalists fuse the supposed reality of one with the representation by the other, thus seeming to share aspects of the "conventional trope" of "yearning for a pastoral past." To avoid this complicity, the anthropologist's task is to penetrate the trope—to go beyond rhetoric, to recognize and find a plurality of discourses, and to uncover the particular meanings of this image of pastoral utopia within both historical and contemporary political contexts. To fuse the supposed reality of the settler-descendant with its photojournalistic representation is to merge the viewer or the naturalist with the object of the gaze, the subject. As Bettina Lerner writes,

> Journalists, as opposed to anthropologists, will never find out the truth about the [Xs] from the [Xs] themselves. . . . Journalists are not trained to be anthropologists. We often, quite inadvertently, ask crude, leading questions, questions whose meaning is dependent on a shared frame of reference between journalist and interviewee. . . I believe it [gleaning the truth] is a job for anthropologists, who have a completely different methodology, and different skills. . . . We should be looking to science to sort out the truth . . . not to the media.[33] (1990:21)

At a time when high-country station families, together with all New Zealanders, are engaged in "nominating certain local practices as definitive of local identity," in a "reactive process of collective self-identification" (Foster 1992:284), researchers must be attentive to the ways in which the agency of pastoral lessees enables them to participate and shape a particular political and cultural process—the objectification of culture (Linnekin 1990)—through the words of those who represent them.

In her comparison of travel writing and ethnographic writing, Mary Louise Pratt argues that by recognizing which "tropes are neither natural nor native to the discipline," we enable ourselves to "appropriate" or "invent" new ones (1986:50). In particular, she focuses on the history of the "discursive configuration" between personal narrative and impersonal objectified description in travel writing, suggesting that the practice of combining them is not unique to ethnographic writing (1986:28). This and other "tropes" shared with anthropology occur also in photojournalistic representations, especially in adventure travelogues where authors render the exotic, no matter how familiar, visible and entertaining. The *Equinox* text is written in richly descriptive language as a reflexive narrative of the authors' experience, and therefore the readers' vicarious experience, in the valley.

Few anthropologists and sociologists have attended to the ethnography of contemporary pakeha New Zealand, and fewer still to rural New Zealand (Carter 1986; R. R. Hall 1987; Hall, Thorns, and Willmott 1983, 1984; Hatch 1992; Mahar n.d.; Somerset 1974[1938]). The high country has been the terrain for representation by modes of discourse other than anthropology and has been portrayed primarily as a pastoral utopia in the antipodes, as part of an arcadian vision with deep roots (Fairburn 1975). The seemingly idyllic, pastoral, close-knit community housed before the stunning backdrop of the mountains in the valley in which I work is not merely a fact of being or of romanticism but a continually living and, consciously and unconsciously, willfully constructed manifestation of identity of a particular category of people. Hall, Thorns and Willmott (1983:60) turn their attention to locality as a focus for research and examine the contemporary resurgence of local identities. They suggest that sociologically informed historical research will enable us to understand the processes involved in the formation and transformation of rural social structures in New Zealand (see, for example, R. R. Hall 1987). In particular, Hall, Thorns, and Willmott (1983) argue that we must ask whose interests have been served by utopian myths, especially those embedded in notions of equality, mobility and the emergence of community.

Rather than seeking to expose what lies behind the well-publicized mystique of the high country, most popular representations buy into the iconography, into those very symbols, thereby pointing to continuous themes and perpetuating the mystique. The articles and documentaries tend to accept and perhaps exploit the themes uncritically and unquestioningly. British explorer and writer, Robin Hanbury-Tenison (1989:196), for example, writes that while land belongs to Europeans, Maoris belong to the land. That sounds good, but the author does not explore this rhetoric and uses Western hegemonic discourse as a way of thinking about pakeha and Maori concepts of ownership. But anthropologists F. Allan Hanson (1989, 1997) and Roger Keesing (1989) have penetrated the rhetoric and provocatively invited attack by suggesting that Maori conceptual frameworks themselves may be partly invented traditions defined by and in opposition to pakeha frameworks.

Writing in 1940 of the attempts within New Zealand literature to find "the local meanings of reality," philosopher Morgan Holcroft speaks of the then existing indifference of the majority of New Zealanders toward their physical environment: "there is a brisk trade in the illustrated annuals which depict the outdoor scene in a somewhat monotonous photography" (1940:82, 19). While acknowledging "a sentimental interest in the country for its own sake," he suggests that "it remains more or less inarticulate." He gives a Samuel-Butleresque example of what is needed through a personal memory of a camping trip at Lake Heron in the upper Rakaia valley:

> It was high summer; the days were bright and warm, and I found my
> pleasure in sitting for hours with my back against a tussock. I

watched the colours change on the mountains across the lake, wondering at the depths which lie between the hard brilliance of noon and
the tender drift of shadows in the dusk. I noticed once again the way
in which the peaks and ridges that are so obviously barren and remote
in full daylight come nearer to the senses in twilight and move, on the
insinuations of tonal change—contributed by the sunset, the stillness
of the lake and the lucid quality of mountain air—towards a moment
of irresistible union with the submerged shapes of mind. At such
times, pondering the curious extensions of spirit and soil, the individual can experience the demonstration of an idea. He is able to know,
with a proof expounded by the senses, that the body and its environment have merely an illusory separateness. . . . Some of us must try,
within the limits of our strength, to escape from easy and superficial
ways of thinking and make a new journey into the wilderness.
(1940:85-86)

As the anthropologist attempts that hermeneutic journey, she moves from
an exploration of overt to latent dimensions of culture. The story of these stations, and others like them, has been well told in documentary films, *Country
Calendar* sequences, newspaper feature articles, and photojournalistic essays.
The high country is much romanticized as an Edenic place or for its idyllic pastoral lifestyle, and consequently is often stereotyped and misunderstood. Today,
such misunderstandings are perceived to threaten a cultural landscape as its inhabitants see themselves in a "present-becoming-past" and actively invite "pastoral allegories of cultural loss and textual rescue," a salvage or "redemptive"
ethnography (Clifford 1986:113, 115) that they cannot produce for themselves
and that *we* may resist as theoretically stagnant, allochronic and homogenizing.[34]
High-country farming families oscillate between Clifford's metanarratives of
homogenization and emergence on the one hand, and loss and invention on the
other.

My analysis of the ways in which high-country station families selectively
evoke and use "the rural life-modes of the recent past" (Gullestad 1989) as symbols of identity illustrates how one community is responding to the increasing
peripheralization of rural culture. They find those very symbols being coopted
by urban people who claim "visual ownership" of the mountains and claim their
stake in public mountain lands.[35] The ruggedness of the landscape, its undeni-
able beauty and its stark altitude highlight it as a particular kind of land; it is
visible from throughout the South Island in a striking way; it is also symbolic of
the distinctiveness of the New Zealand landscape, almost metonymic of national
identity even for those who would never participate in mountain activities or are
unfamiliar with high-country farming life. Runholders and their families react
against the homogenization of identity through the appropriation by others of
their most significant political symbol of identity, namely the landscape they
inhabit, by documenting the fact and process of habitation by humans and domestic stock.

Notes

1. Born in Canterbury, Basil Dowling (1910-   ) has lived in England for many years. Like Dallas and Brasch, he is a South Island poet with romantic temperament whose verse was "a response to the natural world" and for whom land is a "benign Eden" (Jackson and Caffin 1991:388). According to Acland (1975:275-278) Glenmark, leased by G. H. Moore, was one of the most valuable properties in Canterbury. Freehold and leasehold land combined comprised 150,000 acres and carried 90,000 sheep. Eldred-Grigg (1980:113) reports that Moore's great house was rumored to have cost £90,000. The land was divided after the death of Moore's daughter in 1914.

2. In "The Bio-Politics of a Multicultural Field," Haraway discusses *National Geographic* representations of mountain gorillas and "the heterogeneous people who claim them as theirs" as "versions of what can count as nature for nineteenth- and twentieth-century Europeans, Euro-Americans, and—finally—Africans" (1989:263). She examines the ways in which *National Geographic* and recent films of "colonial nostalgia" uncritically play into colonial discourses of race, gender and nature. "Africa remains the heart of the west's unconscious, denied history still in its practices of representations, from fashion clothing to conservation tourism to the images still brought *Out of Africa*" (1989:268).

3. A parallel argument is made by Keesing (1989:25) for Pacific populations for whom "on the eve of European invasion, there were multiple 'realities.'" He writes, "Genealogies, cosmologies, rituals were themselves contested spheres. The 'authentic' past was never a simple, unambiguous reality. The social worlds of the Pacific prior to European invasion were, like the worlds of the present, multifaceted and complex."

4. I use *representation* in a literal sense to mean a nonanalytic portrayal, an evocation of a way of life (Keesing 1987). Stephen Tyler (1986:122, 123) opposes representation to evocation arguing that ethnography should *avoid* representation and be instead a "superordinate discourse," evoking "what cannot be known discursively." Strathern (1991:7-8) provides a useful discussion of "representation and evocation" in anthropology.

5. Most noteworthy is Ngaio Marsh's detective fiction, such as *Died in the Wool* set on a remote sheep station. Carole Acheson (1985:170) writes of the station as the central image in the novel, "symbolizing the multiple role the sheep station has played in New Zealand's history: bringing settlers to the secluded hill country; making sheep the backbone of the nation's economy; and creating a new landed gentry out of the wealthy station owners." Significantly, Acheson (1985:159) quotes the following from Dennis McEldowney's review of Marsh's autobiography: "She has always contrived to write about New Zealand as though she were a visitor, while believing she was a native"; Acheson (1985:164) says that typically Marsh casts her detective hero Alleyn as the outsider. Despite this narrative device, her perspective is less anthropological than one might expect. Acheson concludes that despite Marsh's passion for the land and its role in shaping a national identity and her concern for the Maori people, "she had considerably less sympathy for the pakehas' rejection of British culture, and felt nothing but distaste for the self-imposed parochialism." (1985:173).

6. A distinctive New Zealand pakeha literature has emerged more in poetry than in novels. Few novels are set in the South Island pastoral high country; some were written by non-New Zealanders—Samuel Butler's utopian novel *Erewhon*, Deborah Savage's children's book *A Rumour of Otters* (1986), and Elizabeth Gowan's popular novel *Heart of the High Country* (1985). Butler lived in New Zealand from 1860-1864; an American, Savage lived in Auckland for two years in 1981 and had not been to the South Island; Gowan is a Londoner. For earlier examples written in a Victorian pastoral, feminist

mode, see the romance novels of Louisa Baker (1894) and Edith Searle Grossman (1910). Philip Temple's (1979) historical novel of pioneer South Island back-country life, *Stations*, accepts the primacy of nature and examines differently gendered and generational perceptions of landscape. Essie Summers wrote the first of her more than forty pastoral romances in 1961, published by Harlequin and Mills & Boon. I thank Ann Chowning for bringing her novels to my attention.

7. Holcroft in 1943 wrote that New Zealand poetry was "the creative activity which has reached the highest state of development within our culture" (9). While one cannot point to a specifically high-country poet, Ursula Bethell, Charles Brasch, Allen Curnow, Ruth Dallas, and A. R. D. Fairburn are all concerned with "responding to the suggestions of the New Zealand landscape" and "feel the challenge of our undiscovered landscapes" (Holcroft 1943:84, 88). Holcroft (1943:76) writes of Brasch's *"The Land and the People* [as] more than anything else a warning that the mountains and silent places of this country are still unknown to us; that they must remain aloof from, yet disturbingly close to, our culture until we have learned to include their physical suggestions in the framework of our lives."

8. Most significant is Murray Ball's *Footrot Flats* cartoon strip about farm life, although not specifically high-country life, created in 1975. *Footrot Flats: The Dog's* ~~Tail~~ *Tale* (1986), based on a screenplay by Murray Ball and Tom Scott, is one of several collections of Ball's work in book form. For an analysis see Corballis and Small (1985) who outline the New Zealand myths around which Ball weaves his social criticism.

9. See for example, Constance Gray (1970) and Barbara Harper (1967).

10. Among the voluminous Canterbury accounts are those of Mona Anderson (1963), Betty Dick (1964), Evelyn Hosken (1964), David McLeod (1974), and Peter Newton (1947). Lady Barker's *Station Life in New Zealand* (1883) is a classic, but Barker, who arrived with her husband Frederick Broome in 1865, like Butler returned to England.

11. In her chapter, "Apes in Eden, Apes in Space: Mothering as a Scientist for the *National Geographic*," Haraway (1989:56) examines the Museum of Natural History, *Natural History*, and *National Geographic* as "science for the people."

12. Marilyn Strathern (1991:xiii-xvi) points the way in her discussion of complexity—"the perception of increasable complication" and the "perpetual multiplication of things to know"—as intrinsic to both the ethnographic and comparative enterprise. Her notions of scale adjustment, the scale of observation, of multiplicities, partial connections and perspectives in anthropology's move to a postplural perception of the world are vital for writing anthropology.

13. Speaking with a historian's voice, Renwick (1987:212) challenges anthropologists among others to explore the role of knowledge in the construction of social reality.

14. For station histories see especially David McLeod (1970, 1974, 1980) and more recently Burdon (1987) and Aspinall (1993). For Canterbury regional histories, see as examples W. H. Scotter (1972) and D. N. Hawkins (1957). I consulted Canterbury holdings in social and local history, geography, and literature at the University of Canterbury and the Canterbury Public Library, and public archival holdings (genealogical, settlement and estate records) at the Canterbury Museum and the Department of Lands and Survey. My work prompted the writing of two station histories, both supplemented by oral narratives and based on farm diaries. One of these runholders, both of whom are now deceased, left the history with expectations that his son would complete it. Convention dictates that materials stay with properties, not with individuals.

15. Diary prose and content is formulaic, remaining unchanged over an eighty-year period: for example, the convention of "Self" is used consistently instead of first-person singular "I." The designs of the diaries have changed—from A4 volumes finely bound with paisley endpapers to six-by-eight inch standard-issue diaries from the stock and

station companies; the penmanship too has changed from fine fountain-pen script to hurried ballpoint entries. I have worked with three generations' diaries from the Rakaia properties.

16. The relative shallowness of pakeha history, touching 150 years in 1990, sets it apart from Polynesia including Maori-occupied New Zealand, and Europe.

17. See chapter 5.

18. Diaries documenting the autumn musters during World War II note the "wide beats" that men had to take as fewer men had to cover the same traditional territory.

19. See Hatch (1992) for a detailed ethnographic analysis of social hierarchy in rural New Zealand focusing especially on the gentry and notions of "refinement." Eldred-Grigg (1980) is also useful. See also Scotter (1965:28) with reference to pastoral lease-holders as a class at the end of the nineteenth century. Also see Gould (1970), Fair-weather (1985), Brooking (1986), and McAloon (1996).

20. Comaroff (1989:673) writes of Africa metaphorically as "the African garden" whose contribution to commercial agriculture was part of the imperial marketplace. It served "to reduce the landscape . . . to an ordered array of square, neatly bounded residences (with rooms and doors, windows and furniture, field and fences), enclosure being the condition of private property."

21. This is not a history of station dates, which are systematically documented in records and often not committed to memory. Marcus (1988:4) characterizes such writing by notable family elders as "as an index of concern of those in authority to make a final concrete effort to shape a legacy, to capture for the record the family's reputation in transmission."

22. I had returned to complete a station history and to prepare evidence on behalf of the pastoral lessees to the Waitangi Tribunal (see Dominy 1990b and chapter 7).

23. Thomas (1991) elaborates the distinction between fieldwork, ethnographic analysis and the writing of ethnography.

24. Back in the United States, John and Yva have shared their tape transcripts and screened their high-country photographs for me.

25. Note this from the Canterbury section of Maurice Shadbolt's and Brian Brake's *Reader's Digest Guide to New Zealand*, a coffee-table volume published in 1988: "The sight of a lone musterer and his dogs working a mob of sheep evokes quite the most arresting legend left on a New Zealand landscape by Europeans" (1988:263).

26. In contrast, in 1965 a North American shot the longest segment of his documentary film on New Zealand at neighboring Double Hill. The film's focus on meat-and-wool production as the heart of the New Zealand economy contrasts with the visual aspect of the *Equinox* article, because the former focuses equally on the domestic activities of mother, father and daughter. In the film, concerns are expressed for the future of the farm and the need to keep it in the family as we are told that farming the land is learned by experience, passed from generation to generation.

27. Some of which are being claimed as remedy for other violations of the Treaty of Waitangi of 1840.

28. Shadbolt and Brake reinforce the image. Shadbolt writes: "For visionary gentlemen colonists, the sky was literally the limit, at the least the permanent snows of the alpine interior" (1988:252).

29. After hearing anthropologists' testimony on behalf of Ngai Tahu in their land claims before the Waitangi Tribunal, the New Zealand South Island High Country Committee of Federated Farmers approached me; they recognized my [anthropological] language and asked if I could provide testimony for them (see Dominy 1990a, 1990b for a discussion of ethics).

30. Momatiuk and Eastcott (1978:264) write that pastoralists found their utopia in the high country but also write of the complexity of the "pastoral existence" (1978:258). Robin

Hanbury-Tenison's title *Fragile Eden: A Ride through New Zealand* unfortunately is to be read literally with the bookjacket promise of a tired theme—"the romance of the adventure story with the stark realities of twentieth-century life."

31. A British film crew producing a documentary on Maori land and fishing claims came to interview Hamish. I was told in correspondence from the valley that they "were here for half a day and Hamish took up a minute on film."

32. I have newspaper clippings on the valley dating from 1939 and have viewed a documentary made by the New Zealand Film Unit in the 1950s and another, by a North American, filmed in 1965.

33. Anthropologists in a postmodern era may not be in the business of "gleaning the [singular] truth"; some are attentive to insights provided by feminist critiques of science and alert to the distortions inherent within (see Haraway 1989). Despite allegiance to authority-questioning ethnographies, our invocations of a postnostalgic era are themselves suspect.

34. Clifford (1988:17) writes also that modern ethnographic histories reflect the "historical-political invention of cultures and traditions," a selective, but not necessarily continuous process, as his case of the Mashpee "tribe" illustrates. Much, he says, has been reinvented and revived in complex oppositional contexts.

35. For Britain, Marilyn Strathern (1982:248) has explored R. E. Pahl's parallel concept "the village of the mind."

PART II
FAMILY

Photo 6 View from Turtons Saddle. Glenaan homestead (center) with the Rakaia, Mount Algidus Point, and Glenthorne Station in the very far distance. (See map I-1.)

Chapter Three

Homesteads and the Domestic Landscape

Beneath the hostile heights homestead and farm repose.
—Ursula Bethell, "By Burke's Pass" in O'Sullivan (1997:36)

At the inhabited center of high-country pastoralism lies the station homestead, the farm family's dwelling, and its encompassing domestic landscape—the driveway, cultivated gardens of flower beds and lawns, orchards and vegetable gardens, farm buildings and yards, and tree plantings shaping the sheltered homestead paddocks—that comprise the built environment of the Canterbury high country.[1] Beyond lie the station paddocks sheltered by landforms of high relief and planted shelterbelts of pines and poplars, and even farther removed lie larger higher altitude blocks extending out to the remote and rugged back country. While most of the holdings comprising these properties are Crown pastoral land, leased from the New Zealand government, the station buildings, gardens and cultivated paddocks often occupy freehold land.

Aerial photographs and maps point iconically to consistent regularities in spatial layout that reflect aspects of both social and conceptual systems organizing high-country life. J. B. Harley (1992) treats maps as Derridan texts by focusing on their rhetorical features or devices and their inherent intertextuality; he urges Foucaultian ethnography of modern cartography that acknowledges its links to the politics of knowledge. An intertextual reading of spatial forms suggests that the dominant station configuration is one of encompassment, of boundaries within boundaries, characterized elsewhere as a "geography of enclosures" (Kolodny 1972:55). Such a geography renders space contained, domestic, protected, constructed, cultivated, renders it "country"; it also centers the homestead. Dividing country into "front" and "back" creates its boundaries. My focus is the innermost enclosure, that of the homestead and its immediate grounds excluding the proximate farm buildings, that marks "front" country. The homestead is at the center of a series of layered semicircles, visibly unmistakable from the air. An approach from the ground reinforces this layered effect as one moves into the high country to the homestead deep within. Landscape architect Graham Densem, a nephew of Allan and Betty Dick of Lilybank, nostalgically and clearly recalled for me his childhood visits in the late 1950s:

> I remember the excitement of isolation that the house engendered in a town boy. It was an adventure getting to Lilybank—mentally "driving" car (from the back seat) up Burkes Pass, up the gravel road from Tekapo, over rattly cattlestops, through exciting puddles, juddering over corrugations, "windows up" against the dust if something came the other way, calling from the wind-up phone in the tin shed, then across the thirty-six fords of the Macaulay [River] in Uncle Allan's war-surplus four-wheel-drive truck. That the homestead had to survive when cut off by snow or flood was confirmed to a ten-year-old by the big storeroom and the radiotelephone. The correspondence school room that my cousin Bruce, the same age as me, did his schooling in confirmed that it was isolated. And the power generator that was turned off at the end of the evening. The house was to me a living embodiment of that isolation and survival, and I was aware of it (if less verbosely) then. (E-mail to author, 7 April 1995)

Robert Pinney (1971:155-158) notes that Lilybank's remoteness and location—against the Southern Alps and between the Godley and Macaulay rivers at the head of Lake Tekapo—placed it at the edges of settlement's limits until 1863. Despite the adventure and potential challenge of such isolation, Densem characterized what is special about the station as "comfy." It "felt secure," he told me, with its "set routine" where scones were served at a certain time, where social life, like the physical layout and activities of the station, was ordered.[2]

Cultural anthropologists, influenced by the work of Émile Durkheim and Marcel Mauss, Claude Lévi-Strauss, and Irving Goffman, have explored the intimate association of "divisions of space and social formations" and the mutual dependence of "behaviour and space" as "space defines people" and "people define space"; fittingly, Shirley Ardener (1993:2-3) calls the expression of these social relationships (such as kinship) and structures (such as hierarchical systems) "social maps"; and Henrietta Moore argues that "the meanings of what she [Moore] would call 'spatial texts' . . . continuously shift and are reworked" (cited in Carsten and Hugh-Jones 1995:41). Calling for an integration of symbolic approaches and social production theories, and stressing the approaches of Michel Foucault and Anthony Giddens, Denise Lawrence and Setha Low (1990:460-465) in their review of literature on the built environment encourage explanations in particular of the processual relationship between social organization and dwelling form as it is embedded in larger sociocultural systems (also see Chambers and Low 1989:6; Bourdier and Alsayyad 1989). One avenue of approach for understanding changing housing and social relationships is through an archaeology of structures (see Behar 1986), maps, diaries, and landscape.

Siting Homesteads

Early settlers typically located their homesteads in sheltered areas near streams, within hollows, and in the shadows of hills; frequently the homestead would surrender warmth, altitude and a view for protection from the elements. The old houses tended to ignore the sun and avoid the wind. One elderly woman who had moved to Otago high country with her husband to provide a larger property for their four sons described coming to the sad old homestead: "it had straight rows of pines as shelter so close to the house they blocked the light—it had small windows, small rooms and was very run down. . . . Eventually the house was renovated. It had a concrete foundation and they said it was hard to extend but we did add to the living room and we extended all the windows." Similarly at Snowdon when the Tripp family first came to the property, the stately homestead, sheltered by too many trees against the northwest boundary, got no sun. The rings date the trees over one hundred years. Big rows of trees, three deep around the northwest side, provided shelter for the cottage and vegetable garden, but they funneled the wind in around the homestead. To let the sun in so that the snow melts away, the family has taken down the trees.

Many other factors determined placement of early homesteads—proximity to water and firewood, aspect, land tenure and the limitations of available building materials (see Salmond 1986:61). In *A First Year in Canterbury Settlement*, Samuel Butler offers advice on homestead placement.

> You must put it in such a situation as will be most convenient for working the sheep. . . . All considerations of pleasantness of site must succumb to this. . . . You *must*, however, have water and firewood at hand, which is a great convenience, to say nothing of the saving of labour and expense. Therefore, if you can find a bush near a stream, make your homestead on the lee side of it. (1964[1863]: 118)[3]

Sometimes placement was determined by the land's having been bought from the provincial government as freehold.

Some properties did favor a view (but not always the sun). In his description of the Grasmere homestead in the Waimakariri valley, runholder and author David McLeod writes:

> The house stands, or rather crouches, beside a small glaciated hill in the very mouth of the Cass River where it emerges from its deep-cut valley between the Craigieburn and the Black Ranges. It is a poor place for a homestead, wind-swept and icy cold, and set on soil which is seventy-five percent stones. But oh, what a deeply rewarding view it has down the long slope of the fan to the beautiful pool of Lake Grasmere nearly two miles away! (1974:22)

When McLeod's son, Ian, sought a site to build a cottage homestead, he noted that the freehold did not run up the side of the hill and the flats were "by no means the best spot on which to have built a house" (McLeod 1980:224). Like

many of his generation, he sought an unrestricted view and the warmth of the
sun and negotiated an adjustment in the freehold to do so:

> Ian decided that he would like to get more sun and less frost, not to
> mention a better view. . . . [I]n due course the cottage was built, with
> a panorama of the whole Cass Valley spread out beneath it and sun
> beating straight on to it from early dawn until the great dark bulk of
> Misery cut it off in the late afternoon. Nothing could move in the
> whole wide basin; neither trains on the line nor traffic on the road nor
> station work in the paddocks; not even ducks upon the lake without
> being seen by a watcher from its windows.
>
> There was one snag of course—the wind. The wind that whirls
> over the Misery ridge from the west and, confined by the narrow
> Cass Valley, emerges in a series of violent blasts.
>
> To protect the cottage from these blasts we had to grow some
> trees as quickly as possible. (1980:224-225)

In early days, building fences took priority over improving homes. Now at
the stage of the developmental cycle with disposable income, women work on
their homes and gardens although always with an eye to balancing pragmatism
with aesthetics; often the best site for a homestead in terms of the view will be
too windy and has to be sacrificed; in one instance parents vetoed the architect's
plan for three peaks on the homestead roof for their son and his wife—the reason "totally pragmatic, snow risk."

With fierce winds and bitter cold winters, the Manuka Point homestead especially illustrates this shifting balance between pragmatics and aesthetics.
Originally a 5,000-acre run when it was taken up in 1864, the homestead and
station buildings were built in 1874 on twenty acres of freehold at the conflu-
ence of the Mathias and Rakaia rivers. Over time the rivers shifted to flood the
point; the homestead was rebuilt in 1917 in its present location on the south side
of a 2,000-foot high hillside facing the Rakaia with its shingle cross-hatched by
the four-wheel-drive access route. Sheltered from the nor'west winds but without the benefit of winter sunshine, the homestead was constructed by a well-
known bush carpenter, Gideon Johnstone, who also constructed the woolshed,
from the timber and iron of the original woolshed. In winter the sun shines from
10:30 A.M. until 2:30 P.M., not even melting the frost before being obscured by
the hills behind. To shelter the homestead a dense conifer windbreak was
planted in the 1920s directly between the kitchen and the glaciated Mount Arrowsmith range of the main divide; by 1987 its height entirely obstructed the
view. As Strongman (1984:37) writes, the pioneer "seemed to forgo the wonderful view which he might have had of plains and mountains; he tended to sur-
round his house and garden with trees." The Morrises had replaced the original
kitchen sash-window with two large windows side by side (while preserving the
old wood-burning cooking stove), and in an aesthetic move Juliet Morris wanted
to be able to see her view. During my first visit a bulldozer operator was working with the runholder to lay new four-wheel-drive tracks on the property, and
Juliet convinced Jim that it was time to take down the trees even at the risk of
exposure to the winds. The next morning the garden and pear tree were severely

windblown. The family told me that today the homestead would never have been built in that spot; they have added a wing with full veranda angled to face the sun as much as possible, but their capital has been channeled back into improving the property for livestock, not into moving or rebuilding a homestead. When they purchased Ben Avon after leaving Manuka Point, they opted to live in the station cottage rather than the original homestead, in part because the homestead was rebuilt cheaply and unattractively after a fire, but more significantly because the cottage is well situated for the view, although they wish it were a little bit more up the paddock in a hollow so that the sun would last slightly longer and the view would be slightly better. Regardless of when homesteads were built, varying practical constraints impeded the ideal.

When new homesteads are built, often because of subdivision between siblings, they are placed carefully to minimize the effects of nor'west winds and take advantage of the sun, but proximity to power lines or water supply is more important in determining placement. Cost is still a primary factor (Salmond 1986:61). The most distinctive contrast between the old and the new is not only the placement of homesteads, with new homesteads virtually always standing higher, "situated to make the most of" the view, as one runholder noted, but also their compact design and construction from brick, or concrete blocks rather than weatherboard. The omnipresent veranda so characteristic of British colonial architecture is retained for shade and protection from winter elements,[4] and windows are enlarged to frame and incorporate the landscape into the interior; even additions to old homesteads feature bigger windows, and many have replaced original windows with larger double-glazed ones. Rather than avoiding the scale of the landscape as the early settlers may have had to do, contemporary families want to be able to embrace it as part of their view and blend into it with the architecture and garden design.[5] Exterior colors are tussock yellow or flax or brown or cream, unlike the traditional white, and sometimes they are made of river stone, better enabling them "to recede into the landscape." Similarly, interiors incorporate flecked natural and cream shades in rugs, wallpaper and paint.

The Glenaan family's environmental sensitivity is reflected in their contemporary homestead, with its large windows to bring the outside inside, multiple verandas to bring the inside outside, exterior paint the tawny color of tussock grasslands, roof lines to mimic alpine peaks, and a raised front lawn with a ha-ha, or sunk fence, between garden and paddocks so as not to disrupt the continuity of the alluvial fan as it rolls down toward the river. Whereas Roderick's urban-born wife Pauline told me that the sound of the avalanches in the mountains had made her shudder and that she "never went further than the garden gate" nor to see the rest of the property because she recoiled from the hills, her children and her nieces and nephews embrace skiing, jetboating, flying, wilderness trips, camping and fishing in their recreational lives.

The shifting location and design of homesteads suggests that new generations of inhabitants are less constrained by physical conditions, partly because of improvements in farming technology and changes in New Zealand housing design toward more organic homes, and easier transportation of heavier building materials such as brick and cinder blocks. The road into the Rakaia gorge, still subject to sudden rock slides and flooding fords, is much improved and better maintained with the aid of tractors and bulldozers. Also, all families use four-wheel-drive vehicles, thus lessening their sense of isolation and vulnerability to mishap. These factors enable them to integrate the aesthetic vastness and the ruggedness of the high country into their lives in a way that their parents and more particularly their grandparents, who preserved instead a good outlook through the framing of the trees as opposed to a panoramic view, could not.

Early Station Evolution

Mary Nell, the station manager's wife, came to the original Double Hill property when she was first married in 1908 and kept daily diaries until she and her husband, who came first as a packman at the age of sixteen in 1900, left in 1912 when Double Hill was divided. In her diaries she describes the homestead when she first arrived: "At that time Gid Johnstone and Ted Wolfrey were adding on two rooms for us at the northern end of the homestead which by the way was only one room wide opening onto a veranda a chain (sixty-six feet) long. The cookshop was out from the other end joining a large dining room used by the deer stalkers when there." As one of the original Canterbury runs first taken up in 1858, Double Hill station is classic in its design with its centrally positioned homestead and cohort of buildings. The first manager had moved into a cob cottage as homestead in 1869—two other cottages were to follow with the current frame homestead being built around the third cottage.

Soon after at Double Hill in 1882, the manager built the woolshed with pit-sawn beams, hand-cut rails, and no nails; it had twenty-two stands for the shearers.[6] Thornton (1986:113) has referred to the woolshed as a "vernacular building" that is "an essential part of our [New Zealand] built environment." The stables and the first shearers' quarters of cob, which residents now jokingly call "the five star hotel," were also built in the late 1800s. Mary Nell describes the shearers' cookshop in her notes on the diaries:

> It was a long building with the kitchen and the cook's (at one end) bedroom opening onto a large dining room and behind that the same length of the dining room two bunks high was where all the old shearers slept as it was quieter. . . . The rest of the shearers' accommodation consisted of three rooms with bunks two high but the partitions only went up to the eave. (Nell 1960:4)

Hugh Ensor appointed a manager and his wife to care for Double Hill in 1916 when he purchased it, and in the same year improvements were made to the homestead.[7] At the Depression's beginning in 1930, when many station owners were forced to take up residence on their properties, Hugh Ensor assumed active management of Double Hill, and neighboring Glenrock and Glenariffe, purchased by his brothers-in-law in 1916 and 1917. Prior to this time he and his wife had spent a week at Double Hill. By 1934 twelve permanent men were working on Double Hill and Glenrock, including both Peter and one of his brothers, as well as shearers, cowman-gardener, cook, and rouse-about.[8] Although Mrs. Ensor was not the first woman to live at Double Hill, her husband was the first owner to do so. Changing land legislation reduced the size of pastoral lease properties, resulting in smaller staffs.

In his history of Double Hill, Peter Ensor describes the basic homestead to which his mother, after the grandeur of her North Canterbury property Rakahuri, with its billiard room and fine gardens, first came to live in 1930.[9]

> The old house was of sod walls and snow-grass thatching, later covered by corrugated iron and some weather board covering on the walls and matching lining on some of the inside walls. A long, low verandah, one chain in length faced north with five rooms along it, with a big kitchen and cook's room on the east side, the sitting room on the north and west side going into a small kitchen and bathroom, but no connecting passage to the other rooms. It was all very dark with only some small windows and no glass doors. Again on the west side there was another verandah containing a laundry and big storeroom. These had been of later construction, not cob and thatch.[10] (Ensor 1990:13)

David McLeod echoes the Double Hill diaries in his account of Grasmere and describes its construction:

> The homestead was, in part, one of the oldest-inhabited in the high country and like most of them, had been altered and enlarged. The original two-roomed cob and slab hut, built in 1858, is still contained within an enlarged house faced with limestone from the rocks at Castle Hill. This first hut had a roof thatched with snow grass laid on thin birch sticks crossing the round birch rafters. Bits of the snow grass remain after 115 years and the timber is still as sound as the day it was erected. Wings of timber have been added at different periods and the whole reroofed with corrugated iron. (1974:21-22)

As noted earlier, Mrs. Ensor is admired for rendering the high-country environment more comfortable, muting the primitiveness through hard work, and adapting to harsh conditions as the economy deteriorated. The moral importance of being able to cope replaced elegance as a status marker.

Kerosene lamps provided lighting, and every morning Mrs. Ensor would take away the six or so lamps, wash the globes, polish the stands and trim the wicks. Not until 1948 was the first electric light turned on, when a water-driven wheel drove a six-volt generator, with a landline to the house, to produce power. The generator was later upgraded to twelve and then thirty-two volts with the addition of gearing mechanisms and a bank of sixteen two-volt batteries powering electric lights and fueling a vacuum cleaner, washing machine and electric iron. In 1957 a hydroelectric plant was built two miles away with underground cables to the house to provide a good supply of light and power. A dam was constructed to raise the water level of a stream to operate a low-head turbine and generator that could produce thirty kilowatts of power. Next door the Glenariffe diaries record earlier developments: "Started digging water-race for power plant" (2.vii.53); "Hydro power plant in operation" (12.v.54); and "New pipeline for power along foot of hill finished" (28.x.60). By 1971 power was reticulated across the river to Double Hill and its neighbors.

In the late 1930s when Double Hill divided its management from Glenrock and Glenariffe, new diaries were kept separately. Coincident with routine station activities noted in the combined Glenrock/Glenariffe diaries for these years are those marking the separation from Double Hill and the establishing of the Glenrock homestead for a new family. In 1937, new accommodations, required by law to meet a certain standard, were built at Glenrock as six two-man bedrooms close to the Glenrock cookshop. These entries reveal processes of division when the homestead and station buildings had to be made ready:

> Transport arrived with rock salt, bricks and furniture. (6.vii.38)
>
> Fireplace being built. (19.vii.38)
>
> Reconstructing cow yard. Taylor made gate for same. (13.ix.38)
>
> [Runholders] building yard for pups, killing. (30.iii.39)

Tree plantings were an integral part of the process and, as at Double Hill, they were concentrated primarily around the homestead because rabbits, hares and deer made it impossible to plant trees away from the homestead.

> Planted willow trees. (24.viii.38)
>
> Planting trees in Triangle paddock. Chambers fencing the trees. (30.viii.38)
>
> Finished fencing in the front paddock and planted 500 Douglas firs over the terrace in fenced section. . . . Chambers cleaning out under the shed. (8.ix.38)
>
> Fencing young larches on the bank side of house. (29.viii.39)
>
> [P]ut in some poplars at Glenariffe. (29.viii.39)
>
> Smith making fence round the young trees behind the whare [Maori for "house" or "hut"]. (8.ix.39)

Over the same period of time the Double Hill diaries note tree planting to the west of the old trees beyond the woolshed and stables to provide replacement shelterbelts and timber over time. Some of the Glenrock plantings were milled for timber in the 1980s. And perhaps most dramatically,

Burrows, Wightman and Forrester bringing shed from across the river. (8-10.vii.39)

Burrows constructing the shed. (12-15.viii.39)

Station separation and evolution was ongoing as the families "separated Glenariffe from Glenrock" on 1 July 1943. An understated but startling entry in the October 1944 Glenariffe diaries tells how make-do and accretion built homesteads; it reads: "two bunkrooms moved from Glenrock to join onto this house."

Homesteads Described

From the air, station buildings are identified easily by the intensive, differently hued tree plantings of conifers, willows, eucalyptus and poplar, fast-growing trees that not only define the area around the homestead but also protect it from the fierce nor'west winds coming over the Alps, and the cold southerlies bringing rain and snow. Trees form shelterbelts, distinctive lines running up and across the alluvial fans, although many farm families are trying to break the straight lines and plant native species of trees in response to national environmental sensitivities about their visual impact. Environmental concern for landscape values points to the highly contrasting colors of conifers against the tawny tussock grasslands, the obscuring of landform details and lack of fit with the shape of the hills, the monotonous uniformity and nonindigenous nature of many windbreak schemes, and the dangers of "wilding" (random self-seeding and uncontrolled spread) of introduced species (see Ashdown and Lucas 1987:55-66; Ledgard 1988).

From the air, approaching Double Hill, first settled in 1869 and continuously evolving, and Glenaan, planned from scratch and built in 1974 after separation from Glenariffe, reveals that each homestead is surrounded by the garden with its tree plantings, shrubs and flower beds, as well as the tennis court, swimming pool and vegetable garden this fenced landscape encompasses.[11] These in turn at Double Hill are surrounded by farm buildings and enclosures such as the permanent shepherds' two-room bunkhouse, cookshop, shearers' quarters, hen house, pig house and stables, and farther away, the woolshed, hay barn, killing house, and implement sheds. Double Hill still has the facilities for a large staff, although only two permanent shepherds are on the work staff, but newer Glenaan, worked by a husband/wife team, is scaled back and shares a woolshed, cookshop and shearers' quarters with neighboring Glenariffe, site of the original homestead, and has a shepherd's hut and machine-syndicate operator's cottage to accommodate staff, and covered yards for stockwork. Beyond the properties lie the airstrip, the gentler sheep paddocks on alluvial fans and beyond that the access routes through saddles out to the back country, an expanse of high-altitude tussock grassland leading out to alpine peaks that have been retired from farming or surrendered from the lease over the years (see map 5.1).

As a spatial nexus, the homestead is "the hub of it all."[12] The homestead's central area is the kitchen with an attached dining area and usually an open living room or sunroom with a television, games, and comfortable sofas and chairs (see figures 3.1 and 3.2).[13] Newer homesteads often have a small office or sewing room off the kitchen; older homesteads convert unused bedrooms to office space; one old homestead made a large, central sunny office into a kitchen, turning the original kitchen into a sewing and laundry room. Formal living rooms are often additions and appear as well-lit side wings, often with fine views of the landscape. Bedrooms are usually set apart in wings to the homestead, away from the heavily trafficked central areas of kitchen and dining room.

Spatial divisions neatly reinforce social order. The most critical division is between the front of the house and the back, as the separation between private and public is preserved architecturally. When there were cooks and cookshops and cowman gardeners, "single [hired] men" would not cross the back door into the kitchen, but this began to change in the Rakaia during World War II when station wives began to cook for staff. "Everything" happens at the back door, which became the site where family and farm converge. The back door and back porch where boots are left provide the usual entry to the public/business areas of a high-country homestead; farmers told me that the act of removing their boots marks the spatial transition from farm to home. Typically near the back door is an outside toilet and a large sink, sometimes the washing machine and dryer, the pantry, the freezer, and storage areas. The divisions between the public/business/back part of the house and the private/family/front part of the house are rigid. Shepherds "must go to the back door, not the front door," and they do not go beyond the kitchen unless invited. "I will not have a single boy roaming through the house looking for me," said one woman; her private space is important to her. Graham Densem's memory confirms the layeredness of high-country homesteads. The innermost layer was internal to the homestead itself and was distinguished by the separation between "the public part of the house where visitors went and high-country obligation for hospitality was fulfilled, and the private [areas] where the family slept." Private space maps onto the architectural "front" of the homestead and public space onto the architectural back (figure 3.2). Densem notes that "while I vividly remember the public part of Lilybank, I can't remember the 'front' at all." The Lilybank house, a typical late-Victorian/Edwardian villa modified by progressive accretion, presented its heroic axis of lounge, front door and best architecture to the public; but the axis "became redundant once all access changed to the 'practical' back door and away from the 'heroic' front"—a transformation true throughout New Zealand (Densem, e-mail to author, 7 April 1995). Deriving from an ethic of informality, generosity and flexibility, the shift from the centrality of the front to the back (or sometimes as at Lilybank, the side) may be socially motivated.

When Val and Bob Brown worked out the architectural plans for a new homestead at Glenthorne, they "did things quite differently" by deliberately erasing the front/back distinction spatially in a combined back-and-front door area. The entrance is clearly signaled by the magnificent carved kauri ram's head in the front door.[14] Along the veranda in the back-and-front door area are

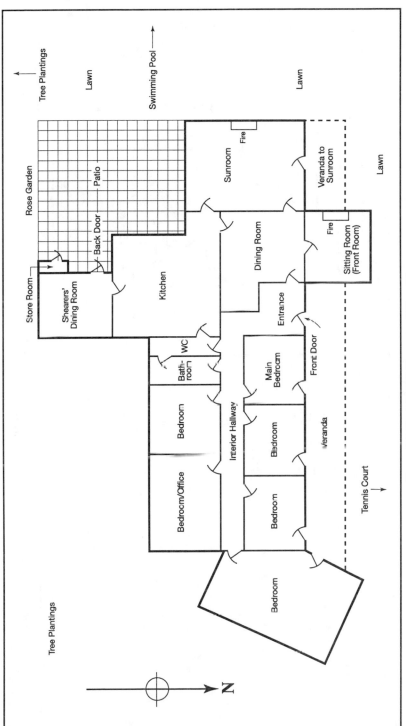

Figure 5.1 Double Hill Homestead Floor Plan
(Not to scale)

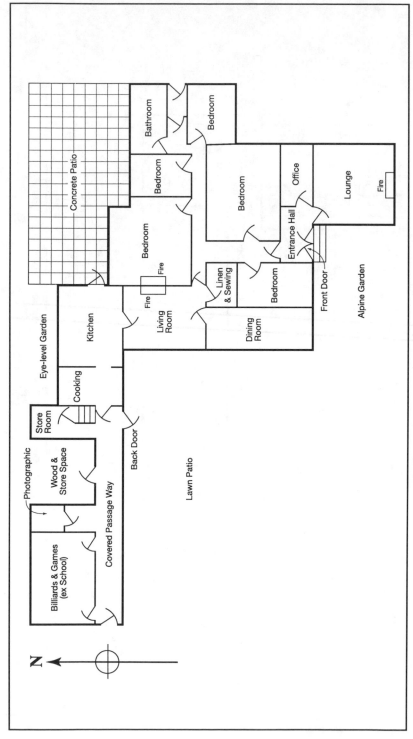

Figure 3.2 Lilybank Homestead Floor Plan
(Dick 1964:15) Reprinted with permission.

the laundry and utility room with benches and space for boots and raingear, the meat safe with cold water pipes running through, and the storeroom. The study had to be by the front door so that Bob could "charge in" in his boots. Val had wanted it a little closer to the kitchen, but since Bob is usually in the study when the children are not home, it wasn't crucial. Off the kitchen are the storeroom and the correspondence-school room. Pocket doors connect the dining and living rooms, and they open to create a large space for family times and close to retain heat in winter. Bedrooms span two floors with a third-floor guestroom and space available for growing children to "spread" into. The potential for expansion and contraction as social needs shift throughout the years is incorporated into the design of the house. Pride in this remarkable new homestead had little to do with aesthetics or scale and everything to do with pragmatics. "It all works—it is a system," Val (whose natal home was Mesopotamia) would say; in the fifteen years they lived in the station cottage, she had done her homework by keeping folders on each room to document her ideas of what might work best.

To build Glenthorne in an ideal location to absorb the view at the head of Lake Coleridge, the original homestead (now a staff cottage) had to be moved to another windier site in November 1985. The new house was positioned in the shelter of the bush and was oriented in two directions—to the mountains in the interior, and toward Lake Coleridge on the down-country side. The view of the woolshed and the yards was important to Val, and she wanted the kitchen windows oriented toward them so she would "feel engaged in life," and Bob could walk easily down to them. The yards are really the center of activity where most of the stock work is done although to outsiders it may seem as if the woolshed is the center of activity. While the homestead may be the hub of station life, the yards are the hub of stock activity; I was told that in the Rakaia of the 1950s and 1960s the flats were "where all the activity was," from where "you could see everything." In location and design, Glenthorne corresponds to salient social forms—the integration of husband and wife and of the nuclear family into the working of station life in a homestead designed to combine home and work, diminished station-staff size, and blurred class boundaries as back and front fuse.

The next layer in Densem's memory was the "house skin—the crucial enabler of normal domesticity during winter cold, summer heat and nor'westers":

> Lilybank had delicious sunshades angling over the windows. I remember them having a big impression on me as a 10 year old [as they were] suggestive of romantic winter snow and burning summer sun to a boy from the more moderate coast. . . . [T]here they are in a photo in Betty Dick's book [1964:16]. (E-mail to author, 7 April 1995)

Cloth awnings deck the western windows in summer and continuous curved-roofing iron awnings protect the western and southern windows "from frost as well as snow" in winter (Dick 1964:64). Densem's childhood sense of this skin layer points to its importance as an insulator, and to the house as vernacular and pragmatic in form, not consciously styled.[15]

Photo 7 Shepherds' quarters at Mount Algidus, formerly the Anderson homestead

Photo 8 Double Hill wisteria-draped veranda, sitting room (left), and sunroom (right).
(See figure 3.1.)

Photo 9 Glenthorne homestead blending into the landscape with native toe-toe plants in front

Photo 10 New plantings in the Glenariffe garden with the Rakaia River and Mount Algidus in the viewshed

> I remember the exciting enclosed corridor at the "business" end of the house—also the back door. It housed the correspondence school room and a storeroom at that time. The configuration as a wing at right angles from the back door was familiar from villas of similar age in town and down country farms—coal shed, laundry, pumproom but at Lilybank it was enclosed with a glazed wall. It all seemed to me at the time so attuned for the heard-about extreme conditions (I never went there in winter). (E-mail to author, 7 April 1995)

Densem notes also that the oblique, offset, asymmetrical layout of the homestead with its side entryway "snuggled" away behind the trees may have been environmentally motivated as a way to shield the homestead from New Zealand's prevailing northwest and southerly winds (E-mail to author, 1 December 1995).

Domesticity extends to the third layer, the garden fence, then beyond to the sheltered homestead paddocks, and beyond those the cultivated paddocks. The homestead paddocks, with their musterers/shearers' accommodation, cottage several hundred meters below the homestead (where Densem's family stayed), farm sheds, dog kennels and surrounding shelterbelts, provided a "special Lilybank noise environment":

> Wind in trees, and in particular, dogs barking. Often at night the dogs (twenty or so of them) would be going to town at the moon or whatever until a distant curse shouted from my uncle in the house two to three hundred metres away would bring silence for a while. Then the dogs would begin again until a rifle shot would ring out, finally bringing silence. (E-mail to author, 7 April 1995)

Densem differentiates the cultivated paddocks on the flats with their unrestricted views from the homestead paddocks with their views channeled by the shelter plantings:

> From these layers outwards "Men," in the number-eight-wire [fence] sense, dominated. It was "Men" who wore boots, shouted at dogs, drove landrovers through impossible depths of freezing river, devised ways of towing them out and being equal to whatever might befall. My Uncle Allan smoked a pipe, wore a tam-o-shanter and big boots, had a brown face and gravelly voice. This layer beyond the domestic seemed full of "Men," all equally brown, who whistled at dogs and jumped over streams in their boots, had meaningful discussions with my uncle, but were never close enough to be names or personalities [to me], just images. (E-mail to author, 7 April 1995)

People of Densem's uncle's generation in the 1950s all "owned the ascent of Everest" with Sir Edmund Hillary and took pride in his mastery of the elements. Densem likened it to "the macho thing" noting that it was gentler than that, rather it was a matter of having to "hold your own with nature." He does not exaggerate the significance of men, boots, pipe smoke, and number-eight wire, and his observations were admired by my Glenaan family as very much on the mark—"he has that right." Hamish Ensor confirmed that when he was a boy in the 1950s shepherds and musterers were still called "men," although a few high-country women with a strong sense of "respect for what came before" still do refer to them as "men." The change from men to boys may reflect historical conditions and generational shifts, having "something to do with the war" when musterers came in from the outside, but also having to do with the lack of births between 1939 and 1945 and the new generation of men who came to populate the high country as shepherds from 1965 or so onward. A month after having met Graham Densem, I was sorting through Glenariffe family photographs. I hesitated at a summer photo taken in front of the veranda circa 1953. On the far left, an eight-year-old Hamish Ensor posed proudly in shorts with very big boots. As I held the photograph out to him, he grinned and told me how special the moment was—"my first boots" he said. His cousins similarly remembered their first boots as marking a critical transformation in a boy's life. He remembers too that his Uncle Duncan at Glenrock would indicate his mood with the number of puffs on his pipe, and the head shepherd would puff away as he decided what to do for the day.

As the back country that "number eight Men" populated gets retired and covenanted for conservation purposes, and the autumn musters grow more infrequent, the distinction between "back" and "front" country that defines "high country" becomes meaningless in a pastoral sense. Simultaneously, as the case of Glenthorne documents, the parallel distinction between "back" and "front" in the homestead also is erased as the nuclear farm family becomes the dominant social form, domestic/family and public/business become more thoroughly integrated, and gender roles are reconfigured as husbands and wives more equally shoulder similar labor.

Alterations and Additions

These homesteads have been expanded and enlarged constantly over the years, and changes in the homestead, gardens, and growth of trees mark the passage and cyclicity of time and serve as chronological landmarks for events. In this way "architectural processes" do coincide with "important events and processes in the lives of their occupants and are thought of in terms of them" (Carsten and Hugh-Jones 1995:39). Mrs. Ensor's daughter-in-law Lou describes the Double Hill homestead of the 1930s only in terms of today's rooms:

> What is the spare room down there was the family's dining room and there was a kitchen behind—this is before the house was altered—with a bakeoven, and the men were fed in the kitchen. The family was fed in the dining room, where we would sit on a cold winter's night. What is now the dining room was the sitting room, and the fireplace is where you now go into the sunroom. (Figure 3.1; Ensor 1990:26)

The station cook prepared meals for the family as well as the staff although they ate separately. This continued until 1942, when improvements to a small kitchen and the addition of a stove made it possible for Lou to cook for her own family. Several years later in 1944 a new dining room for station hands was added onto the large old station kitchen (figure 3.1). Today properties cannot afford large staffs or station cooks, and Lou's daughter's responsibilities are quite different from her mother's. Like many women with a small staff, she cooks three hot meals a day plus morning and afternoon teas for her family and for the two permanent shepherds who eat with the family in the large farm kitchen; on Saturday evenings the shepherds cook their own meal. Casual laborers and workmen are also integrated into family meals. The cookshop is only used during shearing time for the shearing gang's cook to prepare meals, and although once the center of station life, today it is unused for most of the year.

Altered cooking spaces and eating arrangements result from a downturn in the farming economy, with concomitant changes in social relationships such as the spatial diminution of class boundaries between owners and workers, the integration of workers into nuclear family life, and a configuration of roles for some women that circumscribes their activities to the homestead and its surrounds. Elvin Hatch (1992:165) has written of this transformation from the two-table to the one-table pattern as reflecting post-World-War-II egalitarian pressures for social and economic leveling but also as suppressing "open expression of social distance on the one hand while implicitly confirming it on the other." The "one-table" is often large and special, sometimes original to the homestead, and carved of native wood such as kauri.

At Double Hill the addition of a big sitting room with a stone fireplace next to the front entranceway on the northwest end of the house at a right angle to the rest of the house followed in 1950 (figure 3.1). Most homes have such a formal sitting room closed off from the rest of the house and used for large family gatherings at Christmas or Easter and for guests. Peter and Lou's daughter, Elizabeth (Lib) Hutchinson, who lives at Double Hill with her husband Ben and their children, observed how smart the sitting room must have seemed at the time, with its "chapel-like" features; architectural ideas change, though, and she could imagine having extended the veranda around the house instead (figure 3.1). Both the dining room and the sitting room at Double Hill have glass doors, and at Glenariffe the wall between kitchen and dining room was removed when the current generation began to reconfigure the interiors to create more centralized open family space and to provide more light. In 1958 Peter and his wife rebuilt a section of the homestead. They began by removing trees around the house and topping the old tall poplar and pine trees that were too close to the woolshed. The station diaries follow the process closely, and Peter tells the story:

> We agreed to a plan which entailed demolishing all that part of the house containing the bedrooms and the old kitchen and replacing them with five bedrooms, an inside passage including a loo and an office for myself plus some other alterations. . . . We wanted to retain the character of the old house. . . . The first major job was to cut off and get rid of the part to be rebuilt leaving Lou and me to camp in the

sitting room. The idea was to put a wire rope round and pull it down with a big tractor, but at the first pull we saw the whole of the house move so that had to be stopped. We realised of course that the old sod walls were too solid and had to be dug out and what a mess it was getting the roof off with the old snow grass tussocks under the iron together with the possum nests and other vermin. [The builder] became concerned as to how he was going to match up the roofing of a bedroom to jut out at an angle at the far end of the verandah with the rest of the roofline. . . . In the end we had to get a 'dozer in to clean up the mess of the sod walls together with further excavation work for the extension of the house and, while it was on the job, preparing a site for the proposed tennis court among other things. (1990:109)

A big sunroom and fireplace were added onto the west side of the house (figure 3.1). The changes to the Double Hill homestead were radical, but this is not atypical. The expansion was prompted by increasing family size[16] and by better economic conditions in the late 1940s and 1950s resulting from war wool booms.

In March 1992, Peter wrote to me of more changes to the homestead, as his grandchildren began to leave home: "The whole place has been painted. My old office has been turned into another bathroom and a new office has been added on giving much more space for a computer plus more space to store all the paper work which is part of life these days." Children's departures caused similar shifts at Glenrock where runholder Charlie Ensor was moving his study from a room off the kitchen into his son Duncan's room, separate from the house altogether. His mother "Toots" reminded the family that it wasn't Duncan's room at all, but was in fact Charlie's own boyhood room to which he was returning.

Aerial photographs illustrate the formulaic pattern of growth of these homesteads through the years, seemingly "in a haphazard way as interiors changed with the times" with wings and attachments, creating a structure likened by many women to rabbit warrens, in a process that Betty Dick calls "pushing out walls" (1964:34). At Glenrock, Toots Ensor was known for "knocking out walls" and changing the house's shape as her family grew to seven children; she said to me, "As the family grew so did the house." Another woman explained, "As children were born the house grew out, utterly transforming the original cottage inside; I was kept busy with children—I had six over the years." A passage from one of Ngaio Marsh's detective classics tells the same story in its construction of the fictional Mount Moon:

Mount Moon homestead was eighty years old and that is a great age for a house in the Antipodes. It had been built by Arthur Rubrick's grandfather, from wood transported over the Pass in bullock wagons. It was originally a four-roomed cottage, but room after room had been added, at a rate about twice as slow as that achieved by the intrepid Mrs. Rubrick of those days in adding child after child to her husband's quiver. (Marsh 1973[1945]:24)

People were often able to tell me the progression of children who had moved through each bedroom, the oldest remaining child moving into the largest room as his or her predecessor left for boarding school.[17] Commonly covering over old verandas provided additional rooms for sleeping or for teaching correspondence school, or an enclosed hallway to seclude sleeping areas. Older homesteads had verandas off kitchens, living rooms, dining rooms, and bedrooms, often with concrete patios for winter use, as at Lilybank (figure 3.2), and many of the new homesteads follow this same pattern.

In a complex interplay of permanence and impermanence, homestead layouts witness the shifting shapes of nuclear families, adding on rooms and wings, covering verandas, and expanding laterally to accommodate families of procreation and yet adjusting cyclically as families of procreation and orientation oscillate through the generations. In this way, the house, like kinship and its social groups, is similarly processual. Following Lévi-Strauss's concept of house societies in which the house is "a specific form of social organization," Carsten and Hugh-Jones write for South America and Southeast Asia:

> Married couples eventually produce new sibling sets in their children. These siblings are strongly associated with the unity of the house but are also differentiated by the order of their birth. This is often the basis of rank and hierarchy. . . . In a continuous two-way process [of transformation] siblingship becomes affinity, and affinity becomes siblingship. (1995:38-39)

In structure and use, New Zealand station homesteads similarly combine opposing structural principles as lineal agnatic principles of property transfer within the nuclear family from parents to sons compete with ideological commitments to partible inheritance and the equal rights of male and female siblings to belong to family and farm.[18]

Another kind of residential expansion also embodies structural tensions between consanguinity and affinity as parents build a cottage for a returning son (occasionally daughter) and his wife. Loyalty shifts, always, from family of orientation to family of procreation. As this new family of procreation grows, so does the cottage with the addition of rooms. But in many instances the son and his family exchange houses and gardens with the parents and in time, as the parents move down country, the cottage may then pass on to the son's returning son and his wife. Many wives inscribe their individuality and claim to belonging on the homes and the gardens they assume from their mothers-in-law. All families could tell me stories of how this was done, for instance by painting a kitchen purple (an aberration) or taking down wallpaper and ripping up carpets, assigning rooms for different purposes, relandscaping the grounds. The switch is never easy from either perspective. At retirement one widow removed the furnishings of her sitting room from the large nineteenth-century homestead and re-created the identical room in her new home in a nearby village. Many are the stories of parents running out from the cottage at the sound of a chain saw to protect a tree they had planted. Women told me how difficult it was to take over a mother-in-law's garden, and one told me that her mother-in-law would notice with every visit if a plant was moved or went missing; the couple would just respond, "That's right, it's not there any more." Families are mindful of the minutest change in the landscape they know.

The capacity of high-country homesteads to incorporate people is not only structural but also symbolic and extends beyond the incorporation of nuclear and extended families, affines and consanguines. Toots Ensor said of Glenrock, "It was like Paddington Station here often with twenty to a meal. It has always been like that. The walls were elastic. The walls stretch for [my daughter-in-law] also. That is high-country hospitality." An improved road has lessened the need for such elasticity. Still there is space for visitors, especially siblings, who as adults always have the right to return to their childhood home even after their parents have left. Siblings often take turns hosting Christmas as a tradition, as a symbolic gesture, incorporating those who have left back into station life and making them welcome through extensive and concerted preparations beginning months in advance. Homes absorb people easily; bedrooms are always available (often because children are away at boarding school), and because women have to cook large quantities of food for family and staff anyway, an extra person is readily accommodated. Workmen, children's school friends, journalists, and casual laborers are expected to stay. For example, during the fifteen months of building the Glenthorne homestead, Val cooked for the builders. Walls that stretch defy a notion of closed nuclear high-country family, even though compared with their parents' generation today's couples work more closely and exclusively together as farm partners.

Thornton (1986:24) notes also that a century's evolution of country houses through use is apparent in the common practice of making alterations and additions to meet changing needs and circumstances, but houses are strongly vernacular and follow no common trend other than constant transformation. Landscape too shifts, as the river changes course, and patterns of invasive weeds shift. At Glenthorne on the first night of two days of earthquake tremors (at 5 and 7 points on the Richter scale), the Browns drove northwest on the four-wheel-drive track to discover a familiar gut now shingle-filled. Up on a ridge a waterfall had disappeared. Elsewhere a lake came up from diverted water.

The Glenariffe diaries document repetition in patterns of landscape transformation: in January 1945, "Big flood in river tonight, cutting badly into flat"; in February, "Again river and creeks in high flood"; in March, "Saw Commissioner of Crown Lands re flooding of Glenariffe flat"; in November, "River cutting severely into Glenariffe flat, stranding about 300 ewes and lambs and probably drowning some"; in June 1946, "Big earthquake in the night centered near Lake Coleridge. All chimneys damaged and road blocked"; in October 1948, "Main stream of the Rakaia running through Glenariffe flat cutting off outer areas" and "77 percent lambs marked, some still stuck out on flat island." Fifty years later Roderick's son, Hamish, wrote to me of the same intrusion:

> The Rakaia is doing its best to wipe out the river flats and the road up
> the valley above us by coming around the south side of Little Double
> Hill. At great expense we hope to hold it out but it really is against

> nature's wishes to prevent it from changing course, but will give it a
> shot anyway. (E-mail to author, 24 June 1998)

The vernacular form is one of perpetual change in which housing, culture and environment emerge as mutable, having no pure form.

The impression, as Ruth Behar notes in her analysis of a Spanish village house, is one of "a house structure molded by the hand of time" (1986:43) in which "the past and present, given shape in architectonic form, coexist in time and space" (1986:48) and whose diachronic aspects can be discovered through the exploratory process of doing "an archaeology" of the house (1986:53). The Spanish house, unlike the high-country homestead, is broken up into components or pieces as it is divided between siblings in this system of equal inheritance. In New Zealand the house remains whole, and when properties divide, a sibling may be compensated with a new home of equal value. Jane Adams, in her work on southern Illinois farm women, also examines the organization of space and time as a central structuring process through an analysis of homestead architecture:

> Farm structures are enduring; they tend to be remodeled more fre-
> quently than replaced, and many people relate to old buildings as re-
> positories of memories. Buildings therefore can be usefully ap-
> proached as maps to past social forms, suggesting through their
> spatial organization the ways in which the people who lived in them
> ordered their lives. (Adams 1993:92)

Because such architecture mixes permanence and modification, it provides a physical marker against which change and continuity in high-country life can be measured. Earlier lives and times are evident in these old homes even as the spaces are transformed by each generation in a family to meet new needs, and adapt to new domestic cycles, styles, economic situations and technological possibilities.

An aspect of technology enhancing the nuclear family was the introduction of the telephone to replace the radiotelephone that linked the valley's properties after the war. The old radiotelephone linked all the households twice a day as they signed on for messages, and calls out were heard by all. Even grocery lists, called into Methven for weekly delivery on the transport truck, were public. Now families note how much more isolated from each other they are. Improved transportation makes trips to town possible, whether for a child's school game or play or a weekly game of golf. Although this has lessened the mutual dependence of families on each other for a social life, wear and tear on vehicles on a rough and unpredictable road does limit such trips.

Social life still is actively constructed through dinner parties, riding or boating expeditions, woolshed parties, dog trials, skating parties, rugby matches and various school- and farming-related events down country. The size of buildings, from the homestead to the woolshed, can accommodate large groups, and ambitious outdoor events such as gymkhanas and overnight trips on horseback are organized. For instance, Mount Peel, one of four South Island stations with continuous single ownership, celebrated its one-hundred-year anniversary by throwing a dinner party and dance in the woolshed for all Acland descendants, and for all who had ever worked on the property and their descendants; five hundred people attended. Similarly, high-country people, when criticized by others for visible signs of affluence—the pools and tennis courts, the elaborate gardens—will point out that they build these things themselves, that pools were originally put in to control the fires that so often devastate remote homesteads, and that they have to "create their own entertainment," although less so today with improved transportation in and out of the valley. Isolation means that the children have to create their own amusements and seek each other out as friends; when they go to boarding school they often "stick together."

Despite such seeming affluence, houses get the last of the resources because the farm gets them first, and many women wait years for a remodeled kitchen, additional bathroom, or revived front door. At Mount Gladstone, Lois Pitts led me through the station buildings: the homestead and its additions, the garden, the cookshop and shearers' quarters, the killing shed and offal pit, the cottage where they lived when first married (now empty), the cob cottage from 1850 when the first licence was granted, the garage and workshop, and across the willow-banked stream the old (1923) and new (1990) woolshed. The shearers' quarters need work but they "will wait their turn," and "will come behind the house" in priority. The house, she noted, has had to wait its turn also—"since farming is a business, the house always has to come last." She told me that she had to learn to wait and be patient. She pointed to a new front door of honey-colored native wood that her husband had recently varnished for her. In Otago, an elderly woman told me that when finally a big wool cheque of a thousand pounds came in, she stood at the kitchen sink listening to her husband and sons around the table planning a new woolshed, and she got so furious about her house always being at the bottom of the list that she threw the kettle against the wall. The family sent her to the doctor who told her to go home and throw another kettle. Eventually, the house was renovated as they added to the living room and enlarged the windows.

Station families are not always free agents to change homesteads and often have to seek permission for expenditures when the property is an incorporated family land company with parents or siblings as shareholders. Retired parents often call the shots, sometimes even selecting the setting and design of the homestead: one woman had no say in the siting or design of the homestead built upon her marriage; one bride gave up square footage for finished cabinets. The homestead never really belongs to a couple but to the station; rather, they know they will not stay in it past retirement or if a child wishes to marry, raise children and return to farm. Accordingly, many changes are made with the needs of the next generation in mind—selecting a neutral color scheme or not overexpanding a garden.

Gardens and Grounds

Well-planted New Zealand gardens, according to Thornton (1986:24), assimilated the homestead into the landscape. They derived from an English stately-home tradition in which gardens were indistinguishable from the landscape. Perhaps even more importantly for early settlers, as Thelma Strongman argues in *The Gardens of Canterbury*, they were reminders of home, integrating the familiar into the foreign environment: "the idea of the garden as fine art was part of the English culture which was imported into and impressed upon the new province" (Strongman 1984:11). Ngaio Marsh's parodic fictional evocation and Lady Barker's breathless epistolary documentation lend detail to Stevan Eldred-Grigg's (1980:92) argument that the "southern gentry" were "profoundly domestic. They brought with them an English upper class love of home and transplanted it completely." Marsh's ethnographically literary idealization of Mount Moon reinforces the point:

> The house bore a dim family resemblance to the Somersetshire seat which Arthur's grandfather had thankfully relinquished to a less adventurous brother. Victorian gables and the inevitable conservatory, together with lesser family portraits and surplus pieces of furniture, traced unmistakably the family's English origin. The garden had been laid out in a nostalgic mood, at considerable expense and with a bland disregard for the climate of the plateau. Of the trees old Rubrick had planted, only Lombardy poplars, *Pinus insignis* and a few natives had flourished. The tennis lawn, carved out of the tussock hill-side, turned yellow and dusty during summer. The pleached walks of Somerset had been in part realized with hardy ramblers and, where these failed, with clipped fences of poplar. The dining-room windows looked down upon a queer transformation of what had been originally an essentially English conception of a well-planned garden. But beyond this unconvincing piece of *pastiche*—what uncompromising vastness! The plateau swam away into an illimitable haze of purple, its boundaries mingled with clouds. Above the cloud, suspended it seemed in a tincture of rose, floated the great mountains. (Marsh 1973[1945]:24-25)

Reinforcing similar distinctions between domesticity and the wild beyond, Lady Barker describes "the exquisite view" from the saddle as she rode from Broomielaw [Steventon] and began her steep descent to Rockwood for a birthday party:

> Close on our right hand rose the Government bush out of which we get our firewood, standing grand and gloomy amid huge cliffs and crags; even the summer sunshine could not enliven it, nor the twitter and chirrup of countless birds. In front, the chain of hills we were crossing rolled down in gradually decreasing hillocks, till they merged in the vast plains before us, stretching away as far as the eye could reach towards the south, all quivering in the haze and glare of the bright sunlight. The background, extending along the horizon,

was formed of lofty mountains still glistening white against the daz-
zling blue sky. Just at our feet the Rockwood paddocks looked like
carpets of emerald velvet, spread out among the yellowish tussocks;
the fences that enclose them were either golden with broom and
gorse, or gay with wild roses and honeysuckle. Beyond these we saw
the bright patches of flowers in the garden, and nothing could be
more effective than the white gable of the house standing out against
the vast black birch forest which clothed the steep hill-sides for
miles—the contrast was so picturesque between the little bit of civilization and culture and the great extent of wild, savage scenery around
it. (Barker 1883[1870]:91-92)

The harsh tussock grasslands of the high country often seemed "sublime," inspiring settlers with fear and awe. Although folk knowledge suggests that early
settlers eschewed indigenous trees and plants, it is not altogether true, as flax,
toe-toe, and cabbage trees were used together with native plants brought from
England (Strongman 1984:42). Elevation can constrain. A Mackenzie country
woman spoke of "fierce winters and snow" and said that here some people
"don't bother with gardens because it is hard to get things to grow"; she is moving toward planting flowers and creating open spaces with peonies and "bloom-
ing things such as lavenders and roses on a pergola." She has given up on vege-
tables because "you can't get them out of the ground in winter because it is so
frozen." Deep in the Rakaia catchment the garden of newly sited Glenthorne
"will be natives only" and is already marked by bunches of tussock.

Mary Nell in her notes on the diaries writes that the Double Hill homestead, situated on the south side of the river, was a "very healthy place to live—
so open and you could see for miles especially the river away across the flats."
The homestead was fenced, and Mary Nell describes her garden as lovely.
Twenty years later, as Mrs. Ensor transformed the building from "shack" to
homestead, she began to incorporate the landscape into a beautified domestic
world with the addition of French doors and recultivation of the garden. Her
daughter-in-law, Lou, sees both garden and homestead as the results of cultivation, paralleling, she says, but not mirroring, the beauty of the natural surroundings. At Double Hill, while doing outdoor tasks—taking garden rubbish to the
dump, feeding the pigs and chopping mutton for the working dogs—Mrs. Ensor's granddaughter Lib narrated as we went, showing me how the garden is
continually evolving. She and Ben cut down the pines and poplars on the eastern
side of the homestead in 1983, opening the entire area up to light and putting in
tennis courts. Clusters of poplars and firs on the spur above the homestead have
been felled; these hills and their vegetation dominate the old homestead, which
is now painted a different color from the other buildings because "it should
stand out separately." Lib plans to divert the stream to make a pond but does not
know if it will be done "during my time" at Double Hill; it was, in 1994. Behind
the kitchen there is a bricked area with daisies, and the old rose bushes are still
growing well after thirty years. Over the sunroom windows and verandas roses
and wisteria also grow well. She has changed the straight lines of the lawns. The
flowerbeds would have the same flowers in them as in her mother's time, but

finding it difficult to work in her mother's dense beds, she has opened them up. She has added shrubs that would not have been popular then but are more available now, and she has changed the lines, with the flowerbed curving out from the sitting room window into the driveway. The driveway now curves round to the front door, and the old white gate has been replaced by a cattle stop. She wanted very much to have the garden different from her mother's; its transformation is an endless process, one that she says will never be done. She is mindful that if a child comes to farm Double Hill, a wife would not be able to maintain the expanded garden, especially with small children. The developmental cycle of the New Zealand high-country homestead keeps the size of gardens in check.

Betty Dick's discussion of the evolution of the Lilybank garden reflects similar, although earlier, transformations in style:

> We have always cherished our garden, bringing roses and lilies, shrubs and boxes of seedlings, back from almost every trip to town. We have planted cuttings given to us by friends, and delight in watching their incredulous amazement at the intense colours and rampageous habits of everything grown in this clear crisp air. . . . Latterly, however, we have been replacing large garden beds of annual exotics with alpine plants and native shrubs. Tiny creepers clinging to rocks, lichens and mosses have all been transplanted to snuggle under large hebe bushes now almost hedges. . . . We feel now that our home and garden meld into the landscape as though they belong. (1964:37-38)

For many women their gardens are a visible sign of their creative lives' achievements. One woman who built a new homestead with her husband was able to transform a paddock into a garden that is expanding at present from two to three acres. She cooks willingly but would rather be outside where she has "something in which to focus her energies." She and her husband designed the shape of the lawn first, favoring curved edges and distinct garden sections creating contained spaces like rooms: there is a rock garden, an azalea garden, vegetable garden, wilderness garden with pond and gully, and various flower gardens. Aesthetics and pragmatics, as in so much of the built environment of the high country, were combined. The lawn, for example, follows the contours of the land, and the trees throughout the property are valued both for income and aesthetics, a mixture of domestics and exotics, unlike the pine plantations that provided timber for their parents' generation.

Families think carefully about the relationship of the garden layout and design to the surrounding landscape. Dramatic garden expansion at Glenariffe, for example, included a bridge that followed the line of the Algidus hump, echoing it and providing the height from which the entire garden was visible. Facing south, the garden extended to the rear hill/block country bringing it into the garden because "after all they are part of the garden." The guiding principle is to frame vistas, to point attention to them, not by keeping them open, but by directing the viewer's attention through landscaping. Two discrete vistas had been created when I visited in 1995. First, there was a vista from the end of the bridge in a clear line toward the Arrowsmith range with the woolshed in the foreground and framing rows of trees on either side. Second, placement of a pergola on the northern side of the garden created a vista of the mountains on the Algidus side.

Although women assert themselves through the gardens they cultivate, this is a particular meeting ground not entirely gendered as in the past, and reflective of the integration of women and men into farming as a nuclear-family enterprise. Husbands and wives design the gardens together, and either will mow lawns. Landscaping is a joint task, and husbands and sons (although almost never shepherds on this "domestic" turf) wield the machinery when necessary. One woman who was redoing a section of the garden told me, "I've gone as far as I can; now I need men, machines and money." On some properties husbands do the rotary tilling, the pruning and vegetable gardens; on others their wives do. One farmer told me that the vegetable garden is "the prime place where domestic and business come together"; vegetable gardens rather than flower beds fall at the interface of the domestic and farm life. And later in life, retired men garden in lieu of farming as they prune roses and grow flowers, with those who move to cities, like their rural counterparts, gardening on a grand scale.

§   §   §

Geoffrey Thornton (1986:10) describes New Zealand farm buildings as a "memorial to the early colonial economy" founded on agrarianism, which "form an important element in the humanising and transforming of the landscape." They also reflect different social configurations emerging from the changing farm economy, and changing systems of social stratification, as well as an evolving relationship with the New Zealand landscape.

High-country homesteads and their immediate built environment are part of the developmental cycle in two ways as continuity of use and meaning are attached to buildings concurrently with shifts in use and meaning. In their consideration of the concept of household, Robert Netting, Richard Wilk and Erik Arnould (1984:xviii) point out that Jack Goody's developmental-cycle concept "takes no account of history" while opposing perspectives treat the household as "fluid in structure and impermanent in boundaries." Both views can be synthesized in this consideration not of household, but of homesteads. Change is the vernacular.

First, their evolution reflects the stages of the developmental cycle of the family as aging parents move aside for their married children (who will eventually move aside for their children) to take over the farm. The walls stretch and contract as children are born and children leave; within the life cycle of a given family of procreation, rooms are transformed continually through use. As children are born, bedrooms and schoolrooms are created; as they leave the rooms become sewing rooms and gardens expand, reflecting the shifting focus of women's energies over the life cycle. Persistent constraints of isolation, climate and landscape and the continuity of the seasonal pastoral calendar foster regularity of use over the years.

Second, homestead evolution reflects the development of farming technologies, economic cycles and environmental values, as each generation leaves a
distinctive imprint on the design and use of physical space. For example, increasing pastoral productivity (and continuing landscape transformation)
through the use of aerial topdressing, rotational grazing, and improved grasses
means that more work can be done with fewer staff; the economic downturn in
the world wool market makes farming more risky and less profitable, and today
station staffs are pared down as many families run the farm without hired help.
Women without staff are more integrated as farm partners, while those with staff
assume a primary role in cooking, and shift the focus of station life to the homestead kitchen. Changing attitudes to the environment are apparent in the placement and design of contemporary homesteads and the opening up of older
settlement-dated homesteads. Expanded verandas, bigger windows, natural colors and gardens and windbreaks with curvaceous rather than straight lines have
replaced the colder, darker, sheltered homesteads and formal gardens of the past.
The new fondness for indigenous plants, the shift in environmental values, the
use of more glass and light, the preference for curvilinear planting are all characteristic of broader national aesthetic shifts, but the Rakaia properties are particularly interesting places to see these changes because of the continuity of ownership within families and consistency of use.

Although constantly transformed, these buildings endure, but no family or
individual can dare to become attached to a building through which they only
pass, despite (and because of) the simultaneity of its link with shifting pasts and
anticipated futures. Station records and artwork, after all, belong to the homestead, and not the family. In contrast, people's attachment to the station as place
is profound, and, as we see in the next chapter, patterns of property transfer preserve the continuity of family ownership. Even daughters who leave will say
that the natal station is still home, initially with an "H" and eventually fading to
an "h" as they establish their own homes. With this kind of attachment, and the
constancy of family in place, the station homestead and its encompassing
grounds continuously change through a process of accretion and reconfiguration
as each generation makes it their own and leaves its marks for the next generation. The built environment is a cumulative identity marker denoting the continuity of family habitation over the generations as well as the particular historical
and personal experiences of the individuals whose inhabitation moves through
it. The homestead is the families' signature on the landscape. The sense of belonging high-country families share, however, is not based simply on material
attachment to the built environment, but rather on an ideological attachment to
the symbolic weight that family and the continuity of its attachment to property—the larger place, the station—carry.

Notes

1. Lawrence and Low (1990:454) define the built environment as an abstract concept referring to "any physical alteration of the natural environment" to include built
forms, sites, and plans.

2. Judy and Charlie Ensor were telling me how much their girls enjoy coming back to Glenrock and love the security it offers; part of the appeal, Charlie said, is that "it is a secure life." "Secure" evokes the predictable routine station-life demands to which Densem refers. As a town boy, Densem's careful paradigmatic selection of "secure" and "comfy" replicates a recurrent pairing by residents. "It is a comfortable life in the gorge," and the security relates to the "safeness of sameness."

3. Butler's cynicism is evident and off-putting to many farmers. Runholders in the Rangitata valley, where Butler's Mesopotamia is located, disown him because Butler said that he was coming to "double his capital" and they "do not see it like that."

4. Salmond (1986:77) considers the veranda a "classical colonial artifact" deriving in British-settled countries from Jamaica and India. The veranda, sometimes extending around two or three sides of the house, shelters walls from the weather, provides cheap extra living space, protects the front door, and serves as an outdoor room in the warmer months. While offering protection from "the intense heat of summer," the high-country veranda also shelters "the windows from the icy rain, snowstorms and severe frosts during the winter months" (Dick 1964:35).

5. In contrast, a woman in the Mackenzie country defied the advice of a landscape architect and painted her house-trim red saying that "she wants her home to stand out of the environment to make a statement." In resisting ideas about the importance of high-country homes blending into the landscape, she was saying that she wanted her home "to stand apart from it, to be a respite from it, a place away from it."

6. Thornton (1986:111) and Salmond (1986:56) note that timber was the most common building material. In the bush the laboriously created and cheaper pit-sawn timber predated sawmill timber, which was produced quite early in New Zealand. Today corrugated galvanized iron has replaced timber, brick and stone.

7. The Ensor Double Hill diaries begin in 1916; Ben Hutchinson has written the diaries since 1971.

8. Today the properties combined employ four men including the two runholders. In U.S. English it is "roustabout."

9. See the floor plan of the Orari gorge homestead, a classic station well-documented in Harper (1967:75), and typical of the homestead from which Mrs Ensor came.

10. Sod or turf was the most primitive of several available earth materials, dug out of the ground, and typically used in a double row with the space between filled with clay or "rammed" earth (Thornton 1986:15; see Salmond 1986:38 for more detail on sod construction). Thatching was the earliest and least common type of roofing in colonial New Zealand (Thornton 1986:18). Snow-grass or rushes, whichever was available, were used in thatching.

11. The swimming pool was built at Double Hill in the 1950s to replace the old orchard that was ruined by a grass fire.

12. Cf. Pinney's station as "radiating from the homestead" in chapter 5.

13. Many children, unlike their parents, grow up with television and fewer of the evening pleasures that had previously engaged the entire family, such as card and board games.

14. They wanted something similar to but different from the ram's head carved in the linoleum at Mesopotamia.

15. While the vernacular Lilybank house of Densem's time was "a comfortable example of the pragmatic imperative" documentable as a recognizable high-country style, a 1990s Lilybank presents a schismatic change for this particular station, now a hunting lodge with a capital-based imperative. The old homestead has been replaced by the new lodge, just as corporate ownership has replaced family ownership.

16. Peter and Lou had four daughters at the time, ranging in age from seventeen to eight. Other families in the valley had families of six or seven children. Today in the valley, family sizes range from two to four children per property.

17. A youngest son who had left the valley drew a diagram to illustrate which bedrooms each of the children had used. As the youngest, he had been assigned all of them over the years. He had no memory of where his eldest sister had slept. His cousin, also a youngest, told me that her room had often changed and said that she "had lived in all of them, just about."

18. See chapter 4.

Chapter Four

Family, Farm, and Property Transfer

> Why, from Waiau to the mountains
> It was all father's land.
> —Allen Curnow (1997), "House and Land"[1]
> in Wedde and McQueen (1985:197)

As social action and spatial discourse, property-transfer practices and inheritance ideologies protect family ownership of station freehold and leasehold property, preserve family business continuity, and naturalize the attachment of family to country through a cultural logic of sentiment for the station as "home," and through the transmission of epistemologics of country. Patricentric inheritance practices and their differential consequences, in which land and the "opportunity to farm" tend to be made available to sons more often than daughters, create structural tensions in New Zealand high-country families, which must be reconciled to preserve family harmony and estate integrity. Extralocal factors such as tax laws, land and marital-property legislation, developments in farming technology, and international market conditions also constrain the strategies used to preserve residential continuity and congruence between inheritance practices and ideology.

I focus on property-transfer practices and examine their implications for land ownership and station formation, drawing from formal and informal interviews with three generations and their extended families (retired parents and those children, especially sisters and younger sons, who have left) from the Rakaia valley and beyond. Extensive local documentation in daily farm diaries, regional centennial histories, scrapbooks, family albums, wage record-books, genealogies, and the oral histories of individuals, families and stations indicates pride in family attachment and cultural heritage. To illustrate stages in farm and family development cycles, I interviewed contrasting high-country families opting for other property-transfer practices or having less continuity in high-country lands. This is a nexus of spatially dispersed relationships socially and symbolically constituted in a shared high-country identity rooted simultaneously in family as signifier of stability and station as marker of a homeplace.

Inheritance, known as "property transfer," is the primary site where gender differentiation, between brothers and sisters as differently positioned subjects, plays itself out with high stakes[2]—stakes not solely of land as asset or resource or livelihood but also of station as prestige marker, and country as site of identity, as a homeplace. Structural tension between siblings is mediated through complementary discourses of inheritance and sentiment; a reluctance to talk about these practices hides a tension between a surface ideology of partible inheritance but a practice of gendered partibility of assets, resources and knowledge with the opportunity to farm going usually to sons. Families vary in how they reconcile these tensions, but the patterns I describe prevail even in progressive high-country farming communities. In all of these cases, partible inheritance ideology applies and suggests women have equal rights with men (cf. Cole 1971:9), although a commitment to keeping stations intact means that male partible inheritance prevails as men are offered the opportunity to farm, while women are compensated in other kinds of assets. Equality of opportunity to farm the land is guaranteed to as many sons as a property can support.

Several linked analytic challenges complicate my discussion. First, the problematic of analyzing kin relations within and between generations, and of examining inheritance principles and practices in a context where such knowledge is guarded within nuclear families and from the extended family. How do I theorize the culturally sensitive? Second, the problematic of theorizing gender when high-country residents, specifically runholding sons and their wives, deny its significance and discourage its analysis. What do they tell me when they say that gender does not matter, especially when the sisters/daughters of these families who have left, tell me that it does? Third, the related problem of understanding and defending strongly formulaic social patterns in a research context where people experientially like me—urban New Zealanders, liberal academics, feminist scholars—and departed sons and daughters find such a circumscribed social vision "provincial," "closed," or "rigid" in its strong gender differentiation with fixed sex roles and where sons inherit the opportunity to return to the station over daughters. How do I acknowledge and make sense of social traditionalism when the inhabitants deny it and others condemn it?

Sons Who Stay

The progressive runholders with whom I worked most closely represent a post-World-War-II generation. In the Rakaia valley, Hugh Ensor's five grandsons and eleven granddaughters were born between 1941 and 1957; of these four grandsons and one granddaughter stayed in the valley and began managing and owning the properties with their spouses in the 1970s. While farming prosperity in the 1970s enabled stations with multiple sons to increase production and subdivide, the requisite expansion was planned and initiated by the runholders much earlier. For example, in 1953, Hugh Ensor's son Duncan, after selling his interest in the Double Hill estate, expanded Glenrock by purchasing the lease to a neighboring station in an adjacent catchment, an area of 20,000 acres; in 1969 he purchased additional freehold paddocks from Double Hill, which, together with advances in farming productivity from aerial topdressing, increased subdivision of paddocks, and the production of silage for winter feed, made it possible for the property to divide into two, one for each of his sons.[3] His nephew reminded me that "farmers always purchase adjacent land if it turns up—it was too good an opportunity to miss." Both of his sons have a strong attachment to the station and its country, and both admit to never having thought of doing anything else but farming, despite overseas travel, and, in the younger brother's case, mustering elsewhere. One of their wives, like many others, told me that her husband's coming back to this particular place "has something to do with being born here." The brothers understand each other's imperative to return and cooperate to ensure station continuity and survival as well as sibling harmony. Despite working legally split but adjacent properties the brother-brother relationship leads to farming cooperation in lending materials and equipment, working together at busy times during the agricultural cycle—at tailing, the autumn muster, silage making—or in times of family emergency, helping out with grazing when needed, participating in joint economic ventures, caring for children, making decisions for the company, and privileging the rights of each others' children as nephews and nieces in the future.

I supplement my work in Mid Canterbury with data from age cohorts on stations elsewhere in North and South Canterbury, in Marlborough, and Otago. While remaining sensitive to ethnographic detail and the accuracy of narratives from which my analytic points derive, I disguise properties and the specificity of different families' inheritance decisions and practices by adjusting identifying features to create pseudonymous generic stations and by paraphrasing statements. These cases illustrate some of the ways in which families manage property transfer to multiple sons, and the ways in which these sons, as brothers, negotiate station division while simultaneously providing for continuity of family ownership. Although partible inheritance ideology gives women equal rights with men over material resources, the inheritance principles of these properties illustrate the overriding principle of male succession and birth order as older sons stay and their sisters leave.

Inheriting Opportunity

Revealing initiative, the "Downs" runholder and his lawyer decided to form a Land Company in 1969, the year before the pastoral lease was to be renewed, and to implement a run plan. A report on the property was prepared by the Catchment Board, documenting the land (its history, soils, vegetation, geology, erosion), capital (improvements, valuation, stock firm, finance), labor, management (past land use, land capability, stock husbandry, policy, stock movement, field husbandry, plant and machinery), and conservation challenges. The report recommended changes in management practices to overcome conservation problems. A run plan based on the report was drawn up by the Catchment Board, calling for compensation for loss of grazing land to be retired from use— 13,950 acres of land representing 610 ewe equivalents; the loss would be compensated by a subsidy to the run on oversowing and topdressing 1,615 acres of lower country. Additional amounts were included for new fencing and cattle-proof fencing. The runholder's portion was slightly over half of the £20,520. In effect, "the runholder is to be subsidised for the development of his run so that another part can be retired"; subsidies must be sufficient to ensure that the runholder is no worse off from the retirement of the back country and the development of the front country; they must simultaneously compensate for loss of income resulting from lost grazing land, and provide the runholder an incentive for undertaking development work and management changes.

The run plan and the development scheme were worked out to carry 3,000 stock units. With foresight, the runholder had already increased the property's carrying capacity when he switched to pre-lamb shearing in 1958 to reduce stress on ewes and lambs, and enabling agricultural work to continue unhampered in the spring; in 1963 "Downs" began making winter silage when the grass was growing at its best in November and December; aerial topdressing had been introduced in 1953 with superphosphate and clover seed dropped on the fan country. The "Downs" lease was at its lowest value and the freehold on the property at the time was insignificant with low value. The runholder gave his three sons the option to take up ordinary shares in the land company. He lent them the money to buy the shares and held the mortgage. The sons had to earn the shares but had no assets. Their father held onto the preference shares and in his will left the mortgage he held on those shares to his sons. His wife's estate would be left to their daughters upon her death. Each son in turn was offered the shares. As one son explained, "To give the eldest son first opportunity simplifies things," and for their father was a pragmatic gesture most easily preserving the farm as an economic unit and the family name. The eldest could have taken up all the shares, but their value would have rested with his brothers, and he would have had to buy them out. The two older sons each rejected the option of taking up all the shares individually. The eldest son definitely knew he wanted to farm; the youngest was pretty sure that he did. The three boys saw "no winners and a forever debt" in their father's plan. They all believed they had a stake in the place and decided to farm together.

Then in 1970 they had the opportunity to purchase a neighbor's freehold blocks. If purchased it could carry 70 percent of the productive value of "Downs," enabling the sons to double their assets and make two farms. Acquiring these paddocks was crucial "for the whole thing coming off; we couldn't have done it without": If they could do that, then at least two of them could buy out the remaining brother.[4] They went to the Rural Bank with ordinary shares, not worth anything, to purchase the block of land next door. Their father's estate provided the security, and they established a trust.

> "Downs" Station Ltd. had the following financial structure: (1) Preference or A shares which provided voting rights but carried no increase in value were owned by the senior runholder. (2) His three

sons owned ordinary or B shares that provided voting rights and could increase in value. (3) The sons were in debt with the Rural Bank for the purchase of the freehold blocks. (4) Each of the sons had a mortgage owing to their father on their ordinary shares. (Field notes 11.vii.87)

The three sons had land and no stock. They formed a partnership and bought their father's entire lamb drop to stock the new country. They had a clear vision for two farms with two brothers buying the third out but hoped there could be three. The eldest was at home farming; the middle son was studying agriculture at Lincoln College; the youngest was in secondary school.[5] For three years, the eldest worked on the farm for virtually no wages. In 1972 his parents, thinking "there were too many young men on the place," left him to run the property on his own, and went traveling.

Their eldest son says a few things "were bloody good luck." As one son told me: "we wanted to farm and to develop, and we didn't give a continental about finances." They renewed the lease in 1970, and confidence in farming strengthened. Equity and value increased rapidly with a wool boom in 1973. The two brothers, who were both planning their marriages at the time, went back to the Bank to borrow money to enable their parents to leave. Their younger brother came home to work after he finished boarding school while the middle brother was still away at university. The youngest took his value in the family trust, in cattle and stock. His brothers borrowed to stock the farm and buy him out—with the increased value of all their shares. The equity with the most worth was the freehold land.

For the first five years, they farmed well together dividing the labor according to their own strengths and interests—one preferred the stock work, the other the agricultural work. To split the property was always in the plan. One family built a new home two and one-half miles away. The new homestead was meant to balance out the improvement and maintenance costs required by the aging station. They divided the 27,000-acre property on 1 July 1977 into two separately functioning farms—"Downs" and "North Downs"—but remained together under one lease for financial reasons. The legislation under which the lease had been renewed in 1970 based the rental on stock-carrying capacity and provided tenure for thirty-three years. The current lease therefore runs until 2003 at $550 rental. The rent is low because,

> We have only got a very small area of reasonably good [leasehold] country, and not a large area of freehold, but it is a very good piece of freehold. It's actually what demonstrates the significance of a very high form of land development really which is in marked contrast to [a neighbor], which has something like ten times the area of a similar [leasehold] country, but not even twice the stock. . . . Look at the number of stock we run. You look at the breakdown of the two places together ["Downs" and "North Downs"]—you start with 6,000 hectares for the retired stuff . . . the next 3,000 is where cattle and sheep graze over—that includes the high bit where the sheep are—and then

there's only a couple of thousand hectares after that, which is where everything happens. Fortunately, it's very small.

To divide the lease or tamper with it in anyway would mean that legislation passed shortly after the renewal of the [1970] lease would apply. This bases the rental on 2 percent of "Land Exclusive of Improvements," known as LEI, with an eleven-year review. For [our property] whose LEI value is $140,000 it would have meant an increase to $2,800 rent. (Field notes 30.viii.88)

To divide the working of the farm, but not the lease, the older brother says, "we put a mob in yards, counted the lot and then counted out half." Dividing the properties "made it easier." The carrying capacities are equal. As one brother said: "The Trust has worked. We pooled our resources, we built our finances, then we pulled out and split fifty-fifty." In 1987 the two sons bought the last stock from their father and moved from debt into credit.

Elsewhere at "Creek" station a sister told me of her brothers: "there was never any consideration to farm jointly—human nature being as it is, it is too difficult," but such folk explanations should not be accepted at face value and instead may provide the "ideological mask" for "rivalries among the brothers themselves" in a pastoral setting constrained by uncertain variables of climate and economy where formal structures must protect male solidarity and cooperation, and blame is deflected onto wives (cf. Denich 1974:256, 259).[6] People say that brothers will cooperate but their wives will not because wives tend to feel protective of their husbands. The "sisters-in-law explanation" is formulaic, offered usually without provocation, and stated as if obvious. This tension between a man and his sister-in-law (brother's wife), or between sisters-in-law (husband's sisters) is especially acute in instances where properties are co-owned, and the brother/brother dyad is under the greatest stress, although brothers who divide after having farmed together for some years or whose leases are still undivided will give as their reason for dividing, their sons in the next generation—brothers may farm together, but more distant collateral (ablineal) kinsmen such as cousins cannot. Keeping assets evened out in quantifiable financial terms—in calculating carrying capacity and the value of plant and buildings—through careful negotiations is a device to preserve harmony and reinforce equality between brothers. The proffered formulae explain separation in neutral structural terms rather than in personal terms; they also displace responsibility for things not working out from brothers to wives (and potentially to cousins in the next generation), and therefore functionally reinforce the cultural strength of salient working sibling dyads and preserve harmony between primary kin.

In the words of one "Downs" brother, when the two sons took over in 1973, their parents "did not linger on . . . and watch over [our] shoulders but turned the property over to [my brother] and me to farm." Like many of their daughters, high-country parents resign themselves to the inevitability of leaving; they spend their working lives bracing for it. His mother said to me:

It wasn't hard to leave because we did it gradually and it had to be done. We did it gradually over time so it wasn't a sudden wrenching away. (Field notes 19.v.87)

As one relative put it, she (as a city-born woman) may "have had a guts full" of high-country life. For his father it was more difficult:

We had to go, it was very important to both of us that the boys continue to farm, and they wouldn't have waited. [The eldest] might have waited and come back, but [the next son] wouldn't have waited—he would have gone off. We decided to turn the farm over at a point at which the boys were ready to take it on even though it was earlier perhaps than we would have wanted to leave. And we left, we really left—we didn't hang around—we severed the tie. (Field notes 19.v.87)

Their daughter-in-law was struck by their total departure. When she and her husband married and came up the valley, her father-in-law handed over the key and said, "it's all yours now." "I didn't take it in," she said, "didn't realize what he was saying—it took me over a year to come to grips with what it meant. That all this house was ours. [My parents-in-law] are vital people with interests of their own to pursue, which is what they are doing" (field notes 30.vi.87). The children acknowledge how hard their parents had worked with a "basic" house, an erratic electricity supply, no phone, little money, and six children.

All three sons respect their parents' innovative and progressive thinking in estate planning and point to how astute they were in setting up the trusts in such a way to provide themselves with a retirement income. One son said:

It was a clever way of getting both worlds. Dad is a traditionalist in the sense that he wanted one of the six to carry on what he had done. He was hellish hard-working. It was right to split the estate in half and then three ways. Dad had to have security in order to be able to retire. For [my sisters] to share in his estate would mean no monetary value for them since he is still alive. For the girls to borrow against the estate, he would have nothing for himself. It was crucial that Dad and Mum keep control of the estate to meet their own security requirements. Dad never left himself in a position that if a boy went broke it could affect him. We could have, we were pretty cheeky! We would like to think that some of our success up here should be put down to our ability to farm it. (Field notes 11.vii.87)

If the property had been split six ways, and any three had wanted their money out of the property, the others would have found it prohibitively expensive to buy them out. This inheritance principle is cited again and again and is not specific to "Downs." You can "never have one buy two out—it is impossible. Dad's commitment was for the property to remain in the family." For the farm to pass out of the family was unthinkable to this runholder, and in his concern that his sons, all of whom wanted to farm, might go elsewhere, he bought a neighboring property's paddocks and left earlier than he wanted to. Retired parents often stay on a property moving into the cottage as their married son and daughter-in-law move into the homestead, although virtually all high-country families told me that those who "leave their children to it" and build a new life for themselves are respected. Nieces and nephews frequently told me how much they respected these parents for leaving as they did.[7] Their departure was a way to obviate intergenerational structural tensions between father and son, mother and daughter-in-law, and places family continuity ahead of self-interest. Those who love the high country most are able to leave it in this way, I was told, but those for whom it represents social status, find it harder to go.

One son painted another possible scenario that would have served his parents well financially if it had been their primary concern. They might have sold the "Downs," taken what they needed to buy another property to live on, and divided the balance between their children six ways. "No one would have got much in that case." As things worked out, two sons continue to provide their father's salary and paid the mortgage on the property to which their parents first moved after leaving the "Downs." They also had to pay the mortgage on the freehold paddocks purchased from next door. Furthermore, in final estate settlement the sons "will not get a penny" because they were provided with "opportunity" earlier. From the sons' perspective the inequity a sister might claim could apply to them also when one considers that their mother's estate was not used for their parents' retirement. A son noted how odd it is that parents care about being able to leave an estate to their children even at the expense of sacrificing some comfort in their retirement.

In his discussion of wealth and the developmental cycle in a rural South Canterbury community, Elvin Hatch (1992:95) explains that given the regulations controlling inheritance taxes in New Zealand, it makes more economic sense for a young man to buy rather than to inherit his parents' farm outright. As we have seen, sons state that they inherit only *the opportunity* to farm the land—none of this is gifted outright, and on "Downs" and "North Downs," the runholders have moved through the developmental cycle as Hatch describes it; their early years of marriage were marked by mortgage payments to their father for their shares with all earnings being invested back into the properties. Goody has noted in his discussion of family and inheritance that the unity of an agricultural holding is "often achieved at the expense of burdening the productive unit with heavy debts" (1976:2). As time passes and the farm reaches what Hatch calls a "mature stage of development," families are more able to shift their spending from farm improvements to domestic items, to afford new vehicles, home improvements, holidays, possibly the reduction of stock and the hiring of help; at the same time, however, as children reach boarding school age, they incur school fees. While many urban New Zealanders pointed to signs of high-country affluence—private-school education, stylish city clothes, swimming pools and tennis courts, four-wheel-drive vehicles—runholders are quick to point out that their assets are invested in stock and buildings, that cash is not at their fingertips, that they are in debt to parents for stock and the lease, and perhaps most significantly, that while in debt they are not really autonomous in making their own decisions. One runholder, admired for making his opportunity by working his way into the high country by taking up what is commonly called "young man's country"—isolated, remote and often rundown or abandoned stations—said,

> There is a lot of incentive for children to return when they see their parents sitting on half a million or more likely a million dollars worth, at least, of property. What child is going to turn and walk away from that, even if they have to put up with a certain amount in order to have the opportunity to take over a property like that. . . . Since it costs so much to buy into a high-country property, inheritance is really the only way these days for people to get onto one unless they have a very lucky break. It costs so much to buy into one that family ownership is really the only way to be able to do it. (Field notes 14.ix.90)

Hatch (1992:98) notes that landholders are not considered rich by each other: one of his informants told him that "you haven't got the money in your hip pocket" but "you're not tied down" and instead have relative autonomy in which your labor is not directed by someone else. In family corporations or land companies this is not always so, and the trade-off for opportunity is subjection to the land company and its directors. In contrast, a city-born runholder told me "as a free agent I can leave the property without obligations to a family estate or family expectations. I have no constraints, I am free to sell." In 1990 he did.

Sons Who Come to Belong

Occasionally a family has daughters but no sons.[8] An in-marrying son may take the place of a daughter as he farms, and she retains dominion over her mother's homestead and garden; eventually her son may become a focal point and act as the lineal male heir. Such daughters, who stay and work on the station, like those who marry back into the high country, have legitimacy unavailable to in-marrying high-country wives, and authenticity's status enables them to preserve the formulae of social life.

Sometimes when a daughter assumes a property as at "Banks" she will have an equal partnership with her husband in active management—working with stock, making decisions, classing the wool, dealing with stock and station agents. Her capacity to do so depends in part on her household commitments. The property's accessibility to the outside enables this daughter to have a woman in to clean, and a "married couple's" presence means that she can share meal preparation for the hired man and not have to cook for the married shepherd. Her husband refers to his wife as his "partner" and means it in a broader sense than just a "paper partnership." When a daughter (or perhaps a widow) is engaged in stock work as if she were a son, she usually flouts convention but inevitably invites respect if she does well. Resistance and surprise sometimes register in salesmen and stock agents who assume that the man is "the boss." At "Banks," the daughter surprises them by saying, "I am." She is involved in the studs that they run and has "an eye for stock," and men accept and respect her expertise once she has proven herself.[9] She and her husband class the wool at shearing times. She admits that her involvement is unusual and that while it is becoming acceptable for women to do the accounts, it doesn't mean they make decisions. She does.

While it was important to her parents for her to return to her childhood home to farm the property, she added that if none of her children returned she could leave.[10] The children, unlike those from more remote high-country backgrounds, have not attended boarding school because they live close enough to the local school, and they have grown up on the payroll and fully integrated into the farming activities at home. One daughter always wanted to farm but "she has become increasingly reluctant given the resistance to change in the farming community"; she finds it "oppressively traditional." Her brother sees his classmates at the local school as tremendously conservative—"they have no opinions or views—they merely parrot statements their parents might have said such as 'Lange [the prime minister] is a wanker'" or they "drink beer and play rugby—they have no aspirations." The only parallel voices I heard were from those high-country sons and daughters who had left the high country and in so doing no longer belonged, in many cases admitting to their own marginality.

To enable sons to farm, parents sometimes leave either a lowland property or first-generation high-country property for a larger high-country property. At "Hills" this meant sacrificing an intensively cultivated 500-hectares farm and custom-designed home in 1965 for a dilapidated homestead and a 5,000-hectares property so rundown that the stock were too weak to make it back up the hill after shearing. One son told me that at first they couldn't imagine running sheep on tussock. Now he could not leave; the "tussock carries the high country," he says. When he is in the back country, he enjoys its "feel—the sounds of skylarks and of wind in the tussock." He has seen some visitors' physical hesitation at the expanse of landscape as they huddle together at its highest point.[11] Even though lacking a high-country background, the men's care for "Hills" is reflected in the farming choices they have made—leaving a reserve block of unfarmed land and creating variety in the landscape through cluster-planting of native trees to safeguard against "a homogeneous blanket of grass." The younger son narrates the land's history to visitors. Once soldier-resettlement land,[12] the property's paddocks still bear former owners' names, and the brothers have preserved the foundations of the original stone houses. The family applied unsuccessfully to the Historic Places Trust to save an 1890s dam, but it has now been destroyed by flood. Farming continuity from generation to generation is valued even if it means beginning anew. But the affinity for this place in particular, developed in one generation, can be expected to persist in the next. In thinking about the future for their children, the brothers split the partnership. The thought was recurrent: brothers may get along, but cousins may not.

When his sons had left school and were seeking farming opportunities, another runholder bought "Peaks" a 9,000-hectares (22,000-acres) property in 1963.[13] The son of surgeons from Britain, who had come to New Zealand to open a hospital, this senior runholder surprised his parents by wanting "to go farming." He mustered the Grampions, Mount Possession, and up the River Cass before pouring his money into an Otago property; "the high country is special for me, there is nothing else I would rather have done, no other choice." They came to look at "Peaks" when it came on the market, and made the shift, putting all their resources into the property. We were visiting under a huge eucalyptus tree in the stockyards while his sons, a daughter-in-law and a grandson were drafting the wethers mustered in that morning, and I asked him what he looked for in buying the station. "I saw that it was sweet country with sunny faces and some dark faces which you need when it gets dry. I knew how land falls and lies. I saw the potential and we have never stepped back. We moved forward, and the boys worked hard" (field notes 19.ix.90). They had not intended to divide it then.

"Peaks" and "Hills" stations illustrate that high-country properties do change hands. One spring afternoon as I drove many miles up the Awatere valley[14] with Edwin Pitts from Mount Gladstone, he pointed out how the river narrowed and opened out, pointed out boundaries, named stations, identifying those they had absorbed or separated from, and named the families and their occupation dates. Most properties in this valley sold in the 1950s and 1960s—the Muller, Camden, Awapuri, and Mount Gladstone. The drop in wool prices may have affected this flux, and some properties sold because "the sons did not want to go farming." Sometimes a divorce or estate taxes "did people in" or they left a property to six sons, none of whom could buy the others out. Even so knowledge of terrain, of vegetation, of history and commitment to farming is important to the "Hills" and "Peaks" station families despite lack of significant family continuity—so far only two generations—on this country. In this they characterize the generation of progressive high-country runholders in their thirties, forties and early fifties.

While runholders and their families do not see themselves as closed, certain distinctions are salient for the way that they talk about each other as born, and not born, to this country, such as the boss's son, the experienced musterer, the Lincoln College farmer. The terms may overlap but taken separately denote degrees of belonging to the high country. Those who are born to high-country life claim a greater sense of belonging than those who come to belong by buying in; the latter, when successful, like sons who inherit opportunity, make their claims on the basis of hard physical work and success in meeting challenges, as do sons-in-law. They may apprentice as musterer and seek a rough high-country run with development potential, or attend agricultural college, purchase or inherit a hill or plains farm, and eventually scale up by buying a high-country run. This usually demands assuming a large debt, and the runholder will farm progressively to maximize stock-carrying capacity. As much freehold tussock country is cultivated as labor and finances permit. In progressive farming, which invites scrutiny and critical commentary, every blade of grass is said to be measured and technology shapes farming to the maximum. Even so, newcomers think about their location in the high country in parallel kinds of ways to those "born to it," and may claim similar affinities although they are often more willing to sell.

Table 4.1 Double Hill Property Transfer across Generations

Generation One	Double Hill
Ownership	Single owner
Family Size	5 sons, 1 daughter
Migration	2 sons, 1 daughter
Heirs	Multiple in family estate
	3 sons remain
Expansion	Purchase Glenrock,
	Purchase Glenariffe
Homestead	One per property

Property management and ownership take a variety of forms reflecting a commitment to link farm and family. These are most easily categorized as (1) the family estate/trust, (2) the family company, (3) a husband/wife partnership.[15] Many properties commingle varieties of ownership especially in same-sex sibling ownership of neighboring or divided properties. Double Hill was a family estate after the death of Hugh Ensor, becoming a family company managed for the partnership by Peter as some siblings were bought out (see table 4.1), and finally becoming a husband/wife partnership in the next generation when Peter's daughter returned. Like "Creek," "Peaks," and "Hills," "North Downs" is a husband/wife partnership in being an autonomous economic productive unit, but it is also part of a family company encompassing "North Downs" and the neighboring property "Downs." The brothers farm "North Downs" and "Downs" separately, but they and their father hold shares in a land company called "Downs Station Limited." Regardless of the form ownership takes, it provides for continuity of ownership within the family based on consanguineal and affinal ties over the generations. Such ownership contrasts sharply with that of some individuals who have bought into the high country. The Lincoln College farmer who is heavily reliant on extensive subdividing and cultivated paddocks and machinery, and believes less in the traditional muster and sparser grazing in the back country, may be less determined to pass the property onto a son. Many Lincoln farmers told me that there is no expectation that a son will return to farm. From the perspective of the newcomer, who may own a property as an individual or in partnership with a spouse, the responsibilities of those whose land belongs to parents and siblings seem onerous; the history of Double Hill's ownership a generation ago with which I began in chapter 1 provides an apt case (table 4.1).

Within the constraints of different ecological pressures and extralocal socioeconomic factors,[16] family farmers may be differentiated by the varying intergenerational transfer practices used to keep the farm within the family. This means that people sometimes diverge from multiple-heir ownership to keep properties in families and ensure farming as an occupation for at least one son, or that fathers retire early to ensure a son's return. Consequently, table 4.2 shows a dominant pattern for transfer of single-property ownership between

Table 4.2 Property Transfer across Two Generations

Generation	Creek	Downs	Hills	Peaks	Point	Bank
Ownership	Single owner	Single owner	Single owner	Single owner	Family estate, to single owner	Land company partnership
Family Size	2 sons 5 daughters	3 sons 3 daughters	4 sons	2 sons	4 daughters	2 daughters
Migration	5 daughters	1 sons 3 daughters	2 sons	None	3 daughters	1 daughter (deceased)
Heirs	Multiple 2 sons	Multiple 2 sons	Multiple 2 sons	Multiple 2 sons	Single 1 daughter	Single 1 daughter
Expansion	Purchase adjacent run Purchase adjacent freehold paddock Intensification	Purchase adjacent freehold paddock Intensification	Intensification	Intensification	None	None
Division	2 properties Legal separation	2 properties Working separation	2 properties Legal separation	2 properties Working separation Some joint areas Single station name	None	None
Homestead	Creek homestead Cottage New homestead	Downs homestead South Downs homestead	Hills homestead Cottage 2 New homesteads	Peaks homestead New homestead	Point homestead Cottage	Bank homestead
Retirement	Early Remain initially	Early Leave completely	Early Remain initially	Early Remain initially	Early Remain initially	Early Remain until death
Next Generation Family Size	1 son, 2 daughters 4 daughters	1 son, 1 daughter 1 son, 1 daughter	1 son, 1 daughter 2 sons, 2 daughters	4 sons 2 sons, 1 daughter	1 son 2 daughters	1 son 2 daughters

generations, which whenever possible expands a property for division between two sons;[17] in all cases, one of the properties preserves the original station name, and, in some instances, despite a practical separation of land, stock and farm accounts between brothers, the wool bales are sold under the original station name where the wool brand carries an economic value that neither brother wants to forfeit. Some families would split legally if they could, but the cost of dividing Crown pastoral leases and fencing boundaries often prevents this and encourages the formation of family land companies. There is always a transitional period, sometimes lasting for many years, when the property has multiple owners in the form of the family company—fathers, brothers, sometimes sisters; but in contrast to the estate model, where one son might manage a property for life without full ownership, the preferred alternative is to create a mechanism to enable the son gradually to buy out his parents and siblings. In some cases, a third son might be excluded from both land and occupation, although in most cases parents will help him to find a farm elsewhere, or siblings might not be able to remove their shares from the property, or their shares may come in some other form, such as assets. Such cooperative arrangements in land companies will probably not work for the next generation of cousins on adjacent properties should they choose to farm.

Daughters Who Leave

> And the fact there were no mountains meant that there was no solid landmark in the background to refer to when the points of one's personal compass became confused. One's life could not suddenly flow and dissolve. The lights might go out, there might be storms and knocking, and no help in view but mountains seen out of the corner of the eye, as a white fortress; or daffodils seen and known in spring, and yellowing leaves in autumn were certainties that gave meaning and consolation, though one may not realise this until one had arrived in a strange landscape; a spring season where the daffodils and the leaves were already withered; where nothing was known or stayed or could be predicted.
>
> —Janet Frame, *A State of Siege* (1966)[18]
> in McNaughton (1986:146)

Marilyn Strathern (1992:13) defines sentiment as a "special emotion" that "the English have . . . for dwelling on tradition, or for dwelling on what is just out of reach of [individual] enterprise." Such sentiment extends into the postcolonial context in high-country New Zealand, where inheritance discourses can be examined as markers of affect, and as mechanisms for generating sentiment for place and loyalty to the idea of the link between the family name and the station, between family and country. Although a distinction is often made between emotion as private (natural) feeling "not culturally motivated or socially articulated," and sentiment "as socially articulated symbols and behavioral expectations"

(Lutz and White 1986: 409), Catherine Lutz (1992:67) urges us to link private emotion with sentiment as "culturalized emotion"; she and White (1986:417) conceptualize emotion, like sentiment, as simultaneously socially shaped and shaping.

Two contradictory expressions of place attachment—genealogical place attachment, and place attachment enhanced in memory provoked through loss (see Low 1992:168-169)—reveal that "the affective quality of place attachments . . . [is] often accompanied by cognition . . . and practice." (Low and Altman 1992:4-5).[19] The case studies above pertain to sons, and occasional daughters, who stay and experience genealogical place attachment, but what of the women who might be their sisters, the daughters, occasional son, and parents who leave their natal home and experience loss? Being "born to the land" but, as daughters who leave, no longer "of the land," women experience and express varying degrees of connection to and sentiment for the station, and of alienation from inheritance practices as a particular form of property transfer for preserving the link between family name and property. While many women call the station "Home" or "home," and seek another "life on the land" elsewhere, a few realign their affections for the station entirely, noting it as "just something I left behind," a place where gender constraints "closed us out of high-country life." In drawing on the experiences and insights of those children "born to the high country" who have left, both female and sometimes male, I document—from childhood activities, to boarding school, to marriage—the ways in which experiences in and memories of place are concretized and preserved.

The high country's pull is strong for most women born to it, and the daughters from most of the high-country properties that I know often had sought similar environments and a "life on the land" in marriage. One father observed that his three daughters were drawn to parallel places, at the remote ends of rough roads or with other physical landmarks, such as the ocean or a bay, replacing the mountains as a focal point. They married farmers, landscape architects, market gardeners or agricultural agents. One daughter farms on a remote peninsula in partnership with her husband. Bought by her husband's father in the early 1950s, the property is a magical spot with that "end-of-the-road feeling." A five-mile steep shingled road provides access to a homestead encased by rolling hill country on either side of a bay with rare yellow-eyed penguins. For this daughter the sea replaced the mountains. The 1912 farmhouse faces east on a rise within sound and view of the ocean; its magnificent native woods, high ceilings, and wide verandas evoke its colonial past.[20] This property, like many high-country properties, is geographically unique and visually splendid; even so the owners' ideological commitment to equal sibling inheritance transcends "the pull of the land" in this instance. They have three children, two daughters and one son, none of whom at the time of my initial research were interested in farming. They plan for their children to inherit the actual property equally, which they note is unusual. They know that for one to buy the others out is financially impossible, but they are committed to treating sons and daughters equally.

One eldest sister in her forties from a large Rakaia family explained to me that her two brothers' staying on was inevitable because it was the only way to keep the place in the family, and she would be distressed if the station left the family. "That feeling of devastation is totally emotional; I can't explain it." She admits to never understanding the financial arrangements of her friends' and cousins' families, but knows others did things differently from her own family. Other families' inheritance plans were not discussed outside the immediate nuclear family and in many instances were kept from adolescent children. This sister speaks eloquently of her childhood home and of life in the valley: "I hated boarding school. I was desperately homesick, and I ached to be in the mountains." She remembers climbing into bed with her cousin at Selwyn House School and sobbing. She voices a visual nostalgia, and naturalizes her specular attachment:

> It is a physical rather than a mental feeling. Some days I yearn for the mountains. [The] North Canterbury hill country feels pale to me; I needed to learn to see the beauty in things less strong. The Rakaia is very expansive. I have the need to go back. I wasn't weaned; I see this now in terms of real dependency. (Field notes 19.vi.87)

In "weaning," she uses an organic stock metaphor of lambs attached to their mothers, analogous to the biological connection that farmers describe for lambs as attached to their "birth patch"; in a similar way farming families evoke a notion of being rooted in place, of having a natal attachment to country.

After she finished secondary school before marrying, she returned to live at home on the payroll for three years. She helped with her three younger siblings, worked in the house, and is listed in farm payroll ledgers as "domestic"; occasionally she helped her father, but growing up, her labor felt excluded. She continued: "To me it was a man's world and I regretted until I was 16 that I wasn't born a man. I saw myself as a server. My brother and his wife are different in that they work together." She notes other changes in the valley—better roads, more people, her brother and sister-in-law's different stamp on the homestead. "I remember the road across the flats. I regret the flats being washed away and the road changing. My areas are gone; it happened long ago. But there are many pluses for me out in the world."

Her contemporaries were similarly included in station tasks with set jobs. In the farm ledgers, one is on the payroll as a "land girl." Her duties included going "round sheep" during lambing time to check on the ewes. She remembers doing some cooking, the vegetable garden, and milking. She helped her father with the sheep and in the woolshed but was not allowed to dock the lambs' tails. Her father bought her a horse float, and she showed and hunted but did not want to go on a muster, unlike some of her female cousins, especially those "who lived on their horses," who told me how much they would have loved to do so. One, now farming on her own, told me of the huts "out the back" being full of history:

> I once went out with the packie on horseback to the first hut but had to ride back before nightfall; I would never have asked to go [on a muster] and am sure I would have been refused, but it is something I

have always wanted to do. I lived for my horses and loved them and missed them when I went away to boarding school. Most of my cousins loved horses and we lived on the horses on the flat. We thought it a great adventure to ride with the wild ponies (packhorses) down there. I doubt now they were really wild. I remember frosty mornings with cold hands and cold feet riding with my father. (Field notes 14.vii.87)

Her sister quoted above, with slightly more critical distance from this past, bluntly explained horse riding to me: "We rode because we weren't allowed to do anything else—it was all we had to do."

Like two of her sisters and three of her cousins on neighboring stations, this eldest sister married a sheep farmer who lived in very isolated and beautiful pastoral hill country; marrying into similar kinds of properties may make the leaving easier as daughters find husbands in their brothers' and parents' farming networks from boarding school or on the ski field. The eldest sister always saw herself as living "on the land" and expected to marry a farmer. The people she knew at boarding school were "from the land" too. Now on the hill property she does the bookwork, but says she is not "on the land." She and her husband have many community involvements.[21] She returns regularly to the original property with her husband and children to see her brother and sister-in-law. In reflecting on the valley, she thinks it provides a very selfish lifestyle where one can be autonomous and live very comfortably without needing or supporting anyone. "I had to unlearn the things I learned up there. I had to learn to fit in with them [her husband's community]—saying things, the language is different—it took me a long time. [My childhood home] was a sheltered upbringing. I never experienced me. I discovered at 40 that I like being me." Despite her loyalty to the property, to her family, to their inheritance decisions, her ambivalence rests in her critical distance and her recognition of a separate identity.

Her youngest sister imagines that her brothers never had any choice but to return to the property and thinks pressures on children to return are unfortunate. She was never jealous of her brothers and agreed that they should take over. She couldn't bear the thought of them all getting equal shares and splitting the property. She noted that she and all her siblings loved the place, and she always feels welcome, finding little difference with her brother and sister-in-law there instead of her parents. Her cousin feels similarly, and is proud of where she came from—it is part of who she is and she still refers to the valley as home, even though her marital home is on a Canterbury hill-country farm. She is happy that both of her sons have gone to her brother's farm to work in the holidays: it is part of the "family thing" and "it gives [me] much pleasure that the boys [my brothers] are still there, that [my] boys [sons] can be part of that." She thinks of the now-divided station still as one, as home, with her family there.

Their views illustrate how strongly nuclear and lineal sisters' attachment to family is. The linking of brothers and their wives as parallel husband/wife dyads to parents diminishes potential tension between departed sisters and their brothers' wives while protecting the primacy of the marriage partnership. Women who have married in are structurally parallel to their own mothers-in-law, with whom, as we saw in chapter 3, they are in structural tension, with taking over their homes and gardens as its most direct expression; as a working dyad, the integrity of the husband/wife partnership is protected in the responses of returning sisters for whom the homestead door is, quite literally, always open.

These daughters experience acute loss in separation and voice it in a broader cultural logic that mostly acknowledges loss as part of high-country life. To ensure the workability of male-focused inheritance patterns, many (but not all) sisters remain emotionally attached by preserving their link to the station as Home, and transform loss into a challenge to which one adapts, as with other losses that are part of farming. This is not a culture of resistance, but rather one of resilience in which, in the face of environmental challenge and uncertain market conditions, a philosophy of pragmatism generates a rhetoric of "getting on with it," of "making do," of diminishing hardship linguistically through understatement, and in terms of the sparseness of emotional response. One schoolmaster aptly described the high-country character: "they often come with an attitude of 'well, the job's got to be done, so let's do it'."

"I always feel a sense of loss about the valley," said one daughter, now in her forties, who used *turangawaewae* (the Maori equivalent for natal attachment meaning "place where your feet stand") to explain what she meant, and she told me spontaneously that she understands how Maori people feel—"for them it was their Maoriness but for me it was my gender that kept me from the land."[22] We were meeting at afternoon tea with her mother, her husband, and our runholder host. Prefacing her comments, "perhaps I shouldn't say this, but I have to say this, Mum, and I mean no offense," she wondered why the eldest daughters in her region (including herself) married well and did "the expected thing" in "marrying a suitable young man" while the youngest ones weren't as well off. She could see the line up as eldest sisters had the finest outfits. I understood her to be saying that a primogeniture bias applies to daughters as it had for her brothers and may also for her nephews as the eldest wants first pick of which station to take. Her mother quickly disagreed saying that it really reflected the fact that the youngest ones were able to make other choices because of social change. Her daughter suggested they may not have had choices and turning to me said that she wished that the girls who couldn't stay could at least have been given some kind of training, but they weren't—"all they could become were teachers or nurses"; she too nursed, and now remarried to a farmer, she finds the return "felt very familiar." She thinks it is great that today's younger generation is going to university. One of her cousins, an age mate, shifts the blame: "All I wanted to do [growing up] was be at [the property]; I loved the [valley] and didn't want to leave"; because it was hard to think of a life beyond the station and the valley, she resisted her mother's urging her to get qualifications. She rode and skied growing up, and after leaving secondary school traveled to Europe for eighteen months only to come back to the valley to be a ski instructor. Now she too farms in remote hill country.

Daughters born later who grew up in the early 1970s do think of themselves having grown up in a "freer world." One daughter remembers as a girl being able to muster the paddocks with the hired men. Her father's farm diary documents her participation; the entry for 17-19 April 1972 reads "self and [daughter] sorting stud ewes and drafting." She continues to love stock work and to be outside dairy farming; she was miserable when her husband hired a laborer during her pregnancy—she "had six months inside" and hated it. Her parents encouraged her to have a career but she resisted further academic training after leaving boarding school. As a girl, she remembers "following my brother around like a shadow and admiring him." And she felt close to (but has lost touch with) her age-mate cousin, a third son who could not stay; she says "he was never really visible up there" speculating "perhaps he recognized there was no place for him." She and her husband "want the challenge that most farmers seek but not resting on security." With strong feelings about the freedom life in the valley offered to her, like sisters who resented their exclusion from farmwork, she even now thinks of the property as home, often confusing her husband, who doesn't know which home she means.

The cousin to whom she refers had left when his brothers married and returned to the station. As one brother tells the story, "the four of us got married and [my younger brother] left. It was clear that two would stay and one would go. We must have had deliberations. I don't know how [he] felt about it. He ended up with the rawest deal. He had stock and assets. He had the ability to borrow money against his value here. Land and prices were undergoing a steady incline." He was also able to use his parents' house in town as collateral. He comes into his father's will on nonstation things, but the brother notes, "I'm not sure how it will work for him." He concludes, "It was not as easy for him as it was for us since this place was still charging ahead so fast it almost fell over itself," and "he did not get as good an opportunity." His other brother says, "he got the raw end of the deal but admits to having had opportunities that the others did not," but more than that he had to "create his opportunity."

Today, like some of his sisters and cousins, he sees himself as a structural outsider. Like many youngest, he suspected retrospectively when he was very young that there would be no future for him at home; he curbed his expectations and told me that his parents helped him in other ways. Sent away to boarding school at age eight, he remembers his life there more than on the station; an older sister similarly said "I was away more than I was there, away such a lot that I never really left." He always wanted to farm in the high country, but he necessarily "grew out of his love affair," and said that he "has no special attachment to the station any more—it has faded." He was generous and respectful in speaking of his two older brothers and their wives—"it is always hard with four people making decisions—it is to their credit that they have done it"; his comment underscores the centrality of marital partnerships in farming and the acknowledged potential for tension between sisters-in-law. He thinks his father was fair; furthermore, it could not have been easy for his brothers to guarantee their father's income, and he reminded me that "they weren't given anything outright."

Another high-country sister, a middle child, responded differently from her older sisters, by quickly having realized as a girl that there was no place for her and "sorted out other directions" for herself. Atypically, she went to university and studied the humanities, then to teaching college in the North Island where she now lives with her husband and children. Whereas the sister above speaks of her places as gone, this woman's place memories are timeless and fixed. She always has a sense of well-being and familiarity when she goes home. The stability offers a secure world guided by social predictability; such stability is alluring but also inherently conservative.[23] Like many of her cousins and siblings who have left, she notes that when she goes up there, they have little to talk about after catching up on family.

Like many high-country-born women, she speaks of the valley as a capital-H "Home" and Wellington as a lower-case "home," but now that her parents have left the property and she returns to her brothers' homes, it is "somewhere between the capital 'H' and the lower case 'h'." Friends in Wellington are fascinated by her background; the high country is a world they, along with most New Zealanders, know little about. She told me that the valley has always struck her as a unique place, although not to those who remain there. Another high-country daughter from an adjacent valley, now a school principal, said that "her bones will come back" to the station, but now Wellington is where she is from; she feels as if she "doesn't belong" and prefers to stay in a nearby village with her now-retired mother rather than in the old station homestead with her brother and sister-in-law, nieces and nephews.

This middle sister though has strong and explicit feelings about the genderedness of inheritance practices. Her sister and mother told me that she takes it quite seriously that "the boys were favored"; another sister told me that she herself does not feel this way but admits that she is "often oblivious to things." Sympathetically her mother tells a story illustrating the strength of her daughter's convictions:

> [Her brother] was very spoiled. [My husband] once came in saying a rabbit was cornered in the woodpile—rabbits were worth a ten-shilling bounty in those days—and that he must finish his lunch first. [My daughter] finished hers and said she would get the rabbit; she was very angry that it was her brother's privilege to do so. He threw a temper tantrum and was allowed to get the rabbit. She never forgave or forgot. She realized then and there in her growing up that there was no place for her as a girl up there and she developed other aspirations. This episode and the fact that sons would inherit led her eventually to feminism. (Field notes 17.vi.87)

A cousin expressed the same feelings quite succinctly, "It isn't right that daughters can't stay if they want to." Similarly disaffected, an age mate in the valley severed her connections to [her childhood home] without longing, regret, or wistfulness—"it's just something I left behind." She is just as happy to stay away and doesn't particularly like going back there. She said, "When we [she and her sister] married it was as if we no longer existed; when we lost the name we were no longer part of the family." She and her husband thought that her parents were motivated to preserve the farm as an economic unit to perpetuate the family name and reputation through the property. At stake was status and property, not attachment.

Daughters' responses suggest a continuum of loyalty to inheritance practices through the vehicles of narration of loss, of memory, and of sentiment. The affective expressions of attachment are evident in the replication of a lifestyle in similar environments, frequency of return visits through a lifetime, the forging of links through sending their own children back to the station to work, fond memories of a fixed and unchanging landscape often known through horseback riding, detailed memories of the homestead and grounds, a sense of well-being and security deriving from stability produced by the continuity of the farming cycle, and most importantly cooperation with inheritance practices that deprive them of permanent and material attachment despite those feelings of loss signifying attachment. The stability relies upon fixed and predictable social forms dependent upon conventions of land ownership and management.

Property-transfer practices ensure male-focused intergenerational continuity and serve as a mechanism for maintaining the continuity of family and farm, for perpetuating the link of family name and station name and the prestige its history carries. Most sisters, and some brothers, sacrifice their own claims as stakeholders to ensure this continuity. While daughters are schooled in values that disenfranchise them, sons are bound to their birth patch. Inheritance is about ownership of land (more precisely of the lease for the land), especially male ownership, but it is also about opportunity to take up an occupation, and mostly about family continuity on the land. Family farms are characterized by "strong attachment to natal land" as in Susan Rogers and Sonya Salamon's analysis, and "individual, family and farm identity are thus inextricably tied to each other and permanently fixed in space" (1983:542); almost echoing the voice of one of the daughters, they note that country (and I would add epistemologies of country) is sacred and its loss disastrous (1983:543). Disagreements surface not because sons gain materially and daughters do not, but because sons usually inherit the opportunity to farm the land whereas daughters inherit cash, the house in town, or family investments. At stake are land, occupation, and connection to place.

As Robert Hall notes (1987:754) the significance of family lies in "ensuring continuity over ownership of land" in New Zealand. The preservation of family identity is very much at stake in inheritance practices. One son said, "Dad's commitment was for the property to stay in the family." In large families with brothers, girls quickly realize that "there is no place" for them, because, like some younger brothers (and eventually their parents), they are willing to sacrifice personal gain to ensure family continuity. Configured emotionally to leave, they find security in their attachment to the station through family. Such commitments feed social prestige and can be linked to attempts to create a "landed gentry" in New Zealand,[24] to sustain a farming tradition that suggests depth of continuity of habitation and management of country despite merely 150 years of settlement, and to express a form of indigeneity for a settler-descendant population as children return to their natal place.

Reminding us to attend to whereness, whenness, and structures, and to pay attention to the spatial, temporal, and social, Allan Pred (1990:229, 6) conceptually links time and space and urges us also to attend to "tales of local transformation and of the time-space specific interplay of practices, power relations and forms of consciousness." He stresses that "human agents unintentionally and intentionally made histories and constructed human geographies not under circumstances of their own choosing but in the context of already existing, directly social and spatial relations" (1990: 228). Place attachment is concretized in an inheritance discourse that privileges males as farmers and is constructed through cultural mechanisms that, when successful, evoke nostalgia fostered by both memory and a sense of loss for women, and occasionally males.

Influenced by Bourdieu's *habitus*, and Foucault's concept of discourse, contemporary anthropology conceptualizes emotion as ideological practice, as an index of social relationship, and as discourse driven by social practices and behaviors, and located within systems of power (Lutz 1992:7) that determine who stays and who goes in the New Zealand high country; it conceptualizes the spatial similarly as part of a cultural structure, as "'a socially constituted system of cognitive and motivating structures'—a deep structure of personality" (Bourdieu cited in Shields 1991:32). Daughters' sentiment for the high country as home, capitalized or not, and loyalty to family embedded in place is shaped in a context familiar to farming families, one subject to "cultural beliefs that weigh personal rewards against group welfare demands" (Salamon 1992:178). A culturalized public identity negotiated through locating sentiment generates a sense of tradition for a settler-descendant population and is preserved at the expense of an individualized private identity.

The Next Generation

As I write, now at the end of the 1990s, the next generation of sons, mostly university educated, are returning home to farm, while in an era of gender equalization and new land legislation, families face even more complicated decisions as they work out what they call "property transfer" in the fairest way for both sons and daughters, and for themselves as parents who need adequate resources for their retirement. Sons, who have left school recently, like their fathers in the 1970s, work as shepherds at home or elsewhere until they are offered "the opportunity to farm." Despite changes in gender expectations, the current generation of girls growing up in the Rakaia valley seem to respond to a similar pull as their departed aunts in the 1960s and 1970s; those who have left secondary school to study at university have chosen careers in parks and recreation, nutrition, agricultural marketing or environmental fields such as landscape architecture, ecology or conservation work. Noting that this generation has to be more independent as they assume their own educational loans, fathers proudly document their daughters' accomplishments and capacity to earn an income. They stand apart from their aunts for whom options were narrower; as one said cautiously but angrily to her mother and me, "Marriage was our sole option; we were not trained for other things." University networks have made a difference for these girls (and for their brothers) in whom they might meet as marriage partners.

Even so as a new generation of daughters begins to marry, they replicate the outward migration and attachments of their aunts before them. Two vivid indicators stood out when I was back in 1995—artwork and weddings. One couple commissioned Austen Deans paintings for both of their daughters. For a combined Christmas/birthday present, the eldest wanted not a landscape painting but the house painted from the paddocks below. The younger sister's is in the kitchen until she claims it. Meanwhile Deans painted another view from the homestead veranda; not wanting anyone else "to have my view," her mother wanted it, only to be beaten out by her youngest daughter who called Deans and said she would buy it. Her parents admired her building up "quite a high-country art collection," and I admired her concretizing her attachment in paintings of her home patch. As a second indicator, weddings display the essential features of high-country life. Held against extraordinary vistas in the garden of the brides' station homes, their distinguishing features include: a silver dog-whistle as the bride's necklace at the kitchen party; wedding invitations and event programs with a series of high-country sketches— of tussocks and mountains, and dogs, sheep and men; communal pitching of the dinner marquee and flower arranging by local women; family photographs taken in the homestead against a backdrop of high-country paintings; panama hats for the groom and his entourage; exterior wedding party photographs in the tussocks, guest tables named after station peaks, and a large high-country painting or backdrop behind the wedding table.

At the dog trials in May 1995 as we stood at the makeshift bar on the back of a utility vehicle, one runholder caught me up since my last visit, appreciatively noting that my fieldwork was spanning the next generation's return. "Estate planning is the biggest issue on my mind now when one has to be equal to all children . . . if one isn't, a daughter can sue in this day and age." With two daughters and one son, he is trying to figure out what to do. The property—a prize property in the eyes of most—couldn't really support two families because of the expense of dividing the lease and with the new Land Act pending, freeholding land would make this even more difficult because investing in that land would take up capital. "In farming every decision to use capital in one direction takes away from something else." "It's impossible for the farming child to buy out the rest. How does one make it financially possible?" Then too he is aware that he and his wife have to live and while "I don't need to be highly acquisitive I want something, some reward, for all the years of hard work. In farming one's whole life is work." Sensitively and reflectively, he realizes now at fifty that he wants more. A neighbor put it clearly—"in all of this as parents you have to protect yourself."

For the next generation—two daughters and a son in another instance—a runholding couple told me that as things stand they would leave the land and farming opportunity to their son and the stock and assets to be divided three ways between all their children. This might mean that the son would need a mortgage from his two sisters to buy these things. His mother told me that the land would not automatically be his with no strings attached—he has to meet certain obligations in finishing school; she notes that being "Canterbury mad," is not enough—he must "earn his right to be here." This family's inheritance principles favor their son's status as male over his sisters' statuses as older and continue the practices of the previous generation, but they have to be justified and invite family law suits. This runholder's wife, unlike her husband or his brother-in-law who told me he was not ashamed to admit that he would be "quite chuffed" if his son came back to farm, questions these ways. She sees the point of view of daughters—especially her own eldest—feeling that she too should have the right to come here and farm. For her husband the patterns are inevitable because to leave the property three ways would mean that the children would have to sell, and he does not want the station sold. As their son settled into the station cottage (to be followed later by an overseas shepherding stint), he and his wife confessed that we "have no desire to leave the property for a very long time—we love it here."

Another family's developmental cycle is moving toward completion as a son, who has both an older and a younger sister, finished his secondary schooling and like his second cousin came home for a year to decide what he wanted to do before managing a sheep property overseas, finally to return home and take up residence in the station cottage. His mother told me that today children question sons taking over. Her youngest daughter asks if her brother should get the station, and she responds by assuring her that "it will all be evened out" financially. But he will be the one to farm the land. As she and I walked through her spring garden, she revealed this by commenting that "no doubt [our son's] wife [one day] will change it," and she wonders "as the garden keeps getting bigger how his wife with small children will manage it."

Other families question these ways. Resistance often comes from mothers and high-country-born sisters as their own daughters come of age. Ever mindful of protecting families from divisiveness, one high-country daughter—widowed, farming on her own, and respected for her stock abilities—commented on a family that was considering letting the children decide among themselves what to do: "It causes family feuds and I wouldn't want that." Her accountant assumed that her daughter's trust would be used for her marriage and the boys' for farming; when that angered her, he said, "most families do it that way"; she said that she would not:

> It bothers me to think that my daughter would be treated differently just because she is a girl—why should she be? The entire issue causes me so much pain, and I don't know how to resolve it. [My daughter] might marry and leave or might want to come back as a farmer in her own right. [My son] is working down [in the Lakes Country] and [my other son] is in the sixth form at College. Both want to go farming and don't want to pursue university or Lincoln—I worry that if they ever cannot farm they will have nothing to fall back on. (Field notes 14.vii.87)

Her pain is acute because of her dual commitment to sons and daughters in providing both with the opportunity to farm the land and not to create a structural rift within the family by letting them decide. As for many in her generation, family harmony and cohesiveness are nonnegotiable.

Another runholding family's will leaves their estate to their daughter and son with a preferential option that if their children do not wish to farm, the neighboring family station (the runholder's brother's family) can purchase the property's lease at a lower price, without the value of its mystique appeal.[25] Loyalty to family and to community is precious to this runholder, but he acknowledges, as does his brother, that "the constraint on being here and having taken over from my father is loyalty. I know how committed Dad is to keeping this land in the family, this property, and that does bind us. The other constraints are management constraints since Dad has to draw his income from the property first."[26] He and his wife cannot borrow against it; all projects have to be paid for from income. Despite this loyalty, the runholder would never be a station manager for the rest of the family as some farming sons are. In the next generation, settling the estate will be complicated if children of these two properties decide to farm together—both families note how much harder it is for cousins to farm together than brothers.

Bitterly, his sister's husband stressed how important he thought it was to his wife's parents to preserve the farm as an economic unit with prestige value that could perpetuate the family name and the property's reputation. The way to do that was to have divided it only between two sons. He and his wife have three children, a son and two daughters. Even so, despite his own wife's experience, he admits to being "a little bit old-fashioned" in expecting his son to farm rather than his daughters. He would resent a daughter's husband farming the property, whereas he wouldn't feel the same way if a son took over the farm. His wife though said that if a daughter wanted to farm, they would have to give equal amounts to the son and daughter because if they did not the daughter would never forgive them and always resent them. She thinks by rights girls and boys should have equal opportunity. They worry about their son's future because they are still young and have many years left to farm; "when we're through we want to be sure we have the money for a retirement home and to live comfortably." This has not been discussed with the children.[27]

Recently, the second youngest son of four had asked his own father (the eldest of two) if he had always wanted to farm and when he knew he did. Sons with brothers cope by assuming nothing and being modest in their expectations; this second eldest told me he loves high-country farming because it is challenging and allows him to be outside in the mountains, but he isn't sure he will stay with farming since he may not be able to return to the property; as a form of insurance, he was about to begin a three-year degree program for a Bachelor of Commerce in Agriculture. Now, as his father puts it, he "has four sons pounding along behind me and my wife," ages 19, 18, 16, and 9. They do not know what they will do; "it is difficult to balance these things—that is, not giving enough versus giving too much." These matters are often unresolved for the future. His brother's wife similarly told me that she does not know what they will do with their property—they have two sons and one daughter—nor with the family company, "cousins won't be able to work on it the same way and it will have to be split." But these runholders, like their father who came to the high country for his sons, would be willing to sell and move away from the valley in order to give their sons a better opportunity to farm the high country. They recently looked at a much larger and even more remote property.

At dinner one night a daughter said that her university friends told her that she will never have the property because she is a girl. "Is it true?" she asked. In the conversation, which moved from her own grandparents' decisions to speculations about the desires of other children up the valley, she made it clear that none of her female friends would settle for a life up here. Her father was surprised—"are you saying they wouldn't want to marry a high-country farmer?" While her parents talked about back-country women being special and some of their own peers not having known "what they were getting into, and yet you don't see them leaving, do you?" she affirmed her sense of how conservative they all are. When pressed, she gave us one convincing measure of her aunts' and uncles' conservatism—their negative responses to her taking Maori studies courses at university.

Given the farming downturn in New Zealand and changing land legislation, one progressive runholding couple assumes nothing about their children's intentions. Slightly facetiously, their father said that he hopes neither child will want to farm—"then we can sell the farm and take off with the dough. Farming has turned out to be a bit of a mug's game. The future of farming is in the academic part of it, not sitting in the back country moving [fence] breaks." If either their daughter (the eldest) or son does want to return, he and his wife say that they will put the option to the child who stays to buy out their sibling and risk the place being sold. If both wanted to farm, the runholder supposes they might run an auction between them or flip a coin. The only alternative is "to sell 50 percent to each and take the money and run." He told me, "I have been preparing myself from the first brick I laid" for neither child to return although he and his wife would like them to. If their children choose not to return, they would give any family member first rights to buy the property—his brother's children, a sister's child, a cousin or cousin's child. One such cousin had similarly radical responses: "sibling tensions are no good" he said, "and if that happened I would sell off and divide the proceeds between them."

Rogers and Salamon point to inheritance ideologies as culturally determined responses that shape social organization—but, as I have argued above, as discursive conventions they also shape and reflect sentiment—and they suggest that "where the family remains a property-controlling unit of production, such variables as degree of market integration and scale of operation may be irrelevant as either categorical criteria or explanatory variables in discussions of relationships within the family and community. Such patterns of social relationships do not necessarily change as the larger economic context undergoes change" (1983:547). New Zealand high-country station families traced lineally and laterally over three generations provide a comparative dimension to their analyses. That "inheritance ideology amounts to a set of rules defining a strategy for achieving farm/family continuity" (1983:545) links all of the cases where high-country properties are "we [not I] operations."

§ § §

Now to return to the analytic challenges with which I began. How then to theorize the culturally sensitive? Culturally charged, inheritance practices are sensitive precisely because they embody structural tensions and allocate scarce resources. People talk readily but privately; children look around and wonder what their future will be; young siblings and cousins talk to each other, "mapping out grand schemes" behind their parents' backs. At stake in these practices is the preservation of family harmony and the allocation of finite resources, namely the station, and less finite resources, the station's prestige. Relationships are prioritized with the male-sibling relationship prevailing as the primary work unit, and the husband/wife dyad following not far behind. What is sensitive is that sons mostly stay and daughters mostly do not; sons/brothers inherit the opportunity to farm as a resource, which counters partible, egalitarian, pioneer principles that privilege challenge as both the great equalizer and measure of worth, and value achievement over ascription; in the settler context, challenge and achievement become ascription's foil.[28] Hence sons reiterate that they are not given the station outright but rather must *earn* their opportunity, hence the use of a language of inheritance primarily for nonmaterial things such as knowledge[29] and the shift to a language of "property transfer" for material resources. Men who stay fight predominant urban assessments of their opportunities as ascribed and voice in their sensitivities to the inheritance topic unease about the station replicating the English estates their pioneer forebears left behind. As for their departing sisters I do not want to overplay the analytic utility of sentiment nor argue solely for its serving as a cultural plot to reconfigure their emotions; if their self-interest plays a second to their loyalty to family and station integrity, it may also be that status and honor, of family name and station name, are at stake and that their cooperation with inheritance rules preserves that prestige by keeping the station intact and linked to family name.

The metaphoric equivalence of family with station, and identity with country, reflects a fusion of self and family for all players. The station is their signature in a world where mountains are personal landmarks, solid points of reference. In the conflation of station and family name, "social identity is derived primarily from membership in a specific family, and ties to an exclusive household/farm override all others" (Rogers and Salamon 1983:543). What then are runholders and their wives telling me when they maintain that gender doesn't matter? How to reconcile this with the words of a high-country daughter who is glad that "I didn't have brothers" because it meant her family "avoided all the things that go on"? The question is answered for children with the assurance that "it'll all even out in the end." Men and women—as sons and daughters-in-law, as fathers and mothers, as brothers and sisters-in-law—are stewards of a place to which they belong, and where wives come to belong, but which doesn't belong to them; that is what attachment means. Through naturalized attachment, family is the vehicle for nurturing of country. Families entrust sons with stewardship of country, as caretakers for the future; their wives, the women who marry in, are stewards of home and garden. These couples are always aware of transience, of the next generation, of the inevitability of their own departure. Both males and females then experience loss. Parents sacrifice in not selling out and leaving with the capital for their own retirement, or by leaving earlier than they might want to; fathers lose farming, mothers lose homes and gardens. Sons/brothers sacrifice in staying on and forsaking opportunities the urban world might of-fer—pressures to return are so strong that sons are often said to have no options. Daughters/sisters sacrifice by leaving the property (although it always remains H/home to them) but gain instead the opportunity to test themselves, and per-haps to marry back into the high country. Critically at stake in the denial of gen-der as significant is a commitment to mask structural tensions within the family and to deflect tensions between brothers as working partners by adhering to pat-terns of male-focused partible inheritance.

And how to make sense of social traditionalism? Inheritance is a discursive convention with functional consequences. Reliance on set forms preserves cohe-sion, diminishes competition, and dispels tension between structural positions—between brothers and sisters, parents and sons, brothers-in-law and brothers' wives, and wives and brothers' sisters. Family continuity for all is essential and the experience of loss for sisters, and eventually for sons who become parents, is diminished by preserving attachment and yielding social stability that compen-sates for loss—the comfort of being able to return regardless of structural posi-tion. Family is always there, as family and station are conflated over the genera-tions. Yet in practice, social forms can be flexible. Not only do sisters without brothers and widows without adult sons sometimes inherit the right to farm, but a woman who proves herself can take over a station, especially if a son doesn't want it or a father assumes an adjacent property for her. The if-you-prove-yourself-you-can-do-anything rule prevails even in a system with ascriptive in-flections. In responding to a new generation of daughters who may want to as-sert (but have not yet) their right to return over their brothers', parents are taking these changes on as a challenge, an issue to be addressed and solved, one whose resolution is essential if tension in the primary parent/child dyad is to be averted.

Notes

1. South Island poet born in 1911 in Timaru. Like Brasch, Curnow yearned to feel "native to the country" (McNaughton 1986:9) and wanted to discover "self in country and country in self" (Ruth Harley cited in McNaughton 1986:9).

2. The language of inheritance is avoided for property transfer and seems to be re-served for the transfer of nonmaterial things such as mustering knowledge or a top-beat (see chapter 5). I avoid the term "inheritance," which is not theirs, but rather anthropol-ogy's. Inheritance implies gifting in a world of middle-class values, but as businesses stations cannot be gifted—in high-country parlance, they are earned.

3. The financial accounts suggest that the runholder was still paying an annuity into the family estate in the 1970s.

4. In this instance it enabled the runholder to buy a sibling out of part of the lease, but ordinarily the cardinal rule in farming is "don't sell land."

5. One of two New Zealand agricultural colleges, Lincoln College (now Lincoln University) offers a bachelor's degree in agricultural commerce which many high-country sons and daughters pursue.

6. Denich's "Sex and Power in the Balkans" reveals among herding groups "an agnatic core . . . broadened through horizontal links among kinsmen of the same generation" (1974:246). Corporate ties among brothers (and more collateral kinsmen, as in New Zealand with cousins) are essential ecological adaptations and social structures in a context where common external pressures are ever threatening. While not unilineal or tribal, the New Zealand pastoral case elicits remarkably similar structures.

7. One son told me that his perceptions are reinforced as he meets people elsewhere who once worked in the valley and speak so well of them.

8. Outsiders ask me if families with two or more daughters and no sons will avoid family planning and "go for sons," and families with daughters told me that they knew that people speculated if they were "trying for a boy"; they said not. One daughter, annoyed when her mother had such a thought, said to me that surely one could get at this by seeing if people stopped having children after they had a son; while some families did, others did not.

9. She has no interest in machinery or agricultural work and leaves that to her husband and the single man and married couple who work on the property. A shepherd who has been at "Banks" for twenty years, and his younger brother and his wife who have been there for six years, provide help. The younger brother does all of the agricultural and tractor work—the plowing, fence building and so on. Both men are near fifty. She resists having more than one young man as a shepherd—two young boys means no work—"they take off in the tractor and go mad."

10. Like many high-country people, she hopes that one of her children will return but makes no assumptions and exerts no pressure.

11. The sisters-in-law host garden tours for several busloads of visitors each week during the late spring and summer months.

12. State settlement land set aside for balloting by returned servicemen after the wars (see Scotter 1965:436).

13. The freehold is 4,856 hectares (12,000 acres) and pastoral-occupation licence comprises approximately 4,047 hectares (10,000 acres). Heights vary from 488 meters (1,600 feet) at the homesteads to 2,552 meters (8,500 feet) on a major peak.

14. The Awatere is a volcanic valley with basalt further up, unlike the glacial greywacke valleys typical of Canterbury mountains.

15. Husband/wife partnerships are a result of the Matrimonial Property Act of 1976. For an overview, see Angelo and Atkin (1977).

16. In his comparative study of estate inheritance in the Italian Alps, John Cole (1971) identifies a contradiction between inheritance ideology and practice: in one community the estate's continuity is sacrificed to allow for the maximum provision for each offspring, in another the well-being of secondary heirs is sacrificed to ensure estate continuity through a single primary heir. Cole attributes the ideologies to the larger cultural context of which the communities are a part, and suggests that ecological setting determines the actual process of inheritance, which ultimately must make ecological sense.

17. Thirsk (1976:188) notes that the English debate on customs of inheritance was modified by the settlement of New England where, because population was small and land was plentiful, multiple-heir inheritance seemed more appropriate than in England and Wales where partible inheritance destroyed estates. Multiple-heir inheritance in the high-country context has proved practicable when sons are few and additional land or increasing carrying capacity of land is possible.

18. Janet Frame (1924-) was born in Dunedin and lived in Oamaru during her early life.

19. Low (1992:166) provides a useful typology of place attachment differentiating six kinds of symbolic linkage of people and land: genealogical, through loss or destruc-

tion, economic, cosmological linkage, religious or secular pilgrimage, and narrative through storytelling and place-naming.

20. See especially Jeremy Salmond's *Old New Zealand Houses, 1800-1940* (1986) and Geoffrey Thornton's *The New Zealand Heritage of Farm Buildings* (1986).

21. Given station distances from the closest urban center or small farming center, community for her brothers and cousins comprises the inhabitants of the valley, and extradomestic activities mean something quite different. Links outside are either through children in boarding school or through men's participation in farming-based political activities, such as membership in the High Country Committee, the Queen Elizabeth II Trust, the Meat and Wool Board, Lincoln College Council and the like, all of which are concerned with land use and pastoral farming concerns.

22. "It's all turangawaewae, isn't it" asked one sociologist of this data during a presentation at the University of Canterbury. (See chapter 6 and note 5 in chapter 7.)

23. Similarly, a university daughter explained to me that in coming home she likes the stability—things don't change—but although she likes to come home she gets bored. During a brief visit to the valley in May 1995, I was led up to my old room. Everything was in place as I remembered it, and I felt something akin to the well-being this young woman expressed. Here in this remote and stable domestic world, I felt very safe. When taking the turn off into the valley, I always have the same sensation, as I enter a place that is both familiar and relatively unchanging in its social routine.

24. Compare Hatch (1992:134) on the commitment of rural people to historical societies—diaries, old clothes, and photographs; such contexts reflect a concern with what he calls "highbrow" matters and with "refinement." See Eldred-Grigg (1980) for a social history of a South Island elite that defied an ideology of social equality.

25. On the open market, the property would be very valuable precisely because people are willing to pay for the mystique.

26. Both brothers sensibly acknowledge that their knowledge of how much their father wanted them on the property would not stop them from leaving should they decide to.

27. A master vividly illustrated the reluctance of parents to discuss inheritance matters with their children for me during my visit to one of the boarding schools. He was escorting me on a tour with a high-country mother when we encountered her son. As the son was introduced the master mischievously said that as the eldest he "will inherit the mortgage"; the boy looked blank and the master said, "Don't you have a mortgage?"; the boy said he didn't know, and so the master turned to the mother and said airily, "Don't you discuss these things with him?"

28. In his analysis of the British foxhunt, Howe (1981:289) similarly identifies the tension or contradiction between achieved and ascribed status as common to hereditary property ownership.

29. A retired runholder and father of daughters stressed the importance of passing on the diaries to his son-in-law as well as the guidance he could offer; his son-in-law in turn focuses on his own son's developing knowledge.

PART III
COUNTRY

Photo 11 Merino ram fleece, Glenthorne, North Canterbury

Chapter Five

"Knowing This Place": Toponymy and Topographic Language

So
I name names—rocks, flowers, fish:
knowing this place I learn to know myself.
—Peter Bland (1979), "Guthrie-Smith at Tutira"[1]
in McNaughton (1986.252)

In these tussock grasslands, place language used by its inhabitants reveals a cultural order simultaneously shaped by and imprinted on the land. Aspects of language such as technical classifications (legal, geologic and soil) and folk classifications (in toponymy and topographic lexicon) of land define and convey the conceptual systems that in turn shape and reflect the relationship of its residents to the land. An elaborated vocabulary for a total environment that is named with reference to both physical features and human associations (such as personal names and historical events), as well as idioms of orientation, reflects a complex indigenous classificatory system. In his work on "the situated talk of geographical landscapes" among the Western Apache, Keith Basso illustrates how such talk carries information about who a people imagine themselves to be (1988:101); he writes: "Whenever members of a community speak about their landscape—whenever they name it, or classify it, or evaluate it, or move to tell stories about it—they unthinkingly represent it in ways that are compatible with shared understandings of how, in the fullest sense, they know themselves to occupy it." An analysis of classificatory systems embedded in toponymy and topographic representations used by pastoral farmers in the Rakaia valley provides insights into how "they know themselves to occupy it" since in "knowing this place" they "learn to know" themselves.

A lexicon of place names creates conceptual spaces and invites a connotative reading of the grammar of a landscape. Such a lexicon preserves an often unstated and uniquely local history and a sense of a continuity with the past in the landscape as names are "passed down from generation to generation ...

bearing testimony to a very human landscape" (Behar 1986:22; see also Netting 1981:9).[2] By extension, mastery of a complex repertoire of idioms of orientation similarly "establishes one's place" in a cultural world and provides a conceptual adaptation to the complex topographies of a landscape (Wylie and Margolin 1981:15). Such geographic concepts convey a sense of place or a particular kind of attachment to place; for example, the Faroese "have contrived a large world in a small place" by adapting continental geographic concepts to an island world (Wylie and Margolin 1981:43-45), whereas, as I shall demonstrate, New Zealand high-country folk contrive a socioculturally contained world in an expansive place.

The Station

"Country" is the term used most often by runholders to refer to pastoral lease-hold high country and more specifically to their own properties. Today "property" is used in preference to "station" or "run." Writing of earlier times, L. G. D. Acland (1975: 355, 363)[3] and David McLeod (1970:24) use "back country" as a synonym for what is now known as high country for the locality beyond the river gorges, and "front country" for the hill country and runs adjacent to the plains.[4] But today's runholders use "back country" as a complementary term for "front country" by which they mean the very remote, higher-altitude country of their station that is climatically too severe for the stock in winter, and is often above the snowline, where sheep and cattle are grazed in the summer. Such country also includes areas retired from grazing. "Front country" refers to the usually lower-altitude paddocks and blocks[5] used during spring lambing and winter grazing, which are closer to the homestead and usually part of a visible (although treed) topography. "Front" and "back" therefore are defined relative to their proximity to the homestead, not as terms for making a distinction between high country and nonhigh country. Acland's "back" and "front" country have been replaced by "high" or "up" and "down" country in contemporary use. Acland (1975:363) defines his use of "down country" as being the same as that "used (chiefly by people in the hills) to describe the localities near town or on the plains; they also speak of 'down country' people."

Runholders say that in sharing notions of "front" and "back," the "gorge runs are similar from one end of the South Island to the other," with the greatest similarity running North/South rather than East/West. The Mackenzie country in South Canterbury, for example, does not use front/back. Families recognize each other as similar, and these are the men and women "one feels more comfortable talking to"—"it's a social security thing" where in talking to a fellow runholder "he'll instantly pick up on what I'm thinking or feeling"; the link, I was told, is the valley or gorge, and the perception of separation it fosters. Widely separated valleys that isolated early settlements characterize New Zealand topography (Brooking 1986:8).

"Sheep station" or "station," originally meaning merely a stopping place, was used more by the previous generation whereas current inhabitants prefer to refer to their properties as "farms"; they are equally as likely to refer to themselves as "farmers," "wool producers," "lessees," and most recently, "stakeholders" rather than to use the more archaic term "runholders."[6] The "station"—a reminder of an era when, I was told, the merino breeders would sit in their own section of the dining room of the Clarendon Hotel during Christchurch Show week neatly separated from the Dorset Downs people, the Romney people and the rest—has been replaced by the "farm." The terminology, as well as changes in the use and shape of the built environment, reflects the shift from the station of the past with a large hired staff[7] to the station as a family farm unit, with at most a couple of full-time shepherds or a married couple as hired help. As properties have been legally divided between sons, they are also more likely to be called "farms" rather than "stations." The use of the term "farmer" is a way of leveling differences from down-country or plains farmers.[8] People suggested to me that there are fewer social distinctions in New Zealand than in prior generations. High-country women told me that there is a definite generational shift between their families and the previous generations for whom the high-country life had higher "snob" value; this is best illustrated by the inclusion of hired men at family meals rather than in the cookshop of the past. Today "young families couldn't give a stuff about whether a property is a called a station or not."

According to Acland (1975:385), in the nineteenth century "station" originally referred to "the hut, yards and buildings where a squatter stationed himself to work his run, but now [applies] to the whole property, including the stock and leasehold country." It also, he notes, can suggest any fairly large property carrying over 2,000 or 3,000 sheep. For some inhabitants a high-country property can only be called a station if it has Crown pastoral leasehold land and back country or has men go out on an overnight autumn muster; in some instances where a property was farmed as two by brothers, people would note that one half was a station and the other not, even if carrying capacity was equal; back-country land or leasehold land was considered essential. More typically such discussions would focus more on who was "truly" high country and who was not.[9]

"Station" and "run" are often used as equivalent terms although Elvin Hatch and Bob Hall both differentiate the terms. Hatch (1992:47-49) notes that the runholder is a type of farmer but that the terms are used contrastively. He portrays an "ideal" run as representing extensive use of land, located in a remote area at high elevation with steep and rugged terrain, with harsh winters, short growing seasons, shallow soil and little pasture development. Its size ranges from two or three thousand acres to over twenty thousand,[10] with a mixture of land types, and a variety of contiguous blocks at various elevations. It also comprises Crown land held under lease. He notes, however, that local people differentiate the station as a particular type of run—"at the top of the hierarchy of properties" with very large holdings up to twenty thousand acres, and with a staff and operating cookshop. Bob Hall (1987:182) differentiates a sheep station from a run according to two criteria: size—a station occupies more land and has more sheep, and land tenure—a station's tenure is Crown pastoral lease and a run is some other variety of Crown lease; stations are also more likely to be conceptualized as "family properties." Stations are not simply geographical locales but also legal entities and indigenously constructed sociocultural and conceptual units.

Properties commonly are referred to by the station name alone (for example, Glenaan or Double Hill). New names are typically generated when properties subdivide. The names of stations are often the names of old family estates in England, of places in the British Isles, or descriptive names such as Redcliffs, Manuka Point, or Double Hill. A few stations have Maori names, usually place names, often names that reflect distinctive physical features of the place. Kevin O'Connor has written that station personalities are evoked by their given names "whether these be dubbed from the purple and green hills of Antrim, corrupted from misty Gaelic or Maori, or even transposed from the meagre imagination of a mortgage-holding banker. By naming, and respecting names we affirm the bonds that tie us to land" (1989:99). The name of the station is on the gate, mailbox or Automobile Association signpost at the turn-off from the main road to the unpaved roads into the high country, and most significantly is branded onto the bales of wool that go to be auctioned by stock and station agents to the wool-buyers in Christchurch or Dunedin. Also the station name is attached to mobs of sheep at the high-country sales in Tinwald and Tekapo and at the annual Agricultural and Pastoral Shows. Within a name is embedded the history or identity of a station and its family's provenance as well as the breeding lines of stock and their worth.[11] These names are of more significance, it seems, than family names, perhaps because stations can be passed from generation to generation, or sold from family to family, or even remain in a family but with a different family name in the instance of a daughter and her husband inheriting the rights to the lease of the property. Stations may be owned by a family that is incorporated as a land company, an incorporation of father and sons, or two brothers, or even parents, brothers and sisters: in those instances the correct legal title might be Canterbury Station Limited or Canterbury Run Limited or Canterbury Land Company. One sibling might manage it as a family estate.

Bernard Pinney's (1981:6) distinction between a run as "a numbered unit of Crown land" and a station as a "big holding of land, usually radiating from the homestead" and sometimes holding several runs, is the most useful. The run plans of today's family land companies or stations designate the numbers of the multiple runs that comprise them. Early settlers claimed their run or runs by number (often several runs under single ownership comprised a station) and named them as soon as they assumed ownership or residence; as legislation broke up the runs in the late nineteenth century they were subnumbered and renamed as separate stations. But the term is also used colloquially in a variety of ways. Acland (1975:379) notes that "run" was the word that most dramatically changed or extended its meaning through daily usage. Of those meanings that I recognize in use, he includes the country held under a particular lease, a group of runs held by one owner in a station in which the whole area is called a run, leasehold as opposed to freehold, as equivalent to station but not including the sheep as station does. In all of those senses, run emerges as a legal concept referring to the land alone that is managed by the farmer, and station emerges as a cultural concept that includes runs, stock, buildings, and people. It is thus not surprising that families were referred to not only by their surnames but also often by the plural form of the station's name (such as the Glenaans or Double Hills).[12] This may have been a strategy to differentiate families with the same last name (for example, brothers from brothers or male cousins from male cousins), but it was used for all families. When property-transfer practices expand a property so that it can be divided by two sons, one of the properties continues to carry the original station name, and in some instances, despite a practical division of land and stock between brothers and separate farm accounts, the wool bales are still sold under the original station name—the wool brand carries a prestigious legacy that neither brother wants to surrender. In one instance brothers divided the freehold land into two units of equal carrying capacity and divided all of the stock except for the wethers, which run on jointly held pastoral occupational-licence land. As a joint clip, the wether-clip's earnings are divided between the brothers. They market their wool clip under the original station brand because it is recognized and its reputation has economic value; their financial records, however, ensure material fairness by noting which bales belong to which family. In another instance (see chapter 2), when high-country holdings were separated from some of the freehold lower-altitude land in order for a station to become two separately working properties, the original station name went to the property that carried the original homestead, even though it was smaller in hectares and did not carry the higher-altitude back-country land. Again this reinforces conceptions and definitions of the "station" that point to the homestead as its primary referent point and as the center of the station's symbolic system.

Technical Classifications of High Country

Straightforward definitions of the high country are elusive; salient elicited components include altitude,[13] remoteness, difficulty of access, production usually of fine-wooled merino sheep, leasehold occupation, extensive holdings running to thousands of hectares, the autumn muster, and liability to snowfalls and the resulting loss of stock. Former High Country Committee chair David McLeod (1980:9) notes that a definition of the high country first vexed the High Country Advisory Committee when it was formed in 1940 to represent the interests of the runholders in advising government ministers. Were its elements altitude, size, merino sheep, snow proclivity, or leasehold tenure? "There seemed no single fact which linked us all in common interest and we ended by defining a high-country run as a property on which the production of wool and store stock was the main source of income and which might be liable to losses from snow." He describes the range of types of run from the Seaward Kaikouras to the southern lakes. Loosely defining the high country in terms of the nexus between man, dog, and sheep, he links it to marginal environments where the elements are extreme from snow to flood to landslide (1980:10-11).

At once particular, experiential and yet imprecise, his definition of high country eludes the simplicity of comparative typologies of mountain ecosystems that reduce them to altitude, steep gradient or slope, aspect or varying exposure to sunlight, and a succession of vegetation belts or life zones (Brush 1976:126). These characteristics do apply to New Zealand's Southern Alps. So also do the characteristic adaptive patterns of social organization such as communal land tenure and land use that Netting (1981) describes, the processes of political integration that include mountain communities to varying degrees in regional or national political economies, and the ways that high-altitude populations (usually and mistakenly seen as isolationist according to Cole 1978) "balance local resources against outside, regional demands," demands that often increase in proportion to mountain productivity (1978:172), such as tourism.

Following a more technical (but still indigenous) understanding than McLeod and evocative of Netting's focus on communal land tenure, the Grasslands Division of the Department of Scientific and Industrial Research (DSIR) defines the South Island "high country" in "agricultural terminology" as a remote area of high-altitude pastoral Crown leasehold land occupied by large sheep stations, or runs, typically subject to severe weather hazards; management practices are based on extensive grazing of fine-wooled sheep on tussock grasslands. The high country:

> is the area east of the Southern Alps [and west of the Canterbury plains] consisting of properties at high altitude with extensive grazing which are subject to severe weather hazards such as snow loss. Although the number of properties or runs, predominantly pastoral leases from the Crown is small...the total area is large.... The main produce of the area is fine wool, from a total sheep population of about two million, half of which are merino and a quarter merino x Romney half bred. Most properties run some cattle, with numbers increasing rapidly over the last decade. Total numbers are about 108,000, half of which are Hereford, and a quarter Hereford x Angus. (Scott 1977:36)

Bowden et al. (1983:75) note that whether the high country is summer or winter country produces seasonal transhumance. Summer country is cold and difficult, suitable for sheep for only part of the year; stock in winter are grazed on lower land where its blocks are oversown or topdressed. The New Zealand Meat and Wool Board's Economic Service defines the South Island high country similarly as "extensive run country" and calculates the carrying capacity in Canterbury, Otago and Marlborough as 0.9 stock units per hectare. Distinguished from the South Island high country is South Island hill country, characterized by a larger proportion of lowland soil, lower snow risk and less dependence on wool as a source of income (Centre for Resource Management 1983:7-9); it carries three stock units per hectare.

Glenariffe's run plan, a technical document drawn up by the chief soil conservator of the regional Catchment Board for when it was a single unit of approximately 11,500 hectares, provides a "description of the property" in these terms: the plan first differentiates between the "major portion" of the property that is in the "headwaters of the North Ashburton [River]," with the balance, called the "front faces," draining directly into the Rakaia River. The geological distinction between an explicitly hilly "front" country and implicitly "back country" is based on watershed principles shaped by geological activity. It is clear that topography, in influencing the balance of "winter" and "summer" grazing country, affects high-country run management; uneven topography, for example, may create "areas with favourable microclimates" (Centre for Resource Management 1983:11). Winter country is defined not only by low altitude but also by its steep slope facing to the north, often with broken topography where thaws tend to begin (Burdon 1938:156). The altitude of the land is documented as well as the presence of red volcanics in certain blocks, and the presence of fans and alluvial gravels. The thickness of loess covering on "easy and moderately steep slopes" is correlated with elevation and exposure. Below the front faces is "easy to rolling country," which gives way to steep faces "gradually moving to 6,000 feet." Glacial wave action is noted, as are fault lines. A complex analysis of soil type is provided in an appendix but in general, soils are described in terms of their thickness, their weakness or strength of structure, their presence on front faces, easy slopes, catchment location, and their suitability for development. In the report, the long geological and soil history of this landscape is read, as are its conditions for pastoral farming, and its environmental vulnerability in the future. Categories define and reflect patterns of use and proneness to erosion.

Legal classifications are defined by the Land Act of 1948, which created two classes of rural land: farmland, suitable for any type of farming and most typically acquired as freehold land by cash payment, and the Crown pastoral lease, suitable only for pastoral purposes and subject to thirty-three-year terms with perpetual rights of renewal (see Centre for Resource Management 1983:31-53). Almost all of the New Zealand high country is leasehold land with small patches of front country as freehold. Multiple classificatory systems are imposed on high-country land by the act but the most technical is that of land-use capability, a classification system that broadly indicates the suitability of the land for productive use. Taken into consideration are geology, soil type, slope of the land, vegetative cover, extent and potential for erosion, climate, altitude and the history of land use (see Bowden et al. 1983:71-75). Bowden et al. clearly explain that four of the eight land-use-capability classes are arable and four are nonarable: classes I to IV lend themselves to cultivation and cropping, while those with an "increasing degree of limitation" from dryness or shallow soils comprise classes V to VIII. "Land that cannot be farmed at all," in one farmer's words, is considered class VIII land unsuitable for cropping, for general pastoral and production use, or for forestry, and is in the category of catchment-watershed-protection land. Forty-eight percent of the land in the Rakaia valley was class VIII land. At the other extreme, "genuine farmland" is class I and II land, multiple-use land with high cropping, pastoral, and forestry suitability.

In the upper Rakaia valley catchment, seventeen properties have some proportion of their land classified as class VIII, very steep land at high altitudes. This is a region of approximately 2,640 square kilometers, bounded to the north by the Waimakariri and Selwyn catchments, to the south by the Rangitata and

Ashburton catchments, and to the west by the Main Divide (Bowden et al. 1983:9). High-mountain terrain bounds the catchment; the highest peak is Mount Arrowsmith (2,795 meters) and 28 percent of the headwaters exceed 1,500 meters in elevation producing a higher percentage of precipitation as snow than other catchments, slower release of water because of its storage in ice and snow, and a higher proportion of the catchment (30 percent) as bare rock, scree, or permanent ice and snow fields (Bowden et al. 1983:37). The Southern Alps dominate and produce more rainfall closer to the Main Divide (Bowden et al. 1983:29).

In their extensive multiple-volume resource survey of the entire catchment, Bowden et al. begin their discussion of relief: "the Rakaia Basin is bounded by high mountain terrain. . . . [T]he wide shingle riverbeds . . . of the upper Rakaia Catchment are bounded by fans, river terraces, moraines and mountain ranges with broad intermontane valleys infilled with gravel." (1983:37, 39). They then give the altitudes of highest peaks and the catchment headwaters, as well as dividing the catchment into areas of different slope. Such "basin range topography" has been produced by differential uplift and block faulting (Centre for Resource Management 1983:9). Bowden et al.'s image of mountains *bounding* a river as a basin is reinforced by the centrality of catchments or watersheds as organizing principles in defining regions. Altitude provides the sides to the basin and an image of containment with the valley as its center.

Boundary Talk and Toponymy

At its most expansive, "boundary talk" is about the demarcations between neighboring properties, most typically referred to by station names, and is physically externalized by fence lines, visible at a distance to the trained eye as telltale scratches on the landscape. Less expansive and more common is the pervasive exercise of "boundary talk" as a way of talking about specific locales within the property and as a reflection of a folk classificatory system. Blocks and paddocks are two critical ways of differentiating parcels of land within stations as larger noncultivated hillside or back-country "blocks" are differentiated from usually (but not always) smaller, more typically cultivated fan "paddocks" closer to the homestead; both comprise the subdivided properties of today. The subdivision into blocks and paddocks through fencing serves a pragmatic function: it enables farmers to diversify their grasses and supplementary feed as well as to ration and allocate food to different mobs according to their particular needs. Equally important, as Jill Conway has written of the Australian outback, fences "keep bloodlines clear" (1989:41). Subdivision also serves a referential function as it imposes human classificatory systems as a grid of "narrative landmarks" (Rodman 1992) upon an extensive and relatively homogeneous landscape of tussock grasslands; the "linguistic gesture" (Carter 1989:13) of naming the physical features of blocks and paddocks on the grid renders the landscape as a text to be read, as signifying practice, social structure and ongoing social interaction, and cultural production (see Barnes and Duncan 1992:5-8;

Certeau in Frake 1996:241), and as a rhetorical construction (see Carter 1989:36).

Margaret Rodman (1992:649) writes, "Multivocality often involves multi-locality. Polysemic places bespeak people's practices, their history, their conflicts, their accomplishments"; Rodman's framework urges us to examine multi-locality "to empower place conceptually and encourage understanding of the complex social construction of spatial meaning" (1992:640). She sees "narrative landmarks" as both narratives of place told with words and as trees or fences (1992:649). Often, she writes, use values, by which she means "noncommodi-fied dimensions" such as quality of life, predominate in these narratives of place (1992:647); narrative landmarks often signal both exchange (commodified values) and use values. Like Rodman, Barbara Bender (1993:9) introduces a his-torical dimension in which the spatial and temporal are linked in a landscape with multiple meanings that is continually constructed and reconstructed as it links shifting pasts and presents; "it is part of the way in which identities are created and disputed," she writes, "operating therefore at the juncture of history and politics, social relations and cultural perceptions" (Bender 1993:3).

In examining the discursive practice of naming as a way of dividing up the landscape to designate location and create meaningful spaces, I aim to under-stand the runholders' use, conception and construction of place (see Sapir 1912). My approach derives from Vincent Berdoulay's concept of the narrativity of place; he writes "a place comes explicitly into being in the discourse of its in-habitants, and particularly in the rhetoric it promotes" (1989:135).[14] Discourse can be understood in James Gee's terms as: "a socio-culturally distinctive and integrated way of thinking, acting, interacting, talking, and valuing connected with a particular social identity or role, with its own unique history, and often with its own distinctive 'props' (buildings, objects, spaces, schedules, books . . .)" (Gee 1992:33). Barnes and Duncan's (1992:8) use of the term ap-plied to landscape is especially helpful: "practices of signification [constituting] the limits within which ideas and practices are considered to be natural . . . [they are] not unified, but are subject to negotiation, challenge and transformation."

High-country naming patterns reflect use and changing use patterns, per-ception of physical properties, and the settlement processes of inscribing a his-tory of events and ownership. I illustrate this by providing an overview of nam-ing practices of blocks and paddocks for five of the adjacent Canterbury properties in the Rakaia valley.[15] Scanning the names in table 5.1 evokes a physical sense of place—the nature of the terrain and the vegetation, the kinds of farm buildings (all named in terms of use), and the variety of activities in which people engage. Descriptors that denote distinguishing physical, constructed, and social features including use, people, and key events or the circumstances of their construction name blocks and paddocks. The similarity of naming princi-ples across stations, and the use of the same names in many instances ("Tank Paddock," "Bin Paddock," "Woolshed Paddock," "Trig Paddock") point to ex-pected regularities of function, as well as to similarities in the design and map-ping of different stations linguistically. Table 5.1 reflects a classificatory system that emerged from my own attempt to find a toponymic system derived from the exegesis provided by my informants, female and male. For example, "Wedding Hill" was the name attached to a block that was being fenced at the time of the eldest daughter's wedding; it is thus a temporal name, marking a historical moment in fence-building by a social event, rather than marking the social event itself. For its next subdivision, "Twins" marks the time when the daughter's twins were born into the family. "Terrible Gully" was named for the unfortunate death of an injured road worker who is said to have left a note written in his own blood; it refers therefore to an event rather than only to the character of the

Table 5.1 Selected Names of Paddocks and Blocks[a] for Five Stations

	STATIONS	Glenaan	Glenariffe	Glenfalloch	Double Hill	Redcliffs
A. Physical Features	**Shape and Size**	Triangle Little Acre	Square Long Acre	*Little Triangle* *Big Triangle* *Round Back*	*Point* Triangle	
	Location	River Terrace			*Top River Boundary** Top Flat	*Boundary Spur Terrace*
	Natural Features	*Waterfall*	Swamp	*Lagoon Gully*	Tarn Broadspurs Fan* Mt O'Connor*	*Top Cliff Knob**
	Character	*Isolation Confusion*				*Steep Hill*
	Vegetation		Kowhai Cabbage Tree* Tussock	*Scrubby*	Top Flat Trees Scrubby	*Cabbage Tree Kowhai Flat*
B. Constructed Features	**Building**	House Hayshed*		Woolshed Cookshop		Woolshed Old Yard*
	Location	*Bridge*	Front Track	Bridge Stable Creek	Road Block Boundary*	Front Road*
	Farming Features and Cultivation	Bin Tank	Pit Hives Lucerne* Dip Roundup*	Bin Tank Trough Airstrip	Trig Beehive Top Flat Dump Hack Spur Cow*	Tank Airstrip *Summer Country*
	Introduced Flora and Fauna	Top Goose	*Poplar* Stumps	Thistle Stump Stag Hind	First Firewood Top* Willows* Stag	Poplar Lawn
C. Social Features	**Activity and Event**	Donkey Dead Horse			Hack Spur*	Mad Mile Poacher's Creek* *Terrible Gully*
	Family and Workers	*Duncan* Jim Fiona	Bruce Charlie	George	Andrew Don	*Sisters*
	Temporal		*Wedding Hill Twins*			

Notes: [a]Block Names are italicized
*Subdivided into Top/Middle/Bottom or 1/2/3 or Left/Right or A/B

place, in contrast to, for example, "Steep Hill." These are not explicit indigenous meanings although they can be elicited, and most people, when asked, say simply that they name blocks and paddocks by their distinguishing physical features.

An immediate and perhaps predictable distinction between the central analytic categories of block and paddock is clear in table 5.1. The former bears a toponymic system in which physical features such as size, shape, location, character and vegetation predominate as distinguishing markers; the latter system is evenly distributed across a landscape that is managed and constructed, characterized by utility buildings or locales such as woolsheds and haysheds, farming activities, and an association with the inhabitants. Most revealing is a comparison between the indigenous or native vegetative features primarily attached to blocks—kowhai trees, cabbage trees, and scrub—and those introduced or exotic features that are attached to paddocks—poplars, thistles, lawns, and the stumps that remain from firewood trees. Following the same pattern in table 5.2, "Top Goose" and "Bottom Goose" (introduced species) are not at all anomalous as paddock names. This is partly because geese are found closer to the river where food is better, but also because they are not a native species, and are considered pests; of all the paddock names, only these two are original and preceded the division of Glenariffe between Hamish and Alastair.[16] Each year the young "flappers" are shot as part of an organized "goose shoot" engaging the entire valley. Stags and hinds are names attached to both blocks and paddocks and, with deer as an introduced species, are both hunted and farmed.

Fence lines on blocks have a similar link to physical features and often are continuations of natural features, a stream or a ridge, for example. Most dramatic are snow fences that trace the country's contours. I have shown in chapter 2 how Peter Ensor reconstructs the history of place in his Double Hill history by noting the lines of old fencing. Fences also provide him with a starting point for defining the station, serving as the linguistic gesture that enables him to talk about it. Peter Ensor traces one such snow fence that begins along a creek-bed line, now a boundary line between two properties, and runs along the "foot of the hills" for approximately ten miles. Another snow fence (now derelict) runs for sixteen or eighteen miles starting from "the homestead at about 3,500 feet to 4,500 feet following the contours of the country, dropping into Turtons Saddle, over Donald's Hill and Black Hill, then back over the top of Redcliffs and down towards the river" (see map I.1). And another, a boundary fence, "joined the old snow fence on Black Hill going through the big Cookie's basins, all in shingle and rock at about 5,000 feet, then along the range, finishing up down the Turtons Stream opposite the King's Drive in the North Ashburton [watershed]" (Ensor 1990:4). Contours, saddles, ridges, the foot of the hills, the snow line, and spurs are featured as natural signs extended and highlighted by fencing. As extensions of natural boundaries these back-country fences "don't always lead you somewhere." They can, for example, end at a physical boundary such as a creek, a ridge or a crevasse creating contained spaces and enclosing sheep.

Table 5.2 provides a complete, rather than a selected, list of block and paddock names for a single property, Glenaan, together with their size in hectares.

A topographic map illustrating Glenaan's block and paddock boundaries (map 5.1) and the superposition of block and paddock names on an aerial photograph (maps 5.2 and 5.3) supplement it.[17] The names are fluid. Risks are taken as areas are named because sometimes a name is confusing, or not adequately descriptive, or use changes, and another name "takes over." The name for "Cow" paddock no longer exists because a cow is no longer milked; it has become "Hut" paddock, which has since been split into "Hut" paddock and "Middle" paddock between "Hut" and "Donkey." "Donkey" paddock is colloquially called "Horse" paddock or "Chook" paddock depending on the dominant species and "one's thoughts at the time."

Table 5.2 Names of Paddocks and Blocks[a] for Glenaan

		Paddocks (size in hectares)	Blocks (size in hectares)
A. Physical Features	**Shape and Size**	Triangle 6	*Little Acre 14*
			Paddock Hill *1300
	Location	Bridge 2	*Big Stony Creek 138*
		Bottom Creek 5	*Big Flat 280 and Little*
		River Terrace Flats 6	*Flat 65*
	Natural Features		*Waterfall 32*
			High Face 48
			Knobs 24
	Character		*Isolation 53*
			Confusion 32
B. Constructed Features	**Building**	Cottage 9	
		Top/Bottom Hayshed 12	
		Top/Bottom House 9.5	
		Fishtrap 4	
		Dog Motel 9	
	Location	Road 7	*Road 22*
	Farming Features	Bin 6.5	*Trig 14*
	and Cultivation	First/Second Tank 8	
		Shed 8	
	Introduced Flora	Gap 8 [in trees]	
	and Fauna	Top/Bottom Goose 9	
C. Social Features	**Activity and Event**	Airstrip 5	
		Donkey/Horse	
		Cow	
	Family and	Penny 2	*Duncan 32*
	Workers	First/Second Paul 8	*Bruce 22*
		Fiona 7.5	*Darkie 22*
		Jim 4	
	Finance		*Grant *1300*
	Ownership		*Turton*
			Barnard
	Event		*Dead Horse 43*
	Temporal	Top [Doug] 8	

Notes: [a]Block names are italicized
        *Indicates combined size of Paddock Hill and Grant blocks

The names reveal what count as landmarks in this vast and sparsely marked landscape. Again, as in table 5.1, similar clustering of the hill blocks carries names that reflect distinguishing physical features, such as "Waterfall," "High Face," and "Big Stony Creek." The underlying logic behind the exceptions, that is, paddocks carrying names reflecting physical features, invites exploration. The farmer excludes four of the bounded units from his list of paddocks and blocks. These are referred to as a distinctive category of land—"the flats"—reflecting their contiguity to the river. Like the extremes of rugged high-altitude back country, the river is seen as an element "you cannot fight," as something that "finds its own way," suggesting an equivalence of the river with the mountains. "Triangle Paddock" is anomalous because it is close to the homestead although its shape is defined by a natural feature (see map 5.1)—a bluff descending to a stream rather than by an arbitrary fence line. "Bridge Paddock" (named as "Middle Creek" leading into "Top Creek" both of which were never adopted because they were too confusing), moreover, is transitional ground before the saddle leading to the back country via the unimproved "Big Stony Creek Block."

But how can we understand the patterns where names of family members or workers are attached to blocks rather than paddocks, or where they reflect events rather than physical characteristics? Predictably the names of the children of the immediate nuclear family are attached to the paddocks that are close to the house; "Paul" and "Fiona" are a few paddocks removed, while "Penny," named after an infant, is right next to "House Paddock." "Jim" is the salaried, permanent machine-syndicate operator in the valley who lives in a station cottage and is included in most social activities with the station families; it is not surprising that his name is on a paddock, especially because he put in the fence. In contrast, "Bruce," who is a valued farm adviser, and "Darkie," who fenced the block bearing his name, were neither family nor treated as family; their names are attached to more remote blocks, not paddocks. "Duncan" is a lateral relative, an uncle, and his name is attached to a block, not a paddock, but far from the Glenaan homestead (although close to his own). Those names attached to the retired blocks of Turton and Barnard are the surnames of unrelated settlers in the valley who took up these runs. The autonomous names of the runs were incorporated into the station and became blocks, or more typically, "country" as in "Turton's country" or "Barnard's country." Blocks marked by events such as "Grant" (paid for by government grant money) and "Dead Horse" (a dead horse was found there) or "Terrible Gully" have stories attached to them and are inscribed by individual and collective histories, as they sustain the narratives of the past. In summary, blocks comprise all of the back country at furthest remove from the homestead and carry old continuous names through the generations, while paddocks comprise most of the front country. The distance of that back country from the homestead is reinforced toponymically with a set of

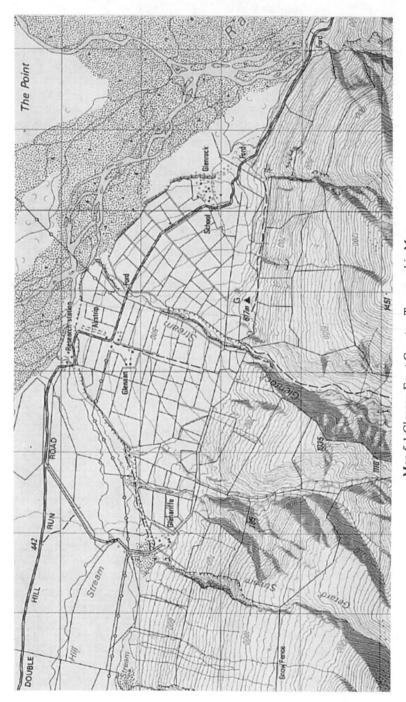

Map 5.1 Glenaan Front Country, Topographic Map
(New Zealand Department of Survey and Land Information 1999b)
Scale 2.2cm=1km. Sourced from Land Information New Zealand data. Crown Copyright Reserved.

Map 5.2 Glenaan Blocks, Aerial Photograph
(New Zealand Department of Lancs and Survey, 1980)
Sourced from Land Information New Zealand data. Crown Copyright reserved.

Big Flat Little Flat

Rakaia River

River Terrace

Fish Trap

Triangle Hayshed

House Dog Motel Cottage

Penny's Road

Donkey Bottom Creek

Cow Shed

Goose

Gap

Tank

Air Strip

Paul

Fiona

Bin

Jim Bridge

Top Dougs

Map 5.3 Glenaan Paddocks, Aerial Photograph
(New Zealand Department of Lands and Survey 1980)
Sourced from Land Information New Zealand data. Crown Copyright reserved.

terms that denote both distance from self literally, such as "Isolation Block" whose fence is "way up the hillside and far away from the homestead," and "Confusion" "because you are confused by the time you get there," or figuratively with nonimmediate kin such as "Duncan's Block," or in terms of uncultivated features such as native rather than introduced vegetation. Proximity to and distance from the homestead is a key point reinforcing and returning us to the central operative distinction between front and back country.

Of course, not all boundaries are of the linear-yet-containing kind marked by the fence lines for paddocks and blocks. Boundaries can be elastic. At Double Hill Lib told me that there is an intermediate zone behind the homestead between the garden and the farm, a wooded area with a back path and a stream; in the front the marker is absolute—a fence and the cattle grate in lieu of a gate separate the lawn and the flower beds from a paddock. Her cousin Alastair defines the farm edge temporally; it is marked by "when I take my boots off" at the back door. His wife Prue stresses that the pony paddocks are not farm, but not garden, and her sister-in-law Belinda marks the boundary of her garden behaviorally—the working dogs are never allowed over the wall or through the gate into the garden. But the family's pig, Potter—in escaping to go "walkabout" up to the back door or into the garage to steal potatoes—is humored; unlike other pigs in the valley, some of which are unnamed, Potter in Leach's (1975) fashion was not to be eaten—his pet status was clearly marked.

Paul Carter, in speaking of the "multiplication of symbolic boundaries" in textual accounts of early settlement days in the Australian outback (1989:153), illustrates that the "strategic deployment of names" by both the explorer and the naturalist was a vital step in enabling a natural world to be known and conceptually bounded as it was transformed into culturally mediated space: "by the act of place-naming, space is transformed symbolically into a place, that is, a space with a history. And, by the same token, the namer inscribes his passage permanently on the world, making a metaphorical word-place which others may one day inhabit and by which, in the meantime, he asserts his own place in history" (1989:xxiv).[18] From a discussion of the toponymic system I turn to a topographic system of surface features as reflected in idioms of orientation drawn from mustering narratives, daily talk, documentary records, and topographic maps.[19]

Placement, Direction, and Containment

Rakaia valley inhabitants refer to it, as did those of all geologically similar Canterbury valleys, such as the Waimakariri and the Rangitata, as "the gorge," a term stressing the entrance to the valley where the river narrows. The unintended effect is to diminish the size of the dramatic expanse of the valley (where the eye could see uninterrupted stretches of twenty kilometers or more) as do the terms "creek" for the (at times 3.5-kilometers-wide) river, and "hills" for mountains (at a height of 2,000+ meters).[20] Some people would say "in this little valley"; the runholder living at Manuka Point on the most inaccessible station in the valley located across the unbridgeable river, diminished the vastness even more by using the term "gully" rather than "gorge." Scale is transformed linguistically through understatement to be less awesome, and the image created renders the natural features protectively containing rather than wild, dangerous and uncontrollable. The topography produces a geography of catchment containment reinforced linguistically, as well as managed in part linguistically through meiosis.[21] Beyond the containment of the mountains, outside of this space bounded by landforms, and "out of the gorge" are down-country people and the rest of New Zealand; here a directional language of verticality is used as a rhetorical device to distance outsiders; for example, one goes "down country" or "down the road" just as one goes "up into the high country" or lives "up the gorge."

The river and the mountains also are diminished linguistically; both are thought of in parallel terms as they serve as markers, demarcate boundaries and sometimes serve as either welcome or unwelcome barriers rather than simply as obstacles.[22] After southerly rains and spring thaws, erosion and runoff from the mountains shed rocky shingle into creeks that dump "porridge" across the only access road as well as flooding the river and frequently changing its braided course. Sometimes it is impossible to "go up the gorge" not because of elevation or steepness but because of the condition of the valley's most significant obstacle and narrative trope, the road. The road is a continuum, paralleling the river's course for much of the distance as you move up from station to station, "going up" to Double Hill or Glenfalloch or "down to" Redcliffs. As inhabitants live further "up the gorge" into remoteness and altitude, they become "more high country," an identity marker that is often contested internally. One "goes into" and "gets out of" Manuka Point, a difficult property to access across a four-kilometer stretch of river, and from the outside one "goes across to" or "gets over to" Manuka Point. It is truly high country.

At the physical, social, and conceptual center of the station is the built environment of the homestead and its gardens, encompassed by specifically delineated territories of either cultivated or noncultivated land ending in and ultimately contained and defined by the mountains and the river catchment they bound as discussed in chapter 3. The dominant configuration is one of encompassment, of boundaries within boundaries. Gardens and forms such as fences and shelterbelts divide the landscape into a named natural world reflecting categories of varying degrees of removal from a humanly constructed world, defining not only economic activities but also ecological and social relationships.[23] Linguistically, I have found that perceptual distinctions, for example, between front and back country, summer and winter country, blocks and paddocks, order the physical world within idioms of containment. These distinctions separate an inner circle of domesticity, including those aspects of the physical environment under human management, from those outside of it, which although less managed are equally contained, and therefore invisible, in this basin-range topography.

Runholders' communicative acts of topographic representation (Basso 1988:101) reveal that, despite landforms of high relief, directional movement within a station is more often described with reference to distance from the homestead in lateral terms, rather than the vertical terms we might expect with the visual dominance of altitude on the horizon (see table 5.3).[24] For example, a shepherd "goes out the back" (but not "out *to* the back") or "out to Turton's country," or "comes into the homestead," but never goes "up to the back country," although he may go "up the hill" and "down to the homestead." Shepherds go "out on the autumn muster," and on the last day of the muster the shepherds "bring the sheep in," and "come into the homestead." For one runholder the phrase was clear as he used the homestead as a way to think about country—"out the back" like the back of a house implies that "you can't see it"; when he took his wife out there for the first time he said to her, "we are out the back now." The distinction between front and back country reinforces the importance of lateral direction over elevation. There is no talk of "up" and "down" with regard to movement between "front" and "back" country. Reflecting pragmatic use, front country is closer to the homestead and back country is further away—they map roughly, but not exactly, onto managed-winter and unmanaged-summer grazing country.

Table 5.3 Idioms of Topographic Orientation

Lateral Placement (on/off)	Containment (in/out)	Vertical Direction (up/down)
Off	In	Up
walk off Donald's Hill *muster off Black Hill* *come off the hill* [people and sheep] *come off the hill* [fences] *bluff off*	*go into the homestead* *sheep* [are] *in basins* *RAP takes in* [this area] *out here through these low saddles* *can't get through that gut* *look down* [a contained area—gully/basin] *down into* [a contained area] *bring the sheep in*	*up the hill* *walk up this creek* *walk up this spur* *up over that spur* *up that fence* *there up to there* *walk up here and back down again* *do a horse beat up the Smite* *top is very round*
On	Out	Down
on Black Hill *on Turton's country* *making a noise on the hill* *walking along the top*	*out the back* *out to Turton's country* *out to Trib* *back round the creek there* *muster through the goat track* *pushed them back* *go out the back* *out on the autumn muster*	*down to the homestead* *foot of Nell's stream* *back down again* *pushed them down* *push the sheep down here* *down the creek*
Motion	Empty	
carry on *walk* [the beat] *follow the fenceline* *follow that spur* *fences don't always lead you somewhere* *covering country*	*sweep that country* *clean this country up* *clean these spurs out* *lifting* [the sheep] *out* *sweep round* *clean up* *hunt* [the sheep] *out* *cleaning round faces* *nice, open little gully*	

Although within the high country this world divides literally (and laterally) into front (visible) country and back (not visible) country the division represents neither a frontier nor a distinction between wild and tame. It is not the frontier identified by Henry Nash Smith (1950:250) as the meeting point in settlement between wilderness/savagery and civilization that shapes American images of the West.[25] Presumably these images underlie Elizabeth Lawrence's (1984:236) U.S. western ranchers' perceptual division between "wild" and "tame" where they see themselves in opposition to the wild. New Zealand pastoralists do not use the term "wild," instead they use the term "the back" to refer to a less managed and transformed, but pastoral, area that is still encompassed within country, within the station. Nor do they think of culture and nature as salient oppositional categories embedded in the relationship between tame and wild; rather the relationship between the categories shifts contextually, as for example the pastoral back country, with its vast and differentiated units of blocks grazed by hardy, sure-footed merinos and walked by musterers who celebrate its challenges, contrasts with a domesticated more managed and transformed paddock landscape closer to the homestead; but this pastoral back country is also managed physically through grazing and fencing, and conceptually through topographic familiarity; left uncared for it would revert to a wilderness that would defy runholders' understanding of what country is.[26]

Deborah Rose (1988:386), in mapping out an Australian Aboriginal land ethic, similarly poses the analogy of (western) wild is to degraded as (aboriginal) quiet is to tame; her interlocutor explains that wild means land that is not cared for and where life is absent; here "quiet country" as tame, domesticated, controlled, nondangerous country—"country in which those who know how to read the signs see human action of the most responsible sort"—provides an appropriate gloss and equivalent cultural concept for high-country conceptions of "country" as containing back and front, not wild and tame. And while Kolodny's (1972:55) psychoanalytic reading of a gendered southern U.S. plantation landscape is not an appropriate reading of the landscape of the high-country station, her idea that the plantation incorporates both the "cultivated and the wild in a single harmonious unit" can be more effectively applied to the station than can Lawrence's oppositional model. Likewise, Carter's attack on the "false rhetoric of frontier history" is useful, despite his tendency to collapse settlers into a single undifferentiated category, since he challenges oppositional conceptualizations of the frontier as a line with nature beyond it and culture inside it:

> The essential function of the boundary is to facilitate communication.
> It enables places to appear and be named. It enables the settler to establish who and where he is. This is my clearing, that beyond is not.
> But this difference does not imply an exclusive opposition . . . the boundary is not a barrier to communication. Quite the opposite: it gives the settler something to talk about. (Carter 1989:158-159)

The situational nature of directionality is evident as people speak from a point of locatedness, a primary point of reference, usually the homestead and the station it represents. Within the valley, lateral movement and idioms of placement (on/off) and containment (in/out) prevail, while between the valley and outside the valley, movement is described in terms of vertical direction (up/down). Eric Hirsch (1995:4, 13, 17-18) differentiates "inside" from "outside" by drawing upon Raymond Williams and his own collaborator Alfred Gell. The Vician inside, "foregrounded actuality," is a kind of placedness that involves "everyday movement," "way-finding," and "navigation," where indexical (subject-centered forms of knowledge) is characterized by a language of involvement and found in "socially shared identities of feeling [people and surroundings] themselves create in the flow of activity between them." I think it glosses onto "high" and "up" in high-country parlance where it derives in part from ethnoecology. The latter, Cartesian outsideness, maps onto "background potentiality," is nonindexical, and implies an "absolute, non-subject centered spatial knowledge," which— while often steeped in romanticism and in commercialism and possession rather than nature and possession—is not a mutually exclusive perception; it seems to gloss onto "down" in high-country terminology where it derives from a natural-science-derived ecological base.

As runholders cartographically narrated the country by explaining its mustering routes, and designating its freehold and leasehold land, front and back country, summer and winter country, and conservation protected and unprotected areas on a series of topographic maps, and as they physically walked the country with me, they were consistent in their use of idioms (see table 5.3). Most critically, when "out the back," musterers talk of "walking the land," seldom "climbing it," and in so doing construct ease of movement and comfort with place. For example, they talk about being "on Black Hill" or "mustering sheep off Black Hill," "walking off Donald's Hill," or of people or sheep "coming off the hill"; one might be "making a noise on the hill," or "on Turton's country" but never "at Turton's country." Once "out the back," as men, sheep and dogs exert effort to go in and out of contained spaces such as creeks, valleys and basins, they use a vertical language. Only when a musterer is already "on" a hill does he (typically) go "up and down" the hill. For example, you walk "up this creek," "up that spur," "up over that spur," "up that fence," "down the creek," and "you walk up here and back down again"; you [in speaking of the past] "do a horse beat up the Smite"; and you "push the sheep down here." Natural features and human constructions (such as fences) that follow such features provide sources of direction. On the tops, the language is lateral again: as you "walk along the top," "follow that spur," or "follow that fence line," "go out here through those low saddles," "can't get through that gut," or "muster through the goat track"; here "the fences bluff off" or "don't always lead you somewhere." In mustering the sheep, the dominant metaphor empties the country as if it is a container: "the sheep are in the basins," and the musterers "sweep around," "they sweep that country," "clean this country up"; also musterers "hunt them out," they "clear these spurs out," carefully "covering country," because "sheep can get away from you."

Movement within the high country is described in idioms of containment significantly reinforced in prevailing nucleated bounded idioms of social relation as the definition and use of simultaneously expansive and divided landforms shape how the self is known. Landscape architects, Michael Ashdown and Diane Lucas (1987:13, 81) have written that the arrangement of landforms such as mountains and valleys create enclosures in the landscape, dividing it into a series of huge outdoor "rooms" or "spaces." Degrees of enclosure vary depending on the landform (1987:23). A sense of land is more present when landscape patterns are more distinctive creating the area's "landscape identity"; this sense of place is emphasized by the primacy of one's daily activity in landscape (Ashdown and Lucas 1987:51). Despite the linguistic construction of boundaries, at the same time, as Roderick Ensor noted, "clarity and visibility make the land omnipresent" in the Rakaia valley. This expansiveness of high-country spaces and limited social interaction with a variety of people means that land is more present here than in more densely settled urban and village communities; equally present in New Zealand, as we will see, are livestock.[27]

Configuring Geography

In *The Road from Coorain*, Jill Conway speaks of reconfiguring her sense of geography:

> It took a visit to England for me to understand how the Australian landscape actually formed the ground of my consciousness, shaped what I saw, and influenced the way a scene was organized in my mental imagery. I could teach myself . . . to enjoy this landscape in England, but it would be the schooled response of the connoisseur, not the passionate response one has for the earth where one is born. My landscape was sparser, more brilliant in color, stronger in its contrasts, majestic in its scale, and bathed in shimmering light.
>
> I realized that the English romanticism I had taken for a universal was a cultural category in which I did not participate. (1989:198, 203)

How does the New Zealand landscape form the ground of its inhabitants' consciousness? In a discussion with a Bureau of Land Management field officer in Idaho, I was describing the intimate knowledge high-country farmers have of their properties and told him of a particular instance on an autumn muster (when sheep are "brought in" from the back country for winter) when the farmer detailed on a contour map the route, or "beat," I should walk. He knew more than the map, however, and supplemented his instructions as most farmers do with reference to particular landmarks, such as a gate, a particular matagouri clump, or rocky outcrop, that suggests farmers know square meters of vast blocks despite the land's scale. Such knowledge, as suggested in chapter 6, is a combination of men's enculturation, of innate skill, and of experience: of "using what my father taught me"; of "being a natural musterer" and "knowing how geography works," having a sense of how the land falls, where sheep might hide and how they move, or knowing where to stand on visually smooth grasslands whose undulations and six-foot tussocks can block the line of sight when looking for sheep; and of experience—"you learn as you go . . . you get used to the terrain." As noted, farmers often told me that one either has stockmanship or not, but it is also part of a (mainly male) inheritance of historically based knowledge of place, intimate knowledge of country. The Idaho field officer contrasted this knowledge with that of the ranchers who run cattle on the public lands he administers; "they wouldn't know how to read a topographic map," he claimed, and have little knowledge of the country they lease. If the difference is as real as he suggests (and it may not be),[28] it may be accounted for by the difference in the U.S. West of grazing cattle that easily can be found in riparian zones from the New Zealand high country of grazing merino sheep that prefer to "run on the [mountain] tops" foraging the land expansively wherever they can find "tucker." "To muster the sheep in" demands "knowing the country," on foot—all of it, no matter how rugged or how high. Already in New Zealand, runholders are noting the loss of this knowledge of back country as land is retired and autumn musters are discontinued. A sense of geography is critical for stock care in remote areas of the high country, and the conditions of altitude must be integrated into one's place-knowledge to farm stock effectively. If toponymy and topography point to an idiom of placement and containment, they point also to an idiom of integration where the mountains must be a lateral extension of country, more than a vertical obstacle.

The ways in which sheep shape perception of landscape, form the ground of consciousness, configure geography, and help shape the system of "narrative landmarks" embedded in toponymic and topographical systems is discussed in the next chapter but is suggested in the answer a farmer provided to a question he posed to me. "What is the first thought that comes to mind when you look at that ridge?" He was pointing to Mount Hutt silhouetted against the western August sky as we drove toward the Canterbury high country. My answer was blandly bleak—I saw only the coldness. He looked at "the tops" (the ridge) and answered, "I'm figuring out where I would put a musterer on the top beat." I asked what he would look for, and he said, "where the sheep would go, if a musterer could get through—it would be easy on that ridge—and where he would bring the sheep as they came off the hill." In his integrated worldview, "you have to include us as part of nature."

§   §   §

Various high-country ways of talking about place define and interweave positionality, use and belonging. My analysis has focused on discursive conventions of place-naming and topographic representation specifically in vernacular idioms of orientation that stress proximity to and distance from the homestead as well as containment and integration. Naming patterns and boundary talk reflect use, perception of physical and constructed features, and the inscription of contemporary events and ownership into a landscape that becomes historicized; like fencing and subdivision, they also serve a referential function. Names reveal what count as "narrative landmarks" and impose cultural meaning on the landscape by transforming it—despite its vastness—into a contained and defined space, place. Legal systems of classification stress location and ownership as well as defining the suitability of land for productive use. And geologists speak of "basin range topography" in which altitude provides the sides to the broad rivers to create an image of containment with the valley and homesteads as the point of reference. Through idioms of orientation, scale is linguistically diminished in its vastness while at the same time steepness is rendered protective through a rhetoric of containment, integration, and horizontal (rather than vertical) directionality. Likewise, the key distinction between front and back country reinforces horizontal directionality and containment, over altitude. It underscores the pragmatic value of such distinctions. And as we will see, place is narrativized in the farmer's product as a fleece tells the story of a year's use of land. Place attachment is most powerfully mediated through stock, as sheep shape the toponymic and topographic systems used by these inhabitants to configure their geography and root themselves firmly in country. These subtle and culturally implicit linguistic manifestations of placement actively "contribute to the formation, maintenance and preservation of the identity of a group" (see Low and Altman 1992:10).

Notes

1. British-born and once-Wellington-based, poet Peter Bland (1934-) takes his title from Herbert Guthrie-Smith's (1999[1921]) meticulously detailed environmental history of his North Island property—*Tutira: The Story of a New Zealand Sheep Station.*

2. Theorists of settled European landscapes from Swiss alpine Torbel (Netting 1981:9) to rural Leon's Santa Maria del Monte (Behar 1986:22-23) to the remote archipelago of the Faroes (Wylie and Margolin 1981) have argued also that a locality's unique lexicon of place names not only enables us to talk about space but also provides "the reference points of a mental map" in which we invest the landscape with meaning (Behar 1986:23).

3. Acland's thirty-eight-page "A Sheep Station Glossary" is compiled from a number of classics in the history of the South Island as well as his own recollection of usage between 1890 and 1910. It provides a detailed consideration of technical, local, and slang words used on the Canterbury stations; Wall's introduction to the glossary notes its potential use for the student of linguistics (1975[1933]:351). For my purposes it is useful primarily for providing technical terms for the pastoral industry and the names for the various features of back-country landscape.

4. Station refers to the entire run, including both freehold and leasehold land, radiating from the homestead and running in excess of 2,500 sheep. The *New Zealand Dictionary* defines the station as "a very large farm for raising cattle or sheep, usually in the outback" (Orsman 1979:1074). Elsewhere the dictionary defines the "outback" as "Australian: the remote sparsely inhabited inland regions." Outback is not a term used in New Zealand; rather the term "back country" is typically used to mean "remote" (1979:70). Hill country is defined as "(mainly in the North Island) high ground, especially when used for sheep farming" (Orsman 1979:513). In the South Island "hill country" was not used to include mountainous country. Mountains therefore become distinguishing features of the high country although its inhabitants refer to mountains colloquially as "hills." McLeod (1970:24) characterizes the "rampart of mountains" rising immediately from the Canterbury plains with barely no foothills as forming a barrier between back country and front country; once those who come from the down country are there it is, he notes, "a different land."

5. "Paddock" provides an example of a British word whose meaning has changed in the New Zealand context, that is, a standard English word "used in a deflected sense" (Wall 1975[1933]:353); in British English paddock means "small enclosure;" however, New Zealanders use it as the equivalent of the "field" in British English (Gordon and Deverson 1985:33). "Block" is another example of how a common word can acquire rural meaning in the New Zealand context, as in Australia; whereas "run" means a large tract of grazing land, "block" means an area of land (Gordon and Deverson 1985:42). Other farming terms include "station," "to draft," "to shed," "to muster," and "mob," and "stock unit."

6. "Station" and "run" came to New Zealand from Australia (Gordon and Deverson 1985:32). Placing geographic naming in New Zealand in the context of "old country" practices is difficult, because, as Wall points out in his sheep-station glossary, those who came to New Zealand from Scotland and England were seldom sheep farmers and did not control a technical vocabulary; instead "what they did do was to take the handiest word they could think of and give it a new meaning. As time went on the word they had chosen changed or extended its meaning" (Wall 1975[1933]:379). Wall presents "run" as the best example of this phenomenon.

7. Hatch (1992) refers to this as a hierarchy of workforce arrangements.

8. A "farm" usually implies cultivation and agricultural production and the term's gradually increasing use in the high country might also refer to the presence of cultivated paddocks growing grasses and supplementary feed such as turnips, straw, oats, choumoellier, and lucerne.

9. For example, Avenel in Otago is not "technically" high country since it is no longer designated as renewable pastoral leasehold land. An officer from the Ministry of Agriculture and Fisheries in speaking of the property said that it is neither isolated (it is nine miles uphill from the tar-seal) nor high in altitude (the homestead is at 470 meters and the highest point 1,000 meters), but then he added there are some high-country properties that are even less isolated in terms of proximity of homestead to road, such as Long Slip or Glendene.

10. I do not translate measurements into the metric system when drawing from published, unpublished and documentary sources that use the former system of British measures.

11. Similarly in East Anglia the name of a country hall does not change regardless of who lives there (Frake 1996:241).

12. This implies that families equate their identities with their station's identity; an alternative reading might be that the "Glenaans," for example is an unmarked possessive gloss for "the people of Glenaan." In either case, station identity is being emphasized.

13. "Altitude," not "elevation," is the preferred term; when queried, high-country people told me that elevation is a geographer's term, not theirs. Some runholders speculated that the term may have come from aviation, for example, "old PC [Peter Ensor] giving the altitude of a peak based on his flying information," and in pushing this with mountain recreationists and linguists I discovered that New Zealanders in general tend to prefer "altitude."

14. Compare, for example, the analysis of their testimony before the Waitangi Tribunal in chapter 7 as politicized expressions of belonging, which illustrate how high-country people proclaim authenticity by inscribing themselves in the landscape and signalling local epistemologies about place as constitutive of identity.

15. In the United States it is common to refer to a piece of land by its compass direction and size, for example, "north forty" is a forty-acre piece north of the main house. In the New Zealand high country, cardinal points are rarely used (except to refer to weather patterns such as nor'westers or southerlies), and size characteristics, reflecting the regular division of land into sections as in the United States, seldom occur. The ir-

regular sizes of paddocks in an area of steepland topography, rather than flat land, might account for this (Robert Kaplan, personal communication). In contrast the undifferentiated seascape of the Faroes produces an extreme reliance on external cardinal reference points (Wylie and Margolin 1981:29).

16. To maintain a property's history, paddock names are retained when properties change hands within families. Proliferation of new names suggests radical development and subdivision of existing paddocks. Peter Ensor found that it is hard to know in Mrs. Nell's diaries where she is talking about; even the creek names have been altered, as Mrs. Nell's "Cascade Gully" has become the Ensor's "Redcliffs Stream."

17. The total area of the eighteen blocks is 1,794 hectares. Of these blocks fourteen average 35 hectares for a total of 494 hectares and two of the larger back country blocks total 1,300 hectares. The twenty-four paddocks total 120 hectares with an additional pair of flat paddocks by the river totaling 271 hectares.

18. Mapping is similar in function to naming. According to Harley (1992:245) "to catalogue the world [through cartography] is to appropriate it."

19. See Wylie and Margolin (1981) for an analysis of Faroese idioms of orientation.

20. "Creek" is typically used as a synonym for the British English "stream." The British English "creek," by contrast, means "inlet," not "small river" (Gordon and Deverson 1985:42).

21. Similarly, George Seddon (personal communication) notes that the rhetorical trope of meiosis is common in Australia where a "wind" is a "draft" and a "forest" is the "bush." Similarly the Scots call their mountains "hills," perhaps resisting their remoteness according to Ardener (1987:41).

22. Geographic notions of what constitutes a barrier as opposed to what constitutes an avenue of communication are strongly culturally coded (Robert Kaplan, personal communication). The notion that rivers and mountains constitute barriers is largely Anglo-European. Relative notions of what is high, in the context of mountains, is also very much a part of the local perception.

23. William Cronon (1983:138) has written that English colonists "reproduced these broad categories of land use [pasture and non-pasture] wherever and however they established farms." He argues that such divisions were imposed on the landscape, creating a "new ecological mosaic that would gradually transform New England ecosystems." Contrastively in the New Zealand high country, unlike in the hill country or on the Canterbury plains, the landforms to some extent dictated the divisions and shaped distinctive landscape values and conceptual systems.

24. This supports Kenneth Hewitt's (1988:14-15) challenge to a powerful "political fiction" of environmentalism" that mountains tend to separate, isolate, and provide barriers and obstacles. We must attend to mountain lands as habitats rather than as geo-ecological zones homogenized by their "remoteness," "fragility," and "danger" (1988:17). He urges us to resist environmental determinism and instead to consider ethnoecological and historical contexts, to attend to how people conceive and value their world, to adopt what David Pitt (1978) calls an "interiocentric" model. Similarly, Epeli Hau'ofa presents Oceania as "a sea of islands with their inhabitants," as "a large world in which peoples and cultures moved and mingled unhindered by boundaries . . . expanding social networks for greater flow of wealth" (1993:8). High-country expansiveness and extended social cohesion defies the boundedness that "remoteness" connotes.

25. See Brinkley (1992) for a review essay on revisionist Western U.S. history.

26. The "unspoiled wilderness" of the U.S. West is, as Frake points out, an oxymoron to the English from whom may derive the idea that "improvement makes the [rural] place" (1996:250).

27. As in areas of the Rocky Mountains in Colorado, the South Island high country as human habitat hosts barely one permanent inhabitant per square mile (Groetzbach 1988:34). Defined by Groetzbach (1988:29) as "young and relatively sparsely settled high mountains" with extensive market-oriented agriculture, forestry, and recent tourism, the Rockies and the New Zealand Alps contrast with "old and relatively densely settled high mountains" such as those in South Asia, Europe, Russia and China.

28. I have not worked with American ranchers and am unable to compare his experience as a field officer with those of the ranchers whose land he monitors. In respect of public lands, the radically polarized and interested representations by ranchers are typified by Wayne Hage (1989) and by environmentalists Denzel and Nancy Ferguson (1983).

Chapter Six

"Getting on with It": Mustering, Shearing, and Lambing

Tussock burned to fine gold, and the sheep bore golden fleeces
By the sudden alchemy of wintry waning sun,...
— Ursula Bethell, "Evening Walk in Winter"
in O'Sullivan (1997:75)

Pastoral high country, once characterized by physical extremes of climate, topography, scale and isolation, provides particular climatic, geographic, and ecological farming challenges to its families. The inhabitants of this once genericized male workplace—of man, dog and sheep—"are united in a partnership to live on the very fringe of habitable land and defy the elements which threaten them at every turn. Snow and ice, fire, flood, avalanche and landslide—we meet them all," writes McLeod (1980:11). Most surely, he romanticizes the implied excess and deprivation through exaggeration, but in a postpioneer world, physical and economic adversity and challenge are retained by settler descendants as components of high-country farming practices and precisely as the source of whatever allure the life might hold. Remoteness combined with the magnitude of the place and the size of staff is "our badge of honor," said a daughter, adding, this is "not tamable land" because of scale, topography, altitude and weather that frustrate domestication. Hard work is ennobling and keeps a semiotic pioneer legacy close to the surface. Certainly, successfully meeting these challenges gives pleasure, and station histories doggedly document recurring hardship despite improved technologies that merely modify this noncultivable and ecologically colonized land. The constancy of constraints provides the conditions from which inhabitants derive their sense of self as a people with a pioneer past constructed from adversity, and as members of a high-country community whose survival depends on individual resilience and initiative combined with teamwork and the sense of interdependence that cushions in times of economic hardship. Increased security derives not from control of landscape but

from familiarity and time depth, from stock knowledge and increasingly sophisticated genetic management.

The threat of early spring snows has influenced farming practices and the
development of farming technologies since settlement in the mid-1800s; technological improvements have not eliminated the threat. Noting extreme variation
in rainfall and temperature as characteristic of the high-country climate, scientists of pasture ecology Douglas and Allan[1] (1992:15) write, "Management has
to adopt strategies to cope with the poor growth seasons and the snow, drought
or flood." Broadening the range of techniques to parry against the uncertainties
of winter and spring weather patterns, they include blade shearing, "which has
been here since day one," and unlike machine shearing in the hill and down
country leaves a residual fleece on pregnant ewes and helps to protect them
against early spring snows; the planting of shelterbelts of *pinus radiata*, poplars,
and Australian eucalyptus to delineate paddocks and to provide protection
against cold southerly winds for stud-flock[2] lambs; and the development of silage,[3] which came later, and enabled farmers to "boost [their] numbers," feed
their mobs, and even increase wool weight during harsh winters and late springs
when the growing is slow. Tractors and four-wheel-drive vehicles have eased
access to the "back country," the area of high-altitude tussock grasslands where
stock graze during the summer; sometimes called "summer country" it contrasts
with lower altitude "winter country" closer to the homestead where most sheep
are wintered and ewes are more protected while lambing.

Douglas and Allen stress wise integration of land resources with the prevailing climatic and economic conditions, noting that "there is no set recipe for
tussock grassland farming" (1992:14);[4] sustainable development programs demand resource identification, strategic planning, and careful management that is
run-specific in what farmers perceive to be "a grand mix of near-natural to
strongly modified habitats" (Molloy 1994:88). Detailed local knowledge of
properties is essential; a Rakaia farmer explained that campers who were dump-
ing rubbish on the river flats at Redcliffs did so because "they don't know that
the land is valuable, that [Willie Ensor] uses it, that every square inch counts."
Sheep and grass have to be managed and checked throughout the year, as sheep
rotate through cultivated paddocks and blocks. They require balancing available
grasses (subject to weather patterns, especially wind, rain and snow and helped
by aerial topdressing) with sheep's nutritional needs. In the spring, hill blocks
and grass paddocks are topdressed with superphosphate, and cultivated paddocks are planted, for example, in choumoellier or kale, root crops such as
swedes or turnips, new grass (cocksfoot, rye grass and timothy), and leguminous
pasture plants (white or red clover, maku lotus, and lucerne). Fences are built
and maintained; paddocks are sized to maximize available nutrition without
waste. In winter, supplemental feed such as hay or silage must be calculated so
that adequate quantities are produced and the appropriate mobs rationed accordingly. Like all New Zealand farming, its logic has more to do with balance and
constant assessment of the cost/benefit ratio than merely organizing farming
around the agricultural cycle, although farmers aim to do what they think "is
right, regardless of cost or benefit." The bottom line is productivity and sustain-

ability within defining market conditions,[5] running maximum stock units without compromising grassland or fleece quality. It is growing the best wool with the finest micron (fiber diameter) for those aiming to "fine up" their merinos and with the heaviest clean fleece weight for the highest price. The land's value is measured by its capacity to continue to provide over the generations. All of this concerns balance, agonistic resilience in adversity, aggressive cultivation of challenge, and adaptability to change. At stake is ecosystem sustainability in which livestock domestication is a dynamic player and management of hawkweed, woody species and rabbits replace weather as the main concern (Brown 1993:325). Naturalizing conventions and discourses prevail in which the human players culturalize nature and naturalize culture in ways that script them physically, sensually, emotionally, cognitively, and socially as part of habitat.

The autumn muster, shearing the sheep, and spring lambing and its associated tasks of tailing (or docking), castrating, and vaccinating are critical pastoral productive processes, routine activities that, as the Comaroffs have illustrated for Tshidi, create persons while persons create themselves, and "transform human energy into a vital political economy" (1992:135, 137). Against the precise mimetic detail of mustering, shearing, and lambing, I decode these traditional practices as embodied experiences signifying cultural identity.[6] Each is labor intensive and structurally and symbolically important for the organization of social life, for the preservation of continuity of the past in the present, and as a marker of cultural transformation. These seasonally cyclic events occur, of course, within a context of routine activities, all of which sustain husbandry and contribute ultimately to the production of wool from grass. They reflect how pastoral leasehold land—not as land transformed through cultivation but as land to which runholders have only a surface-right relationship—is simultaneously specific and expansive to high-country farmers through being walked.

Mustering In

The seasonal use of extensive back-country tussock grasslands with their low-carrying capacity most distinguishes high-country merino farming from hill- and down-country farming. In autumn—either April or May depending on a property's altitude and latitude—sheep are "mustered in," brought from remote summer grazing country into the station's front country. Autumn-muster narratives predominate in station and family histories, autobiographies, short stories, station and farm verse, and novels.[7] Peter Newton's (1947) foreword in his musterer's memoirs, *Wayleggo,* describes the musterer's job, the work of sheepdogs, mustering-gang composition, camp-life routine, and the country's proportion and character. Such accounts tell us how essential mustering is to the distinctiveness of high-country farming.

Peter Ensor prefaces his mustering narratives with a description of the visible front faces of Double Hill, Glenrock, and Glenariffe, and of the back country, which accounted for two-thirds of the combined properties. Three brothers—Roderick, Duncan, and Peter—would "muster in" together as their sons and son-in-law, now brothers, cousins and neighbors, still do. Peter describes the furthest boundaries of the faces coming down onto the south side of the Rakaia as well as the fence lines marking the boundaries between the properties, giving altitudes of the main peaks and of the two most significant saddles—Macintosh's of 3,000 feet and Turtons of 4,000 feet.[8] Today Macintosh's provides access to the Glenrock and Redcliffs back country, and Turtons access to the Glenaan and Double Hill back country. In the early Double Hill autumn muster of the early 1940s,

> [T]he traditional mustering line was six days around Double Hill, with six or seven men plus packman and four horses. The first day the men climbed out from the Homestead then mustered the Smite [River] down to the Smite tent camp, halfway down the Smite. The packman and horses had sometimes over twenty miles to travel around Glenfalloch via the Lake Stream, then up the Smite to the tent camp—a long, hard day for heavily loaded horses. The sheep were hunted further down Smite faces.
>
> Next day the men mustered down the Smite and around to the Homegully Hut and holding paddock, about two miles above Lake Heron, and then around the face towards the Swift River, leading up to the Clent Hills Saddle at about 5,000 feet—a long slow drive for both the pack team and sheep. The Rock Camp Hut is just over the saddle facing north.
>
> Fourth day for the pack-team is downhill but hard travelling down a creek until it joins with the north branch of the Ashburton River, coming out of Petticoat Lane, then going into Turtons Stream where Comyns Hut is situated. Comyns Hut is the only original hut still standing.
>
> The fifth day on Double Hill is from Comyns up to Turtons Saddle and at 4,000 feet into Glenariffe, finishing up at Double Hill on the sixth day. Glenrock camps are, or were, Redcliffs [now Willie's homestead] then over MacIntosh's Saddle . . . to MacIntosh's Hut, then on down the Swift River to the confluence of the North Ashburton and the Swift. Two or three days of Glenrock country is mustered from Cookies' [Hut]. (Ensor 1990:5-6) (See map I-1)

Peter's history stressed familiar routings, often following streams or ridgelines, altitudes and distances, mustering-hut locations, and the difficulty of access for the packman and packhorses. The last muster on this scale was in 1968 after which much of Double Hill country was closed up. On an August 1988 flight over this country, Peter's nephew from Glenrock, Charlie, pointed out the same features to me, following the land in terms of the old mustering routes, and pointing out landmarks destroyed by avalanche, such as Rock Camp hut, as well as fencing lines.

For Rakaia families, the autumn muster persists as a focal point of back-country pastoral activity. Because topography does not change much, the mustering beats remain constant over the years, as do the paths taken by sheep and men; such physical traces provide unexpected degrees of continuity with the past. Property and fencing subdivision may change the routes slightly, as may scrub growth or unstable scree slopes, but even these transformations depend on the contour of the land and predetermined beats and, most important, they must consider sheep movement or else the stock will smother against new fences. Musters are rarer, cover far less country, and, when done, are much shorter than in the period prior to the early 1970s.[9] While some properties have overnight musters from five to seven days, many runholders "bring the sheep in" in several days or, perhaps, an overnight muster. Land retirement plans and the surrender of Crown pastoral lands have decreased the area of back country used for sheep and cattle grazing. Cultivated paddocks, aerial topdressing, and silage and hay production have made up for the loss.

At Erewhon, where the muster used to take thirty-five days, helicopters have made a difference because "now you can fly over and the men don't have to bother climbing for ages to go into basins where there are no sheep." Usually, the country cannot be mustered effectively this way. When the National Film Unit asked a runholder if he had ever mustered by helicopter, he explained his answer to them to me:

> I tried it for a muster for one day, and it didn't work. The reasons it didn't work—you don't see the land, you can't keep an eye on how it's changing and what's going on. You have to sit down for twenty minutes when you get dropped in at 8,000 feet because the altitude changes your oxygen and breath levels. You can't see the terrain the same way; you can't find the sheep. It doesn't work. (Field notes 3.iv.87)

Given the land surfaces, which appear smoothly undulating to the naked or un trained eye, it is hard to understand that when standing on a hillside the matagouri or tussock or shape of the land itself can block the line of sight. On some properties, two-way radios link musterers, enabling one man to tell another where he can see sheep left behind above or below, but the use of radios violates a sense of "what is proper for staunch musterers." Jokingly noting that "real musterers don't need radios," a runholder explained that "you are looking after your own patch," and two-way radios "get in the way of this and interfere with the experience."

Now on occasion, when "spotting or straggling," some runholders save time by using a helicopter to drop them into the back country; they then "walk out," droving out of the summer country, for instance, the cattle with their smaller numbers. A Rakaia runholder said, "if you are dropped off by chopper and left, it is a wonderful experience. There you are and it is absolutely quiet." I felt some sense of this at Glenaan in May 1995 when Hamish and Belinda's son, Paul, and Hugo, his friend from the Awatere valley, were dropped off to bring the cattle in:

> Bondy, the helicopter pilot, picked up Paul, Hamish, Hugo (and me) in the paddock immediately below the homestead at 7:00 A.M. . . . . Took off in semidarkness, full moon two days on the wane. Hame and Paul in the front to look for cattle, Hugo and me in the back. . . .

Took off over the Glenaan paddocks—crisp, clear, green, neat and all in place. So, so green, the paddocks. Headed up Stony Creek [Glenrock Stream] toward Turtons [Saddle] and perfectly over [see mapI-1].[10] I was on the right hand side looking at Double Hill country. Ached from incipient tears. Velvet. Still. Thought of Peter's memories. Over Turtons Saddle, which is technically "the back." Thought as we flew over how much the desolation appeals to me and then thought about the gorge families wanting to be buried in front country where they have roots and know best; whereas for me, I have no claims to domesticated front country. Freehold line runs by the shingle scree in Stony Creek. So front country can be undulating and untopdressed, unimproved. The country surprised me from the air—always steeper than I can recall, smoother than I would imagine, and contained. . . . I breathed deeply to manage my queasiness from the petrol fumes, from the unfamiliar sense of suspension.

The creeks serve as reference points for giving directions. Last night, the instructions focused on Mutton Gully, Turtons Stream, and Round Hill Creek (map I.1). The cattle were further out than Hamish had expected. Saw a huge mob, then some more down in the riverbed. Dropped both boys off together, quite high up [on Round Hill Creek], because Bondy had trouble finding a suitable spot to land and had to go down on a spur in half light. Then we lifted up and went on to Mutton Gully, after a circuit up Turtons and then up Round Creek, which was quite full of water, toward Clent Hills Saddle where we circled and flew back to Turtons. The boys will have to cross it several times. We flew up Mutton Gully and saw six cattle. Hame pointed out Comyns to me (with two structures) and where Rock Camp would have been but we saw nothing left. So quiet. So vast. So true to an image of containment from top to bottom. That is what the landforms suggest with their catchments and basins and saddles and spurs and ridges—the critical distinguishing features. The hills were identified for me on the basis of basins and scree slopes. Tussock cover is [visually] gentle.

[On the way in] Hamish told me that Petticoat Lane is his favorite spot. "Deep and beautiful country. Rough [to walk]." (Field notes 19.v.95)

The alluring qualities of solitude, enhanced by the scale and emptiness of country were similarly expressed by a high-country daughter, now an environmental activist, who told me, "it is open space, a vast quilt, open space devoid of human habitation."

Distances covered are vast, and "taking a beat" (or horizontal section) means finding one's way more or less along a contour across scree slopes, above or below sheer rock faces and gullies, along ridges, and down spurs. Beats can be up to one mile wide and ten miles long (Newton 1947:12). The rule of thumb is to make noise sporadically (usually when up on a knoll) to move the sheep forward while letting other musterers know where you are, to stay close to a ridgeline if possible, and to follow sheep tracks since sheep "know the best way to go"; one runholder told me of a road surveyor in South Canterbury who used their tracks to guide him across the land. Often a musterer and his dogs have a sense of where sheep are likely to go based on prior years. Even so musterers are obliged to zigzag behind them, heading for ledges and high knolls for the best view of wandering sheep below or in dips and gullies, as well as to be seen by other musterers above and below, who must know at all times where the others are. Not knowing the country can lead to one being "bluffed" and having to backtrack up and down to find a way through terrain deceptively smooth at a distance but rough on foot. "The men figure the country out on the ground; they do not pore over maps." Rather than risk being bluffed most musterers will climb a thousand feet; during one premuster evening meal, musterers were said to face the same conflicts as pilots—"be old or bold but not both."

Mustering the back country, more than any other aspect of high-country farming, demands tough physical exertion and detailed visual knowledge of experientially familiar terrain. Each shepherd in a mustering gang is responsible for pushing the sheep out along a "beat," with his five to seven dogs. Mustering is really a way of harnessing the dog's natural predatory instincts for our use; even so a shepherd has to be prepared to move about on a beat—"the sheep don't come to you." In fact, "that is what high-country mustering is all about— the sheep are afraid of men and dogs." Dogs are bred for the type of work they do. Heading dogs, known also as eye-dogs, run out silently making a wide sweep in front of the sheep and bringing them back to their master by the force of their eye; they often can "hold" sheep wherever required. Huntaways "hunt sheep" by driving them from behind with their bark. Dogs work as a team with a musterer, and, like the musterer, they are valued for their capacity to tolerate extremes of terrain and climate, their ability to work independently and yet follow placement instruction sharply, and their daring in going where no one else will go. Like sheep, dogs also mediate how the country is known.[11] Dog stories are integral to mustering tales. Elaborated are a dog's pedigree, and skill in finding and herding sheep. Considered neither stock nor pets,[12] the working dogs are the measure of a musterer's worth; like a good musterer they must know how to handle sheep in an environment where sheep are afraid of humans and tend to shy away from men and dogs.[13] These skills, I was told, are important in "our kind of country" because when a musterer misses hidden or cunningly elusive sheep "they are lost to you forever" in large blocks where they will die in the winter snows.[14]

At dawn on Glenmore station on the muster's first day at the headwaters of the Cass River up against the main divide in Mackenzie Country,[15] Jim Murray outlined six separate beats, identifying significant ranges, peaks, saddles, valleys and spurs. In assigning beats, a runholder or head shepherd assesses each man's ability and the steepness and hardness of the country, and the quality and mix of a man's dogs, as well as fairness in giving each a turn at top, middle and bottom beats. Jim told the men where to go and what to do by indicating a direction not to go in, and identifying a ridge to stand on, a spot to wait at, a pocket where sheep might camp, and tricky areas from past years. The men listened, very rarely double-checking what he had said but seeming to follow his condensed directions. He told the men where he or other musterers might be spotted or joined up with along the way. On one snowy morning, drawing from experience, he suggested to the musterer assigned the top beat to take overalls and a book because he would have a cold wait along the way. On that first morning, everyone set off with his hillstick seemingly at top speed.

Only going on the musters could convey to me the land's scale and the extent of experience it demands. My letters, based on field notes, elaborate the complex mechanics of a muster—preparation and food supplies, the logistics and itinerary, the daily routine of hill and hut life—as well as the cast of characters in the mustering gang, the conversations and the jokes. Jim Murray is fourth generation of his family at Glenmore and in 1987 was on his "20th muster":

> The logistics of the Glenmore muster were astounding. Some of the supplies were taken out to the huts in the Toyota the day before the muster began. For our trip in, Jim, Ron the cook, and I climbed into the cab of the Toyota Land Cruiser, five musterers stood with our remaining supplies in the back, and an enclosed wire trailer packed with 35+ snapping and snarling dogs was towed behind.[16]
>
> The first day at Glenmore after lunch at the homestead, we drove out twenty miles or so up the Cass River along the shingle and over the braided strands to Tin Hut where we stayed for four nights. The sounds and smells stay with me, mostly—the sounds of the dogs barking and yelping, often in the night setting up a howling chorus that a shepherd would have to still, the rustle of the tall pine shelter belts surrounding the huts, the perpetual rush of the braided river and of the falls at Waterfall Hut where we spent our last night, the 'wayho' of Jim's voice echoing down from the ridge tops as he hunted out sheep. At night I heard the 'wayhos' captured in the mountains still. And the smells—well, mostly of dog pee with all those dogs running to the truck every morning to urinate over the wheel wells, heading for my tent if they could,[17] for the hillpacks, the boots, the hut, the woodpile, anything vertical that they could foul by getting past Ron's broom. By day five the Toyota was acrid. The persistent odor of raw mutton—I never learned to like its smell—used for dog tucker, sides of mutton in sacks, which daily was chopped with an axe and thrown to them on their chains in front of the dog motels—metal drums under the pines. The scent of whiskey, the nightly ritual of it following dinner, seven mugs of whiskey and a pitcher of water.
>
> Mostly I remember my sense of frustrated inadequacy and of awe. It came from the waiting, but also from not being able to go where the men went because I wasn't fit enough to keep up or experienced enough to find my way through the bluffs and crevasses. With time one can always climb up or down to get around, although often you don't know which way you should climb to get around— you can, for example, go uphill and still be bluffed at a gut as I was on my first day, or go down and not be able to get up the other side because of steep loose shingle. So on day three the sensible decision was made to leave me behind, which meant I was often alone in the riverbed waiting and straining to stare at hillsides, to see if I could see man or dog or sheep.[18] When I did find them (magnified with my 135-mm camera lens) it was by spotting a single file of sheep

stretched out like a fragment of cream-colored string against a steep scree slope with a man high, high up above directing his dogs below. The dogs do so much running, much of it on shingle, that they get footsore with bruised and cut pads. Each man had five or six dogs so that occasionally they could leave one behind at the hut to rest for a day and heal. Amazing creatures, these working dogs—they are crucial, "stars of the event, the heroes of the show," Ron said, and yet not pampered. . . . From this distance they were dark pinpricks often completely nonvisible without fieldglasses. . . . Much of the waiting was at 2800+ feet amidst tussock, matagouri, paradise ducks, jagged hills and blue nor'west skies. . . . But I found out musterers do a lot of waiting too. Roderick Ensor told me later that once upon a time men who smoked were preferred as musterers because they would sit and have a cigarette while waiting for the men on other beats to hunt the sheep down to them. Jim Morris offered another reason, "they are preferred so the sheep can have a spell, as with droving, so they don't hurry the sheep—it's not good to hurry them—and the sheep can go along at their own pace." Having to wait for a mate to hunt sheep out of a bluff or spur is part of the job. In a couple of instances when I was waiting for a musterer to come through on his beat, I gave up and went on, fearing that he had already gone through; in both he came through more than two hours later.[19] My amazement reflects, I suspect, lack of appreciation for how much of what these men do is a product of experience. They have been walking hills for years and what seems steep to me doesn't seem insurmountable to them because they are practiced. . . . I needed another runholder though to tell me after I had left Glenmore that the men are hurting—that while they are fit and experienced it is still hard work. (Letter from the field, 28.iv 87)

Vital to good mustering is the "capacity to know where stock will go," combined with the skill of working the dogs to maximum effect in a range of terrain and weather conditions. One high-country-born man told me that as with stockmanship one either has mustering ability or not, and that a mustering sense is also part of an inheritance of historically based knowledge of place, of having an intimate knowledge of country. "In this environment, skill is the ultimate leveler." This man came home to muster for two years at the age of nineteen but had mustered smaller blocks before then. Mustering is not taught but developed through serving an apprenticeship on several properties. The first time one might take the bottom beat and see the sheep come down a particular spur. The next year "you might be given a top beat with directions on where to go, for example, to stand on a particular knob" for the best vantage point. "You are guided by your predecessor to where the best knob is. You wouldn't take the time to find out for yourself when they pass on their knowledge." So he concluded that mustering is learned, but you have to have an aptitude for it also. Like farming in general, mustering engages a critical tension between innate aptitude and skill derived from experience that directs their movement on steep land, as well as their knowledge of the mutual workings of country, stock, and dogs.

As we walked in the Awatere valley, a young musterer, who returned home for experience before attending agricultural college, narrated his first muster at age fifteen. "You follow sheep tracks and ridges mainly for the best ways down and along. You learn as you go," he said, "you get used to the terrain and take long strides looking ahead [not down]—you can't be too careful picking your steps, but you do miss steps occasionally twisting an ankle or tearing a ligament." Musterers are said to have an ideal build—slight with strong muscular legs, wiry but not too short or too tall. During a tailing muster in 1990, the runholder noted that the hired man was "a natural musterer," by which he meant that when placed on a block he knew what to do without instruction even though he had never been there before. To illustrate he said of a young manager from another valley that because he "knows how geography works"—meaning he has a sense of where to stand to see the most in a vast block and where sheep are likely to string off—he could be placed in the block and "know where to go and what to do." Stock knowledge can compensate for lack of particular geographic knowledge. "Common sense is much of what it is about," according to Hamish. "It's about understanding the principles of the big picture, understanding the objective." Knowing a particular "patch" of land through experience is one component for being a good musterer, but the visual is important too because "you can see a lot from one spot with fieldglasses." Despite the scale of the land, runholders know vast blocks in detail and "go to the same knob year in and year out, and drink at the same creek"; this was apparent when I was given instructions—landmarks would be a fence or a knoll, a cabbage tree or outcrop, even a rock that otherwise might be mistaken year after year for a prone sheep resting on a hot day. One runholder told me on one such occasion that in giving me instructions he was "using what his father had taught" him.

In-marrying women who work on the farm have to acquire the knowledge that seems both innate to and experientially inherited by their husbands. At Glenaan Belinda and I talked about her mustering knowledge while walking in afternoon mist on our way through Trig Block to push ewes and lambs through the gate into the next block (see map 5-2). She told me that Hamish initially would give her seemingly vague directions for a mustering beat and send her off. I knew what she meant because I too found his directions for following a beat condensed and coded—so much was assumed about my knowledge of how the land falls, how sheep behave and where sheep go. I would push for more detail, wanting specific predictions on what might happen; mustering is not predictable though, and ultimately one has to have a sense of what to do when it is not. Belinda learned by experience, cumulating knowledge year upon year; she learned more by mustering the blocks on her own, as she has done increasingly in recent years. But she told me that her husband knows the country in a way that she does not; he finds it hard to imagine what it is like to not know it in the same way, as one who has grown up there.

The lay of the land—the distance of back country from the homestead and its topography—excludes women. Musterers are mainly male, and daughters seldom go on musters, although parents are proud when they do and in recent years three Rakaia daughters have been out. Varying reasons are given for the taboo against girls—the specialness of the event for men, the sleeping arrangements in the huts, the lack of walking fitness that girls have. One daughter (in university) recently took the top beat with her boyfriend, a shepherd, and found it much harder than she had thought it might be—it was cold, she had to wait a lot, she got anxious, and ate little. She told me that she found it hard to keep up. Her mother told me at the time how her daughter had been "shocked at the distances and the speed with which the men cover the terrain," and her father explained to me that "the muscles a musterer uses are familiar to them and stay in shape."

My own experience on the Glenrock muster took me through Macintosh's Saddle for several days mustering from Cookies Hut and then into Macintosh's Hut about which Peter wrote. To provide a sense of the scale, I extract from field notes condensed into a letter home about a muster with Charlie Ensor at Glenrock:

> On Charlie's muster I slept in the hut in a top bunk where the junior people go; senior musterers, packies and cooks go on the bottom. We took some leisurely days, and Charlie explained how musters used to be done, pointing out the terrain to me, explaining beats, discussing the history of each of the huts, telling me how the pack horses used to be loaded and used (they only stopped using them about six years ago).[20]
>
> The final day we mustered Black Hill and Willie [Charlie's brother from Redcliffs] and the two shepherds from Double Hill came to help. Black Hill is very steep and bluffy, often closing off the road below with rock falls. . . . Charlie gave me a manageable [without dogs] beat of my own to walk—a top beat, between 5,000 and about 6,000 feet. . . . I set out from MacIntosh's Hut (2,800 feet) with Charlie and Mike [his old school friend from St. Andrew's who calls himself an "occasional musterer"] following a fence steeply up the hill to well over 5,000 feet. Although I kept by the fence line, when I got to the top I wasn't sure that was where I was meant to be with sheer rock above me and a grassy basin defined by steep shingly spurs. I puzzled over my topographic map, and decided it was the only way to go. Once over there was another basin much the same as the first, beautiful because it was wider than I had expected, but slightly marred by my anxiety. Down the shingle, through the next basin, up the next shingle spur, and I was in sight of a magnificent tussock-covered flat. The flat was glorious and I reveled in the ease of walking it, the thrill of being there, getting there, seeing a mountain tarn in the distance, being up high for once, seeing Black Hill, seeing over the tops and down over to Lake Coleridge and over to Peak Hill and then up the Rakaia and Wilberforce and over to Algidus and Glenthorne beyond. The summit rose from another angle up to my left with tussock in front and another hill rising on the right and then dropping on the other side with sheer bluffs where I could hear Charlie's mustering calls and the bark of his huntaways. I followed the fence and dipped down into a saddle overlooking Double Hill and Glenariffe country, and headed across the flat toward the tarn with the nor'wester pushing hard against me. After lunch I set

off through the lowest saddle to find the spur that Charlie told me
would lead off the hill and down to the road. I thought I'd found it,
noting from my topographic map that it gradually got steeper. There
was no sign of Paul who was sitting up on Donald's Hill spur (he said
later it was hard to sit, nothing was flat) for several hours until he
could drive the sheep down. All the sheep that have been pushed
across the hillsides come down this spur, so on I trudged. Where it
was steep, I stuck to sheep tracks, assuring myself that it was the
right spur. At times I was on hands and knees to avoid being blown
sideways by the gusts. At other moments I was convinced that I was
coming down the wrong spur and would be bluffed, that I'd get stuck
and be forever embarrassed if they brought the helicopters out after
me, that I would have a night in the tussock hunkering down behind a
matagouri bush, that I would break a leg, that I would have to turn
around and backtrack, retracing my steps to the hut where we began
our climb that morning. The perk I got when I jumped down onto the
gorge road was worth every second of anxiety. The men were still
droving thousands of sheep off the hillsides, and I sat out of sight behind the matagouri, on the other side of the road by the river for the
better part of an hour and a half with my binoculars fixed on them.

All the sheep, all 4,000+ of them came down Black Hill onto
the gorge road about a mile down from Glenrock homestead, whereas
at Glenmore, they were mustered each day down onto the riverbed,
and then gradually wove their way down the river toward the upper
paddocks, where eventually we were met by Ann [Murray] at the end
of the fifth day—all of the ewes miraculously emerging from the riverbed and blending with the hundreds coming down off the spur of
the last hillside, where they had been pushed by the men working
their beats along the faces. The ending is quite spectacular and even
the musterers had their cameras ready. (Letter from the field, 28iv.87)
(See map I.1)

The days after that were spent, drafting and drenching and crutching[21] and ended
similarly at Glenaan on the first day of May taking the ram to the ewes to start a
whole new cycle. While the sheep have all been mustered into the yards, the
runholder is able to look over the mob closely, drafting lighter stock off to go on
better feed.

The elderly miss the "busy feeling" of the old musters; gangs stayed longer
and played cricket and golf—"today they are in and gone. It created a stronger
sense of community and kinship then." Like shearing activity, the seasonal muster created social relationships that defined high-country "life" as cohesive, dynamic, and more densely populated during these transitory moments. The muster
in particular bridged class distinctions between runholders and shepherds at
varying phases of the life cycle, while simultaneously reinforcing class categories through friendship networks as one man's son would apprentice to his father's old classmates; it linked properties as musterers casually elicited information on how things were done elsewhere and passed on news. These social
dynamics are clearly illustrated in the selection of one South Canterbury runholder's mustering team—good men, smart, clever wits, careful fit workers.

Photo 12 Jim Morris of Manuka Point drenching newly purchased Corriedale wethers at Glenfalloch in the autumn

Photo 13 Waterfall mustering hut up the Cass River, Glenmore, South Canterbury

Photo 14 Charlie Ensor with working dogs above the Swift River, Glenrock muster

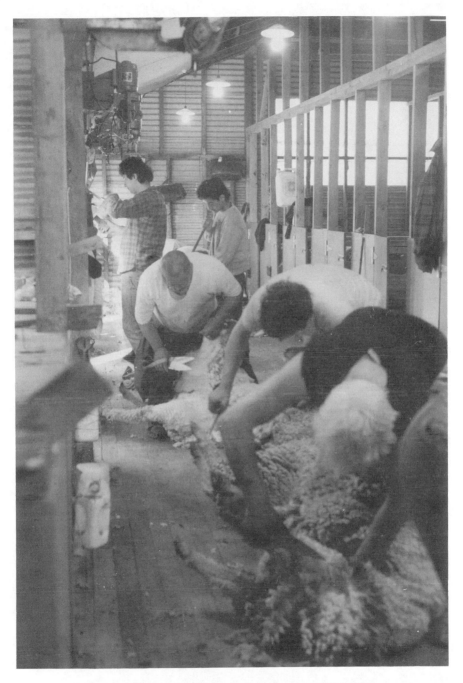

Photo 15 The Karaitiana blade-shearing gang at Glenariffe

Photo 16 Merino stud ram, Glenthorne, North Canterbury

Photo 17 "Throwing" the fleece from the machine shearing board to the wool table, with sheep in the holding pens, Mount Gladstone woolshed, Marlborough

Photo 18 Tony White classing wool, Glenariffe woolshed

Photo 19 Blade-shorn sheep in the counting-out pens, Glenariffe woolshed

Photo 20 Belinda Ensor earmarking a lamb during tailing time, Glenaan

Two were his own young hired men: one was a verbally quick Christ's College-educated fellow with experience on two of the Rakaia stations; the other was the son of a kiwi fruit farmer with modest land holdings in the North Island, a young fellow who has dreamed of working in the high country since he was a small boy, and gradually, had acquired a team of dogs. His family thinks he is crazy for working in a "cold bleak end-of-the-earth sort of place." Two of the other men also were contrasting types: one was the runholder's nephew, a Christ's College graduate, and in line for the family farm with his brother in Waiau; the other, thirty and engaged, has established a small deer farm after mustering up this valley for twelve years (he too has worked in the Rakaia) for the money toward "his own patch." Joking references to inherited wealth and private schools, and runholders' situational code-shifting between formal talk in the homestead and at mixed-sex events and colloquial talk in the yards, woolshed and back country, situationally dissipated structurally inherent class tensions.[22] Ten years after my initial work, as runholders' sons are returning to farm, the tensions between them and the hired men are less easily dissipated.

Despite the return of sons, families told me with regret that this is country their children will never know, now that more land is retired and musters become nonexistent on many properties; some runholders in their forties have never mustered the land their fathers knew. At stake is what Harvey Franklin astutely recognizes as the social function of New Zealand's farming, recognizable to the Rakaia farmers to whom I showed this passage:

> It persists as a way of life that its participants seek to defend. The meshing of politics with farming persists not only because of the profound influence farming exerts on the export trade and hence the growth and stability of the whole economy but in addition because the farming community is a social body—diverse and not always united—which has its own ethos and beliefs and dearly held objectives that it seeks to defend and advance. The interpenetration of economic and social issues attached to any discussion of farming introduces an irreducible degree of ambiguity that lends confusion to all analyses. . . . [I]t retains a social importance . . . because of the inestimable value attached by the community to private enterprise, which, in this case, retains close associations with the family unit. (Franklin 1978:135)

Structurally important, the muster still binds the back-country runs and families in mutually interdependent ways and continues to encode station life in country. Brothers and neighbors muster in together, shepherds are exchanged between properties, beats are passed from generation to generation, and women contribute in vital ways by preparing the supplies as did their mothers-in-law before them, in some instances sending out duffs (boiled puddings) in the same honey tins. Perhaps most significant, by continuing to walk on the land, runholders continue to "know it," to experience its evocation of heritage, to embody its sensual immediacy, and to protect the singularity of their stewardship of high-country lands. The loss of this fading and historically formulaic practice saddens them and threatens to break the tight bond between family and station where inheritance of knowledge and skill is said to be crucial in managing so many stock effectively in such vastness. Seemingly paradoxical, as scale is lost, community is lost.

Shearing the Fleece

A culmination of a year's activities, shearing the fleece off the sheep is "harvest time," with runholders calling themselves "wool growers" or "wool producers." The quality of the fleece—its weight, staple length, fineness, color, texture, its contaminating vegetation—records the condition of the stock and the land on which they have fed. For many, shearing the ewes marks the transition from winter to spring, and in the Rakaia valley it occurs between August and October; farmers estimate that half the properties shear in the spring rather than in summer as in the past.[23] Most properties in the valley are still "feeding out" supplemental hay or silage, which they do until the end of September or when it runs out. Pre-lamb "blade shearing" rather than machine shearing of ewes is the rule on these Mid Canterbury properties although some to the south in Wanaka and around Lake Wakatipu commonly use cover combs in machine shearing with similar effect;[24] in contrast to machine shearing, blade shearing leaves more residual wool on the sheep, protecting them against early spring southerlies and the snow that falls even as late as December. The sequence of shearing in the valley is determined by the order of lambing, and yearly the same blade "gang" moves from property to property. In the past before prelamb shearing, the gang would work from the bottom to the top of the road, shearing at the highest altitude last. Regardless of the sequence, shearing, like the autumn muster, provides continuity with past pastoral practices, links properties as information is exchanged about others through the shearers, and enhances social interaction with its labor intensiveness.

Historical Note

Mrs. Nell's Double Hill station diaries from 1910 to 1911 reveal a different shearing schedule and larger scale operation, but the principles are very much the same.[25] Shearing began in the summer on 19 December 1910 and ended on 3 February 1911. A total of 29,601 sheep were shorn representing the combined stock from present-day Glenfalloch, Double Hill, Glenariffe, Glenaan, Glenrock and Redcliffs stations.[26] The acreage comprised two runs (118 and 119) and totaled 113,500 acres (Acland 1975:316). The diaries list workers' names and their jobs. A large staff was on hand; twenty shearers are listed in the diaries as well as a wool-classer, two woolpressers, three woolrollers, a "carry away," three fleecepickers, a butcher and brander, a cook, a cook's mate, a penner-up, a shed shepherd, and the boss of the board. Descriptions of the specific jobs are in the following sections of this chapter.

Some selected entries evoke life on Double Hill at shearing time in 1910-1911 and suggest the kind of ethnohistorical detail that station records preserve, to enable a reconstruction of farming conventions, of the quotidian, and of social historical details:

Sat. 17 Dec.—Filled shed in evening. Shower from Sou West. Fine Day. Sou'west wind. Les [husband] & shepherds culling wethers. Ross [the waggoner] went to [Iron] store[27] and brought shearers. McLean and James gardening. [Harry] Rushbrook [packman for several years] getting workshop ready. Self baked and washed. Got letter from Mother, Ethel & Xmas card from Mrs. Morgan, also Xmas present from Mother, Ethel and Maude.

Sun. 18 Dec.—Fine day, Nor'west wind. Worthington [shepherd] went to Blackford. McRae [shepherd], Berry [musterer] and Ross went to Algidus. Surveyors shifted camp to station. A[lfred]. Comyns [boss of the board] arrived at 4 p.m. from Snowdon. Shearers rolling up all day.[28] Wrote to Mother.

Fri. 6 Jan.—Fine Day. Sou'west wind. Shearing all day ½ bred wethers.[29] Ross went to bush for wood but the wheel of the dray fell to pieces in the river coming home. Ross got washed downstream, & Nugget the shafter was nearly drowned.[30] Fagan [musterer] & Berry brought up rams from Gunn's. Self went to yards most of day where Les and shepherds were drafting Redcliffe hoggets. 7,956 sheep shorn.

Tue. 10 Jan.— Fine Day. Sou'west wind. Shepherds mustered from station to Smyte. Scott [Tommy Scott, the shed shepherd] & Woodley [musterer] took sheep out over Turtons Saddle. Ross Anderson, & Os [shepherd] carted in hay per motor car. Les doing odd jobs & mustered Lower Flat in afternoon. Self very busy with housework. A joke, just a glorified sludge.

Wed. 1 Feb.—Fine Day. Sou'west wind. Shearing all day. Waggons went to store with wool. Leslie & shepherds keeping ewes up to shed. Self & Dick [son] went to yards in morning and down to top flat in afternoon. . . . Seed birthday cake for Lad [Leslie's brother, shepherd]. Wrote to Leo & Mrs. Fagan. 27,983 sheep shorn.

Fri. 3 Feb.—Fine Day. Nor'west wind. Sou'west storm from 4 p.m. Les and Alf squaring up with shearers all day. Finished shearing at 10 p.m. Self washed. Stuart went to store with wool. Ross cutting crops till the reaper broke down. Shepherds doing odd jobs. Worthington left for holidays. (Nell 1908-1912 Station Diaries)

The Double Hill entries in these years point to both the remarkable scale of the shearing operation in duration, in size, in labor intensiveness, and the complexity of its division. The size of shearing mobs, like the scale of mustering, is linked to the expansiveness of country. Shepherds were mustering sheep off the hills from the furthest boundaries of each of the stations (entries note going through both Turtons and Macintosh's saddles to the back country), filling the shed, drafting and culling, and taking the mobs back out to their respective paddocks and "countries." Besides shearing-related duties, the shepherds, the gardener, the wagon driver, and station manager Leslie Nell continued their routine daily and yearly duties: carting firewood in and matagouri out, shoeing horses, carting in hay, cutting crops with the reaper, fixing fences, and killing. Mrs. Nell's diaries give a sense of some social life—the horse races, a birthday, the surveyor coming to tea—as well as social interaction on the station, friction between the station cook and the shearers' cook, for example. Throughout she systematically documents the comings and goings of workers, visitors, and family, suggesting regular contact among the gorge properties. The weather, health matters, letters and presents sent and received as markers of links into and out of the gorge are carefully noted. Her own domestic and farm-related duties include picking gooseberries and cherries, boiling red currants for jam, making beer, baking, washing, ironing, sewing, housework, drafting in the home yards, making fancy work. Elsewhere in the diaries we learn that she rides her pony, raises a pet lamb, transplants cabbage plants, and takes photographs of shearing at Double Hill.

In 1930 the shearing moved to the Glenrock shed because the shearers' accommodation was better, and the transportation costs for the bales slightly less; before this the ewes were shorn mainly in the Double Hill shed and the dry sheep at Glenrock (Ensor 1990:14). In 1937 the final shearing tally was 21,550 and 523 bales of wool. By this time the Double Hill shed needed upgrading, the accommodations for shearers improving and new sheep and cattle yards erecting since the old yards were too far from the shed (Ensor 1990:40). As of 30 December 1939 the combined properties were running 26,960 sheep including lambs, and 164 cattle. Then by February 1940, Double Hill was run separately from Glenrock and Glenariffe when their leases were transferred to Peter's brothers Duncan and Roderick respectively.

Years after Leslie and Mrs. Nell had left Double Hill, shearing continued to follow similar routines for the runholder and shepherds—a combination of shed duties and the mustering in and taking out of sheep. Peter Ensor thinks back:

> Shearing was finished in good time this year—actually 28 January [1941]—and the shearers paid off. There was no contract work in those days [it was introduced in 1947] so paying off the eighteen or twenty men with their individual tallies on time was quite a job, with everyone trying to get away as quickly as possible. With the help of Duncan and Rod, we would finally say goodbye to the gang.
>
> With a fairly fast gang working and shearing the ewes, organization had to be up to scratch to keep things going smoothly. A day's diary entry of 6 January was an example: "Cut out 2 tooth ewe mobs—between Creek's mob—Camp paddock mob and started on Glenariffe flat [a location] ewes. Duncan, McGrimmon and Chisholm mustered Glenariffe flat mob and brought to yards.[31] McKenyse &

Sinclair mustered Top Long into Camp paddock. Emerson and Hampton brought Camp Paddock ewes to yards before breakfast. Two-tooth mob out to Twitch Paddock. Between Creeks and Camp Paddock ewes to Triangle Paddock. McGrimmon and Chisholm up to Double Hill to muster Middle flat in morning." (Ensor 1990:34)

The Woolshed

While the shearers start their day "on the board" at 7:30, the farmer always begins the day earlier. Before shearing, all the sheep have to be "mustered in" to the yards. They are often drenched for parasites, and sometimes they are drafted into smaller mobs on the basis of age. Old merinos may be culled for sale down country. The farmer's obligation is to keep the shed full of clean, dry sheep for the shearers. The best shed can hold enough sheep for an entire day of shearing in case of rain. Once the sheep are in the shed, the presser assumes the responsibility for moving the sheep from pen to pen and ultimately into each shearer's catching pen. In the shed, farmers keep an eye on how the sheep are handled by the shearing gang, but with contract shearing most are careful not to hover. Pens should not be crowded because overcrowding can cause "pen stain" as manure-covered rumps brush against other fleeces,[32] or it can cause a smother as sheep lose their footing and can be trodden to death. Very few farmers will allow the use of a dog in the shed and most abhor the practice. They watch too for careless shearing; the shearers must work fast, but not so fast that they cut the sheep or shear unevenly or with second cuts to the fleece. After shearing, which leaves sheep weakened for a day or two, the farmer has to get the mobs back onto good feed quickly to "recharge their batteries." Shearing, especially the machine shearing used today on some gentler-country properties, stresses the sheep as the animal works without full fleece to keep warm in spring weather.

A shearing day consists of four two-hour "runs" from 7:30-9:30, from 10:00 until 12:00, from 1:00-3:00 and from 3:30-5:30. The shed runs to the minute. During breaks, shearers roll and smoke a cigarette or sharpen their blades; blades last for about 1,000 sheep. Morning and afternoon teas are served promptly at 9:00 and at 3:30 at the shed; and lunch at noon and an evening meal at 7:00 are served in the cookshop.[33] At Glenariffe the gang is housed in basic shearing quarters near the woolshed and yards, and the cook uses the cookshop adjacent to the homestead to prepare meals. Often nine, occasionally ten, shearers are in the gang, with three shedhands on the board, a woolroller and a "wool-classer" working on the wool table, a "presser," and a cook in the contractor's employ. Contractor Paul Karaitiana's gang of ten can blade shear 900 to 1,000 merino ewes in a day, averaging together 220 merinos in a two-hour run; some merino fleece cuts more easily than Corriedale, but merinos are slightly slower and more expensive to shear since they have extra folds on their necks, some more than others depending on breeding schemes.[34] Blade shearing moves much slower than machine shearing, with a good blade shearer able to shear between 120 and 160 sheep on a good day compared with 200 sheep for a machine shearer. In machine sheds, loud radio music often blares and the constant noise of the machines hums above the sheep hooves on the shed gratings; sheep are more nervous in a machine shed showing sensitivity to the machine noise, the sunlight, and the shadows created by constant movement. Many, although not all, blade sheds are quiet and evocative of the past.

Shearers keep their own informal tallies as they pull sheep from the pen, and strategically leave the most difficult sheep to pull out until immediately before the break to give themselves that extra minute or two in order to maximize their tally. At the end of each "run" the farmer tallies the sheep as he releases them from the "counting out" pens and enters each shearer's total into the station tally book. Today on contract, the contractor pays shearers for the total number of sheep they shear so the pace they set is steady and demanding.[35] A fleece comes off the sheep in a single piece, is grabbed quickly by a shedhand, known as a "rouse-about" and "thrown" with an expert flick of the wrist to land spread out on the classing table where it is rapidly "skirted" by another shedhand and classed by the wool-classer. Teamwork, a collective blend of expertise and coordination and the essential social formation at this harvest time "hasn't changed at all." Nor has the routine of station life for a shearing gang changed. While the shearers emphasize how hard shearing work is as one attempts to maximize one's efforts in an attempt to balance speed with care, the contractor's wife who works as cook emphasizes the financial risk confronting him as he attempts to beat the weather and the road conditions from job to job.

In part because of scale, speed is of the essence in a shearing shed, and a well-designed shed operating on a "gravity flow" principle enables the process to work in a direct line from one end of the shed to the other. Despite differing ages and floor plans, all sheds—typically rectangular with the woolroom attached as a wing from the middle or the end either in a T-shape or an L-shape—contain a number of discrete areas: (1) from outside, sheep move through a series of holding pens with raised slatted-timber flooring until they end up in the "catching pen" from where the shearer retrieves each animal; (2) the woolboard, or shearing board, is softened with lanolin over time and colored with spots of blood, manure and wear patterns from use, and each shearer has a "stand" on the woolboard and "porthole" out of which the shorn sheep slides down a ramp into the "counting-out pen"; (3) with wooltable and press, the woolroom is often at an end of the woolboard in the older sheds and in newer sheds the woolboard is often a raised platform in the center of the shed, which saves the shedhands from bending down to pick up each fleece and reduces the distance they travel from each shearer to the classing table.

The earliest New Zealand woolsheds, built to cope with large numbers of sheep and to keep wool bales dry in remote areas, were patterned on Australian ones, usually made of machine-sawn timber and occasionally of stone or masonry; often sheds were clad in corrugated galvanized iron as they are today with what Geoffrey Thornton (1986:111), mistakenly evoking the visual over the experiential, has described as an "unhappy visual effect." However, Thornton rightly notes:

The woolshed is, in its architectural form, the most striking symbol of the New Zealand pastoral landscape. . . . Sometimes it is the sheer size that impresses. Other woolsheds have a delightful arrangement of form giving interest to their composition. . . . We can even accept the ubiquitous corrugated iron as a legitimate and remarkably permanent cladding for walls, especially when painted in the traditional red oxide. Certainly as a roof material it has proved its worth, painted or not.

One should not overlook the complementary features of any woolshed: the assemblage of yards for drafting sheep. Where there are unpainted weathered timbered posts and rails they form a most worthy accessory that frequently helps to meld the woolshed structure into the general landscape. . . . [T]he mostly unselfconscious design of these structures has led to vernacular building and an essential part of our built environment. (1986:113)

In *Erewhon*, Samuel Butler (1987[1872]:24) claims to be refreshed by the "semblance of antiquity (precious in a new country)" evoked by the cathedral-like woolshed "with aisles on either side full of pens for the sheep, a great nave, at the upper end of which the shearers work, and a further space for wool sorters and packers" (1987[1872]:24), although he noted that the oldest shed in settlement at the time was no more than seven years old. Woolsheds still have this effect, encoded as their wooden interiors are with the cumulative smell of sheep and the knotches of shearers gone by. The cultural significance of the woolshed may also derive from the role it plays, like the yards and the tailing yards, as a physical and conceptual intermediate space between uncultivated pastoral land and the homestead: as the ultimate container for the expansiveness of stock activity and human labor, it is the physical site for harvesting a product, the fleece, and for concentrating the labor force (farmers, family, shearers and classer); and it is the conceptual site for distilling the landscape and pastoral activities of the year into fleece. It is sensual both in terms of its warm sweaty lanolin and ovine excretory smells, the sounds of hooves clicking on the grease-stained slats, and blades moving against each other. "Hanging around the shed" during shearing time reveals much about the human/animal interface on a property. In the yards and in the shed itself, the sheep come as close to the homestead as they ever do. Fusing farm and homesite in the built environment, the woolshed is also a communal site for social activities, such as dog trials, family reunions, dances and sometimes weddings.

The Fleece

Wool is the farmers' primary product both in quantity and in the value it carries on the market. The fleece precisely reflects the condition of a year's nourishment and of farming practice. The factors considered in valuing wool are the weight of the fleeces—measured both as a greasy fleece and in terms of its yield as a clean fleece—and its micron.[36] While some farmers obtain certificates enabling them to "class" their own wool, most of them pay a classer, the highest-paid worker in the woolshed, to do the job. The classer examines the fleece as a whole, taking into account the finest wool around the shoulders and the thicker wool toward the rump. Fleeces are expertly folded and tossed into "bins," categorized usually in terms of main-line fine, average, and strong as well as second grade or inferior wool. When full, a bin is pressed into a bale, which is clipped shut, branded with the name of the station, the number of the bale in sequence, and the classer's insignia. In the record book, the number of each bale and its contents are recorded; this information is sent with the shipment to the woolstore. In addition to the main line of fleece, there are bins and bales for belly wool,[37] topknots, skirting wool, sandy and seedy backs if they are present, and "daggy" wool (clots of dirt around the hind quarters) and "pizzle [urine] stained" wool from the wethers.

When the wool reaches the woolstore, its site of connection with the market system, the manufacturing potential of the clip is tested and the buyer assesses the standard of its preparation for sale. Two core samples grab a section of most of the fleeces in a bale. A horizontal core sample is taken for the buyers and goes on show. Buyers inspect core samples in terms of their testing specifications, appearance and touch. The vertical sample goes for testing that records the yield and micron. If the wool has been classed well, the bales for a line of fine merino wool will produce a test result that is the average of the microns of the fleeces in the bale. If marginal fleeces have been included, they can affect the core sample, and lower the value of the entire bale. Half a micron can make a difference of a few dollars per kilogram and several dollars per sheep in price, even more with superfine fleeces; a bale can hold up to but not over 200 kilograms in weight. Poorly skirted fleeces and inconsistent classing can hurt the farmer, but if too much of the fleece is skirted he can also lose money by producing less main-line wool.

Turning fiber, such as wool, into a standardized commodity is difficult in comparison with the production of synthetic fibers because the growers are working with an animal of a certain genetic potential managed with human labor in a specific environment. Wool production is transformative as it converts grass into fiber through the medium of the sheep. The fleece signifies the landscape and the careful balance of nourishment, provided by the farmer and the climate, for the fleece to reach its full potential. Simultaneously it is a measure of ovine excellence and the social prestige of the property.[38]

Full sets of wool samples indicate the condition of a property. When buyers examine the samples prior to the auction of the wool clips, they read flock genetics, the condition of country and their mutual interaction, as well as the skill of the farmer as grower and classer. The wool reflects a series of decisions made by the farmer as he treads that line between "cultivating" the product, and giving in to biological and environmental conditions at the interface of what farmers refer to as the natural and the cultural. His capacity to "get it right" depends upon numerous decisions: which stock to sell, which rams to keep or cull, when to put the ram to the ewe, where to put the ewes for lambing, when and when not to intervene in lambing, how much feed to give, how much to skirt off the fleece, where to draw the line between fine and medium and strong wool lines in classing. And even if the farmer "gets it right," "in the game of farming" climate and market conditions—conceptualized similarly—"may not be on his side."

Let me illustrate the market intricacies. During the Wool Auction at the Christchurch Wool Exchange in October 1990, hundreds of lots were selling so fast that woolgrowers had to make crucial on-the-spot decisions. Should the wool go in this sale or be held until the next? Between the two wool sales was a national election (resulting in the dramatic ousting of the Labour party by the National party) that might affect the value of the New Zealand dollar; should it lose value, it would be to their advantage. At a sale in Timaru the previous day the wool prices were down, especially for fine merino lines between 17.7 and 18.3 microns. A family could hold a line of especially fine wool, or all of the bales, out of the sale and gamble on the market getting better. In addition, they could place on some of the lots a minimum price reserve that auctioneers had to get for the lot to be sold. Or they could decide, as one did, to instruct the stock and station company to make the decision to sell the wool or to "pass" if the price offered was not high enough, as happened to one of the station's sale lots. As it turns out, the buyers had been impressed with the property's three bales of superfine merino at 16.7 microns; it was good in color with a whitish, greyish cast to it, clean and fine in diameter, with good length of staple, strength, evenness of crimp, and lack of vegetation. The bales "topped the sale," and the farmer and I spent the afternoon examining each of the fine wool samples in the buyers' shed for a comparison. The gamble to sell paid off in a year when wool prices had dropped dramatically because of the release into the market of stockpiled Australian wool, the high value of the New Zealand dollar, the reduction of foreign exchange available for spending on nonoil imports in oil-importing countries during the Persian Gulf crisis, and the withdrawal of two of New Zealand's most important woolbuyers, Russia and China, whose wool markets were in disarray in the aftermath of Perestroika and the Tiananmen Square massacre.[39]

Similarly, by resituating actor-centered analysis in ecologically driven anthropology, Robert Netting has written that the alpine Swiss peasant householder was "confronted continually by critical choices" (1981:40). Netting's neofunctionalist description of "making a living" in a subsistence economy of mixed mountain agriculture, called *almwirtschaft*,[40] portrays a generalized population in a state of homeostatic equilibrium, while allowing for an internal dynamism where human and livestock populations and environment are interdependent:

> Although the tasks and the tools of survival were common, the decisions on how to allocate time and effort, whether or not to sell a cow or buy a meadow, and what risk to take in the continual guessing game with the weather were ones that directly affected the family's livelihood. Everyone needed the same counters to play this game, but individual skill, knowledge, and luck influenced the outcome. (Netting 1981:40)

Managing or cultivating stock to grow wool is using what one knows of nature
in its multiple senses—weather, feed, genetics and breeding, animal behavior—
as well as the dynamics of market conditions to make both work together in
one's favor. The job, as Alastair Ensor put it to me, is all about balancing and
averaging costs and benefits; like others, he said that farming is really about the
law of averages both in terms of calculating feed and in terms of the decisions
made as wool is classed. As with mustering, it means knowing the formula but
engaging with deviations. Working in the woolshed then highlights the centrality of classificatory systems in farming whether one is breeding stock or producing wool. Sheep-station families live with constant uncertainty, subject to the
vagaries of the weather or the market and are engaged in a constant struggle to
"do one's best" with the stock and land they know while acknowledging that
even that is not enough to ensure success.

Lambing and Loss

One challenge provided by the extremes in climate includes snowstorms, "the
hazard of the high country" (Gardner 1971:200) whose aura "has depended upon
its reputation for hardship" (McLeod 1972:153). Snowstorms provide a way of
talking about the uncertainties of climate (including floods and droughts and
devastating nor'west winds) and a way of thinking about the uncertainty of market conditions. Runholders often made the analogic link between weather and
the market as external forces against which control is futile and minor modification possible, and speculate that the high country is coping better than most New
Zealanders with the current economic crisis because they are "geared for" uncontrollable factors that characterize high-country history, such as variable
mountain-weather conditions, and boom-and-bust market cycles.[41] Their responses to parallel constraints of geography, climate, markets, and land-tenure
legislation are adaptive, transformative, creative and resilient.

Falling most acutely at the intersection of fierce weather conditions and
farming productivity is spring lambing, a time of vulnerability and of labor-
intensive activity where social insurance and farming smarts are imperative.
Lambing begins at Glenaan Station when the pregnant Corriedale ewes are taken
to protected, out-of-the-way hill blocks to be left alone to lamb. On 29 September 1990 the ewes were taken to Confusion, Waterfall, Isolation, and Duncan's
blocks (see map 5.2) to begin lambing on 6 October. The superfine merino ewes,
bred to carefully selected pedigreed rams, are treated like a stud flock and placed
in the most sheltered paddocks close to the homestead; careful treatment of
stock correlates with their worth. In contrast to other pastoral cultures such as
Scotland, merino lambing is distinctive in its need for independence, and the
farmer seldom intervenes unless he is working with a stud flock where the ewe
is valuable both for her fine wool and her progeny; orphan stud lambs will be
hand-fed or put onto a lambless ewe whereas flock orphan lambs might be left
alone "for nature to take its course" because the ewe's "inability to lamb naturally" might be passed on.[42] Not interfering is a deliberate part of farming man-

agement. This the Glenaans told me is "very much a high-country thing" and that "it gives nature its best chance to work in a productive way."

Concerned that "all of this must seem incomprehensible" to me, Hamish and Belinda worked to help me reconfigure my emotions. I was socialized into a culture of loss, while I was simultaneously prodding to understand the cultural logic of breeding. During one of these lessons, we went round the lambing paddocks after especially bad weather to pick up dead lambs:

> Belinda and I took the quad [four-wheel motor bike] up the airstrip to the top paddock just beside the Bridge paddock and gathered several dead lambs. This is a less sheltered paddock with no elite merinos in it. The weather (snow yesterday and cold weekend) made lambing more stressful. Some of the dead lambs had been picked over by the seagulls. White blots on the green of the paddocks, smelling of rot. They seemed too far away from life for one to think of them as lambs any more and the numbers made the singularity of a life less compelling and immediate. Lambs were lifted by their rear legs and placed in plastic containers on the front; as they accumulated they were moved to the trailer. (Field notes 1.x.90; see map 5.3)

To protect the biological integrity of the paddocks Belinda would take the quad to the edge of a paddock at some distance from the main mob. She picked up the lambs she could reach directly and walked in lightly to get the rest.

> We moved from the top paddock and through toward the Bridge paddock where the cows were all gathered. . . . From there we moved to Jim's paddock with 22 dead lambs. These were the weaker sheep. Live lambs watched with their mothers, staying close as they followed them across the paddocks. Some were suckling. Some mothers would lick the lamb's tail.
>
> Down the airstrip again to the next paddock on the western side and through that to the very sheltered paddock just below the house. Only one was there; Belinda said the shelter made a significant difference. We reversed our steps and looked in on the cattle where there were two calves—one close to its mother, the other a black one asleep on the grass. Belinda checked the trough to see if water reticulation to the paddock was working.
>
> We went to the horses' paddock around the hut and picked up five lamb bodies including "lambchops" or "little big head" whom Hamish had pulled out of a ewe on Saturday (when it half snowed and rained all day). The lamb was placed in the airing cupboard to warm up and taken back into the paddock to be with its mother. They fed it milk from the mother in a bottle for the colostrum. The ewe did not take the lamb back, and it developed pneumonia, dying in the night.
>
> Then down to the dump, which is on the north side of the road by Stony Creek roughly where the stream dumps out into the river. The dump is over the edge of the cliff and looking down I could see dead sheep and lambs and smell the stench. As we hurled the lambs off the back of the quad we counted them up for a total of 32 which

didn't seem to surprise Belinda. Hamish expects an 85% lambing rate
from the merinos.

The matter-of-fact, but noncallous, response to death measured in numbers is
cultivated and reinforced so much so that they worked to cultivate it in me.
Belinda reminded me constantly that I couldn't "get soft about the lambs" because "you couldn't farm if you did." Although stud lambs are ear-tagged nu-
merically for individual identification, I was told not to individualize the flock
lambs by memorizing a telltale mark; in the tailing process the gang called one
small lamb with a brown patch on his back "Wee Dinkums"; we all began to
take note of where he was in the process because he was so easily differentiated.

Snow losses always hover as a threat. In *Station Life in New Zealand*
(1883), Lady Barker devotes Chapter XX to "The New Zealand Snow-storm of
1867" at Steventon Station (Broomielaw) on the south bank of the upper Selwyn
River in the hills between the Waimakariri and the Rakaia Rivers (see map I.1);
not only is this letter the most frequently cited from *Station Life*, but it is the
most-often-repeated snowstorm narrative in New Zealand literature, weaving its
way into successive settler accounts and mainstream published histories.[43] Toward the end of her story Lady Barker begins to calculate the loss at half the
flock and all, or at least 90 percent, of the lambs.[44] This, she notes, cannot compare with the sufferings and losses of those further into the distant "back-
country" ranges, or those on the plains where sheep had taken shelter under high
riverbanks where "the tragedy of the creeks was enacted on a still larger scale"
(1883:173). As a closing device it is standard in such accounts simultaneously to
factually enumerate the losses while diminishing them against the greater losses
elsewhere; like stock and land, emotions are managed. For example, of the July
1945 snow David McLeod writes, "Compared to the plains and foothills we es-
caped fairly lightly, for there was only a foot at Grasmere and, being a southwest snow, it did not deepen much higher up; but it was followed by three weeks
of some of the severest frosts we ever had" (1980:72).

In November 1987 I received such an understated letter from Belinda at
Glenaan. She begins,

> Three weeks ago [13 October] we had *a rather* unexpected snow,
> which was over two feet at the top of the airstrip and over eighteen
> inches on the lawn. *The worst aspect* of the snow was that we were in
> the middle of lambing and calving. All the cows are calving in the
> paddock and we had a few cows with milk fever, one died but we
> saved another five by *pouring bottles of this and that* into them like
> magnesium and calcium. *Quite a few of* our merino ewes particularly
> the older Mount Cook ewes [of good pedigree, known on the station
> as "elites"] got sleepy sickness; *they weren't very easy* to save. We
> had the tractor going around all the paddocks with a snowplough so
> the stock could get at the grass. The snow was around for a week, but
> *we were only without power* for two days and the telephone just over
> twenty-four hours. *We weren't as badly off as you* were recently with
> your [U.S.] snow. (Emphases added)

If we compare her letter with Hamish's station diaries of the time,[45] we find in the latter a factual documentation of loss, ending with the routine killing of mutton:

> 13 October—Started snowing at 6 a.m. 37 cm at house and 56 cm at top of paddocks by 2 p.m. Power and phone off.
>
> 14 October—Snow ploughed for all stock in paddocks. Phone restored 1:40 p.m. Power restored 4:30 p.m. Approximately half snow gone by 5:00 p.m.
>
> 15 October—Worked on cows with milk fever, 5, plus 5 ewes with sleepy sickness. Snow ploughing second round.
>
> 16 October—Worked on one cow that didn't get up. Cut up dead cow for dog tucker.
>
> 17 October—Picked up snow deaths. 5 old MA ewes. 55 merino main mob lambs 15 merino elite lambs. 2 calves. 1 cow. 1 yearling. 1 2-year heifer. Killed mutton.

The entries illustrate pragmatism fused with the humanitarianism necessary for sustaining husbandry.

Hamish explained to me that the paddock is "a total environment" where any human step into a paddock at lambing time changes it. A ewe picks her own spot to lamb, and once the waters break, the spot is defined and demarcated. Lambs know where they are born and have a homing instinct, which is why they resist mustering and head back to familiar country. The Glenaan tailing muster in 1990 when we brought in the ewes and their lambs from the steep sunny north-facing "lambing blocks" to the yards illustrates these challenges and the processes of mustering on a much smaller scale than the autumn muster.

> We mustered the sheep through two very steep blocks—Duncan's (30 hectares) and Dead Horse (43 hectares)—and into a third paddock-sized block—Trig (14 hectares)—and from there they went directly into the paddock in preparation for tailing. . . . In the first block the gate was at the bottom of the hill, and in the second the gate they needed to go through was half way up, although there was another at the bottom; we needed to know where fencelines and gates were in order to position the sheep for movement from block to block. . . . Hamish split the familiar and the unfamiliar across the beats to accommodate my presence and Marty's. [See maps 5.1, 5.2, 5.3 to trace mustering route.]
>
> The best mothers hold their ground the firmest, which makes mustering them and their lambs difficult. This year the musters were harder than Hamish and Belinda remembered them being in the past because easterlies blew most of the days and made the sheep drift in the wrong direction [merinos tend to walk into the wind and the yards were to the west]. Also because of the breeding schedule the lambs

> were especially small. . . . Strategies to get them to move are hitting
> the fence noisily, tapping the backs of ewes with the stick, as well as
> "wayho-ing" and clapping hands.
>
> [Eventually] we drove the ewes and lambs from the paddock
> and down the lane toward the yards. Belinda drove the Land Rover
> around the fence line of the paddock and to the back, and then we all
> waved rattles (empty plastic oil containers with a few stones inside)
> and yelled and clapped to move them forward and away from us. The
> dogs ran back and forth along the back holding the line. Then we
> pushed the ewes and lambs down the lane, all pushing hard behind,
> and drawing the scrim [mesh netting] out behind them at the final
> moment past the cluster of pines beside the shed and into the sheep-
> yards and then from pen to pen and into the shed where the ewes and
> lambs were drafted. (Field notes 5.xi.90)

To muster ewes and lambs is particularly challenging because "these hill country lambs have never had human contact and are likely to make a break for freedom to the country they know." If accidentally left behind, "a lamb will attach
itself to its patch and may even mother up to a tree." The instinctive connection
attaching lambs to their birthplace as land imprints upon them similarly roots
farming families organically to the station. Metaphorically human connection to
territory is in the blood. Furthering a link only made exogenously, boarding-
school masters would refer to the colleges as "holding pens" for high-country
children who (like sheep) would be sure to return to their patch.

This documentation, mine and theirs, and experiences of loss—sometimes
of an entire year's lambing "drop" in the case of snow and of the lambs on the
flat as it washed away—promotes practicality and naturalizes resilience. Burdon, for example, has written, "it was realised (in 1867) that storms were part of
the scheme of things and must be expected at greater or lesser intervals"
(1938:98).[46] Formulaic phrases reflect a prevalent and progressive ethos of "getting on with it," and linguistically create a capable, coping mentality that moves
people forward, and is illustrated, in the phrase—voiced often—"and so I had to
get on with it." A woman spoke of the "plain bloody slog" of domestic work in
midcentury noting that "you had to do it or it doesn't get done" referring to getting up at 3:00 A.M. to light the stove and cook chops for the musterers. And her
daughter-in-law, a generation later, used the words "you must go with it" to
stress the importance of adapting to climate and environment. Encoding landscape in character, a boarding-school matron portrayed children from high-
country farms as "practical, responsible and capable"; "they have been depended
upon to be sensible . . . and seem quite mature"; they "can't control the weather,
can't kick, it affects their attitudes and creates a steadiness in the boarders."

§   §   §

Implicit and reinforcing farming and life philosophies reflect a sense of having
little control over environmental processes[47] and yet of continuously and progressively evolving farming practices in a boxer shuffle with, rather than
against, them. In prose considered "high flown" and dated by some farmers,

McLeod (1980:246) claims that his fellow runholders have no illusions—"day by day they and the animals that they have tamed do battle against wind and water, fire and flood, heat and bitter cold. . . . They do not seek to conquer nature, only to live with her upon her terms, learning by trial and often costly error what she will tolerate and what resist." He continues, "This has been the history of the high-country stations for more than 100 years—the gradual learning of nature's rules in a land where there was no [European] pre-history to guide . . . grudgingly at first . . . but ever more widely, the self-discipline which is required to make us obey the rules of nature has been accepted as necessity, and with this discipline and our courage and ingenuity we can look forward" (1980:246).[48] One farmer in reading this passage said that it was "a load of crap," the generational rhetoric of those who "farmed for Mother England"; perhaps he recognized a colonial rhetoric that claims to value skill and enterprise over social position (Ritvo 1987:79). Bob Brown (1993:325), in addressing the twelfth grasslands conference, sees the serious threats of hawkweed and rabbit invasion to sustainable pastoral use as equal to the weather. McLeod's portraits of the high country, like those of his contemporaries, are destabilized as part of a senior generation's nostalgia for a singular past, a past in which the tweed-clad runholder managed the station while leaving most of the physical labor to the staff.

"High flown" and "a load of crap" in romanticizing hard work perhaps, but David McLeod's critical nexus of sheep, men and dogs "united in partnership" within the constraints of geographic scale, climatic extremes, and fluctuating markets hints at a critical configuration for an anthropology of high-country grassland pastoral communities. Like dogs and men,[49] sheep as a more critical resource than land in agropastoral communities traverse that land, but sheep, especially high-country merinos, pick the routes, creating persistent traces on the landscape. Merinos transform the grass to fleece, mediate between the land and the product, wool, and as Arnold Strickon has suggested for cattle "ranching complexes" (1965:255), between humans and the environment.[50] Merinos are remarkably transformative agents in this landscape. They hold up very well. Until recent diversification they have been the most reliable resource in a dynamic environmental field in which country, stock and humans engage equally in complex interaction.

Eugenia Shanklin and Riva Berleant-Schiller (1983:xv), as well as Tim Ingold (1980), focus on the relationship between livestock production and the social arrangements they create and preserve within the broader context of the political, economic, symbolic and ecological implications of livestock; and while noting that the cultural ecology aspect is best developed in anthropological studies,[51] they urge us to attend to "the ideological and ethnic identity correlates" of these systems (Shanklin and Berleant-Schiller 1983:xvi). They invite consideration of the consequences of the conditions of country and stock for the formation of cultural identity and spatiality.[52] Indeed if "the way men relate to animals can be used as a key to read about the way human beings conceive of themselves and the ultimate meaning of their own lives" (Willis 1974:7),[53] and if, as Mary Hufford (1992:249) illustrates, "we find one species, human beings, using the territorial signals of other species . . . to lay claim to a variety of landscapes" then merinos no less than working dogs provide a way of conceptualizing a particular kind of placement in country. Blatantly, what they signify in their centrality is, as McLeod suggests, a measure of skill, of discipline, and of resilience. But through breeding schemes and increasingly sophisticated biotechnological techniques, sheep are the device for fine-tuning pastoral responses to markets and the device through which farmers work within unyielding country that limits innovation in ways that preserve a seemingly bold-faced continuity while simultaneously dislocating it in ways that reflect the italicized instability of the country they farm.

Practical philosophies and farming techniques reflect also peoples' containment with their stock within an environment that both creates, and is created by, high-country farmers and that, in turn, leads to and reflects an attachment to land based on both the idea and actuality of its rugged extremes, its uncontrollable weather patterns, and its degradation by invasive plants.[54] When set against the ethnographic record, narratives of loss, embedded in poetry and local oral narratives, as well as in documentary and published materials, and the development of stock management practices serve as creative responses to climatic, environmental, biological and market-based uncertainty and assured fluidity. Taken together with other discursive practices within the ethnographic record, they can be examined anthropologically, as another high-country trope that contributes to a particular understanding and construction of identity at a time in New Zealand when high-country station families are defining themselves actively within nationalist discourses as "people of the land."[55] They see themselves aligned together with their stock and their dogs, as contained within the environment and created agonistically through the challenges it provides. Here as one farmer said and others echoed in a variety of ways indicating both genetic affinity and naturalized resilience, "One learns to be at one with the environment. You go with the environment. You can't fight it . . . you take it on the chin."

Notes

1. I incorporate the work of pastoral scientists but do so knowing that their expertise is often challenged by runholders. In reading a draft of this chapter, one runholder questioned my incorporation of Douglas and Allen by reminding me that they showed poor judgment when they wrote in a myxomatosis submission that an Otago run "didn't have a rabbit problem" and was "properly run."

2. Progressive properties are diversifying through stud-flock lines (distinct from main lines), pedigreed superfine lines of stock, in which particular rams are selected for breeding to "an elite" ewe flock.

3. First used at Glenariffe station in 1963 as a form of insurance against harsh winters and late springs, silage is essentially "grass preserved for winter" through the anaerobic fermentation of finely cut grass compressed in large covered pits where the acid/pH content is sufficiently high that bacteria cannot grow. After the winter, the grass begins growing again usually about 20 September. The grass is cut when it is about a foot high (usually on this property around 11 November), as high as possible but before it goes to seed or goes rank. Once cut down, it is raked to partly dry and mechanically gathered and

cut and put in the pits. One farmer said that making silage is "like harvesting every-where" and in the gorge it is labor intensive requiring one to mow, the rake driver of the forage harvester, two or three lorry drivers to carry grass to the pit, and a tractor and driver to compress the grass in the pit. Farmers differ in how dry they think the silage should be. The machine-syndicate operator told me that grass is like fresh apricots, silage like dried apricots or muesli, and hay like Wheatbix; if grass is 80-90 percent moisture, then silage might be 60 percent and hay 10-20 percent moisture. Glenaan station, in 1990, had three silage pits but by mid-August had only opened two; the third could be left for another year, but once open the exposure to oxygen means that it has to be used that year or resealed (although one "loses in doing it") because aerobic fermentation will begin. Silage is rationed carefully and daily as the machine syndicate manager "fed out" be-tween July and September, but not to all the mobs; for example, as of 17 August the sta-tion was feeding the hoggets and two-tooths on grass, the merino ewes and wethers on hay, and the Corriedale ewes on silage.

4. See Gary Hawke (1987) and Brian Easton (1992) for convenient reviews of cur-rent economic conditions and the history of agricultural policy.

5. See Mike Floate's *Guide to Tussock Grassland Farming* for a useful overview of the ways in which "pastoral farmers must . . . use the most efficient, the most economi-cally viable, the most ecologically sustainable systems which also have the flexibility to integrate with other uses" (Allan Kane in Floate 1992:2). See especially Douglas and McRae (1992). Also see O'Connor (1987), and O'Connor et al. (1990). Some runholders rejected these sources as uninformed, trusting instead their own knowledge.

6. In instances where our work increasingly has possibilities as "applied hermeneu-tics," such as in advocacy work (Myers 1988:609, cf. Dominy 1990b), our informants may take particular responsibility for certain kinds of accuracy. After reading some sec-tions of a draft, an informant told me that he was concerned that "where you get one or two farming facts wrong the wrong people . . . [agricultural scholars] will hone in on that and fault the entire work for the wrong reasons—your lack of knowledge about farming rather than your analysis about our way of life." I followed his suggestion that various farmers proof this chapter for accuracy in farming details.

7. Especially rich in their detail are Peter Newton's *Wayleggo* (1947) and *High Country Days* (1949). See also David McLeod's accounts of his earlier years as a mus-terer and as a runholder at Grasmere in the Waimakariri valley. A. E. Woodhouse (1950) edited a collection *New Zealand Farm and Station Verse, 1850-1950*.

8. Macintosh's is known as Redcliffe Saddle on topographic maps.

9. Nor is it unusual for musterers to take out a pillow, and for some bosses to sup-ply a generator for electric light and a radio.

10. The language of flying must be differentiated from the language of walking as the 'copter went "right down to Boundary Creek," "up over Double Hill," and "up over the saddle."

11. For a comparative study of place attachment, see Hufford's (1992) analysis of foxhunting in the New Jersey Pine Barrens in which she traces the construction of place through the movement of hounds and foxes in a Chaseworld.

12. When I returned to Glenaan in 1990, we caught up on station pets, especially those working dogs that had died since my last trip. Slaughtering an animal for food, putting a flock ewe out of her misery, and ending the life of a sick working dog or a horse differ in technique and emotional cost. I was told that to put a ewe out of her misery would not be difficult in that one "wouldn't even need to think about it" because she was one of many, whereas it's very different in the instance of a sheepdog or a horse "who has worked for you." Shooting an animal or slaughtering it is immediate and therefore easier to deal with; these things, however, are never done easily, and I was told by this runholder that "my capacity to do it sometimes frightens me, that the capacity to take a

life is a relatively uncomplicated and straightforward thing, but the nearer the animal is to the homestead, the harder it is to do." In the case of one sheepdog, riddled with cancer, it was so difficult that euthanasia at the veterinarian's surgery was selected. Working dogs and household pets are also disposed of differently; on this property they were buried along a fence line bordered with pines one paddock removed from the homestead; dead livestock—lambs, sheep, and cattle—are thrown into the dump, although children often negotiated to protect aged "pet lambs" from such a fate. Killing is both very routine and variably complex for different runholders and shepherds, and critical distinctions in modes of killing made by runholders suggest a continuum based on use, singularity, and proximity to self and the homestead. See Grandin (1994:1354) for a discussion of the ways in which humane slaughter may be equivalent to euthanasia, that is, "a humane death that occurs without pain and distress." See also Vialles for an ethnography of abattoirs that defines "meat" as a combination of slaughter and other cultural constraints (especially 1994:55-60).

13. See Neil Rennie's *Working Dogs* (1984).

14. Newton writes: "I pay tribute to the unsung heroes of the sheepdog world—dogs unknown except in their own district, but who by their courage, brains, and faithfulness under the severest of tests—the shingle tops of the South Island high country—proved themselves the veritable kings of the canine world" (1947:23-24).

15. Glenmore, a property of 50,000 acres, runs 11,000 sheep; its highest mustering peak is 8,000 feet and the homestead is at 2,400 feet. The runholder had just finished renegotiating the lease on the property; none of the land was retired. In the description that follows, only the summer ewe country was mustered—Jim and his two station hands had mustered the wether block the week before. The snow risk is high with snow around the homestead for two months a year, and the summers are very dry in December and January. Jim reckons that using the back country we mustered saves him three months of feed over the course of a farming year. After reading this last sentence, a runholder said to me "for the average runholder that's what it's all about. It's absolutely critical to save feed here. At [home] to replace the one month [the sheep are out the back] would mean we would have to hand feed and purchase that tucker. We can't communicate what it's worth."

16. For eight people and five days (with an additional two rain-day's allowance) Jim's wife, Ann, did much of the advance food preparation.

> She has a basic list, but when she was first married Jim guided her. In addition to organizing and packing supplies, she baked five puddings (rice pudding, Mississippi mud, apple-and-raisin, berry, apricot), two egg-and-bacon pies, boxes of cakes (gingerbread, fruitcake, and currant cakes) plus tins of biscuits. Every egg was individually wrapped in newspaper, and she organized crates of beer, and sacks of potatoes, carrots, parsnips, cauliflower and silver beet, as well as several sides of mutton, ten loaves of bread, sausages and other staples. The men eat a lot at the end of a day, but I did too and craved the camp oven's cooked meat and vegetables and potatoes. (Letter from the field, 28.iv.87)

The following month at Glenrock, where there were fewer of us, the supplies went out in a wire trailer attached onto the front-end loader of the tractor driven out by the packie over Macintosh's Saddle and down Cookies Flat to Cookies Hut because the men both mustered (walked) in and mustered out on foot.

17. The men slept in a hut, but I slept in a tent outside to protect the integrity of the muster for the men. I ate meals with them and socialized around the table after supper. At

moments, it seemed odd to be out in the frost, in the rain, and through a dusting of snow, when there was a spare bunk inside, but I benefited too from privacy.

18. Later reading David McLeod's account of his first muster in *Many a Glorious Morning* softened my embarrassment.

> My first day's mustering was rather a fiasco—and a cold one at that. I still had only one dog and obviously wouldn't be much use on the hill, so I was sent, as is usual in such cases, to go to a certain place and wait. Anything more agonising for a learner I can't imagine. He goes to the place all eager and keyed up. He waits an hour, and not a sign does he see of men or sheep. He waits another hour. He is sure he is in the wrong place. He is sure he has failed to see the other men. He is sure they have forgotten him. He is sure he will get the sack. He goes through agonies of anxiety and indecision, and in the end, when he has just decided all is lost and he must go home, he hears faintly on the wind the sound of barking dogs and a tiny figure appears on a rocky outcrop a thousand feet above him and a fait "Yahoo" drifts down to him. (1970:46)

19. Again my embarrassment was eased when I learned that the men also "get anxious, not knowing if you've waited long enough." I heard stories about musterers who had fallen asleep.

20. Horses are no longer used, rather, supplies are taken out by four-wheel drive vehicles or tractor. Improved tracks and better vehicles, such as Land Rovers and Toyota Landcruisers, mean that musterers can get out to the back country quicker than on foot.

21. Full crutching with machines removes the fleece around the hindquarters and down the insides of the two hind legs, and the back of the udder; its removal facilitates mating and keeps the sheep freer of dags (wool and dried dung). It is done in late autumn, usually after mustering in April, and immediately before "the ram is put to the ewe" for breeding.

22. Occupying the border zone of class convergence, men adopt linguistic forms associated with the manliness of the working classes whereas, as Susan Gal has pointed out for English speakers (1991:181), women adopt respectable phonological forms linked with higher-ranking classes.

23. At Ben Avon, further south in North Otago, the wethers are shorn at the end of November with a few left until after Christmas at weaning time. Not everyone pre-lamb shears with a range from late winter to early summer.

24. Hamish drew these analogies for me: (1) machine shearing is like sending you out with no clothes on; (2) machine shearing with combs is like sending you out with underwear on; (3) blade shearing is like sending you out clothed but with no overcoat. Halina Ogonowska-Coates in her tribute to blade shearing, *Boards, Blades and Barebellies,* documents how catastrophic machine shearing was for the South Island high country when introduced early in the century; slightly less generous than Hamish, she equates the extra layer of wool left by blade shearing to a woolen singlet (1987:25). Some runholders talk of switching to machine shearing with cover combs if the blade shearers raise their rates.

25. I have selected dates from the middle of the Nells' time at Double Hill (July 1908 to March 1912) to avoid the possibility of shifts in the farming routine immediately subsequent and prior to management and ownership transitions. When Double Hill was divided in 1912, Leslie Nell was running 35,000 sheep.

26. The territory would have stretched from Lake Stream in the west to Terrible Gully in the east and from the Rakaia River on the north to Mellish Stream and Boundary Stream on the south.

27. The Iron Store was a shed on Peak Hill Station that marked the crossing point across the Rakaia and Wilberforce Rivers; it provided storage facilities for supplies and outgoing wool bales (see map I.1).

28. In preparation for the shearers, the shepherds would clean the cookshop and shearers' quarters with brooms and buckets in hand. These quarters were still standing but unused in 1987; see chapter 3 for Mrs. Nell's description.

29. Half-bred sheep usually originate from Merino-Leicester, Merino-Lincoln or Merino-Romney crosses.

30. Eight horses in pairs were hitched to shafts of the wagon; the number of horses helped to ensure that if one pair lost its footing in quicksand, another might be on firmer footing. A gig or spring cart was used for lighter transport.

31. Jock McGrimmon was a seasonal man whose wife became station cook. Peter Ensor notes that the accommodation for a married couple was "pretty primitive" and that until Mrs. McGrimmon arrived "cooks were a problem," but she "was a very pleasant woman and good cook, so things went well for a year or so until they departed" (1990:33). Hugh Chisholm came mustering for the season. He was a brother of Bill Chisholm of Molesworth. Later Hugh worked for the Land's Department as a pastoral land officer (1990:33). Bert Emerson, musterer and permanent hand for several years, "was rough as bags in a lot of ways, but good to work with, and he would tackle anything," according to Peter (1990:30).

32. For this reason, on some stations ewes are off feed for half a day, rams for a full day, before going into the shed for shearing. Some stations leave the lights on overnight to discourage the sheep from lying down. Most runholders dag their sheep (remove clotted wool from hindquarters) before shearing in order to save on costs.

33. Peter Newton (1949:47) in his account of life as a musterer on a typical (but disguised) Canterbury high-country station calls the four two-hour runs the Australian system and dates the introduction of this shorter shearing day into the high country in the 1940s. From the mid-seventeenth century on, tea with sugar became an indispensable substance for the work break, especially for rural workers (Mintz 1985:141). Most high-country properties shear their sheep under full contract, which means that the gang brings their own cook and supplies with them and the station provides mutton, traditionally one sheep for every 1,000 shorn.

34. Both Corriedales and merinos are considered fine-wooled sheep and fall into three grades of fineness. Fine merino wool is measured as 20 microns and finer; fine Corriedale wool is measured as 26-27 microns; extra-fine Corriedale wool is 25 microns and finer (Classer Registration Committee n.d.:17). The Rakaia properties were changing their flocks from exclusively Corriedales to exclusively merinos during my early field-work.

35. The blade-shearing tally in 1988 at one station was 3,037 of which 667 were merinos. The shearing rate for the farmer was $7,315 for 3,037 sheep at a rate of $219.45 per hundred for full contract shearing plus the classer's fee.

36. The weight of clean wool expressed as a percentage of greasy wool is a measurement called yield (New Zealand Wooltesting Authority n.d.:3).

37. Some properties may combine bellies and, for example, floor sweepings across categories of sheep.

38. Cf. Ritvo's concept of bovine excellence in *The Animal Estate* (1987:46-47). Elite cattle signaled a shift in the rhetorical function of animal husbandry in which stock became part of a rhetoric of self-assertion and display encapsulated in agricultural shows for elite families, "ceremonial reenactments of the traditional rural order" (52).

39. See, for example, the lead editorial entitled "Rural Fortunes" in *The Christchurch Press*, 10 November 1990.

40. For discussion see Hugo Penz (1988).

41. As Eldred-Grigg (1980:190) indicates, a sudden economic recession hit Canterbury in the 1970s; he cites Brian Easton, "the 1970s was a disastrous decade." Then record merino-wool prices in the 1990s and "more room to move" financially provided a cushion.

42. These ewes produce a product of value—lambs and fleeces—rather than being the product itself, however their genes are preserved or not through the success of their progeny.

43. Such as traditional station histories depicting settlement years and the late nineteenth century (Samuel Butler, R. M. Burdon and Constance Gray) and the twentieth century (David McLeod, Peter Ensor).

44. Acland (1975:231) documents her husband's loss at 4,000 out of 7,000 sheep including almost all of the hoggets.

45. Such detailed logs of stock losses and snow fall can be consulted in the future to understand patterns (climatic or wool production or economic, i.e., wool prices) or, for example, to indicate to farmers how much silage might have been consumed by how many stock over a given number of weeks of winter.

46. As indeed happened again in 1895, 1903, 1908, and 1918. McLeod (1980) writes in detail of the snows of 1939 and 1945.

47. David McLeod gives voice to it in this way: "Men who live among the mountains are constantly reminded that nature is always more powerful than themselves" (1980:244).

48. Struggle is reflected in the titles of two high-country histories, David McLeod's *Kingdom in the Hills: The Story of a Struggle* (1974), and Peter Ensor's "Many Good Years, Some Not So Good: A History of Double Hill Station" (1990).

49. Cf. Terry West (1983) who places animals over land as the critical resources for Bolivia's Aymara and similar agropastoralist communities.

50. Strickon underscores an economic/ecological pattern built around features of grazing of ruminant livestock, dependence upon the money-market economy, and extensive use of land and labor.

51. In the Alpine context see, for example, Netting (1981) who focuses on "cultural coping behavior" in a given ecosystem.

52. For an examination of the shifting properties of Tshidi Barolong cattle as "total social phenomena" that "linked a material economy of things to a moral economy of persons" in varying "economies of signs and meanings" throughout the colonial encounter, see Comaroff's and Comaroff's (1992:127-154; 144) historically interpretive and political-economy-based analysis, "Goodly Beasts, Beastly Goods."

53. From his analysis of Evans-Pritchard's consideration of cattle in the lives of Nuer, Willis (1974:13, 21) reminds his readers that "their social idiom is a bovine idiom," as cattle provide a Nuer "with a wealth of poetic vocabulary which he uses to endow both his social life and the world of external nature with meaning"; cattle *bridge* the world of society and nature.

54. For parallel instances on the U.S. Great Plains, see essayist Kathleen Norris (1993:170): "But these places demand that you give up any notion of dominance or control. In these places you wait, and the places mold you."

55. See, for instance, the book cover of Wedde and McQueen's *The Penguin Book of New Zealand Verse* (1985); it reads "We are not anywhere, but somewhere. The context of where we are is defined in this anthology by traditions conveyed in the Maori language, and by a complete re-reading of 'New Zealand poetry'."

PART IV
CONTEXTS

Photo 21 Runholder Hamish Ensor with Ngai Tahu elder Trevor Howe

Chapter Seven

Asserting Native Status

> For the descendants of the colonisers as well as those of the colo-
> nised, the history of the colonial encounter is an ineradicable and a
> formative experience. It must be confronted, not denied; met in its
> complexity, not forced into manichaean oppositions; understood, not
> simply resisted. This is especially true in New Zealand now that a
> new nationalism is developing around the rhetoric of post-
> colonialism. (Williams 1990:12-13)

With some exceptions, the anthropology of colonialism and postcolonialism
has tended to neglect British settler descendants as its focus and to ho-
mogenize their various expressions of cultural and national identity as derivative
and singular extensions of British culture overseas.[1] Regardless of where we
locate hegemony, Maori and settler-descendant discourses (as well as anthropological discourses) interpenetrate within national arenas, and ongoing processes
of identity formation should be viewed dynamically as historically, geographically, and culturally situated rather than singularly unidirectional.[2] I resist the
tendency to universalize the discourse of the West as it understands "Western"
people as a generic category, and I approach late-twentieth-century Pacific Anglo-Celtic high-country descendants with an anthropology that juxtaposes and
blends Eurocentric with indigenously derived ethnographic categories and
meanings. Even within pakeha New Zealand, a heterogeneous discourse about
cultural identity predominates, a discourse shaped by encounters with the particularities of land and a variety of indigenous "other."[3]

My field research challenges stereotypes in the scholarly literature about
the aridity of pakeha conceptual systems as primarily materialistic, individualistic, and homogeneous; it suggests the need to explore the ways in which elabo-
rating the symbolic nature of land is shared with *te iwi Maori* although expressed differently. From the nineteenth-century land wars to contemporary
Maori land claims, including those of the South Island Ngai Tahu against the

area of Crown land under study, understandings about the land have been central in forging cultural identities, both tribal and national, in New Zealand for both Maoris and pakehas, rural and urban. The importance of a spiritual connection to land for the construction of Maori identity has been celebrated in contemporary Maori literature,[4] recognized in anthropological and historical writings about Maori life, asserted in the renewed expression of cultural identity in *Maoritanga*—the Maori sovereignty movement—and formally presented to the Waitangi Tribunal.[5] Our understanding of the symbolism of kinship and land for pakehas is limited by comparison.

The statements of high-country farmers in a land-claims case before the Waitangi Tribunal suggest that their evidence, although culturally located, is not only a self-conscious politicized referential expression of belonging of one set of pakeha voices, but part of a larger process of claiming and sustaining vital connections to the land through a new, more explicit, evoked discourse of authenticity. The high-country landscape as a physical and cultural site is a central metaphor in the conceptual systems of its inhabitants and provides them with a way of thinking about and constructing their sense of self, while pointing to an emerging rhetoric of primordial affinities based in attachment to place. Following Ashdown and Lucas (1987), I use landscape "in the broadest sense of environment, encompassing physical form and all natural and cultural processes and interactions between them. It may also be considered the character of land as perceived, shaped and experienced by a society generally inhabiting a particular place."

Many of the runholders with whom I worked were active in the South Island High Country Committee of Federated Farmers, established in 1940 as the advisory body to the Minister of Lands, with elected officials from each high-country region sitting on the High Country Committee. I attended local section and national committee meetings and visited and interviewed members on their properties throughout the South Island. The Committee has operated with a greater sense of urgency in recent years because, as Elvin Hatch (1992:37-43) documents in his discussion of the changing position of agriculture in New Zealand, the emergence of an urban-based economic elite and the movement of the agricultural sector to the periphery has diminished both the influence and prosperity of runholders. They have responded by appropriating a discourse of stewardship and conservation, of oneness with a culturally conceptualized "natural world." In addition, conservation, environmental and recreation interest groups such as the acclimatization societies, Royal Forest and Bird Protection Society (1984), and Federated Mountain Clubs (1983) actively assert their interest in public mountain lands. Globally, with mountain ecology and sustainable development under scrutiny, such critical tensions between cultural-heritage conservation and natural-area management dominate contestations over and definitions of mountain protected lands. The Committee's primary concern was the claim before the Waitangi Tribunal of Ngai Tahu against the New Zealand Crown and the *iwi's* (tribe's) call for remedies in the form of high-country pastoral leasehold land: it consulted with Ngai Tahu and government ministers, monitored the hearings, and selected three high-country people to represent the South Island high country before the tribunal. Given my research on the aspect of high-country identity embedded in the inhabitants' relationship to land, the Committee asked me—in my role as "professional outsider"—to give testimony documenting their connection to land (Dominy 1988). I analyze the high-country evidence as a politicized expression of belonging.

In the New Zealand context, both te iwi Maori and various settler-descendant rights of cultural identity compete in the present as local peoples seek definition within an ideology of postcolonial "bicultural consensus" distanced from the colonial past (Mulgan 1989:150). In such a democracy, these "two indigenous cultures," but especially the aboriginal minority, must "be guaranteed the resources to maintain and develop their own culture" (Mulgan 1989:149) as they formulate authentic local identities. Paralleling orientalism with an implicit occidentalism,[6] however, Mulgan notes that the "denigration of Western culture can go too far" (1989:45), and he begins to resist the homogenization of pakeha culture (by refusing to equate the Crown with pakehas as treaty partners, for example) as well as that of Maori (by noting its basis in distinctive communities [iwi]).

James Urry also speaks forcefully for the multivocality of the terms "pakeha" and "Maori," underscoring the idea that "the terms are part of the political discourse of this country and thus open to critical enquiry" (1990:20-21); he asserts that both Maoris and pakehas in New Zealand are active (although differently positioned) participants in an industrialized nation-state "derived from the European transformation of agrarian society" (1990:21) including both Maoris and other agrarian peoples who settled New Zealand.[7] His is an important point, and my intent in exploring the connection between landscape and settler culture is not to adopt what Jock Phillips has called "a naive frontier hypothesis, which simply assumes that it is the frontier that creates a new people" (1990:133). He urges us to resist the sense of pakehas as "cultureless" and asks that we "trace who these people were and where they came from . . . [and with what] inherited cultural baggage" (1990:133). I would add that we cannot assume that settler cultures are merely derivative.

Ashcroft, Griffiths and Tiffin have identified a site of conflict in postcolonial literary cultures—the collision of "the backward-looking impotence of exile and the forward-looking impetus to indigeneity" (1989:136). They remind us to attend to the problems engaging European settlers as they negotiated relations with new landscapes: "constructing indigeneity" and asserting difference from an inherited tradition in negotiating between "the imported language and the land"; they urge us not to render unauthentic the processes of creating a sense of belonging.

Turning to documents set against the backdrop of my field research in the South Island and the High Country Committee's participation as an "interest body" in the Waitangi Tribunal hearing on the Ngai Tahu claim, I follow Allan Hanson's directive that "our analytic task as anthropologists is not to strip away the invented portions of culture as unauthentic, but to understand the process by which they acquire authenticity" (1989:898).[8] Nicholas Thomas, in noting that processes of identity construction are "not somehow contrived and insincere," argues that scholars now have "naturalized the artifice of invention" (1992:213).[9] In the Pacific, anthropologists have examined these processes in terms of ethnotheories of similarity and difference (Linnekin and Poyer 1990), the politics and construction of tradition (Jolly and Thomas 1992), and engagement in identificatory discourses of custom or rhetorics of tradition (Lindstrom and White 1993). Extending the theoretical dimensions of this literature, Thomas writes:

> Hence what is important is not so much the categorical fact that difference provides a foil for identity as the actual histories of accommodation or confrontation that shape particular understandings of others and thus determine what specific practices, manners, or local ethics are rendered explicit and made to carry the burden of local identity. (1992:213)

I focus on an instance of the explicit assertion of belonging in which oral evidence alone must carry this burden: the 1988 testimony of high-country runholders before the Waitangi Tribunal, describing their attachment to land. These data demonstrate the ways in which high-country people voice their sense of belonging when land is at stake and participate as particular pakehas in the rhetoric of emergent nationalism apparent in the tribunal proceedings as an ongoing social drama.[10] While noting that the explicit voicing of an affinity and identification with the land comes at a time when runholders perceive themselves to be potentially displaced and threatened with loss, I examine the rhetoric as a moment in the process of striving to acquire and, equally important, as conveying authenticity. Moreover, I point to some of the constitutive elements comprising a high-country discourse of authenticity as the shape of their affinity to land is voiced. As the 1840 Treaty of Waitangi is recognized as the founding document of the New Zealand nation, the moment marks a "necessary move in the direction of a post-colonial mentality" (Renwick 1991:20).[11]

The Waitangi Tribunal

In 1975 the Treaty of Waitangi Act set up a tribunal to "make recommendations on claims relating to the practical application of the principles of the Treaty [of Waitangi, 1840] and, for that purpose, to determine its meaning and effect and whether certain matters are inconsistent with those principles" (Orange 1987:246). Although stressing the principles and spirit of the Treaty rather than the texts, the tribunal is required to "have regard to the two texts, English and Maori, of the Treaty; . . . where ambiguity or doubt exists on interpretation considerable weight should be given to the Maori version" (McHugh 1988:13).[12] Therefore, its recommendations have cultural and symbolic as well as political significance.

The purpose of the Treaty—as an international treaty of cession, but not absolute cession, between the Queen of England and the chiefs, subtribes and people of New Zealand—was to "secure an exchange of sovereignty for protection of rangatiratanga" (New Zealand Maori Council of 1983, cited in Kawharu 1989:xvi-xvii). *Tino rangatiratanga* as it might have been understood by the tribal signatories meant "tribal control of tribal resources" or more precisely "evidence of breeding and greatness":

> Here, "breeding and greatness" allude to the two main criteria for leadership: primogeniture (generally male) and proven ability. "Evidence," for its part, turns on the concept of "mana". Mana is that power and authority that is endowed by the gods to human beings to enable them to achieve their potential, indeed to excel, and where appropriate, to lead. It is in the nature of a spiritual contract. (Kawharu 1989:xix)

Kawharu succinctly captures the interpretive dilemma surrounding the treaty: "For the Maori, power was to be *shared*, while for the Crown, power was to be *transferred*, with the Crown as sovereign and the Maori as subject" (1989:xvii, emphasis in original).

Especially at issue is article two of the 1840 Treaty of Waitangi in the Maori version of which "The Queen of England agrees to protect the chiefs, the subtribes and all the people of New Zealand in the unqualified exercise of their chieftainship [tino rangatiratanga] over their lands, villages and all their treasures [*taonga*]." The passage in the English text reads: "Her Majesty the Queen of England confirms and guarantees to the Chiefs and Tribes of New Zealand and to the respective families and individuals thereof the full exclusive and un disturbed possession of their Lands and Estates Forests Fisheries and other properties which they may collectively or individually possess as long as it is their wish and desire to retain the same in their possession."[13] Judge Ashley McHugh, chair of the tribunal for the South Island claim, uses the Waitangi Tribunal's *Muriwhenua Fishing Report* (New Zealand Waitangi Tribunal [hereafter NZWT] 1988a:179-181) to specify the criteria that underlie Maori thinking about taonga as distinct from "property":

> Maori extended their deep sense of spirituality to the whole of creation. . . . To the pre-European Maori, creation was one total entity— land, sea and sky were all part of their united environment, all having a spiritual source. . . . In Maori terms these resources were possessed. . . . All resources were "taonga," or something of value, derived from gods. . . . Taonga were either gifted or wrested, never sold. To buy and sell was an entirely western practice and when finally Maori engaged in buying and selling, they were behaving in a Western way within the colonial design and system.

In interpreting the meaning of the English and Maori texts of the Treaty, the tribunal's most significant ruling in the Muriwhenua case accepted the approach that the treasures of the ancestors include the forest, fisheries and language.

Bicultural in composition, the tribunal often convenes on the *marae* (ritual arena) of the group filing the claim. It is not responsible for the making of law but functions as a forum for airing grievances against the Crown and as a commission of inquiry for investigating or inquiring into the merits of claims.[14] It is empowered to make recommendations to the Crown with respect to compensation. Additional legislation has broadened the tribunal's scope. In December 1985 the Treaty of Waitangi Amendment Act of the Labour government increased the tribunal's membership to seven[15] (and, again, in 1989 to seventeen) and extended its powers to allow grievances to be considered from any point since 1840. Under the 1986 State-Owned Enterprises Act several government departments were replaced with state-owned commercial enterprises; this required transfer of certain Crown assets to enterprises such as Forestcorp, Landcorp, Coalcorp and the Tourist Hotel Corporation. Pastoral leases remained under the jurisdiction of the Crown. The Treaty of Waitangi (State Enterprises) Act of 1988 empowered the tribunal "to recommend the return to Maori ownership of any land or interest in land transferred to a State Enterprise" (McHugh 1988:5) and protected from transfer those lands to which Maori had claims before the tribunal.

The tribunal has become the site where the claims of competing interest groups converge. These claims on the pastoral high country, which is under the jurisdiction of the Crown because of its high multiple-use values for production, scenic and conservation purposes, provide the context within and against which the leaseholders write. The most powerful claim about the role of land for their sense of identity is that of Ngai Tahu.

Ngai Tahu Claim and the Kemp Purchase

In the claim of Rakiihia Tau and Ngai Tahu Maori Trust Board against the New Zealand Crown, Ngai Tahu people seek remedies for the Crown's failure to protect rights guaranteed to the tribe by the Treaty of Waitangi. Their nine-part claim is solely against the Crown and pertains to eight areas of land purchased from Ngai Tahu as well as their dispossession from their *mahinga kai*. It is based on the Crown's failure to allocate land to the tribe after promising to set it aside as reserves.[16] Ngai Tahu assert not only that the Crown imposed its rights of preemption to acquire their land extremely cheaply but that some land was confiscated without agreement or compensation. They also contest the Crown's denial of their right to lay claim to pastoral land on the same basis and scale as Europeans. Thus Ngai Tahu assert that the Crown's actions caused the loss not only of their economic base but also of their chosen way of life.

According to the Treaty of Waitangi, action cannot be brought against private owners, only against state-owned land. Paul Temm, counsel for Ngai Tahu, in opening the case said:

> Ngai Tahu . . . do not seek to regain one square inch of land that has been bought and paid for and worked for years by their fellow countrymen. . . . They do not ask for the plains of Canterbury or the suburbs of Christchurch or the city of Dunedin to be restored to them—

as in justice they might well do. They know that is not practical. Instead they say that there is throughout this island Crown land which
can be measured in millions of acres. It is to that land that they point
and say: "There is our remedy." (Cited in Booth 1988:86)

This is the basis for the claim on Crown pastoral leasehold land in particular;
Ngai Tahu claims include 2.6 million hectares of South Island high country
(one-tenth of the nation) held in 1988 under Crown pastoral lease tenure by approximately 360 sheep farming families of European descent.

This is the oldest claim in New Zealand. In 1849, Matiaha Tiramorehu
wrote to the lieutenant-governor: "The owners of the land are discontented with
the portions allotted to them. . . . This is but the start of our complaining to you,
Governor Eyre. And although you should return to England, we shall never
cease complaining to the white people who may hereafter come here" (Evison
1986:26-27). Ngai Tahu continued to seek recognition of their land rights
through numerous petitions, parliamentary inquiries, court proceedings and
through royal commissions, most significantly under Smith and Nairn in 1879-
1881 (whose records were locked away until 1979), under Mackay in 1887, before joint committees in 1888, 1889, and 1890, and in 1921 under Jones, Strau-
chon and Ormsby.

This is also the largest claim in New Zealand, covering an area of roughly
34.5 million acres (seven-tenths of the South Island and more than half of the
land mass of New Zealand) as Ngai Tahu seek compensation and restitution of
lands to include monetary payment, ownership of Crown pastoral leasehold
land, and fishing rights. They seek not only to "manage their own due share of
the country's resources for themselves" (Evison 1988:52), but they seek also "an
effective partnership with the Crown in the management and control of [the
mahinga kai] that remain, including fisheries" (Evison 1988:45) and in the
"economy of our traditional territory" (O'Regan 1989:262). They hold the
Crown responsible for protecting and restoring their natural resources.

Of particular interest to high-country runholders, because it involves much
of the land currently comprising the Canterbury and Otago high country, is the
aspect of the claim concerning the disputed boundaries in the 1848 Kemp Purchase.[17] Ngai Tahu understood the purchase to extend from the coast to an inland boundary along the foothills of the Southern Alps extending from Mount
Grey to just north of Dunedin and excluding areas such as the Bank's Peninsula
and Lake Ellesmere (figure 7.1). The Crown understood the purchase to extend
from the coast all the way inland across the Alps to the boundaries of the Arahura block (1860) on the West Coast. This disputed area, known as "the hole in
the middle" includes not only the pastoral high country but also national parks
and freshwater sources of many of the southern lakes. Ngai Tahu ask for involvement in the administration of national parks so that they might "exercise
absolute authority in the Maori historical and cultural interpretation of the parks
to the public" (O'Regan 1989:257). Henry Tacy Kemp's deed was signed by
thirty-six chiefs who were promised reserves set out later by Commissioner
Mantell, reserves averaging only ten acres per person (in contrast to reserves for

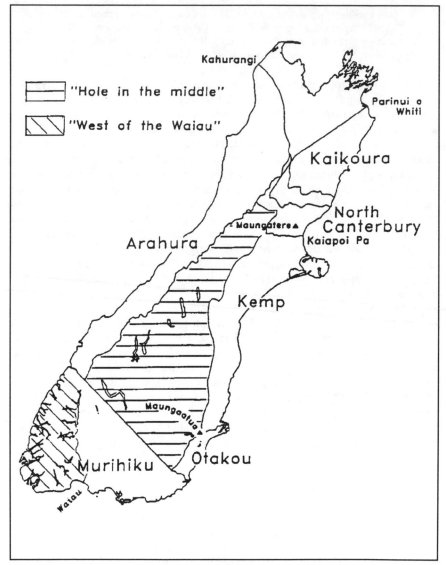

Figure 7.1 "The Hole in the Middle"
Reproduced with permission of the New Zealand Waitangi Tribunal (1991:7, fig. 1.2)

Europeans of fifty acres) (Evison 1986:23).[18] Ignoring Kemp's instructions, Commissioner Walter Mantell neither visited Ngai Tahu settlements nor marked out the promised reserves, "ample portions of land for their present and prospective wants," before the negotiations (Evison 1986:20, NZWT 1991 2.4:53).[19] Most of Kemp's 20-million-acre purchase was transferred to the New Zealand Company, then to the provincial governments of Canterbury and Otago; eventually the land was sold to European settlers at which time "the food-rich waters were gradually drained or fenced off, and so the mahinga kai were mostly lost" (Evison 1988:25).[20] One of the most controversial, the Kemp Purchase elicited complaints within months of its signing; eleven grievances were filed before the tribunal.

During the hearing, the Crown mentioned "Third Parties" to the dispute (NZWT 1988b K1.1f.21) and cited the *Muriwhenua Fisheries Report*: "The resolution of one injustice should not be seen to create another." Referring to high-country pastoral runholders, it noted "we feel Ngai Tahu's statements have been unsettling for a community that generally has shown support" (NZWT 1988b K1.1f.21, 23). A particular aspect of the claim indeed unsettled the run-holders. As one farmer wrote, "Using pastoral leases as a remedy looks just too easy a solution for the government and in fact every Joe Bloggs in the Street" (letter to author, 22 June 1988). The runholders argued that using pastoral land as remedy would entail a liability for Ngai Tahu. Administrative costs for pastoral land, even with amended leases, would exceed income because of environmental management costs and limited profitability from pastoral farming (O'Regan 1989:258). But in seeking management and control over the "economy of [their] traditional territory" (O'Regan 1989:262) through "an effective partnership with the Crown" (Evison 1988:45), Ngai Tahu hope to gain a role in decision-making about land-use practices in these upriver catchments. Ngai Tahu Trust Board Chairman Tipene O'Regan argues that these vital practices have implications for Ngai Tahu mahinga kai downriver (1989:258). They hope also for the restoration of—"the cultural and historical association with that vast southern landscape which is the tribe's spiritual home" (O'Regan 1989:259). High-country leaseholders, unlike hill-country and plains farmers, have a stake in these proceedings.

Filed in August 1986, the claim was followed by seven amending claims during the next two years; the tribunal was constituted in June 1987; the hearing began with the claimants' case in August 1987; it closed at a ceremony held in October 1989. The tribunal's findings on each of the grievances were released in a 1,280-page, three-volume report in February 1991;[21] the tribunal did not address the question of remedies because its role "is to determine whether, and to what extent, the Crown has acted in breach of Treaty principles and the extent to which the claimants have been detrimentally affected by any such breaches." It is then left to the parties "to negotiate a settlement of any proven grievance" (NZWT 1991 1.7:27). Some recommendations were proposed.

High-Country Submissions

Three high-country people represented the High Country Committee of Federated Farmers, which acted as an independent third party before the Waitangi Tribunal. Their statements reveal the substance and some of the logic of the runholders' opposition to the use of Crown pastoral leasehold land as remedy for the Ngai Tahu claim. In a letter to me, a committee member noted that in their evidence the runholders would stress the historical importance of the land to them and "how we feel as though we are the indigenous people of the high country" (22 June 1988). They wanted the tribunal to know what "we are all about and what our world means to us" (letter to author, 2 February 1989). Their evidence attempted to demonstrate the intensity and particularity of their affinity for, and identification with, the land they farm and inhabit. To this end they sought the independent testimony of "our anthropologist" to lend external legitimacy to their assertions.

As an ethnographer, I am a double witness in this account: witness to the lives of high-country people and witness to (and in) their involvement in the Waitangi Tribunal hearings. Before the hearings, and independently of them, I had been investigating aspects of cultural identity embedded in high-country people's relationship to land as expressed in the inheritance patterns, discursive conventions and symbolic formations, and farming practices, discussed in earlier chapters. Their testimony and my research illustrate the notion of landscape as a place where humans make meaning and create a world through experience.

In mutually reinforcing testimonies, Hamish Ensor, Iris Scott and Jim Morris each claim powerful connections with the land. As chairman of the High Country Committee and a third-generation member to own and farm a pastoral property in the Rakaia gorge, Hamish Ensor presented evidence on four issues. He began by suggesting an understanding of Ngai Tahu's relationship with pastoral lands (he acknowledged trails through the Rakaia valley to the west coast for greenstone), and provided evidence on the depletion of resources (tussock grasslands are threatened by introduced flora and fauna), freely given access to pastoral leasehold land in most instances,[22] and his sense of the inappropriateness of using the Crown's interest in pastoral leasehold land as a remedy for any claims justified before the tribunal.

Engaging primarily in a legal rhetoric of contractual obligation linking him to land, Ensor also provided a review of the Land Act of 1948.[23] In reference to Crown pastoral leasehold land, he referred to Section 66 of the act: "A pastoral lease shall entitle the holder to the exclusive right of pasturage over the land comprised in the lease, and a perpetual right of renewal for terms of thirty-three years, but shall give him no right to the soil, and no right to acquire the fee simple." Ensor stressed that the pastoral-lease system was designed to create security of tenure, as well as "a special relationship with the Crown"; he underscored the "sanctity of the lease documents" (NZWT 1988b P22[b] 7.9; 3.4). He measured leaseholders' commitment to the land as expressed in the value placed on long-term security of tenure guaranteed by the Land Act. He did not mention that "fair annual rent" was a contentious issue in discussion of high-country pastoral lands. Those groups with an interest in public mountain lands assert that concessional or "peppercorn rentals" of 2 percent fall well short of the 6 percent administrative costs to the government. Rental values for pastoral farming are determined as a percentage of the land exclusive of improvements (LEI), a valuation-based rental system that is market-oriented. The Land Amendment Act of 1979 set rent at 2.25 percent of LEI with a two-step phase-in period, in which reviews of rentals established by the Land Amendment Act of 1970 occur at eleven-year intervals.[24] As of March 1983, pastoral leases yielded a rent of $179,688 (Kerr 1984).

Ensor made it clear that he did not question the historical bases of Ngai Tahu claims but wanted to comment on remedies that impinge on "the rights in perpetuity of an independent third party," such as the runholders (NZWT 1988b P22[b] 4.3). He asserted social connection to land by measuring the continuity of inheritance patterns, demonstrated by leases as patrimony passed down through generations of farmers acting as custodians of the land.

> If any group of New Zealanders can claim to be the indigenous peo-
> ple of the pastoral lease land perhaps it is the lessees themselves as
> they are the only people in the history of New Zealand to have actu-
> ally settled on and worked the land in question. My people, regard-
> less of race or creed, including members of the Ngai Tahu tribe[,]
> consider themselves to have the indigenous feeling of the high coun-
> try. In many cases the occupation by these lessees extends back over
> four or five generations. (NZWT 1988b P22[b] 7.10)

Richard Mulgan, in asking if pakeha have an equal right to call the country home, for example, notes that farming is a "dynastic, not a personal activity" (1989:70) and comments that the strength of commitment to a pakeha extended family is seen in attitude to land.[25]

In the Rakaia valley, six sons and a daughter of four farmers returned in the 1970s to what have become, through expansion, development, and surrender of land, seven properties. As illustrated in chapter 4, high-country inheritance patterns reveal a variety of forms of management and ownership of properties reflecting an inheritance ideology linking property and family. Regardless of the form ownership takes, it provides for the continuity of ownership within the family, one that is based on kin ties over the generations, as parents create opportunities for their children, usually sons, to buy them out. Daughters who marry out do not often think of the family farm without thinking of family being in that place; they return throughout their lives and often live in similar environments. Remember that one woman had told me of an emotional devastation that she cannot explain but one that often motivates women to accept the inheritance opportunities of their brothers rather than forcing siblings to buy each other out or having the property's lease leave the family.

Ensor's emphasis on settlement and working the land as a measure of connection was distinct from Ngai Tahu expressions of connection to mahinga kai in the high country, areas that they knew but did not inhabit or work; his connection parallels aspects of permanent Ngai Tahu settlements. Ensor was saying that the high country, as settled land, had primacy for its current inhabitants in a way that it did not as mahinga kai for Ngai Tahu.

This primacy of continuity through descent is also measured economically, in terms of financial investment in what high-country farmers and lease documents define as "improvements" (for example, buildings, tracks, pasture plantings, fences), but not in terms of its cultivation, which is prevented by the Land Act. Although Ngai Tahu may seek land compensation to re-establish the economic base lost through depletion of their mahinga kai, high-country farmers see pastoral leases as their economic base and "share a common desire to preserve the very delicate balance between production and conservation on high-country land" (NZWT 1988b P22[b] 5.3). In this way, Ensor pointed out that pastoral lands demand a high degree of management that the leaseholders—through their expertise—are equipped to provide.

Building on his legal argument, Ensor stated that the perpetual right of renewal provided for by the Land Act "contributed to the preservation of the landscape" (NZWT 1988b P22[b] 5.4). Underscoring his sense of the concerns of today's farmers to protect high-country lands from exploitation by introduced species and damage from cultivation, he linked high-country concerns to those of Ngai Tahu and urban-based environmental and recreation groups, and acclimatization societies.

Ensor especially underscored the importance of conservation issues to high-country people, citing his own appointment to the Queen Elizabeth II National Trust, established by Parliament to oversee the development and protection of open space. He also pointed to general high-country support for the Protected Natural Areas Programme, established in 1982, whose teams identify sites of specific scientific interest and conduct surveys of tussock-grasslands flora and fauna with high protection requirements worthy of reserve status (NZWT 1988b P22[b] 5.5). In these ways he alluded to the multiple-use value of high-country lands for production and for scenic and conservation purposes. He stated that "lessees appreciate that their land has high public amenity values to all sectors of the community" (NZWT 1988b P22[b] 6.2). With this statement, he attempted to persuade other constituencies whose access to high-country lands would not be ensured under Ngai Tahu ownership. In conclusion, Ensor noted that pastoral leasehold lands were held by the Crown to protect the wider national interest.

The *Ngai Tahu Claim Report* (NZWT 1991 23.2.2) took exception to the lessees' refusal, expressed in this evidence, to believe Ngai Tahu assertions that "spiritual links are any greater on pastoral lease land than that on freehold land" or are greater in comparison with coastal and river margins where permanent Ngai Tahu settlements were located. The tribunal noted,

> [T]hese contentions overlook the fact that when the Kemp and other purchases were effected by the Crown, requests of Ngai Tahu to retain extensive areas of land which would have included some high country, were wrongly denied by the Crown. Ngai Tahu were left with no high country land and virtually no other land. They were in no position to engage in pastoral farming whether in the high country or elsewhere. But European settlers, by contrast, were enabled to take up extensive runs of many thousands of acres. (NZWT 1991 23.2.2)

The tribunal responded with economic logic, comparing types of land in terms of farming potential rather than considering the implications of the unique topography of the high country for shaping identity.

The next high-country statement serves as a "communicative act of topographic representation" in its focus on a geographic landscape and provides clues to the "ideational systems with which [landscapes] are apprehended and construed" (Basso 1988:100). In her statement, Iris Scott—a pastoral lessee—also addressed both the issue of remedies and the importance to lessees of retaining the Crown as lessor under the present system of tenure (NZWT 1988b P22[c]). Emphasizing belonging through familiarity, her submission documented the relationship of farmers to the land they worked, land that they understood, and that they farmed with the benefit of both traditional and modern agricultural and environmental knowledge. She used her property, Rees Valley Station, Glenorchy, to illustrate that their system of management relied upon "the specialised knowledge of local climate and the likely response of the environment" (NZWT 1988b P22[c]:2). It is continually evolving in step with, and within the constraints imposed by, nature. She reified nature as she talked about her respect for and interest in it. She spoke of the specificity of "traditional high-country farming" and its reliance "on nature to a greater extent than most types of farming" (NZWT 1988b P22[c]:2). Her discourse is far from generic; instead it is punctuated with assertions of a detailed knowledge of landscape. During the course of my fieldwork I had repeatedly heard parallel assertions. A retired farmer said: "I knew every inch of the place. You had to." His son said: "We are caretakers. We are for the country as a whole, for the next generation as opposed to managing for the day." And his nephew said: "You know the land you walk." One farmer described in detail the hues of color in the glaciers at the headwaters of the river and the effects of light on perception of distance. The farmers could identify every physical feature and sheep track from the air. They could, for example, instantly recognize remote scree slope in a 100,000-acre area captured in an aerial photograph.[26] But this detailed knowledge exists within the national context strategically introduced in Ensor's evidence in which local identity is claimed to serve the national interest: the pastoral lease symbolizes a relationship of shared ownership between the runholder and the Crown in order to "preserve the land for the benefit of all New Zealanders." This is further reinforced by Rees Valley Station's openness to visitors. Scott concludes:

> High country farmers have the role of guardians. The Crown has a role in protecting non-commercial aspects of land management. The special knowledge we have of our properties and our sense of sharing in ownership is of enormous value in the protection of land for future generations as well as present day benefits. Long term security of tenure is vital for wise land management. (NZWT 1988b P22[c]:5-6)

Iris Scott's evidence is congruent with other knowledge-based claims to land. Runholders see knowledge as a form of cultural and ecological adaptation that they claim enables them to maintain the balance between agricultural production and environmental conservation on a particular property over the generations. Legislation and inheritance patterns provide the necessary continuity for stewardship. The latter ensure the transmission of "local knowledge" from generation to generation.

A quick narrative detour to my data illustrates the ethnographic context from which such testimony derives. An eloquent statement comes from a "youngest son" who did not return. He said, "What inheritance is all about, really, is heritage—inheritance of knowledge. It is a fragile environment—you have to know it." Runholders stress the value of the particularity of knowledge on a given property and cite weather patterns, terrain, geological history, the location of wetlands and vegetation, and the patterns of stock movement as spheres of knowledge. Environmental extremes—the scale and rugged topography of pastoral high-country lands, and the sparseness of people—accentuate, but do not determine, the critical nature of detailed knowledge of place (Ashdown and Lucas 1987:51). As I illustrated, mustering the back country to bring in the sheep for winter, more than any other activity in high-country farming, demands full knowledge of the terrain.

A lessee who, unlike Ensor was not "born to the high country" and unlike Scott did not "marry into the high country," authored the final submission. As a young high-country lessee, Jim Morris was more explicitly emotional in a statement that attempted to illustrate how his relationship to the land defined his identity as a high-country farmer whose "feeling for the land and for the people who also live and work there is of an order that the Maori people would understand" (NZWT 1988b P22[d]:1). Obviously, this position has its challengers, and Morris knew those pakeha stereotypes of high-country people that he opposed. For instance, Morgan Holcroft writes:

> Some of us who are not Maori may also feel, in undisturbed remnants of bush, what Maoris saw and felt in forest still unexplored. Such experiences are never completely real; they occur too close to boundaries where the trees begin to dwindle and disappear, and are mere intimations, felt along the nerves, and gone with a sighing of branches in a rising wind. The most they can do for us is to take us a little closer to an understanding of what may be the spiritual element in the Maori relationship with the land. (1990:122-123)

By situating runholders at the margins, Holcroft asserts a greater cultural authenticity for one experience over the other. In this same essay, he also homogenizes the categories of te iwi Maori and pakeha by asserting that, while the former can speak of ancestral and spiritual concerns vis-à-vis the land, pakehas "saw only practical needs and requirements, *as farmers still do*" (Holcroft 1990:121, emphasis added).

Morris challenged myths about high-country inhabitants: that their history is static, that high-country folk know only the affinity of possession for land, that Ngai Tahu and high-country people have a markedly different feeling for land, that the romance of back-country living is without physical challenge and hardship,[27] and that its inhabitants derive their connection solely through the privilege of birth and marriage. His claim to knowledge was through experience—working with the successive bosses, managers, shepherds and wives who populated the high country—and not through inheritance. Like Ensor and Scott, he pointed to the Land Act of 1948 as responsible for a system of tenure that was intended to balance farmers' needs and the Crown's interest in erosion control with the benefit to the nation of preserving the productive potential of the land. He also pointed to the evolution of knowledge in high-country life as a way of distancing his generation from those of the "pioneers with guts and foresight and dreams that made the first moves and also the first mistakes" (NZWT 1988b P22[d]:3). A transformed relationship to the land was claimed, signifying the importance of land for identity.

At stake for Jim Morris was the way of life, linked to land, people, and work, that was his whole reason for being there. He closed his testimony with these words:

> After 25 years working in the back country as a shepherd and then after a lucky break, as a lessee, I still look every day with a feeling of awe on the mountains, the rivers and the bush that make up our high country lands. My hope is that this awe, felt no doubt by many men and women, will transcend so called cultural differences and unite us, so we go into the next decade as one, with the best management of our fragile resources as a collective goal. (NZWT 1988b P22(d):4)

Jim Morris's evidence—which the tribunal considered moving (NZWT 1991 23.2.4)—asserted that high-country people shared an evolving way of life defined around place and people's relationship to place as pastoral farmers. While acknowledging a material affinity of high-country farmers for the land as expressed in its economic value, he elaborated a spiritual affinity, in which connection to the land and identity was inseparable. Morris's testimony challenged stereotypes about the aridity of pakeha conceptual systems and suggested the need to explore the ways in which the elaboration of the symbolic nature of land is shared with Maoris, although it is expressed differently. For example, recall the sister, natal to the high country and now married and living elsewhere, who had spoken to me of aching to be in the mountains: "It is a physical rather than a mental feeling. Some days I yearn for the mountains." Her words suggest that landscape is both a physical and conceptual place constituting identity.

Stephen Levine has identified two surprises in the runholders' submissions. First, he notes "how anomalous [these] sentiments appear within the non-Maori culture, in which restraint and detachment are much more common than intensity of commitment" (1990:5). Second, he notes "Claims about the primacy of land and tradition, moreover, have been the more or less exclusive domain of Maori protagonists ever since evocations of 'loyalty to Empire' began to lose their appeal" (1990:5). Within the national arena of contested identities, these politicized and self-conscious expressions of belonging on the part of high-country farmers reflect an "apparent convergence of affinities" between non-Maori and Maoris that for Levine has the potential to unite and to divide. Optimistically, he concludes, "The atypical submissions of the high-country sheep-station farmers, rugged settlers able to articulate ties to the land without embarrassment, to some extent do point the way toward a cultural reconciliation between two co-existing peoples" (1990:6). A more pessimistic conclusion that such expressions may divide them is clear as he directs his readers to "the impli-

cations of cultural and territorial displacement arising from one people's appropriation of another people's language and self-imagery" (1990:6). In this sense,
high-country assertions of belonging must be counterpoised with highly public
claims of te iwi Maori about "the primacy of land"; such assertions of place-
bound identity, of localism, in a politicized context, such as the tribunal, risk the
accusation that in their construction some "localities can be frauds" (Relph
1991:101).

The worst-case scenario is illustrated by an additional submission. A non-
high-country farmer representing the Otago branch of Federated Farmers made
this final submission, independent of the submissions on behalf of the High
Country Committee of Federated Farmers. To the embarrassment of the Committee, this errant submission seemed manipulative in its overt wielding of a
rhetoric of white indigenization and its appropriation of a Maori symbology. The
submission appropriates Maori language, exploiting the social modality of *tangata whenua* (person or people of a given place), of mana, and of the canoe, to
position pakehas in the high-country landscape. Maori "feeling for the land" is
paralleled by a "white 'hands in the soil' feeling," a rather inappropriate descriptor given that pastoral leasehold land is not ordinarily cultivated, and in light of
the distinctions drawn by Iris Scott with other kinds of farmers who do cultivate
the soil. He writes "we have some Mana not from the land itself but from the
work we have done to improve [*sic*] it for those who come after us, as our ancestors of three or four generations did before us." We are reminded that whites
have ancestral land in Europe and Maoris in Hawaiki and in New Zealand, but
the author makes a distinction as he talks about looking at mana and ancestral
land from a European point of view: White mana does not come from ancestral
land but rather from "their own deeds and actions . . . and from the aroha he puts
into his land. The longer we live on or care for the land the greater the Mana
from it." Finally, he envisions a canoe that "will get nowhere unless the brown
and the white work together" (NZWT 1988b P29:2). The farmer does appropriate Maori symbology but fails to make it his own except insofar as he, like Ensor, stresses "working" the land as the essence of pakeha connection. The notion
that mixing labor with land is necessary to make claims of appropriation derives
from characteristically nineteenth-century European ideas (Ward 1989:8).

The Waitangi Tribunal's Response

The Waitangi Tribunal's report on the Ngai Tahu claim ruled that serious and
repeated breaches of the Treaty of Waitangi extending over a twenty-year period
of purchase negotiations reduced Ngai Tahu to near landlessness and must be
redressed:

> The honour of the Crown can only be restored by a settlement which
> recognises the magnitude of Ngai Tahu's great deprivation, sustained
> over more than a century. Only a large and generous response by the
> Crown will suffice to redress the wrongs done to Ngai Tahu and lay

their numerous grievances to rest. No less will serve to restore the
honour of the Crown. (NZWT 1991 24.5.6).

While finding in favor of many of the Ngai Tahu claims, the tribunal left the
determination of "large and generous" compensation by the Crown to negotiation between the tribe and the Crown but recommended a grant of one million
dollars to cover the cost of future reparation negotiations as well as a grant of
$399,168 to the Ngai Tahu Trust Board as compensation for the cost of bringing
the claim before the tribunal.

Warning readers of the *Ngai Tahu Claim Report* that "The narrative that
follows will not lie comfortably on the conscience of this nation" (NZWT
1991:xiii), the tribunal was measured, firm, and direct in its commentary:

> The Crown, through its agents, rode roughshod over Ngai Tahu's
> rangatiratanga, over their right to retain land they wished to keep,
> over their authority to maintain access to their mahinga kai. Instead
> of respecting, indeed protecting, Ngai Tahu's rangatiratanga, the
> Crown chose largely to ignore it. In so doing it acted in breach of an
> important Treaty obligation, and has continued so to act to the present
> time. (NZWT 1991 2.4:78).

In regard to the grievances about the western boundary at issue in the "hole
in the middle" area of the Kemp claim, the tribunal found that Ngai Tahu agreed
to sell the plains, not only to the foothills, but to the west coast. The tribunal
upheld the Ngai Tahu grievance pertaining to mahinga kai. It found that the
Crown entirely failed to fulfill the terms of agreement between Kemp and Ngai
Tahu by not providing ample reserves for their present and future needs—
including their villages, homes and gardens—and by not reserving their mahinga
kai. This interpretation is reflected in the tribunal's not restricting the definition
of mahinga kai to "cultivation"—as suggested by Kemp—but in finding its
meaning in those places where food was produced or procured (NZWT 1991
17.1), the meaning given to it by Ngai Tahu at the time.[28] European ideas about
aboriginal property were found to have prevailed in prior rulings on Ngai Tahu
grievances about mahinga kai (NZWT 1991 2.4:67). In finding mahinga kai to
be the tribal resources in and on the land, in the forests and in the rivers, lakes
and sea, and in the sky, the tribunal considered them basic not only to the Maori
economy but to the whole social fabric of tribal and intertribal life (see O'Regan
1989, cited in NZWT 1991 2.12).[29] Seriously disadvantaged by their tiny allocation of land holdings, Ngai Tahu were unable to compete with European settlers
who gained control of thousands of hectares in the pastoral system (NZWT 1991
2.4:76).

In respect of the high-country community, the tribunal noted in the record
that the farmers' evidence was given in a spirit of good will, and "indeed sympathy" toward Ngai Tahu, even though in some cases not supporting certain remedies that Ngai Tahu were seeking for their grievances (NZWT 1991 23.9). The
remedy at issue was land. In its findings, the tribunal suggested that land vested
in the Crown and state-owned enterprises, such as pastoral leasehold land or

national parks, might feature in remedy to Ngai Tahu as they seek to reestablish their rangatiratanga. Such land, much of it marginal with a high conservation component and with primarily scenic, recreation, environmental and wilderness qualities, has "intangible" value to Ngai Tahu as tangata whenua, but it will not provide an economic base.[30] Urging good will on all sides and in response to runholders' concerns, the tribunal noted that it "has no reason to believe that, were the Crown title to pastoral leasehold land to be vested in Ngai Tahu, they would be other than sensitive and caring for the proper conservation of this high risk land" (NZWT 1991 24.5.1). But, the runholders ask, how are the Ngai Tahu to guarantee this?

Pastoral leasehold land is virtually the only land left to the Crown to give. The runholders say they have no reason to believe that today's Ngai Tahu, or any other category of New Zealanders, would be sensitive to the land's needs. In discussing this possibility with me prior to the hearing, runholders expressed concern about "a lack of understanding on the part of the government of what we are really all about, why we are here and what the conditions are" and posed the critical question: "But what if Ngai Tahu freehold and sell off the land?" They maintain that "the soil here is too sensitive to be in the hands of one [group]," that is, Ngai Tahu. These runholders are engaging in a strategically spatial rather than imperialist discourse, one in which not only the status of boundaries, but also the protection of landscape and cultural values is at issue. This kind of contest about whose rights to land prevail has implications not only for identity but also for land management and resource control.[31]

Tipene O'Regan, told the press that the tribe will seek a mixture of returned land, cash and shared control of resources as final settlement. Then Minister of Maori Affairs, Winston Peters, concerned in preventing "an elite being compensated for a historical grievance while the people at the bottom got nothing," called for an economic blueprint from Ngai Tahu, "a total economic plan," to show how settlement money in the form of a development fund for both "Maoridom and the nation" would be used.

§   §   §

The Waitangi Tribunal provides a dramatic forum for the postcolonial encounter in New Zealand between the iwi, the Crown, and various categories of pakehas at a time when these cultural identities compete for legitimacy in a dynamic discursive field of contested meanings. High-country lessees *and* Ngai Tahu, the "postcolonial" *and* the "postindigenous," vie for cultural authenticity in an arena best described as a site where they "improvise local performances from (re)collected pasts, drawing upon foreign media, symbols and language" (Clifford 1988:14). The lessees resist inclusion as settler descendants in a static, generic, imperialist discourse, by acknowledging their changing relationship with land through the generations and their differences from other pakehas. Ngai Tahu resist assimilation into a homogeneously white nation-state, as well as inclusion in a static, generic discourse of "otherness." Both parties articulate instead the dynamic, multifaceted nature of their being in a polyvocal, postmodern world where cultural-identity construction is richly nuanced, fluid and situationally specific. The high-country farmer no more claims land based on an appropriation of Ngai Tahu symbology than Ngai Tahu appropriate white notions of ownership in seeking restitution. In their testimony both parties resist the notion of reified culture as continuous tradition.

In *Fear and Temptation*, literary critic Terry Goldie (1989) provides a cultural analysis of white colonialism and its idioms of domination by comparing the representation of the indigene across the white postcolonial literatures of Canada, Australia, and New Zealand.[32] Differences between the representations are insignificant, Goldie argues, because "the game, the signmaking, is all happening on one form of board, within one field of discourse, that of British imperialism" (1989:10). Goldie's focus is the unidirectional process of white strategies of "indigenization" in which white settlers either penetrate the land or incorporate "others" through appropriation of their symbols. In both cases the appropriation of land is at issue: "The indigenized white is sanctified by indigenous mysticism and is able to enter the formerly forbidden regions of the alien land" (1989:146), and "through the indigene the white character gains soul and the potential to become of the land" (1989:16).[33] By homogenizing and placing in opposition both "indigenous" and settlement culture across the white commonwealth,[34] Goldie's structuralist approach emphasizes the generic quality of an imperialist discourse and suggests by extension that the high-country submissions are appropriative of land by claiming tangata whenua feelings.

In that runholders' opposition to the use of Crown pastoral leasehold land as remedy for the Ngai Tahu claims does not invalidate the claims, it does not fully fit Goldie's description of a white strategy of indigenization in which land is penetrated and native claims are rejected. Counsel for the High Country Committee stated:

> As third parties affected by this claim, pastoral lessees do not wish to interfere in the historical justification of the claim by both the Crown and Claimants other than to point out the consequences of their action to runholders using Crown lands under a perpetually renewable leasehold title. (NZWT 1988b P22[a]:26)

To the extent that the runholders hoped that the Crown would establish that Kemp purchased the "hole in the middle" according to the conditions set out by New Zealand's founding document, the Treaty of Waitangi, the logic of their opposition is legal. Their claim depends upon the system of land tenure created by the Land Act of 1948. This system protects their rights as lessees in perpetuity, and was intended by the state to protect soil and water values and guarantee wise land management by balancing production and conservation values for the nation. These are also the grounds for an environmentally based opposition to granting Ngai Tahu as landlords the ownership of pastoral leasehold land as compensation from the Crown.

What of the second white strategy of indigenization, identified by Goldie as the process of incorporating "others" [and their land] through the appropriation of their symbols? Such scenarios represent the kind of verbal strategizing that Mark Williams might have had in mind when he described the "psychologically devious need among the descendants of the settlers to validate their appro-priation of the original inhabitants' land by a further act of appropriation . . . [of] the unique values of indigenous culture" (1990:13). To what extent can this be said of the self-representation of those runholders speaking for the High Country Committee?

While high-country lessees do not argue for the same authenticity as Ngai Tahu, they do try to establish a discourse of authenticity in which they voice their belonging *to* land, a concept that has been called "landship," and which carries its own set of obligations to land (O'Connor 1989:101). Theorists in an-thropology, history and cultural criticism complement my perspective by noting the ways in which narratives about identity are shared, explored and negotiated as local (in this case Ngai Tahu and high-country) epistemologies are reconsti-tuted in the Pacific.[35] They resist the inclination to polarize contemporary indi-gene and settler descendant. As Alan Ward warns:

> We tend for convenience to talk of two sides, Maori and Pakeha; however, both were complex societies and cultures and were becom-ing increasingly more so. There were never just two viewpoints, Maori and Pakeha. . . . Neither culture was static, neither was entirely "traditional" by the time the Crown purchases in the South Island were taking place. (1990:152)

Nor is either "culture" static in the present, for colonial and postcolonial encoun-ters, as James Axtell (1985:7) has noted, are "an interweaving of mental selves, and the images which . . . people have of one another are an important aspect of their encounter." And too generations are divided. Runholders explicitly con-trasted today's family farming to that prior to World War II when "the whole game was boom and bust. That's why we had many absentee lessees. Often just a manager would sit here, munching away, having no idea what was going on in the business world. That was to the detriment of the land. During the Depression many went under, bust, then somebody else would take a gamble on the lease, a real Russian Roulette."

The logic of the runholders' opposition to the use of high-country lands as remedy was not only legal and environmental, but also cultural. They attempted to demonstrate the shape of their affinity for, and convey the strength of their identification with, the land they still graze, inhabit and transform. To this end, they sought my testimony to lend legitimacy to their assertions. In their evi-dence, they engaged in a spatial, rather than a purely temporal, discourse one where place is a rhetorical construction;[36] in "writing worlds," place is not sim-ply reflected mimetically but rather constituted rhetorically (see Barnes and Duncan 1992:3). A number of constitutive elements comprising a high-country discourse of authenticity emerge. The high-country submissions speak of an ongoing and constantly changing relationship to land, rather than making re-course to continuity with the past. They adopt a collective rhetoric of distinct-iveness as they speak of their particular reliance on a reified nature, rather than using a generic discourse of similarity with other agrarian and urban whites, including their forebears. They link the continuity of their presence over several generations in the high country to topographic and environmental knowledge, rather than with ownership and control of resources alone. They speak to the advantage of shared (Crown leasehold), rather than individual (freehold) ownership, of their suitability as caretakers for the national interest in leasehold lands, and of the need to acknowledge their complex similarities to, and differences from, Ngai Tahu.

To argue for high-country indigeneity is not to argue for the same indigeneity as Ngai Tahu. The referential content of the discursive practice of presenting evidence about attachment to land, taken together with, for example, instances of ways of talking about "country" suggests that the landscape of high relief is constitutive of boundedness and identity; the "rooms" of high relief (Ashdown and Lucas 1987) map onto cultural identity, an identity in which high-country families differentiate themselves not only from Ngai Tahu but from other settler descendants, including their own forebears. The boundedness of space, embodied in images of containment like the mountains and the valleys ("gorges") they define, can be understood as a rhetorical device intended to locate oneself vis-à-vis others.

Notes

1. In the Pacific, historical ethnographies (Dening 1988; Sahlins 1985, 1995) have explored the colonial encounter between traditions but have emphasized the universalizing discourse of the West and have stopped short of the present. The anthropology of colonialism has paid insufficient attention to the anthropology of white settlement societies. Vincent Crapanzano's (1985) work in South Africa and Bruce Kapferer's (1988) and Peter Read's (1997) in Australia are notable exceptions, for anthropologists typically give voice to the silenced and the indigenous rather than to the colonial discourse that presumably speaks for itself. In Australia, Gillian Cowlishaw's *Rednecks, Eggheads and Blackfellas* (1999) focuses on outback racial relations between cattlemen and Aborigines. Veronica Strang in *Uncommon Ground: Cultural Landscapes and Environmental Values* (1997) reveals variations between outback homesteads and simultaneously maps spatial borders and markers representing the various players on the cattle stations, from wealthy landowners, to managers, to Aboriginal stockmen. She emphasizes that Europeans are separated from the land whereas Aborigines share a social and spatial order characterized by equality and homogeneity, one in which interaction, rather than separation, characterizes their relationship with the land.

2. We would do well, as Martha Kaplan suggests for the colonial encounter in Fiji, to view the postcolonial encounter also as a field of plural articulations, as the "spaces and areas of practice where the processes of articulation and the contestation of articulations between cultural systems are ongoing" (1989:18). Similarly, Ann Stoler (1989:136) writes, "colonial cultures were never direct translations of European society planted in the colonies but unique cultural configurations, homespun creations." See also Cooper and Stoler (1989:609-610), and Knapman (1988:213).

3. Cronon (1983), Crosby (1986), and Fisher (1980) illustrate how transplanted peoples are rendered vulnerable to the influencing effects of distinctive geographic and cultural environments, and of distinctive landscapes and indigenous populations.

4. Literary works, such as Patricia Grace's *Potiki* (1986), Keri Hulme's *The Bone People* (1986) and Witi Ihimaera's *The Matriarch* (1988), eloquently explore contempo-

rary Maori spirituality as a crucial aspect of identity; in these works of protest and affirmation (see Sinclair 1992:283), it is evidenced in attachment to the land (tangata whenua)
and the importance of the past. Cast in a literary idiom is Witi Ihimaera's "idyllic voice
of the pastoral" (Williams 1990:115) in the *Matriarch*, a powerful novel, balanced as
Karen Sinclair (1992) notes, because it does not merely romanticize "a calcified past":

> Waituhi. It was the close kinship the whanau [family] shared with
> one another so that we never lived apart from each other. It was the
> place of the heart. This place of old wooden shacks and scrub-
> covered foothills. This place where the Waipaoa was wild in the win-
> ter and strangely menacing in the summer. This place of the painted
> meeting house, Rongopai, with its eaves sloping to an apex like an ar-
> rowhead thrusting at the sky. This place of people growing older,
> where flax and flowers grow untamed in the plots where houses once
> had been. This place of the village graveyard where the tribal dead
> slept in the final resting of the body. This place, this Waituhi, was
> family. The whanau was my home. The love and affection they held
> for each other were the ridgepoles of my heart. The sharing and en-
> joying of each other were the rafters. And within these walls and
> roof, my heart was shared with my whanau, so closely intertwined
> that I never ever wanted to leave Waituhi. Taku manawa a ratou ma-
> nawa. My heart was their heart. [Ihimaera 1988:107, cited in Wil-
> liams 1990:115-116]

As a nostalgic longing for a preindustrial past, the passage serves as a mode of resistance
to modernity, one characterized by Williams as quite similar to the writings of English
and New Zealand novelists of the 1920s and 1930s, such as D. H. Lawrence and A. R. D.
Fairburn. See also Murray (1998).

    5. For example, in examining the 1985 claim of the Muriwhenua people against the
New Zealand Crown, Waerete Norman considers:

> Various sets of relationships: groups of Muriwhenua people tied to
> each other and to their resources of land and sea, measured over time
> by layers of generations back to a common canoe and to an even ear-
> lier people than themselves. . . . It is about turangawaewae, tangata-
> whenuatanga, mana, or in the words of the Treaty, "tino rangati-
> ratanga." It is about the "object" of rangatiratanga, the resources of
> the people: all that enabled them to survive and to flourish since me-
> dieval times. It is therefore about the physical and the material; but is
> equally about the spiritual and the esoteric, or in the words of the
> Treaty, "taonga katoa." [1989:209]

For obvious reasons in a bicultural context, Norman does not translate or italicize Maori
words. Drawing on his translation of the Treaty of Waitangi, Ian Kawharu (1989:313-
314) translates as follows: *turangawaewae,* literally "standing place for the feet," i.e., the
rights of the *tangata whenua; tangata whenuatanga,* exercise of proprietary rights over a
given place; *mana,* authority, prestige, sovereignty; *tino rangatiratanga,* the unqualified
exercise of (their) chieftainship; *taonga katoa,* all (their) treasured possessions. Kawharu
(1989) uses "Pakeha" as a synonym for the Crown. See also New Zealand Waitangi Tribunal (1988a).

    6. See also James Carrier (1992).

7. Literary reclamation of history such as Ihimaera's *The Matriarch* (1988) and Maurice Shadbolt's *Season of the Jew* (1986) and *Monday's Warriors* (1990) intertwine a multiplicity of conflicting and overlapping Maori and pakeha voices within shared historical and national contexts; taken separately and in juxtaposition, these novels illustrate that the nature of the colonial encounter in the nineteenth-century New Zealand land wars was not static, or unidirectional, or oppositional. In Ihimaera's work, according to Karen Sinclair (1992:304-305), the past and present are merged, as are pakeha and Maori modalities, creating a cultural coherence that is "not illusory" nor "mythical" and illustrative of the provisionality of history. This multiplicity makes the writing of authors like Ihimaera (and by extension Shadbolt) an effective means through which contemporary identities can be negotiated.

8. In a response to my consideration of the ethical dimensions of having submitted ethnographically based testimony on behalf of white settler descendants to the tribunal (Dominy 1990a), Stephen Levine (1990) raises a related issue embedded in my testimony—that of arguing for a parallel (but not greater) authenticity of high-country people's connection to the land (with Maori connection) within a national context where that relationship is assumed not to exist. As I have argued, "my submission to the tribunal was intended to argue for recognition of . . . cultural difference as nuanced rather than sharply oppositional between Maori and Pakeha" (1990a:23). I continue to explore this thread not by "testing authenticity" but by examining the shape of emergent authenticity claims of runholders. For responses to Dominy (1990a) see Handler (1990), New Zealand Association of Social Anthropologists (1990), and Urry (1990).

9. Hanson (1989) of course was referring to "the making of Maori culture" as part of an expression of political ideology, a process that Hal Levine (1991:444-445) has called "a rhetoric of ethnic politics" in which the "invention of culture" serves as a "rhetorical instrument." Levine urges that the process be examined in the context of ideological production. Both Maori and pakeha assertions may be viewed in this way. Hanson (1997:207) further makes the case that "the study of ideological aspects of culture is not less empirical than the study of those apparently (but only apparently) 'harder' realities of economics and politics."

10. Appropriately, Victor Turner (1974:33, 35) has also called the processual units of social dramas "social enterprises," that is, "public episodes of tensional eruption."

11. During the 1990 sesquicentennial, no fewer than fifteen books contributed to what Belich (1990) has called the "Treaty industry" in New Zealand publishing. Those publications by Orange (1987) and Kawharu (1989) are outstanding.

12. See Belich (1990) and Kawharu (1989:xi) for discussion. See Kawharu's appendix (1989:316-321) for his annotated translation of the Maori text as it might have been understood in 1840; he provides the original texts in English and Maori also.

13. See the first schedule of the 1975 Treaty of Waitangi Act, reprinted in appendix 1 of the *Ngai Tahu Claim Report* (New Zealand Waitangi Tribunal [hereafter NZWT in notes] 1991).

14. Following Hobsbawm, Adrian Peace calls such commissions of inquiry or review tribunals "modern theatres of control," noting that as such review bodies "consistently articulate their impartiality, they go to great lengths to broadcast their independence, they heavily invest in the rituals and the symbolism which underscore their political abstemiousness and moral integrity" (Peace 1993:190). Even so he notes that their decisions often support the status quo.

15. Under the 1985 Amendment, the tribunal consists of the Chief Judge of the Maori Land Court, and six persons, of whom at least four are Maoris. The governor-general on the recommendation of the Minister of Maori Affairs, who consults with the Minister of Justice on these decisions (McHugh 1988:6), appoints these individuals.

16. These land claims, known as the "Nine Tall Trees of Ngai Tahu" include: Ota-kou (Otago), Canterbury, Banks Peninsula (including the French, Port Cooper, Port Levy, and Akaroa purchases), Murihiku (Southland), North Canterbury, Kaikoura, Arahura, Rakiura (Stewart Island), and the mahinga kai. Harry Evison (1986) and contributors (1988) and Tipene O'Regan (1989) provide an overview of the Ngai Tahu Claim from the perspective of the claimants.

17. Of 360 pastoral lessees represented by the High Country Committee, 324 are on the land comprised in the Kemp Purchase (NZWT 1988b P22[b]2.2). See the *Ngai Tahu Claim Report 1991* which details (NZWT 1991 8.1-11, 17.1-7) and summarizes (1991 2.4, 2.12) the grievances, findings and recommendations of the tribunal pertaining to the Kemp Purchase and mahinga kai, respectively. Mikaere (1988) documents the Ngai Tahu response to the 1848 purchase under the leadership of prophet Te Maiharoa. References pertaining to NZWT draw upon Crown submissions catalogued as Document K or high-country submissions catalogued by the tribunal as Document P22. All citations refer to paragraph number except in instances of testimony that provided only page numbers.

18. Testimony in the Ngai Tahu hearings focused extensively on Commissioner Mantell's conduct. Both Evison (1988:28) and Orange (1987:174) discuss Mantell's re-gret over his initial role and his later attempts to make amends.

19. I follow the indexing format of the tribunal indicating chapter and section num-bers in my citations. Where sections run for several pages, I have included page numbers also.

20. The Ngai Tahu Claim Settlement Act of 1944 was meant to address those claims of broken promises under Kemp's deed; Evison asserts that there are claims also arising from not following the Treaty of Waitangi (Evison 1986:43).

21. Two additional reports, on the sea-fisheries claim and on 108 ancillary claims raised during the hearing, were to be released.

22. Realizing that some charges of denial of access by extremists did not match his own experience, runholder John Chapman conducted a survey of his own region in the Mid Canterbury high country to provide evidence of a high degree of public recreational use of the twenty stations he included and to illustrate, more importantly, that pastoral use is not incompatible with recreational use. Seldom were requests for access refused, and tenure appeared not to influence the runholder's decision. A range of services was pro-vided including accommodation, search and rescue, advice and directions, and maps. He also interviewed recreationists and discovered that his findings concurred with their ex-perience; in particular they explained that when refused access they preferred an explana-tion. Speaking to an international audience at the East-Asia Pacific Mountain Associa-tion, Chapman said that many runholders enjoy the presence of recreationists because it "reinforces and refreshes your own perception that you live in a beautiful and interesting environment" but the returns diminish when runholders find that they are no longer grant-ing a favor but instead are expected to provide access and services as an obligation (1996:209).

23. See New Zealand Department of Lands and Survey (1948). Currently under re-view, the legislation is discussed in the next chapter.

24. See New Zealand Department of Lands and Survey (1979).

25. Mulgan seems to be speaking particularly of New Zealand Europeans. As Sonya Salamon (1992) has illustrated in her comparative analysis of German Americans and Irish Americans in *Prairie Patrimony*, European farmers do not conceptualize their ties to the land in the same way. Rogers and Salamon (1983) in a co-authored compara-tive analysis of two sets of contrasting French and American farmers find a range of variation in inheritance strategies but stress uniformity in seeing farming as both a way of life and an occupation. They write that family farmers are concerned with "satisfactorily transferring from one generation to the next the skills and values they associate with

farming as well as the material resources required to practice them" (1983:535). For further discussion, see chapter 6.

26. These are only assertions, however. Analysis of toponymy, boundary talk, and vernacular idioms of orientation used to talk about movement in space reveal cognitive components that these assertions merely suggest (see chapter 5).

27. As an *American Ethnologist* reader noted, reference to histories, genealogies, economic fluctuations, and narratives of success and hardship are richly present in Ngai Tahu discourse and seemingly sparse in the runholders' testimony. Such references—especially to themes of economic, climatic and environmental challenge, such as isolation brought by rivers flooding and washed-out roads—predominate in pakeha documentary records, oral histories and station narratives.

28. According to Alan Ward (1990:157), matters of interpretation regarding the meanings attached to words in the context of tribunal hearings demand the attention of historians who must distinguish "the lived reality, as apprehended by the actors of the time," from that "understood by later actors who placed their own constructions on what had happened."

29. While Ngai Tahu argued that Governor Grey was fully aware of the tribe's dependence on mahinga kai for their survival, the Crown argued for a limited meaning of mahinga kai, stressing its specific mention only in the Kemp Purchase, and argued essentially that Ngai Tahu abandoned their traditional resources and moved voluntarily into a changing society and economy with its new food resources (NZWT 1991 2.2:160).

30. The tribunal's most specific recommendation was that the Crown vest all of its South Island greenstone (*pounamu*) interests in Ngai Tahu ownership and control. It was recommended, however, that current mining licenses should run their normal course.

31. As John Hayward notes:

New Zealand is not a homogeneous society. We are a nation of identifiable groups whose culture, experience, age, sex and education result in our holding differing priorities and preferences for the way in which land and water is to be used. Until such time as these values are dealt with in a systematic and explicit manner our land use choices will result in something less than social justice. (1987b:27-9)

32. See Dominy (1991) for review.

33. In a chapter entitled "The Natural," Goldie explores the textual images of the indigene as environmentalist, "an emissary of untouched nature [who] fears the ecological dangers of white technology," suggesting that this image preexisted in the semiotic field of the explorers (1989:36). Given their nomadism, he notes the irony of the link of the indigene and the land. There is no irony, however, unless one assumes that only permanent habitation or ownership of land implies connection (Mulgan 1989:34).

34. I use italics for *indigenous* to specify Goldie's use of the word and have avoided its use except in discussing it as a site of contested meanings of identity; instead I use the preferred Maori form *te iwi Maori* or the tribal name when I refer to the precolonial settlers of New Zealand. Marianna Torgovnick (1990:20) writes that using quotation marks to treat "*primitive* differently from abstractions such as *Western* implies that the societies traditionally so designated do not, and perhaps never did exist—are simply a figment of the European imagination." Goldie's (1989:5) notion of the indigene is quite similar because the indigene exists as an image, a signifier, a representation behind which lies the reality of imperialism, oppression which "awarded semiotic control to the invaders, and since then the image of 'them' has been 'ours.'" Richard Mulgan (1989:20) opts for "pre-colonial aboriginal peoples" rather than "indigene" for peoples whose lands were

settled by colonial settlers; he notes that the distinction between indigenous and exotic is "relative to a particular time."

35. Keesing (1989) has argued that both aboriginal and settler descendants engage in an ideology of attachment to and spiritual significance of the land. Similarly, Paul Carter (1989:325) moves Australian aborigines into the same historical space as Europeans, "a space constituted culturally, according to social, economic and above all, intellectual criteria."

36. In *The Road to Botany Bay*, Paul Carter (1989:350) argues for a spatial history of settler society, one in which we seek intentions and the invention of a point of view or panoramic eye, rather than an imperialist history in which we seek chronological origins. He suggests that we have suppressed spatiality in our own Western historical consciousness and urges us to recognize its form and historically constitutive role rather than focus on its content. Perhaps most significantly for my argument, Carter argues against a diorama history, a "model of historical progress which has equally obscured a fundamental dimension of the colonizers' history" and argues instead for attention to the making of spatial history as settlers were "choosing directions, applying names, imagining goals, inhabiting the country" (1989:xx-xxi). Thus places were invented, not found, through naming processes that described not a physical, but a conceptual, place (Carter 1989:51).

Chapter Eight

Legislating a Sustainable Land Ethic

Grass springs sweet where once thick forest
gripped vales by fire and axe freed to pasturage;
    —Ursula Bethell, "The Long Harbour" in O'Sullivan (1997:30)

While my South Island interlocutors, like Ngai Tahu and Australian Aboriginal groups, also call their place "country," I would not argue that pastoral high country is a sentient environment to pastoral families.[1] But I do want to illustrate, through an analysis of ethnographic and textual materials, what kinds of active resource managers high-country people are as they respond to a transnational rhetoric of sustainability. Their conception of "country" contests predominant reductive and binary models of production/conservation and economic/visual resource and suggests a far more complicated dynamic between scientific and cultural paradigms of sustainability than has been acknowledged.[2] This dynamic is captured explicitly in the internationally driven top-down concept of equitable sustainable land management with a dual commitment to both cultural and ecological diversity as defined locally, formulated as part of Agenda 21, Chapter 13, "Managing Fragile Ecosystems: Sustainable Mountain Development," at the United Nations Earth Summit in Rio de Janeiro in 1992.[3] I examine an emergent land ethic by exploring the legislative arenas within which discourses of sustainability are defined and by examining the relation of sustainability to "country." While acknowledging competing aspects in the positions of various stakeholders in the New Zealand high country, I focus on one category of players—the runholders—and attempt to articulate their evolving land ethic. The ethic is part of an immediate ecosystem and responds to Deborah Rose's plea for the development of an indigenous Western land ethic not in the wilderness or in exotic places (and minds), but "in our own back yards, farms and stations" (1988:387). I aim to elicit the cultural components of a remarkably transnational and yet strategically local high-country understanding of sustainable land management.

To provide a historical context, I trace transformations and sociopolitical currents in Crown land legislation as it shaped the pastoral-leasehold tenure system, focusing especially on the Land Act of 1948 and the land classification system it established. A plural history in which various constituencies articulate ties to mountain lands is often voiced in terms of legal conventions or commercial and technical designations. This history displays the complexity of competing interests that typically interact and intersect in making policy that shapes sustainability. These conflicts must be examined within the context of changing political parties and market forces in New Zealand farming and shifting values regarding, and definitions of, nature and culture,[4] land and nation. The idea of sustainability, then, is contested, processual, and political.

The contemporary focus of my analysis is on the effects of government restructuring with the election of the fourth Labour government in 1984, on a series of subsequent legislative initiatives for land-management reform (such as the 1991 Resource Management Act and the 1995 Crown Pastoral Land Bill),[5] and on high-country inputs and responses to the concomitant studies and legislative initiatives.[6] John Marsh argues that because "farmers may not take account of impacts of farming which are not directly reflected in prices and costs," their calls on "non-market costs" in natural systems must lead to legislative intervention that will restrict such use in order to ensure that they be sustained (1994:16). Inevitably, then, sustainability must be defined and controlled through legislation. While sustainability operates as a dominant value at the international level (Bradsen 1994:99), it remains "an elusive target" locally (Marsh 1994:16).

The regulatory arena of land legislation has defined the conditions of high-country occupation, ownership, and management, and reveals continuously conflicting values between runholders and various national players in these public lands. My purpose is not to intrude on the terrain of scholars in land-resource management who can best assess the relationship between land-tenure legislation, land management, and the degree of range degradation in the South Island (as does the Martin Report),[7] but rather to illustrate that changes in legislation mark key tensions in New Zealand national culture between constituencies competing to define the high-country landscape, and its management, occupation, and ownership. The values at stake include commitment to pastoral use, to freehold and leasehold tenure of pastoral lands, to public recreational access, and to nature conservation, including landscape preservation and species protection, and to a much lesser extent cultural heritage (as in historical or pioneering) protection. A rhetorically consistent and oppositional tension emerges between the protection and preservation of a less culturally mediated landscape, often summarized simplistically as a tension between production (pastoral use) and conservation (nature preservation and protection), and the protection and preservation of pakeha mountain pastoral culture and its landscape.

Early Legislation: Production and Economic Sustainability

Initially pastoralists were attracted to Crown lands outside settlement blocks because Crown licences (as they were known), issued for varying amounts of time depending on the province, were generally cheaper than other lands; by 1865 "virtually the whole of Marlborough, Canterbury and Otago, including Southland, was . . . registered and stocked up as sheep or cattle runs, right to the limits of the forested and permanently snow-capped Main Divide" (Centre for Resource Management 1983:33, citing O'Connor and Kerr).[8] Beginning in 1876 with the abolition of provincial governments, pastoral lands were under the jurisdiction of a central government that "was largely ineffective in preventing the degradation of the tussock grasslands through the combined effects of fire, sheep, snow, depression, rabbits, cultivation, war and insufficient knowledge and capital" (Kerr 1984:25); these effects were apparent by the 1880s, coinciding with falling wool prices, and continuing until the 1950s (Centre for Resource Management 1983:36-37). Under the 1877 Land Act, licences were auctioned as their terms expired and sold to the person bidding the highest annual rent, for up to ten years, with the preemptive right to freehold 320 acres around the homestead; the system persisted until the 1948 Land Act (Centre for Resource Management 1983:35).

Management of South Island mountain lands led the government immediately after World War I to commission Leonard Cockayne to "make an economic investigation of montane tussock grasslands," the results of which were published in a series of articles in the *New Zealand Journal of Agriculture* beginning in 1919 (McCaskill 1969:154). David McLeod (1980:16-17) explains that a Southern Pastoral Lands Commission was appointed in 1920 to look into burning of tussocks, overstocking and continuous grazing of sheep without improvement, increasing numbers of rabbits, and land tenure. These issues persist in addition to concerns over the damage to pastoral grasslands caused by introduced hawkweed[9] and Canada geese, and the intrusion of exotic conifers into the visual landscape. Responding to the commission's report, an amendment to the 1924 Land Act restricted burning at certain periods and encouraged more attacks on rabbits by runholders. McLeod notes that little else was done at the time, and in thinking over the thirty-year management of his property, Grasmere, he writes that he "made use of every available square yard, however rugged or inaccessible, and of every plant that sheep would eat, no matter what its value might be to the environment as a whole . . . slowly coming to realise the part that depletion and nutrition played in the struggle" (1980:17). In the 1940s some farmers worked with the commissioner of Crown lands and the Land Settlement Board to reduce rent paid through livestock reduction. In the Rakaia valley Double Hill reduced its rent from $1,150 per year to $750 in 1948.

In 1937 Molesworth, the largest single holding in the nation, was abandoned because of rising costs and falling production, and the Crown took over much of the station to "reduce the degradation and erosion of these lands and to achieve sustainable land management" (South Island Working Party on Sustainable Land Management [hereafter SIWP] 1994:84) at a time when rabbits were

Photo 22 *Hieracium* taking hold of tussock

yet again in crisis numbers and high-country farming, after eighty years of extensive grazing, promised to become uneconomic (see McLeod 1975). The Lands and Survey Department, developed from the department originally concerned with surveying Crown lands and leasing them to settlers, was the administrative body, but its local administrators, the commissioners of Crown lands, were surveyors, not specialists in pastoral use. The simple system used to determine tenure was to lease a run to the highest bidder at auction. Rents, varying widely among properties, were based on sheep numbers. In 1940, seeing their future foreshadowed, the runholders met with the minister of lands, who approved the High Country Committee as an advisory body on all matters concerning the South Island high country. It comprised representatives from each of the provincial land districts,[10] and in 1945 it was incorporated as the South Island High Country Committee of Federated Farmers. The minister also agreed to appoint one high-country man from names submitted by the High Country Committee to each land board as seats were vacated.[11]

Legislating Rehabilitation: The Land Act of 1948

Legislative advances in the 1940s and 1950s provided the administrative framework for rehabilitation through such acts as the Soil Conservation and Rivers Control Act of 1941 (creating catchment boards) and the Rabbits Act of 1955. A key piece of legislation, the 1948 Land Act, created the current system of pastoral-lease tenure for Crown land, the terms of which determine high-country land use and figure heavily in runholders' claims to security of tenure. The minister of lands introduced the act saying, "It may be necessary for some control to be exercised over the type of land contained in the lease for soil conservation purposes to prevent erosion and regenerate some of the hill country contained in the lease" (in Kerr 1982:4). The tussock grasslands were at a low point, and public concern for soil conservation shaped the Crown's reluctance to allow for the permanent alienation of the high country; even fertile lowlands were threatened by high-country erosion (see Cumberland 1981 for a geographer's view).

The act replaced pastoral licences with leases that confer the following rights and obligations on lessees: a lease perpetually renewable at thirty-three-year intervals with "fair annual rent" fixed by the Land Settlement Board,[12] and "set at a rate per 1,000 stock units of unimproved carrying capacity—adjusted for location, stock performance, and other 'special factors'" (Kerr 1984:26); the exclusive right to pasturage over the land comprised by the lease but with no right to soil and water, wild trees (and shrubs), introduced animals and scenery, and no right of freehold; de facto trespass control; restrictions on stock numbers, and burning of vegetation, and cultivation, cropping and grassing of land, with stock numbers and adjustment of boundaries subject to the permission of the commissioner of Crown lands. Control of rabbits, adoption of improved technology and management, and the availability of finance mainly from the reinvestment of farm income accompanied the act (Kerr 1984:25).

The legislation gave security of tenure to land classified by the Land Settlement Board as "land suitable or adaptable for pastoral purposes only" (New Zealand Department of Lands and Survey 1948 S 51.1) and facilitated rehabilitation of the high country (Kerr 1987:3) by providing "occupiers with the confidence to invest in long-term management strategies" (SIWP 1994:84).[13] Insecurity of tenure has often been cited by high-country lessees as the source of environmental deterioration.[14] In *Spirit of the High Country* lessees note that the Land Act provided both "a real sense of ownership" and a "conservation ethos" (South Island High Country Committee 1992:19), but the authors of *Pastoral High Country* argue instead that scapegoating insecurity of tenure became part of high-country mythology (Centre for Resource Management 1983:40), and pastoral scientists Douglas and Allan agree, acknowledging that economic conditions, limitations of technology, and overgrazing were more critical (1992:13). Following the Land Act, "the history of the hill and high country . . . has been one of dramatic improvement of vegetation, rising stock numbers, intensification and diversification" (Centre for Resource Management 1983:48). Prices peaked during the Korean wool boom in 1950-1951 but were undermined by a waterside workers strike in 1951 that stopped the sale of wool. Run management for soil conservation purposes promoted development of pastoral runs in the 1960s (Centre for Resource Management 1983:49); lowland development by runholders was subsidized in return for retirement from grazing of pastoral leases on severely eroded mountain ranges, especially class VII and class VIII high country; this measure was accompanied by careful control of animal stocking and by noxious weed and animal control. A marked shift from extensive grazing to rotational grazing and greater subdivision of blocks improved productivity and marks an organically based understanding of land management. Despite a focus on soil conservation and grasslands ecology at this time, productivity remained the primary goal and led to the development and intensification of production and use in the land-development movement of the 1950s, 1960s and 1970s through aerial oversowing and fertilization (Isern 1992). Farmers told me that subsidies also promoted production and quantity well into the 1980s and in so doing shaped people's images of high-country farmers for the worse.[15]

Freeholding Farmland and Protecting Multiple-Use Lands

In 1970 rent was made reviewable every eleven years but only after the thirty-three-year leases had run their course. Because the thirty-three-year leases would be due for renewal in the early 1980s, the Land Settlement Board and the lessees began to consider the basis for establishing a "fair annual rent." The Land Amendment Act of 1979 switched to a valuation-based rental system, with the rental rate for pastoral leases at 2-¼ percent of the value of land exclusive of improvements with a two-step phase-in period (see Kerr 1982:4).[16] In 1981 lessees, concerned about the impact of revised rentals based on the value of land, persuaded the government to set up a Committee of Inquiry into Crown Pastoral Leases (Kerr 1984:27). The "Clayton Committee" recommended phasing out pastoral-leasehold tenure by reclassifying suitable land as farmland and "establishing a tenure called 'multiple use' land for areas within pastoral leases which, in the public interest, ought not to be permanently alienated" (in Kerr 1984:27). Many who claim to protect the public interest believed that the thirty-three-year lease term had made runholders the beneficiaries of highly concessional rentals, but they also believed that eleven-year intervals were still too long given rapid inflation. Many argued that the committee protected the pastoralists' interests above the public interest; runholders, however, noted with distress that their input had not been sought.

Early in 1983 Federated Mountain Clubs organized a weekend seminar on "The Future of Pastoral Leasehold Lands," with contributions by all of those with an interest in Crown Lands. Explosive newspaper headlines such as "South Island Land Grab" and "Huge Profits in Crown Land Grab" headed stories that suggested millions would be put "in the pockets of a select group of South Island farmers" who could freehold "picture postcard" settings such as lakeside lands that are invaluable (*New Zealand Times* 9 and 16 November 1983) and elicited angry responses from the Minister of Lands, Jonathan Elworthy, noting that lands when sold would be done so at market value, and only land reclassified as farm land could be purchased (*New Zealand Times* 23 November 1983). The move toward freeholding had been supported by the minister in his address to the 1981 Hill and High Country Seminar, "Are pastoral leases really necessary?" He urged the reclassification of high-country land from pastoral to renewable leasehold, which carries the right of freehold, but with 4 percent rental, thus necessitating a move to freehold for many farmers. Taking a strongly economic line, Elworthy argued that the pastoral lease was a constraint to production. Circulated to Federated Farmers was a letter of response on their behalf to the *Times* by Des Gregan, a former valuer and land administrator, that provides a critique of the kinds of media distortions so angering to Elworthy:

> The recent changes in Land Settlement Board policy providing for greater liberalisation of freeholding rights over pastoral land, far from depriving recreationists and conservationists of their rights and desires, provide a unique opportunity for the separation and resumption by the Crown of the Land considered suitable for multiple use or reserve status. No land may be freehold before full reports have been considered by the Land Settlement Board as to what land should be retained.
>
> Firstly, land reclassified for freeholders will not include lake or river frontages that are invariably reserved. Secondly, the values of areas reclassified as "farmland" and subsequent sale are determined by the Valuation Department, an independent authority, as full market values taking into account all factors which may influence the value of the land—including "picture postcard settings."
>
> Not many runholders, under the economic circumstances prevailing will be able to face the costs involved in freeholding but where they can this may be expected to lead to more intensive development and subsequent subdivision which can benefit New Zealand. (Gregan 1983)

The Land Settlement Board did not endorse the Clayton Committee recommendations but, in a series of resolutions put forward to the minister of lands
in April 1983, preferred, "(a) the retention of the existing form of pastoral lease
(b) the facilitation of partial reclassification of suitable land within leases; and
(c) the protection of conservation and recreational values of significance" (in
Kerr 1984:27). Kerr notes the practical effects of these recommendations, including the gradual reclassification and freeholding (on the lessees' initiative) of
at least part of most leases; the covenanting of land by the Crown for conservation, recreation, or other purposes; and continued restricted tenure for pastoral
use of land not reclassified or covenanted (1984:27). Freehold title would only
be available "in a manner which does not compromise identified conservation or
recreational values of significance" (in McSweeney 1983:53).

The initiatives for recalculating the basis for rents on leases to force farmers to freehold particular lands within their leases and for reclassifying the pastoral high country during the 1970s elaborated the distinction between farming
land designated for production, which was proposed for freeholding, and conservation land designated for preservation. Farming land fit an earlier model of
sustainability in which economic production based on a model of extraction of
resources (i.e., soil) took primacy, while conservation land fit an evolving model
of sustainability in which environmental preservation based on a model of ecological balance (i.e., species) took primacy. Legislating new classifications that
fixed the distinction between productive freehold land and multiple-use conservation land promised to carve up the landscape into categories defined in terms
of different uses and value, and in terms of simultaneously competing discourses
of sustainability. Government restructuring of the administrative mechanisms
for owning and managing high-country lands has been ongoing through the
1980s and 1990s and has reified these distinctions. The protection of natural and
recreational values has replaced productivity on the national agenda.

Contemporary Legislative Initiatives: Conservation and Ecological Sustainability

High-country lands comprise 6 million hectares or 22 percent of New Zealand's
land area of 27 million hectares. Of this, in 1994, 2.45 million hectares of land
(tussock grasslands, peaks, glaciers, rivers, lakes, and some native forests)—
approximately 48 percent of the South Island high country, 20 percent of the
South Island and 10 percent of New Zealand's total land area—were held as
Crown pastoral leases with a total of 341 pastoral leases carrying approximately
2.8 million stock units. The balance of Crown land is 3.5 million hectares, consisting of the Department of Conservation estate and national parks (New Zealand Commissioner of Crown Lands 1994:10; South Island High Country Committee of Federated Farmers 1992:2). Tussock grasslands once covered 25
percent or 5 million hectares of the South Island; together with braided rivers

they cover one-third of the South Island and incorporate distinctive landscapes, special plant species and rare animals.

Conservationist Gerry McSweeney and soil scientist Les Molloy note that these tussock grasslands contain "a unique group of plants and animals adapted to temperature extremes, drought, heavy snowfalls, fire and even to erosion of the unstable mountain ranges" with little environmental protection (1984:2). They are concerned about the threat to these grasslands posed by pressures from agricultural development and freeholding, as well as pressures from hydroelectric development, irrigation development, exotic forestry, tourist villages and ski areas (1984:3). While high-altitude lands have been protected through retirement programs, low-altitude tussock grasslands and high-country wetlands remain at risk, they argue. McSweeney and Molloy note that pastoral-lease administration has focused primarily on farming, rather than on the protection of natural and recreational values; they urge the securing of reserves in tussock grasslands and share the view of nonfarming constituencies with concern for the public interest in the high country that the Land Settlement Board "overwhelmingly reflects the political, departmental and farming interests on it" (cf. Centre for Resource Management 1983).[17] In their view, the election of the fourth Labour government in 1984 reflected Labour sympathies for the public interest.

Within the Ministry for the Environment, Landcorp (Land Corporation) and DOC (Department of Conservation), together with the Land Department and the Department of Survey and Land Information (DOSLI) (derived from the former Department of Lands and Survey), are concerned with pastoral leases (see figure 8.1). From the perspective of groups such as the Federated Mountain Clubs, this division of responsibility was an improvement over administration by the Department of Lands and Survey, and the Land Settlement Board with their presumed pastoral bias (see Henson 1986:24). It suggests a shift from a preference for pastoral use of these lands to an accounting of a diversity of values and uses (Hayward 1987a:43).

Protecting the Public Estate and the Fourth Labour Government

In September 1986, the Cabinet decided to implement a partnership between Landcorp and DOC with the former responsible for commercial farming and land-management operations, and the latter for the identification and protection of conservation values in high-country lands. This separation maps onto that between production and conservation. Pastoral leases and licences were to be administered by Landcorp together with a number of farms and unalienated Crown land, but the leases remained under Crown ownership with the corporation serving as agent. As the branch of the Ministry for the Environment that deals with planning and policy advice and the monitoring of the environmental effects of policies, DOC's main role is nature conservancy, including both a management and an advocacy role "looking after the public interest in the public estate for the intrinsic values of that estate, to allow the appreciation of the

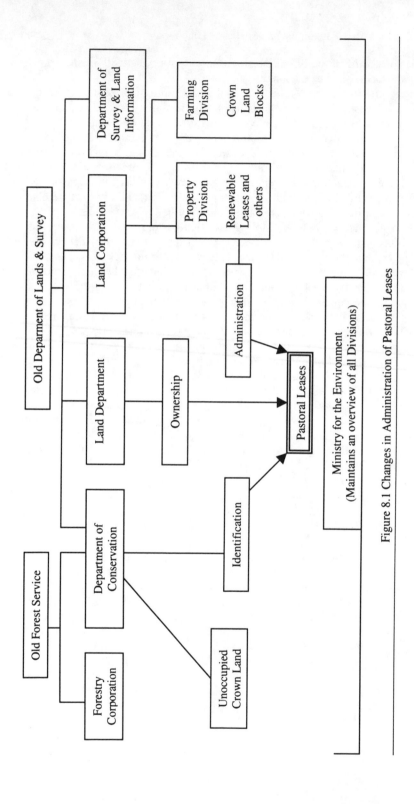

Figure 8.1 Changes in Administration of Pastoral Leases

estate, to permit recreation on it and to safeguard the future options regarding it" (Woollaston 1987:53).

Parliamentary Under-Secretary for Conservation Woollaston emphasized that the separation of conservation and preservation objectives from production objectives underpinned the establishment of DOC, and noted that the intensity of feeling surrounding the administration of high-country lands is overproduction versus conservation values (1987:51).

> The debate from the public's perception became one that involved not just the use of or access to public lands; it also became a debate about the preservation of a valuable part of our national self-image, our national identity. I don't want to suggest though, that only those that live in towns and look through their centrally heated windows at the Southern Alps have any sort of emotional attachment to that land. Those involved in production from that land identify just as strongly with it collectively and I think much more strongly as individuals. They become, in a good sense of the word, very possessive of the land. I think the symptom of this has been the increasing identification of Crown lessees as "owners" of their farms and the land they lease. (Woollaston 1987:52)

For precisely these reasons, the division of production from conservation distressed the High Country Committee. Referring back to the 1948 Land Act, High Country Committee chair Hamish Ensor noted that "this was plainly a recognition of the fact that, within that line, production and protection should go hand in hand to the benefit of the nation" (1987:69). Ensor's concerns were shared by Chris Kerr, a management officer of the Tussock Grasslands and Mountain Lands Institute at Lincoln University, who noted that "land protection, land management and soil conservation are indistinguishable" (1987:8); in either case, at stake are soil, water, and vegetation, all of which former land-tenure legislation (such as the Land Act of 1948) was designed to protect (Kerr 1987:5).

Even more distressing to runholders was the uncertainty of negotiations over marginal strips along streams and rivers, plant and animal pest control, and the Protected Natural Areas (PNA) program. Riparian strips three meters or more in average width were understood by the government to be excluded from transfer to state-owned enterprises such as Landcorp. Provisions in the State-Owned Enterprises Bill (section 24.2b) and the Conservation Act (section 64.4) dictated the exclusion, presumably to provide public access or for the protection of river banks and water quality. The government in 1987 indicated that it planned to eliminate taxpayer funding for the control of weeds and pests,[18] but runholders could not carry the burden of this control, which totals $15-25 million per year;[19] John Aspinall states that some farms currently spend up to 25 percent of gross income on such control (1996). Local and regional pest-control authorities with a separate authority focusing on national pest problems seemed likely (Kerr 1987:2).

The PNA program, established in 1982, was meant to "identify and protect representative examples of the full range of indigenous biological and landscape features in New Zealand, and thus maintain the distinctive New Zealand character of the country" (SIWP 1994:63). Here aesthetics become an integral part of what is sustainable. Teams were to identify the sites, which would then be managed through a voluntary arrangement between DOC and the lessee. The PNA program was implemented slowly with no completion date targeted and a presumed shortage of funds; many farmers had moratoria placed on lands with potential PNA designation, removing that land from farming use and complicating their ability to plan or sell leases. As one runholder noted, "Protected areas should be everyone's asset, not the farmer's liability alone." A danger of PNAs for runholders is that they can increase tourism, leading to potential disruption of stock management and increased land degradation from human use.

Similar in purpose to the PNA program is the Queen Elizabeth II National Trust, which protects landscape features on private land by accepting gifted or bequeathed land and by open-space covenants. Established by act of Parliament in 1977, the trust provides, protects, and enhances open space, defined as "any area of land or body of water that serves to preserve or to facilitate the preservation of any landscape of aesthetic, cultural, recreational, scenic or social interest or value" (cited in Clendon 1988:23). The National Trust is of special interest to leaseholders because it is "able to provide a legally binding means of protecting special landscape features, in perpetuity and independent of government or commercial interests" (Clendon 1988:23). The trust usually assists with fencing expenses and with legal and survey costs incurred in registering a covenant agreement on a land title. At stake then "in the evolution of balanced high country land management" are both nature conservation and agricultural development (McSweeney 1983:54). By 1994 Gerry McSweeney was claiming nature conservation as "our only sustainable land use" because "a young nation such as ours draws on natural icons to establish our identity," trade and tourism depend "on our clean green image," and nature tourism sells "active experiences" to visitors (not of the "thrill and kill" kind) (1994:58-62).

An additional player with an interest in the public estate is the recreationist whose voice is heard most loudly through Federated Mountain Clubs. While arguing that the pastoral-lease system was fairly effective when it first evolved, the spokespeople for such groups say that current changes in land use demand changes in land tenure. They favor more surrender of high-country lands to the Crown rather than retirement, where lands remain ungrazed but within the lease. They favor access to class VIIe (severely eroded class VII lands) and class VIII lands also but claim that runholders argue over these classifications. An equally powerful spokesman is University of Otago botanist Alan Mark of the Royal Forest and Bird Protection Society (1985). He argues that the classification "pastoral" is meant to apply to land with clear agricultural value and no recreational value; national values are embedded in high-country lands, and these values must be met first by fully assessing the public interest in these lands. He, too, favors the surrender and compulsory destocking of VII7e and VIII lands if necessary, though he acknowledges that this practice might leave uneconomic those runs for which these lands occupy a large percentage, noting that the idea "gets the backs of farmers up" (Alan Mark, personal communication, 15 June 1987).

Legislating Sustainable Management: The Crown Pastoral Land Bill of 1995

In reviewing pastoral-lease tenure, the 1994 Martin Report maintained that it "is not achieving sustainable management and does not provide the flexibility to make the necessary changes toward ecological sustainability and economic viability"; the report called for a review of pastoral-lease tenure and aimed to make freehold "all land not required by the Crown for the public interest" (Marshall 1995:4). Of the four objectives outlined by the report—promoting sustainable land management; transferring the state's productive assets to the private sector; protecting the public interest in nature conservation, recreation, access, landscape, and cultural and historic values; and considering the Treaty of Waitangi—I will focus on those concerning sustainable land management and freeholding.

The Resource Management Act of 1991 (RMA) defines sustainable "management" and subjects all land regardless of land tenure to management constraints ensuring sustainability of "natural and physical resources." This means managing the use, development, and protection of natural and physical resources in a way, or at a rate, which enables people and communities to provide for their social, economic, and cultural well being and for their health and safety while—

> (a) Sustaining the potential of natural and physical resources (excluding minerals) to meet the reasonably foreseeable needs of future generations; and (b) Safeguarding the life-supporting capacity of air, water, soil and ecosystems; and (c) Avoiding, remedying, or mitigating any adverse effects of activities on the environment. (Resource Management Act II.5.2)

The act refers to matters of national importance such as preservation of coastal features, protection of outstanding features and landscapes, protection of habitats for indigenous vegetation and fauna, preservation of public access to shorelands, and the relationship of te iwi Maori with their taonga.

Reinforcing the RMA, then Minister of Lands Dennis Marshall sought to address land degradation, specifically evident in the encroachment of weeds, pests, reduced productivity, reduced profitability, and reduced capacity to maintain inputs; to "clarify accountabilities for the condition of land and to create incentives for sound land use practices" in part by making certain parcels of land freehold in order to motivate farmers to adopt sustainable land-management practices; and to increase the resilience of land by freeing it from the lack of diversification that pastoral leases ensure (1995:5). Marshall worked on the Crown Pastoral Land Bill of 1995 to bring about land-reform policy that ranged in its considerations from increased freeholding to the government's taking back pastoral leases altogether. He built on prior reviews of the tenure regime and in particular came to favor a proposal creating three categories of land: "farm" land for freeholding, "restricted use" land retained by the Crown and managed under lease for a range of both production and protection purposes, and "conservation" land to be placed in the Conservation Estate (Marshall 1995:3).

The bill outlines the procedure for seeking tenure review in which a runholder can initiate purchase. The Martin Report, after scrutinizing pastoral-lease tenure and noting that lessees are reasonably content with the status quo, urged that tenure review progress rapidly precisely because it provides a strategy for improving sustainable management in the high country (SIWP 1994:87). Ecological sustainability, as defined by the RMA, is said to take top priority in these negotiations. As runholders understood this, it meant that all leasehold land is "up for grabs since it will begin on a level playing field," that classification is gone (for example, class VIIe and class VIII land), and that the central issue is the method by which the price is set for freeholding. As one runholder said to me: "No farmer in his right mind is going to trade in a 2 percent rent for a 10 percent mortgage," but the Crown "wants to work this out because it is costing them money" (field notes 6.v.95).

On a property that has initiated this process on an interim basis pending review of the bill two issues emerged in the early stages of the review: public access and the valuation of what might be sold. The family noted that they were undergoing the review process not in order to gain freehold, but rather "we are in this to resolve issues about the RAPs [Recommended Areas of Protection][20] and the uncertainty that DOC has imposed on us." With the "RAPs on hold," the runholder said, he wanted them "to make up their minds." The family was told it was critical for them to specify what they wanted out of the tenure-review process; they were told repeatedly that they should be no worse off at the end of the day in either financial or productive terms. While I was there, the lessee consulted with Ngai Tahu to see what kinds of specific demands on these lands they might make with the Crown; their representative had no specific demands and acknowledged that even if burial sites were present, they would best remain undisturbed by being unacknowledged. Like the lessees, the Ngai Tahu representative did not feel that all land should be open by right to a public. Similarly, Tipene O'Regan, chairman of the Ngai Tahu Trust Board, does not trust public ownership. He cuts through the "kiwi taste" for the absolutist "ideological landslides" that have dominated tenure reform in recent years and aligns his position with the farming community: "It's one of the reasons why I like high country field days, and why I like dealing with people who really do work the land, rather than sitting around and philosophizing about it" (O'Regan 1994:63). O'Regan characterizes the Eastern Polynesian people who came to New Zealand as "habitual interventionists with the environment" and says that their production ethic worked in an environment that was rapidly self-healing (1994:64). Over time, he suggests, they were "forced into a relationship with their environment based on sustainability" (1994:65). Sustainability, he argues, is "not really as a concept preservation of a resource. That is, preservation for preservation's sake. . . . It is the preservation for use. It is conserving and caring for them

for use" (1994:65). Conservation, then, is "wise use and protection of the repro-
ductive capacity of the resource."

Members of the High Country Branch of Federated Farmers met in Timaru
on 15 May 1995 to discuss the Land Bill on its way to a Select Committee.[21]
The runholders were generally supportive of the bill, but three clauses received
their attention. Clause 20 of the Crown Pastoral Land Bill aims "to promote the
sustainable management of reviewable land" and to facilitate

> (i) The restoration to full Crown ownership and control of reviewable
> land that has high inherent values; and (ii) The freehold disposal of
> reviewable land capable of productive use; and (iii) The creation of
> appropriate public rights of access to and enjoyment of reviewable
> land.

Runholders noted that the bill does not define "productive use" and does not
specify what "the enjoyment" of lands might mean. "Inherent values," after
much discussion, was glossed as meaning (natural and physical) conservation
values, and the discussion turned to consideration of compensation, with the
suggestion to add a clause reading "where a determination adversely affects sustainable management, the financial loss will be equated."

As was often the case in such meetings, my input was invited and I suggested that the high-country community might write in the collective self as part
of inherent cultural values. During a field day on sustainability at Mount Peel
station, consultant John Tavendale mapped out the following mission statement
for the property and its owners since 1855, the Acland family:

> To manage the property in an optimum Physical and Financial man-
> ner with financial returns not to have precedence over good standards
> of improvements, sustainable pasture management, yet ensuring that
> the property will continue to be farmed by the Acland Family. (New
> Zealand Conference on Sustainable Land Management 1994a:49)

Sustainable ownership as a resource is critically at stake in this statement.
Clearly these are not the cultural values intended by the legislation. The Martin
Report differentiates three kinds of resource values, all of which are designated
as economic—use values (benefits derived by society in either an active or pas-
sive way), option values (preserving options for future use), and existence values (values held by people willing to pay to keep things in existence) (SIWP
1994:12). The report gives primacy to yet another value, primary or intrinsic: the
basic ecological characteristics of systems that are the "'glue' that holds everything together" in such a way that the value of the ecosystem "will exceed the
sum of the [economic] values." The concept is akin to anthropologists' understanding of culture as superorganic, except that ecology has replaced culture.

Clause 14, "Discretionary Actions," authorizes the commissioner of Crown
lands, when considering tenure review applications from lessees, to have regard
for "ensuring (so far as is practicable) the protection of the inherent values
(other than recreation values) of the land." As the minister of lands explains

(Marshall 1995:17-18), the commissioner can take into account not only soil-conservation values but also "nature conservation, landscape, historical and cultural values." Historical and cultural values receive no elaboration in his proposals, however. Some farmers were concerned that this clause "can stuff up a run—production will not win out over conservation."

Clause 31 was considered the most important, because it empowered "the imposition on land being disposed of of covenants intended to ensure sustainable management" (Marshall 1995:iv in explanatory notes). Runholders read this clause as a blank check to the commissioner regarding covenants but noted also that it extended the categories of land that could be freeholded and would elicit opposition from nongovernmental organizations (NGOs).

Shared by Ngai Tahu and the runholders is a diachronic integrative, interactive model of their relations to environmental processes in which sustainability is "an *outcome* of systemic processes that link people to one another within a community, to their natural environment, and to other communities" (see Lieber forthcoming, emphasis added). As Lieber underscores, what is to be sustained is a particular kind of relationship between a population and an environment; here (and throughout the Pacific) social relationships are at stake and land is a template for the familial. In contrast, urban-based environmentalists and NGOs argue for preservation of a presumed static past.

Sustaining Aesthetic Landscapes: Preserving Open Space

NGO opponents of the Land Bill, who also seek to return high-country lands to an undegraded state, vigorously oppose the freeholding it suggests. Just as the profoundly modified British moorlands (also burnt and grazed) seem to have exerted a spell on Marion Shoard's protection advocates (1982:57), so does the New Zealand high country exert a similar spell for some, that is, as a site for discovering wilderness.[22] Shoard argues that people are not only herd animals but also loners, hence the desire of the wilderness lobby for the open space of the moorlands (1982:58). She extrapolates eight components of wilderness: wildness (the antithesis of domestication), openness (its emptiness and the dominance of the sky), asymmetry and homogeneity (simplicity with no obvious pattern, silence, and solitude), height (demanding physical exertion), freedom to wander at will (liberation and tracklessness), the absence of human handiwork (an "appearance" of being untouched by humans), relics of ancient man (historical monuments), and wind (Shoard 1982:59-60).

Similarly, a high-country daughter argues not for the sustainability of resources but for the sustainability of landscape, the solitude of expansive tussock grasslands, and of an open-space aesthetic (cf. Norton 1991:16). Lesley Shand, an active conservationist in the Royal Forest and Bird Protection Society, celebrates openness, homogeneity, nakedness, and wilderness as domesticity's converse:

The real issue of the high country rarely gets aired yet drives the passion which fires people who know the back country and understand it. . . . It was summed by Bernie Card, (once Field Officer in Lands and Survey and then the head equivalent in Landcorp), with what he said to me after the Awatere Valley Hearing part of the Clayton Report—"Landscape." I agree with him that landscape incorporates many things. The real threat we face is the loss of those *inimitable, irreplaceable landscapes*—great distances, sweeping vistas and with them goes the natural vegetation, space and the feeling you are seeing a living massive 3D oil canvas—but it's *real*. Those vast distances uncluttered by buildings and in the most part without outward vestiges of colonisation—introduced trees.

I am talking of low altitudes [in the high country]. Where else in lowland areas can you find such untampered with space. The Land Bill commodifies and turns the high country into real estate, and allows the landscape to be chopped into blocks. Smaller blocks are what domesticated humans used to town sections can cope with mentally. They cannot cope with the open space. It's unmanageable in their eyes so it's turned into tidy little blocks of domesticity.

People's imaginations must instead be fired by the concept of OPEN SPACE. That to me [would be] the greatest loss of all imposing [the] clutter of domesticity on a landscape so beautiful in its nakedness. You really see the form of the country. The underlying geologic forms that are the coat hanger of the present landscape are there for the wondering at. You can imagine and speculate about the great forces that created those forms.

I dread the thought of clutter for it. The high country will lose its inscrutability. (Lesley Shand, personal communication, 12 May 1995, emphasis in original.)

She refers to a pamphlet produced by the High Country Public Lands Campaign in May 1995[23] as a call to arms to save the high country from a "sell-off" by "killing" Marshall's Land Bill, and by blocking privatization and permanent alienation through "unconstrained freeholding" of "hundreds of thousand of hectares of the high country now owned by all New Zealanders." Federated Mountain Clubs has referred to the Land Bill as "The Last Great Public Land Carve Up" (Barr 1994). Arguing that covenants are insufficient, the pamphlet says that the bill "marginalises conservation" and fails to protect the high country's "remaining indigenous character . . . from continued burning, grazing and farming use." It "fences nature into a corner" by allowing only areas of (arguably) "high inherent" conservation value to be allocated to the Department of Conservation and thus neglecting "large wildland areas important for ecosystem protection and recreation" that should be part of the public conservation estate. For the coalition, the Land Bill's major purpose should be to "safeguard nature conservation, landscape, public access and other Crown interests," and the responsibility of the commissioner of Crown lands is to "protect natural character and indigenous vegetation and wildlife habitat." Sustainable in these terms is the presumed continuity of the past, continuous with an indigenous, timeless landscape to which New Zealanders have access, which section 2 of the Conservation Act of 1987 attempts to define: "Conservation means the preservation and protection of natural and historic resources for the purpose of maintaining their *intrinsic* values, providing for their appreciation and recreational enjoyment by the public, and safeguarding the options of future generations" (emphasis added).[24]

Of primary value for sustainability is a particular kind of heritage, identified by the Royal Forest and Bird Protection Society as the land forms, vegetation and wildlife of the high country that are unique and distinctive, that is, endemic to the place. At stake with the proposed privatization is the protection (sustaining) of "the mountains and tussock lands, sweeping valleys and dramatic landscapes of this region." Like Lesley Shand the Society seeks to take advantage of a naturalized historic moment when they might preserve an unbounded visual landscape, like the British moorlands, in which a "network of extensive parks and reserves to protect the natural areas" might be created (Royal Forest and Bird Protection Society 1995:1). "Outstanding wildlands" comprise this unbounded landscape, the components of which are areas of recreational significance, "the Southern Lakes," "the rolling tussocklands of the Lindis Pass area, the mountainscapes of the McKenzie Country, and the vast braided rivers and gorges of the Rangitata and Rakaia, Waimakariri and Clarence Rivers" (Barr 1994:26).

Cultural Diversity and Community Sustainability

Legislating sustainable land management has taken a new twist in the 1990s. Such legislation is necessary, according to Australian lawyer John Bradsen, because without it the two sets of forces illustrated above will prevail: material forces (economics) and nonmaterial forces (values, attitudes, and beliefs) (1994:100). Bradsen argues that the former sidelines ecological systems, ignores land as part of nature, and lacks a sense of the community (as distinct from individuals), while the latter is full of contradictions, inconsistencies and wishful thinking. Bradsen suggests on the basis of models in South Australia that the best legislative models empower, organize, and guide communities (1994:102). Community has become the third force in the sustainability equation as community-based collaborative models of ownership emerge.

In New Zealand the Rabbit and Land Management Programme provides such a model and has established the prototype for future initiatives. Established for the period 1989-1995, and funded with $25 million from the central government, the regional councils of Marlborough and Canterbury, and farmers from these areas, the program was a comprehensive response to pest and noxious weed devastation with its goal "to achieve ecological, economic and community sustainability in the dry tussock grasslands." Involved were farm families in the program area, the Ministry of Agriculture and Fisheries, and an advisory committee made up of those with direct high-country involvement; 400,000 hectares of land were selected including ninety-eight farms with especially badly rabbit-infested lands. The program responded to the nexus of problems created by rabbit and hawkweed infestation, the stresses of a highly variable climate, and the declining financial viability of high-country farming. It focused on rabbit control (through poisoning, shooting, and fencing), "whole farm" plans (with a focus on property plans and good land management), and semiarid-lands research involving collaboration between landholders and researchers in a variety of organizations (New Zealand Ministry of Agriculture and Fisheries 1988).[25]

Reminiscent of Aldo Leopold's definition of the land ethic as a "community instinct in-the-making" (1969:403), Bradsen's view is entirely compatible with the international goals of the Mountain Agenda for developing approaches to sustainability that "empower mountain communities to exercise more control over local resource management and conservation" and to recover and foster "the cultural expressions of mountain peoples" whose *"cultural diversity provides a basis for sustainability"* (Mountain Institute 1996:13, emphasis added). The not-so-extraordinary parallel between cultural diversity and biodiversity, between community sustainability and ecological sustainability (and, as I will argue, between cultural identity and country) prompts us as anthropologists to imagine how we might find a way to enter these dialogues on sustainability by factoring human communities into biodiversity.

My approach is shaped by Robert Netting, who homeostatically jump-started political ecology in his *Balancing on an Alp*, where he attended to conditions of land tenure, the distribution of land, and its economic significance as social and cultural facts "grounded in history and perpetuated by custom and law" (Netting 1981:14; cf. Lieber 2000 for another longitudinal analysis). In taking those components into account along with environmental possibilities and the specificity of subsistence systems, Netting (1981:40) conceptualized the social world as part of the ecological arena and directed attention to the significance of land regulation (as well as intensification and expansion) in shaping the allocation of certain resources (1981:42). For smallholders, some kinds of resources lend themselves to communal management (Netting 1993:173). In the Swiss Alps, where Netting worked, communal land tenure was essential to smallholders' management of land in a profoundly modified environment; while ranchers and pastoralists are not smallholders in his terms (1993:3), the less-modified New Zealand Alps similarly may continue to benefit from a form of communal land tenure and management.

Comparative cultural ecology, environmental historian Donald Worster suggests, invites us to look at the landscape (for example, an instrumentalized river and its social consequences) in order to see "the interplay between humans and nature and to track the social consequences it has produced—to discover the process by which in the remaking of nature, we remake ourselves" (1992:63). Worster asks not *if* human beings dominate nature, but *which* humans dominate nature. If the sustainable land ethic rejects individuality and individual ownership and management of resources in favor of Crown ownership and management to preserve the public estate, it might recraft community, too, not by compartmentalizing land into categories of freehold and Crown land (or categories of production and conservation), but by imagining a different kind of communal ownership—characteristic of but distinct from European alpine tenure patterns—at the district or regional level.

Taking Ownership of Sustainability

The most vocal voices for freeholding in the high-country community argue from a systems-based approach to sustainability in farming or land management. Here the interaction among indicators of sustainability provides the measurable components into which sustainability breaks down: financial (profit, risk and capital), social (employment, knowledge base, community effects and values) and ecological (soil, water, and ecological quality and nonrenewable resource use). These indicators are aspects of a range of sustainable land uses including conservation, pastoralism, forestry, and commercial recreation. Fusing conservation and diversified production in sustainable land management is said to be achievable through processes of local ownership, meaning ownership of problems and of codes of practice (A. Ensor 1994:79-80). "Practical pastoralists" will have to join forces with skilled advisors, agencies, financiers, and politicians; secure tenure and assets must be assured; ownership and the preservation of tradition are incentives to long-term planning; financially robust operations should be sustained; biological controls for hawkweed and rabbits should be introduced; and outside interests should be rejected unless people buy the privileges of ownership. Above all the "pastoral future will depend on farmers' ability to understand, take ownership and address sustainable land management" (Brown 1994:40). These farmers and the constituencies they represent have adopted an explicitly science-based sustainable land ethic in which "the answer lies in building strong farmer/science/agency partnerships" (A. Ensor 1994:80).

As a plan of action this approach is entirely consistent with the international Mountain Agenda of wanting to empower mountain communities to "exercise larger control over local resource management and conservation and generate income in sustainable and equitable ways" (Mountain Institute 1996:26). In *Spirit of the High Country* and in "Sustainability in the South Island High Country" (South Island High Country Committee of Federated Farmers 1992, 1994), the high-country community demonstrates the importance of protecting local people's interests, recognizing their knowledge, and supporting and initiating long-term monitoring of the environmental, economic, and social impacts of their actions. Above all, the agenda calls for local communities to participate in "all decisions that affect their natural resources" in locally driven programs (Mountain Institute 1996:22). Some, like former High Country Committee chair Alastair Ensor, see New Zealand as a pioneer: "In this regard New Zealand might get it right—it's small enough and focused enough with the contemporary shifts framing the debate to have the edge on the world in terms of claiming it is clean and green [although] with nitrogen runoff, we might lose that edge." He thinks that the "ultimate measure" of sustainability is in water and runoff.

The community has been proactive in the face of challenging social, financial, and environmental constraints in recent years. Farmers note that in the 1980s (and before) it was "all production, production with no concern for environmental issues whereas now, environment is the critical factor"; acknowledging that "farming management is not a static option, farmers state that past financial concerns must be replaced with equal attention to ecological and social concerns" (New Zealand Conference on Sustainable Land Management 1994a:50).[26] With so many interest groups making claims on these lands, farmers refuse to stand passively by and let others call the shots; in fact they are working to outsmart urban rhetoric by quantifying it. They are developing computer modeling for measuring components of financial, ecological, and social sustainability and for surveying and monitoring vegetation (Aubrey and Ensor 1994).[27] The computer model STOCKPOL is used to ensure that specific options for farming are biologically feasible; another computer model, RANGEPACK, calculates and projects economic outcomes (New Zealand Conference on Sustainable Management 1994a:56). In the Rakaia, together with a local-level Landcare group and some funding from the Ministry of Agriculture, farmers are monitoring approximately one hundred species of vegetation in twenty sites per property, examining three to five sites per property per day. They selected a range of sites—with varying altitude, and aspect, and including unimproved and improved country, as well as back and front country—and worked with a list of salient species such as hawkweed, blue tussock, snow tussock, and sweet vernal. They defined an area one hundred by one hundred meters and drew a line through it to do a species count. They enter the data into a computer (graphing it on three axes) to produce a baseline against which to measure change.

An advocate for the valley's monitoring project believes that these data will provide definitive evidence against people who argue that areas are degraded by stock. He gave me the example of one hill on his family property that environmentalists declared tussock grassland, and he explained to me that they don't realize that isn't its original state—it has tussocks because it is grazed and also has superphosphate applied; with grazing removed, the tussocks would not maintain themselves. An "authentic natural state" therefore cannot exist. Other farmers told me that while computers measure what actually is happening physically, management decisions are often made "from the gut," from intuition, "from an instinct for farming." While "ag-sci types struggle to understand" the computer programs, they "come easily to the farmers who understand intuitively what it is about." A farmer said that such a program "gives one the vocabulary to notice indigenous vegetation," thus taking care of "information holes" in their systems. He said that it has provided farmers with an opportunity to learn about what they don't know rather than to voice what they do know. Another farmer in the Rakaia valley quietly and confidently asserted that the best measure of land degradation is the condition of his stock, as the ultimate measure.

In the 1990s the shift to a discourse of sustainability allows for a move away from landscape and closer to country in the most recent stage of the sequence in "landscape as sustainable"; the concept has been imposed on the high country as part of an international agenda to manage mountain ecosystems, and farmers, while recognizing the need to actively embrace and define this top-down concept (to make a global ideological movement theirs), shared their doubts about it with me; "it's the in-term, but it hasn't been defined," "what does it mean to be sustainable?" "what is to be sustained?" "for whom is it to be sustained?" In this hermeneutic vacuum they are responding locally to sustainability as the newest colonialist mentality (Charlie Stevens, personal communication), and seizing collective agency by pioneering computer software to measure the concept and move it beyond rhetoric. Their actions take ownership of the concept.

An Indigenous Land Ethic: Sustaining Local Communities

A now-influential Pacific literature theorizes cultural identity by emphasizing its fluidity and constructedness, proclaiming the situatedness rather than the inherentness of its authenticities, and helping to jettison threadbare essentialized understandings of culture as accretive, consensual, static, and coherently indigenous; indeed indigeneity is a pastiche (Keesing 1993). Similarly, an indigenous state of nature is also a pastiche, and "country," like cultural identity, is as much a construction as an essence. Just as theorists of cultural identity reject a biological model of culture as species (Jackson 1989), so also must theorists of place reject a biological model of a "natural" landscape as having fixed, albeit diverse, inherent features. And yet it is precisely inherent and intrinsic values that clauses 14 and 20 of the 1995 Land Bill and the 1987 Conservation Act objectify, essentialize, and specify as needing the protection afforded by sustainable land management. At stake in the complex maneuverings to define sustainable land management are competing ideas about what these values are and which form of cultural landscape should prevail in high-country lands.

The truth is, as novelist of place Wallace Stegner remarks, "a place is more than half memory" (1994:51), and nostalgia for the way places used to be is a sign that "we have made a tradition out of mourning the passing of things we never had time really to know." He cites Wendell Berry

> and his belief that if you don't know where you are you don't know who you are. He is talking about the kind of knowing that involves the senses, the memory, and the history of a family or a tribe. He is talking about the knowledge of place that comes from working it in all weathers, making a living from it, suffering from its catastrophes, loving its mornings or evenings or hot noons, valuing it for the profound investment of labor and feeling that you, your parents and grandparents, your all-but-unknown ancestors have put into it. He is talking about the knowing that poets specialize in.

Stegner's call is to preserve place by sustaining habitation, not through nostalgia or replication of false authenticities. He tells his readers to be still, to belong, as indeed the current generation of Rakaia families have sought to do. And he, the poet, provides a formula for the sustainable in his own land ethic: "Only in the act of submission is the sense of place realized and a sustainable relationship between people and earth established." Stegner's western land ethic has been attacked by multicultural critics, suggesting that the substitution of "place" or "nature" for "culture" in Jean Jackson's title "Is There a Way to Talk about Making Culture without Making Enemies?" is equally risky when applied to the environment.

Preservation is not straightforward and knowing what is to be preserved seems to rely on rootedness and realizing that a country of pastoral lands is also a pastiche, like identity. In positing that people treat valued landscapes as "shrines to the past," David Lowenthal has written that people's preferences for past over present landscapes derive from "erroneous perceptions" that fail to acknowledge that such pasts (like identities) are complex and fluid accretions of time periods (1982:93). Lowenthal explains why people revisit these valued landscapes in memory—because the past is highly malleable through mental processes of selectivity and imagination, and because we can imagine a false continuity through landscape (and perhaps solitary escape in landscape) that counters the fragmentary nature of our lives in late capitalism. While Lowenthal addresses a primarily visual or representational landscape, rather than land in its more overt physical, geographical sense, his concept of valued landscapes resting in the valorization of a mythical past is equally applicable to conservationists' concerns for nature resources with high inherent value and to conventional discourses of sustainability with their emphasis on ecological continuity and preservation of an idealized, past balance of self-sustaining resources free of human intervention. Contemporary political, economic, and ecological pressures in the South Island preclude the continuation of a discourse of landscape and demand a return to treating this terrain on the terms of its managers and owners, the high-country community, for whom this place has been "country," an inhabited site invested with cultural meanings.

Jim Morris's reflections, although not typical, are provocatively resonant of Stegner's and Lowenthal's situational sense of place. He believes that the world cannot be sustainable in its original form because change is essential to its condition, that sustainability time spans should be lengthened and land use slowed down to a minimum to ensure the same potential for future generations; sustainable use in any land "rests in the hearts of men, not textbooks and science," because technology cannot be relied upon to solve the problems of overuse in the present (Morris 1994). He urges a return to rotation through paddocks and back country rather than cultivated paddocks and to mulching and fallow lands to "give the land more of a chance," practices that he is experimenting with to control hawkweed and rehabilitate the soil on his Otago property. In particular he attacks the profit motive sustained by the ideology of economic growth by urging lower expectations in terms of productivity and by using the horse as a way of returning to and preserving an endangered land ethic that celebrates animal husbandry, the soil, and the local community (Morris 1996b:176-178). Stegner says to be still, to belong; Morris says to follow Stegner's lead. Morris's thoughts, as dated as they may seem—he acknowledges that they may sound crazy—are reflected in the community-based, interactive project of legis-lating sustainable land management for pastoral lands at present and in community-based, local-level land care groups. His analogy of the land to the human body, similarly (and momentarily) sustained by drugs in the form of fer-tilizers, gives one pause as it suggests a series of linked analogies paralleling the historical progression from production to conservation to community in land legislation—land : body :: natural/biological diversity : cultural diversity :: country : cultural identity. If the analogy holds and dominant cultural metaphors become ensconced in land-management policies, Bradsen's legislative under-pinnings in community and the Mountain Agenda's commitment to the simulta-neous preservation of *linked* biological and cultural diversity may provide Aotearoa/New Zealand with the grassroots model for an innovative sustainable land ethic.

Notes

1. Like other theorists working in the anthropology of place, Deborah Rose (1988) returns cultural agency to our understandings of ecological systems. She asks that we attend to the political economy of knowledge and increase understanding of our role as moral agents in the systems of which we are a part. Drawing on her own ethnoecological studies in the Yarralin/Lingara area of the Northern Territory of Australia, Rose invites a shift in perception to see how Ngarinman people understand human life as existing with "a living and conscious cosmos," one that Elizabeth Povinelli (1993), in her work with Belyuen in the Cape York Peninsula, has revealed as a sentient environment, and which her interlocutors call "country."

2. See John McPhee (1971) for a philosophical consideration of conflicts and con-vergence between discourses of conservation, wilderness, development, and hydraulic engineering. See Dominy (1997a) for an Australian case study.

3. As a global network, the nongovernmental Mountain Forum is committed to promoting and implementing the Mountain Agenda. The Mountain Forum's webpage can be found at <http://www.mtnforum.org>. The regional Asia/Pacific Mountain Forum has as its focal point, ICIMOD (International Centre for Integrated Mountain Development), with its network on sustainable development of mountain and upland areas of Asia. Its webpage is <http://www.icimod.org.sg>. See Mountain Institute (1996).

4. Kevin O'Connor has defined culture in this instance as "the impact of work on environment by a people acting under the impulse of a continuing tradition," but he un-derstands such culture to be adaptive and creative, not "slavishly mimicking" one's grandparents (1989:99). As he notes, "Continuing culture also requires a continuing envi-ronment." In the Australian Alps, the term "cultural heritage" is used instead. For an exploration of parallel issues in the context of the Australian high country in New South Wales and Victoria, see Scougall (1992).

5. See New Zealand Government (1991, 1995).

6. Textual data include the 1991 Resource Management Act, the proceedings of the 1994 New Zealand Conference on Sustainable Land Management convened at Lincoln University (1994b), the comprehensive "South Island High Country Review" produced in the same year by the South Island Working Party on Sustainable Land Management, the new Crown Pastoral Land Bill (revising the 1948 Land Act), the extensive reports of the Rabbit and Land Management program, and farmer initiatives in computer modeling such

as Project FARMER (acronym for "Farmer Analysis of Research, Management, and Environmental Resources") of the Rural Futures Trust (Aubrey and Ensor 1994).

7. Commissioned by the ministers of conservation, agriculture and environment, the "South Island High Country Review" is known as the Martin Report after Graeme Martin, chair of the South Island Working Party on Sustainable Land Management, which authored the report.

8. The Tussock Grasslands and Mountain Lands Institute, dissolved in 1988 and replaced in 1993 by the Centre for Mountain Studies, has published extensively on pastoral-leasehold land, focusing on tenure, management, and sustainability. See its Centre for Resource Management (1983:31-54) for a history of land tenure.

9. These include: Mouse-Ear Hawkweed, King Devil, Tussock Hawkweed, and Field Hawkweed (South Island High Country Committee of Federated Farmers 1992:14).

10. In 1983 369 runs under pastoral lease were distributed among the provinces as follows: Marlborough 15 runs with one representative; Canterbury 122 runs with three representatives; Otago 200 runs with three representatives; Southland 25 runs with one representative (McSweeney and Molloy 1984:5).

11. Land boards were superseded in 1948, but high-country representation continued on the newly formed Land Settlement Board.

12. A chief pastoral land officer was responsible to the Land Settlement Board, which, in turn, was under the minister and Department of Lands and Survey. The board could reclassify land. Section 167 of the 1948 Land Act gives the minister of lands the right to set aside Crown land as a reserve even if it is subject to a pastoral lease.

13. The implications of the wording are unclear now although in 1948 it is likely that pastoral use was the only conceivable meaning intended. As Kerr asks (1987:3), "Is it intended that pastoral land be used exclusively for 'pastoral purposes' and thereby exclude all other uses?"

14. Underlying the legislative dependence of scientific resource management of tussock grasslands in New Zealand has been an implicit bias toward the tragedy-of-the-commons model, which tends to assume that the "users are selfish, unrestricted by social norms of the community, and trying to maximize short-term gains," but, as McCay and Acheson point out, contextual factors must be considered in any attempt to generalize from this model (1987:7). The argument has worked to the runholders' advantage in securing them the tenure that undermines extractive, nonsustainable productivity. See also Netting (1993:185) for a complex reading of the relationship of security of tenure to investment; he writes that "smallholders cannot wittingly destroy their own resources and thereby ruin the future livelihoods of their offspring" (1993:333).

15. This kind of ecologically compromising pastoral activity is linked to local intentions realized through global markets.

16. In contrast, in the United States the formula is more complicated and also the subject of bitter debate. "The formula consists of a base value of grazing on public land adjusted by indices reflecting current year land lease rates, cost of production and beef cattle prices. Annual increases or decreases of fees will be limited to no more than a 25 percent change from the previous year's fee. The fee will not, however, be lower than US$1.35 per animal unit per month (AUM). AUM is the amount of forage consumed by one cow and one calf, one horse, or given sheep or goats in one month" (in H. Ensor 1993:20).

17. The composition of the Land Settlement Board at the beginning of my fieldwork was: minister of lands (chairman); three representatives of the Department of Lands and Survey; one representative each from the Treasury, the Ministry of Agriculture and Fisheries, the Valuation Department, and the Rural Bank; and four private members (all farmers). Alan Mark (professor of Botany and advocate for Royal Forest and Bird Protec-

tion Society) and Alan Evans (former Federated Mountain Clubs president) were invited to attend.

18. Weeds include nassella tussock, broom, gorse, nodding thistle, ragwort, burdock, and sweetbriar. Pests include rabbits, possum, pits, feral deer, cats and ferrets (South Island High Country Committee of Federated Farmers 1992:16.)

19. Earlier, Prime Minister Muldoon under the National Party eliminated Tax Payer Input for the same.

20. RAPS were areas created by the preliminary ecological survey work completed as part of the Protected Natural Areas Programme and were defined under the Resource Management Act. While some lessees participated in having such areas designated, others did not. Action on RAPs has been suspended.

21. See New Zealand Ministry for the Environment (1995) and Marshall (1995) for documents under discussion.

22. See also Graber (1976). Graber's "wilderness ethic," distinct from Leopold's garden-based "land ethic," is an urban phenomenon that, she argues, is out of touch with the means of rural livelihoods (1976:114).

23. The campaign involves the Royal Forest and Bird Protection Society, Federated Mountain Clubs, the New Zealand Deerstalkers' Association, the New Zealand Fish and Game Council, and Public Access New Zealand.

24. Crown Pastoral Land, 86-1, defines "inherent values" as natural resources (as defined by the Conservation Act of 1987) and recreational, cultural, and historical values (Marshall 1995:2). Runholders referred to such areas as the "Crown jewels."

25. See also the *Report of the Rabbit and Land Management Task Force* (New Zealand Rabbit and Land Management Task Force 1988).

26. See also Molloy (1994) and Morris (1994).

27. For example, the Martin Report resists definitive statements but expresses concern for the possible decline of organic matter, nutrient levels, and soil pH (SIWP 1994:28). In response to the report's conclusions about nutrient imbalance on unimproved country, the South Island High Country Committee of Federated Farmers (1994) provided specific calculations for balancing nutrient losses by artificial inputs.

Epilogue

Calling the Expanse a Home

Now, vainglorious,
He calls the expanse a home and awful Nature, friend.
——Ursula Bethell, "By Burkes Pass" in O'Sullivan (1997:36)

Intent on romanticizing neither their landscape nor their way of life, high-country families understand country not only in visual or panoramic terms but also in grounded interactive terms where cultural practices embody socially and geographically situated experience, knowledge, and skill. They resist the idyllic representations and pastoral nostalgia that often characterize modernist literature, art, and media portraits of peripheral zones such as theirs. In this sense landscape is not for specular consumption, a commodity process Allen Batteau has analyzed in national-park formation in the Appalachians as "appropriating nature" (1990:100). The lessees who shaped my understanding of location in, and connection to, place taught me to see landscape not solely as scenery with its distinctive textures, colors and light, but equally as inhabited by and embodied in stock and humans. I learned to look at a hillside with an eye for the pinpricks of sheep and cattle, for faint traces of fence lines and tracks, for a musterer's potential beat. I learned to see the inscriptions of people and stock on country, and I have sought the inscriptions of country on people and stock.

In *Imposing Wilderness* Roderick Neumann (1998:20) writes, "The representation and appreciation of landscape, then, initiated the development of an insider/outside duality, where the outsider commanded all-encompassing visual control over a nature free of human labor." He draws upon Raymond Williams's division of the landscape into the two spheres of practical and aesthetic at the moment of transition to industrial capitalism, and he points to the emergence of a duality in which the insider travels *in* landscape, whereas the outsider can only travel *through* landscape. In this way, the runholder who works country does not engage in the separation and observation that characterize the outsider's visual consumption (cf. Williams 1973:129). Working country is a way of "achieving a bodily knowledge of the world" and connecting with place that unseats environmentalist celebrations of nature as a "world of original things" (White 1996:172).

Similarly, Simon Swaffield (1993:61) in his sensitively postmodern exploration of the high-country landscape as an Umberto Ecoesque roselike symbolic figure demonstrates that its meanings are historically shifting, unstable, plural, and overlapping. Those meanings have shifted from "landscape as picture" (1777-1900), to "landscape as landform, soil pattern, regional setting" (1900-1960), to "landscape as scenery" (1960-1970), to "landscape as environment" (1970-1980), and finally to "landscape as experience, symbol and ideology" (1980-1990). Most recently landscape has become a site for identity construction (1990-1995), and at the end of the decade, it takes the form of capitalized nature through sustainable development and biodiversity conservation. Swaffield notes that landowners and managers, whom he defines as having some kind of control of land in the high country, tend not to use the term "landscape" at all; he is right, and I note that these meanings of "landscape" above apply to their sense of "country," the preferred term. "Visual ownership" and the mystique of the high country are external constructions, modes of imaginative appropriation, imposed on a landscape that is being commodified as scenery in ways alternative to pastoral farming, and commodified as an urban retreat from modernity through environmentalism and recreation; human and stock habitation are considered intrusive in the landscape, and scenery in its visual sense exclusive of the pastoral presence.

When I returned to New Zealand in May 1993 to participate in an East Asia-Pacific Mountain Association symposium at Lincoln University, I learned that the South Island High Country Committee had responded to an emergent language of "resource management," "multiple use," and "sustainable development" by producing their own high-country coffee table volume, large enough in size, according to the chairman Bob Brown, to make it difficult to shelve. Widely circulated and displayed, *Spirit of the High Country: The Search for Wise Land Use* was distributed to national and local government bodies, lobbying groups, stock firms, and to libraries, secondary schools and banks throughout the nation. The twenty-six page, glossy, photographic essay makes the richness of high-country life and affinity for the land explicit (and desirable) by stressing the mutuality of production and conservation. To redefine their public image, the Committee writes in direct, practical prose, "Like most things in life, it is a matter of getting alongside other people to see where they are coming from. We hope that this publication helps to achieve that" (1992:1).

Their title *Spirit of the High Country* asserts farming resilience and fortitude through challenging climatic and economic conditions, as well as the kind of attachment Ruth Dallas expresses when she writes that her spirit "fills the familiar valleys" and is "folded deep in the hills" (in McNaughton 1986:174). The connection the Committee makes is both strategic and sincere as it implicitly takes on some of the linked questions that have defined my analysis. How are local epistemologies of place constitutive of identity? How does the physical high-country environment and the experiences through which it is known frame who a people imagine themselves to be? How might their cultural existence in all of its aspects—from the ecological to the social, from systems of production to systems of signification, from its latent, unvoiced to its overt and expressively voiced qualities—be understood as patterned, motivated and cognitively coherent in a bicultural nation state? How is country an extension of its people, and a people an extension of country? In exploring these questions, I too have sought to get alongside these families, as they strategically reassert their kinship with culturally induced "nature," "to see where they are coming from" and in doing so to understand their experientially based concept of country, "habitus" in Pierre Bourdieu's sense of the term, and the multiple contexts from which it derives and to which it responds.

Throughout I have tried to remain ethnographically grounded as I have explored the relationship between physical setting, social activity and people's cultural constructs as together they comprise newly indigenous understandings of country. As illustrated especially in my discussions of toponymy and topography, and of the high-country submissions before the Waitangi Tribunal, I have sought to test and challenge those indigenous understandings of self presented implicitly in language use, and more explicitly in rhetorical constructions to an interested public, culminating perhaps in the High Country Committee's *Spirit of the High Country*. In analyzing high-country legal testimony in the Ngai Tahu land-claims case, I documented how the runholders speak about and construct belonging and suggest that high-country geography, as a central template in the conceptual systems of its inhabitants, provides them with a way of thinking about their cultural distinctiveness. The high country is a point of origin rather than location. In drawing upon an array of materials from geological maps to resource surveys to vernacular categories to conversations with local people, I examined the discursive practice of naming and its use as a way of dividing up the land to designate location and create meaningful spaces, as well as to understand high-country inhabitants' conception and construction of place. Here I elicit the semiotic qualities of narratives by transforming boundary talk into its cognitive components. Social cartography is measured from the homestead; thus, communicative acts reveal that despite landforms of high relief, people speak of "coming into" and "going out" from the homestead, and these divisions override geomorphologic divisions of down and up. The distinction between front and back country reinforces the importance of placement, direction and distance over altitude. Reflecting use patterns, front country is closer to the homestead and back country is further away, mapping respectively onto winter and summer grazing country. As argued, beyond the containment of the mountains, outside of this space bounded by landforms, and "out of the gorge" is the rest of the nation, both rural and urban; a language of verticality is used as one goes "down country" or "down the road" just as one goes "up into the high country" or lives "up the gorge" [valley]. As inhabitants live further "up the gorge," deeper into remoteness and altitude, they become "more high country." Ways of talking about place specify not only location, but also use and belonging. Knowing the place (knowing the "where") means knowing the self (knowing the "who").

Knowing Country

High-country sociocultural practices are defined not only by the constraints imposed by the physical environment as Mona Anderson's *A River Rules My Life* attests, but also by a geographic space that is shaped into "country" by its inhabitants' social and conceptual experience. Visually and in practice, the high country is a pastoral landscape not a nondomesticated wilderness. The interplay between physical geography and humanly constructed country is readily apparent in agricultural practices and philosophies that selectively combine traditional and progressive techniques. While the basic principles of pastoral farming remain relatively unchanged from those outlined by Samuel Butler in his 1863 directive tract *A First Year in Canterbury Settlement*, they suggest a continuous shift, peaking in the 1970s toward greater management of land through more intensive cultivation and technological intervention, and the introduction of biological measures for the control of invasive species in the 1980s. The station has become a farm. These changes include more and better forage for stock throughout the year with greater subdivision of blocks and paddocks, intensive topdressing, the production of silage as supplementary winter feed, and the creation of run plans that have closed off to stock those remote leasehold areas at the highest elevation, and have set off recommended areas of protection for wetlands and species preservation. While progressive farmers leave agricultural college armed with the language of stock units and maximization of profit, the knowledge that is most explicitly valued and culturally elaborated is best described as stockmanship. Essential to the stockmanship in which one "knows animals" is high-country mustering.

A good stockman knows where stock are likely to go, and a good musterer "knows how geography works." Without exception, runholders and shepherds explained that mustering ability is innate, like the eye in a good working dog; people who do not have it would have been culled like sheep before they ever could "go out" on an autumn muster. The principles are the same as those for the smaller blocks where all shepherds start out: don't get ahead of the sheep above, make lots of noise, and cover the country. Covering the country means knowing where to be positioned on a knob to be able to see up and down, and more importantly it means being willing to zigzag up and down the hills regardless of how tiring the extra steps might be. Knowledge of stock movement, and being able to move like stock, is crucial. Merinos, for example, especially older ones, can be cunning. Even though stockmanship is believed to be in large part innate, all farmers impressed upon me the significance of one man passing on his local knowledge of the country to another in ways that naturalize social experience. A musterer does not invent his beat; it is assigned, and while directions given seem vague and terse, they are condensed with strategic significance.

Inheritance patterns, which provide for male-focused intergenerational continuity, serve as a vital mechanism for passing on cultural knowledge of "the country" and of stock movements within this country. Clearly, inheritance is about patrimony and property transfer, especially male ownership of stock and freehold land, and of the rights to a lease. Estate planning typically ensures that all children will receive equally, yet it usually ensures that sons will have the opportunity to stay on the land because the integrity of the estate rather than the interests of individual heirs is often at stake. While sons usually inherit the opportunity to farm, daughters inherit other kinds of assets, such as family investments or cash. Inheritance patterns provide a system in which the continuous transmission of cultural knowledge is preserved from generation to generation. A young man's apprenticeship begins seriously when he finishes school. Every man has to serve his apprenticeship, ideally by working on a variety of other high-country properties, under the guidance of his father's old schoolmates, as well as by working at home sometimes under his father's head shepherd, eventually to take his place. When I returned to Canterbury in the antipodal spring of 1990, one son had returned home to work for the year before going further afield for his farming experience. Another was leaving Christ's College to go home and work for the year until he decided "what he is going to do." In another valley, both sons were working on staff during my September visit; one was about to go to Lincoln to study for a commerce degree. By 1998 seven out of seven sons, from seven properties, were either in agricultural college or working as shepherds.

The Routine of Sociocultural Existence

The station has been my analytic unit, but its edges are conceptually complex and culturally elaborated in many ways: through the importance attached to its physical boundaries, to continuity of ownership, and to its name and reputation. Boundaries delineating the station often coincide with the nuclear family and suggest that the high-country sheep station is really the family farm and not, as in the past, a managed estate. The shift from a system of absentee owners and managed properties to owner occupation began in the Rakaia when the three Ensor brothers took up farming three generations ago. Station diaries and journals from the 1930s indicate large staffs—several shepherds, rabbiters, a station cook, a teamster and later governesses and "domestics." The size of the stations has been reduced through retirement programs and the introduction of run plans, and through subdivisions of property into separate nuclear units by splitting male-sibling bonds. The division may involve a legal division of a pastoral lease, or where that is not feasible, a separation of stock and financial management. One property has bought an additional lease and another the paddocks from next door to sustain second sons. Sometimes, but not often, two brothers, even if married and with children, may farm a property together; this is difficult and unlikely to succeed. As properties have divided, decreased land holdings and improved carrying capacity in individual stations graze more sheep on less land. Staffs are smaller. Today the largest property in the Rakaia valley has two full-time shepherds. The station cook is now the runholder's wife, and on some properties, the hired men cook at least one meal a day for themselves. As the farming economy tightens and the New Zealand dollar drops in value, more high-country women are taking the place of a hired man in the paddocks and in the woolshed. Although the division of stations suggests salient brother/brother dyads, continuity of residence on a property from generation to generation suggests salient father/son dyads. While many parents leave the property when they retire, others move from the homestead to the cottage, until their grandson returns and marries, displacing them from the cottage and beginning the developmental cycle again.

Station families are reputed to be cliquish and snobbish with impenetrable social networks, a consequence not of attitude but, I argue, of historical legacy, the specificity of pastoral farming conditions and demands, and social isolation. Physical remoteness constrains social interaction and scatters individuals thinly across an open, extensive, and sometimes inaccessible landscape while also demanding interdependency in times of need and fostering respect for privacy precisely because of that interdependence. Isolation also dictates the contexts for social interaction and shapes social activity with farm and family as the primary spatial and social units that define daily interactions within and between the nuclear family and hired men. Neighbors, both kin (for example, a brother or a cousin) and nonkin, who inhabit the same valley or share the same access road, are usually members of a geographically recognized community. Stock and station agents, telephone repairmen, the weekly transport and mail truck, the farm adviser, a child's correspondence-school teacher—as members of the institutions that provide vital services to isolated people—may break the social routine when they pay a visit.

Ritualized social activities defined by the farming community or the boarding schools or the national calendar punctuate farming life and operate to structure lives also. Few families opt out of these events regardless of the degree of pleasure they might take from them. Social activities are oriented around outdoor sports, especially horseback riding, skiing, and jetboating. Families try to work to free holidays or weekends when children are home from chores. The push to finish tailing by the Christchurch Show in November and to finish silage by Christmas is an attempt to free up January for time with children. Often children who are home during a busy time put on their work clothes and boots and pitch in as they go on the payroll. Neighbors and relatives know about each other's children: how well they have done in school, what exams they will sit, when they are rowing or playing in a rugby game. People work hard at knowing about each other's children. Commitment to family is "what life is all about." Beyond that, trips to town or to the dog trials, the agricultural and pastoral show, a high-country field day or the ewe fair take these families into a more intensely social world comprised of other high-country families who know what to say to each other. While social events dot the calendars so do overlapping school events. As children grow older, they are encouraged to aim for success in sport as a particular kind of challenge. A glance through the Christ's College register reveals recurrent lists of high-country names under sports photos. Also valued is school leadership, rewarded through the duties of prefect or head prefect. Boarding schools are vitally cohesive, as high-country children are well represented in rugby and rowing, two of the more respected sports, and parents travel long distances in inclement conditions to watch their sons play. Two men in one valley and a brother-in-law who graduated in the same year were in the first rugby fifteen at College during their secondary school days. Sons and daughters follow fathers and mothers in school residence houses and sports teams, although contemporary families make difficult decisions as they consider both state and private schools as options for their children.

Children's age cohorts sort parents into social groups. Between 1941 and 1957 a generation of seventeen children was born into the families of then three stations in the Rakaia valley. In interviews with that generation, now scattered mainly in the South Island with three in the North Island and one in Australia, they spoke of their childhood in terms of their age mates. Same-age and usually same-sex children linked properties together even in instances where they attended different boarding schools from their cousins. The links between children were especially apparent at marriage when a cousin and friend might be asked to be a maid of honor or a best man. Later in the life cycle, the same cousin might be selected as a godparent. Since the age span was in some cases wide within a given property, the children saw themselves falling into two generations. A similar pattern has replicated itself today with the older children who are now finishing boarding school and attending university or coming home to work linked in different age-sets from the younger children who ranged in age from two to seventeen in 1987 and from five to twenty-eight in 1998. Parents with younger children find themselves together at school events and take turns running children home from and back to boarding school. Social boundaries remain tightly defined and integrated as much from circumstance, familiarity and habit as by choice. If physical atomization defies regionalism and fosters localism, free movement and integration along the spine of the Southern Alps create bonds that are reinforced even within the urban environment. In this way mountains, like Epeli Hau'ofa's Polynesian "sea of islands" are points of connection rather than separation (1993).

Working the farm is the dominant cultural practice. People talk about where they are in the farming cycle at any given time and what needs that creates for labor and for cooking. Ideas are fixed about what is possible on the land. Unchanged daily and annual routines organize lives around the demands of the agricultural cycle, modified in turn by the weather. Farm diaries record the minutiae of daily life in detail, which provides an unbroken link with an ancestral past. Sound memories of familiar country and an intimate understanding of the logic and repetitiveness of the farming cycle enable farmers to reconstruct sequences quite accurately. Entered also are statistics—numbers of sheep or cattle bought and sold, numbers of lambs marked and tailed, numbers of sheep shorn. In reading old station diaries, I am surprised not so much by contrast as by constancy. Now, as then, the pig and hens need to be fed each day, winter firewood needs to be cut and stacked, sheep droppings shoveled out from under the woolshed grates, dogs run, mobs of sheep moved from one paddock to another, fences mended. On rainy days farmers manage accounts; they once filled out large paisley-bound ledgers in fountain pen with the names of employees, their jobs, their wages, their taxes; but now rainy days are as likely to be committed to figuring out the Goods and Services Tax or entering farm accounts into the

computer. Much more mustering and coming and going into the back country
fill the pages of station diaries in the 1930s, 1940s and 1950s before land was
scaled back. But the names of creeks, of hillsides, of some blocks and paddocks
remain much the same. Categories of sheep requiring different management
practices remain constant. Shearing (although now in August rather than January) and tailing are labor-intensive times. The Christchurch Show, the local dog
trials and agricultural and pastoral show, the stock sales continue and remain a
focus. Homesteads are altered, trees felled and planted, gardens expanded and
redesigned. The Landrover still gets taken down to town once a year for a war-
rant of fitness. Farm diaries record the coming and going of children to boarding
school in a regular pattern, and the cold snowy southerlies and dry dusty
nor'westers are documented as respectively they move over Turtons Saddle or
down the valley.

The routine of farm and family suggests the constraint of stasis that station
families resist through constantly seeking new challenges. They might be improved stock management, such as breeding a finer or cleaner fleece or higher
lamb yield, or mastering computer-software programs for computer modeling in
land management. Members of the current generation, like their parents, are
pragmatic innovators. In a world where much remains the same, they seek always to move forward and in this way perpetuate pioneer, colonial British
strengths of entrenched hardwork, pragmatism and moderation that were revived
in the 1930s (cf. Brooking 1986:44, 47).

The introduction of electricity and of the telephone, and improvements in
the maintenance of the road are significant changes in the Rakaia valley that
alter routines and ease old challenges. Large freezers, electric washing machines, microwaves and other "mod-cons" make life easier for women but still
the routine of cooking regulates their lives. Mona Anderson said of Mount Algidus that it had changed from her day because of the introduction of these ap-
pliances; but one of her successors still cooked for twelve shearers plus her family for fifteen days each spring, while minding her four children, teaching them
correspondence school, and managing the household. Men and women travel
more with improved road conditions. Children can come home from school
more often. Trips to Methven to the garden club or to play golf are habitual.
Increased involvement in the Agricultural and Pastoral Association, the collie
club, or the High Country Committee is eased. But this is a shift in intensity
more than in type of involvement. Peter Ensor in the 1960s chaired the High
Country Committee and made trips to Wellington and to Ashburton on behalf of
the runholders; his brother Duncan was president of the Corriedale society and
of the Royal Agricultural Show. In this valley, voluntary and political involvement has always drawn out the inhabitants for participation in local and national
affairs. Despite improved access, one still has to think about the road. There is
no corner shop and the drive out is time and wear and tear on a vehicle. Improved telecommunications in the 1990s through facsimile machines and elec-
tronic mail outspeed the weekly transport-truck run. In spite of the changes, the
gorge families still construct the lives they live; they create their own activities,
and without complaint construct meaning in a vast environment that does not

provide it for them. Here beyond the television and the newspaper or magazine, there is no escape into mass culture.

Focused social and emotional energy is invested in immediate nuclear households. Commitment to one's spouse is total and divorce is said to happen less often than in cities. In the words of one adult daughter, "It is too complicated to get divorced. You work and look for other solutions," accommodating differences, not so much to keep the property together but because "it is an ideal that you stay as a unit, because the farms work as units." For those women who are actively involved in farmwork outside the house, much pleasure comes from being able to work with their husbands on shared tasks. Another woman, who defines her world within the garden fence, chose to face the new homestead toward the yards and the road so that she could see what was going on at the farm; her husband had selected a site facing away from the farm and across the valley. Irrespective of whether women and men actively farm together or whether they have a sharply delineated sexual division of labor, their daily lives are punctuated with each other's presence. In these highly routinized days, meals and morning and afternoon teas ensure that husbands and wives see each other throughout the working days. This was not always so as historical records make clear, especially when men were "out the back" for long periods of time, but it is undeniably the pattern for contemporary farm families. The spatial blurring of domestic and public domains is continuous and exceptional. The painful absence of children at boarding school from age ten or eleven (from age eight in the 1950s and 1960s) until the end of secondary school strengthens the husband/wife dyad and accounts for how often women and men named their spouse as their "best mate" (friend) or as "coming first." It may be partly because of children's absence that high-country breaks from work revolve around them. Trips to town always include a stop at the school to visit even if only for twenty minutes during a lunch break. School events are seldom missed. Although infrequent, weekends when children come home are treasured and visitors are discouraged then and during school holidays, which are family times. In 1987 when I had a leave-of-absence to begin long-term fieldwork, I was encouraged not to arrive during January because of the school holidays, although as our ties have deepened, the restriction no longer holds. This is a child-focused society and lives are defined by the family's developmental cycle.

Because the physical environment defies transformation and control through management, runholders' linguistic and cultural practices evoke adjustment to and engagement with place. While the ruggedness of cold, harsh, bleak country is acknowledged, it is seldom challenged or exaggerated. The relationship of runholders and their shepherds to their country is irreducibly adversarial or oppositional. They work throughout their lives both consciously and unconsciously to create a niche for themselves within the landscape. Their language is peppered with cliches of resilient resignation: "You can't think about it," "You've got to get on with it," "You can't look behind, only forward." In a vast environment, people move forward by controlling their domestic environs and their stock absolutely; they do not expect to make a lasting or visible dent far from the homestead, rather they survive in spite of the conditions with the

expectation of moving forward or holding ground but never of moving back-
wards. The farming life here is continually talked about as if it is "an opportunity," and the daily motif is one of "challenge." Always high-country inhabitants
look for a challenge. In this sense, their pioneer legacy of achievement is unbroken.

§ § §

When I returned to the Rakaia in 1990, the majestically beautiful scale of the
country and the utopically remote and constant quality of station life surprised
me yet again. Scale consistently defies my memory—I cannot take it away with
me nor retain my sense of it when not in it. Photographs do not capture it because they crop off the periphery, frame the landscape in miniature, and because
they portray landscape selectively as scenery, as visual. I found myself on this
fourth research trip, as on the first, reluctant to go to town, and turning off the
main highway up the gorge road toward the Arrowsmiths was always a tremendous relief, like going home. I took comfort in the (for me) imagined safety and
seeming stability of this place; I took comfort in coming home as much to my
field family as to the gorge, remembering it as much through sounds as through
vision—the alert barking of the working dogs in their kennels as I turned by the
mailbox to head up the drive, the constant proximate nor'west winds in the pine
breaks, and the distant gentle, the sometimes rough, rush of the Rakaia River as
it gauged rainfall and alpine snowmelt. The pull of the high country draws back
sons and daughters to live and visit, draws back its inhabitants after trips away
and overseas with a predictably steady and magnetic force. Even those like me,
who have no claim of belonging, are drawn back.

   On each return to the Canterbury high country, I find that I have forgotten
what the valley is like. Certainly, some of the allure has worn off with each trip,
as the unfamiliar becomes familiar, and the exotic less so. The illusory utopic
quality of station life began at times to feel provincial and stifling to me. Life is
public, and yet also acutely nucleated and private because people are careful not
to "live in each other's pockets." It hums on with unerring predictability. The
social boundaries are rigid and unyielding; Mary Douglas's (1982) notion of
"strong group," "strong grid" seems applicable in a way that I had not noticed
before.[1] Some people in the valley would ask me: What will you find to write
about to fill a book? or Aren't families everywhere the same? It was difficult to
say that even the assumption that social units elsewhere are families marks a
late-twentieth-century people as distinct. This is a world where social structures
and roles are clearly defined. Women and men marry, have children, and grandchildren. Their work lives are defined by the regular demands of the agricultural
cycle and predictable and predictably unpredictable climatic cycles. The stimuli
that frequent interaction with radically different others excite, are absent. Lack
of awareness and of comprehension of difference yield a formulaic homogeneity
in dress, social habits, assumptions, outlook, and language that are hard to defy.

   These passages on my personal reentry to the field evoke what continues to
surprise me visually, sensorily and experientially in this place despite its ethnographic familiarity. They evoke the ways in which the families' affinity for the

place and their sense of security have begun to become through habituation my own. And they are evocative of the stigmatized quality of formulaic patterns of social life. My own ambivalent sentiments about the rigidity of this world were echoed by the sons and daughters who had grown up here and left, often those with the harshest assessments and revealingly acute external perceptions, of high-country life. One couple who would never return to rural Canterbury spoke of its provinciality, of the exclusivity of its networks, of the narrow notions of what is acceptable and unacceptable. A university daughter, who does not want to return to live, told me that she liked the stability; she comes home "and nothing's changed," but after a while she gets bored. Other sisters asked if I had noticed how "they" all dress the same, and all use the same formulaic expressions.

In his analysis of sentiment, place and politics among the Pintupi of Australia's Western Desert, Fred Myers (1991:286) provides what he calls a "social ontology" in which he links "the negotiated quality of Pintupi daily life and a regional system based on extensive individual ties of shared identity"; he ethnographically derives the "transcendental" from the lived world of daily experience. His analysis is appealing to me because the theoretical vocabulary he engages to discuss a small-scale, spatially dispersed, egalitarian society defined through the mythological construction of The Dreaming can be productively applied in a postcolonial context to its presumed converse—pastoral farmers, descended from nineteenth-century Anglo-Celtic settlers, whose ancestors' wealth derived from a mercantile economy, who participate aggressively in a global-market system, and who must come to terms with a colonial legacy of dispossession in a postcolonial settlement state. Unlike the generic indigenous categories of Australian Aboriginal or Maori peoples, high-country families are "not the natives of choice" (as Richard Handler [1990] so aptly put it) and are often genericized themselves, as a southern gentry, as pakeha elites, or as European or Anglo-Celtic interlopers in Aotearoa/New Zealand. My ethnographic cases engage these alpine settler descendants whose rural-elite status is fading. The emergent quality of their identity, like their environment, as constantly negotiated deserves attention.

This places the anthropologist in a curiously slippery spot. One is not expected to be kind when one works with those who are "not the natives of choice," but to be sharply critical seems an unfair response to the kindness and hospitality of a host community that is infinitely more complex and emotionally layered than stereotypes suggest. From the subaltern point of view, to be sympathetic to "my natives" opens me to criticisms of being co-opted, of being blindly gullible as a North American outsider, and of overromanticizing people and place. An Otago runholder cautioned me precisely on this point. As chair of the High Country Committee, he urged me to provide a corrective to romanticized images, "to put on a negative hat," and to say things, as I may have done, that may not be comfortable for the high-country community to hear. In this way my "objectivity" would be enhanced, and my work could be "of use." An integrated analysis of behavioral, linguistic and symbolic forms when applied to a so-called "elite" settler-descendant population does in some sense bring anthropology back home as we cast our analytic net over those who on the surface, as pakehas, seem much like "us" (I assume a homogeneity—and hegemony—of audience) and yet can be approached usefully as people concerned with belonging and keeping, with blood and land, with family and farm, as a people struggling to create a dynamic sense of their own lineally defined and historically derived cultural identity with links to place. My intent has been to mediate polarizations between "traditional" and "modern" societies (see Jolly and Thomas 1992) especially in a context where "under conditions of domination, self-representations are constructed oppositionally" (Keesing 1993:588).

Today indigenous materials are used to document, sustain and create cultural heritage, and to provide insight into the cultural values of the Southern Alps at a moment when cultural and traditional land-use issues are at stake, and the conflicts over the management of Crown pastoral mountain lands seem endless and irreconcilable as they reveal competing rhetorics of nature conservation and biodiversity preservation. Policy aspects in the environmental regulatory arena pertaining to the human impact on mountains as well as in the changing symbiotic relation of mountain environments and human populations are centrally important (cf. Allan et al. 1988; Salzman 1991). Environmental, socioeconomic and cultural systems shape and influence each other and within this interaction constituencies compete in mountain areas; none of these systems, including the ecosystem, is static. We need to understand the different and overlapping cultural systems and environmental concerns of those who engage in extractive or consumptive activities (forestry and range management) and those who engage in preservation (conservationists). Their differences need to be interpreted, not assumed or polarized. Cronon writes, "the choice is not between two landscapes, one with and one without a human influence; it is between two human ways of living, two ways of belonging to an ecosystem" (1983:12), but it is between *more than* two landscapes, two human ways of living, or two ways of belonging in a pluralized field of ecological narratives. Finally, the transformation of mountain and rural ecosystems and their socioeconomic aspects includes the urban creation of the outdoors by recreationists, tourists, and overseas investors.

Ngai Tahu land claims before the Waitangi Tribunal (1988-1990) provoked high-country identity claims to place embedded in continuity of settlement and intensity of place attachment. At stake also is environmentally sustainable development that takes into account both natural resources and cultural heritage. Such a focus examines mountain-grassland cultures not in terms of ecological anthropology with its emphasis on material conditions[2] but in terms of place attachment, defined by Setha Low as "the symbolic relationship formed by people giving culturally shared emotional/affective meanings to a particular space or piece of land that provides the basis for the individual's and group's understanding of and relation to the environment" (1992:165). As the "conservationist" replaces the "pioneer," ambivalence persists in the perceptions people have of these mountains and their inhabitants. Mountain pastoralists find themselves part of a process of rural peripheralization in which their alpine vision (embracing human habitation in the frontier) and national visions (linking national identity to a vast wilderness empty of human habitation and needing protection) collide (cf. Grenier 1992). Parallel processes occur in the Australian Alps where graziers find it necessary to evoke the importance of their cultural heritage to the Australian ethos (see Dominy 1997a; Good 1992a, 1992b; Scougall 1992). Such concerns afflict other alpine transhumant[3] ranching communities, especially in the U.S. and Canadian West (Trigger 1996). Family farms are under severe economic pressure and in decline especially in light of the removal of government subsidies in the 1980s, and corporate agriculture and tourist development is on the rise.

Writing from the perspective of an interested New Zealand public who owns these leasehold lands and "must look at what's in it for us," journalist Bruce Ansley (1994:25) identifies the newest players in those constituencies interested in high-country lands. They are wealthy overseas buyers primarily from Asia and more recently the United States. Faced in some instances with unsustainable land in a state of ecological collapse, especially in the semiarid rabbit-prone Mackenzie country, runholders are forced to sell their freehold and leases. Ansley cites figures provided by the Campaign Against Foreign Control of Aotearoa, based on figures from the Overseas Investment Commission, that suggest that six high-country stations sold out to foreign owners in the three years between 1991 and 1994, involving 70,000 hectares of "our best scenic territory"; Ansley suggests that those sales have been kept quiet (Ansley 1994:18). They include some of the best-known high-country stations— Lilybank and Flock Hill, for instance; Ansley calls the former "one of New Zealand's high country legends" (1994:21). When Ansley was writing, Erewhon, the station across from Butler's Mesopotamia, and its neighboring Mount Potts, were also on the market.

Flock Hill High Country Resort, Grasmere Lodge, and Lilybank Lodge now have websites for prospective tourists and conferees as these consumers participate in an economy of weekend spectatorship.[4] Selling difficulty of access and views of "Canterbury's rugged high country," Flock Hill's High Country Explorer Tour carries tourists from Christchurch by coach to the foothills, by jetboat up the Waimakariri to the station's eastern boundary, and by "Your Mercedes Benz Unimog All Terrain Vehicle" through the 35,000-acre property and along a section of the "original stage coach road" to lunch in the Lodge's garden restaurant. With its "Small Luxury Hotels of the World" seal, Grasmere Lodge sells itself and freezes its past as a "traditional New Zealand high country station," "nestled in the mountains . . . . a country retreat of unrivalled charm and distinction." Web browsers read its history to learn about "former owners of this historic farm" after whom the seven guestrooms (with en-suite bathroom) are named. This included David McLeod who visited yearly until his death in May 2000 and, we are assured, "understood the need for farms to diversify these days."

Furthest away from its sheep-station history, and most geographically remote of these properties, is "luxurious" Lilybank Lodge for "elite and discerning guests" with nightly charges of NZ$560.25 per person (double occupancy) including a "gourmet 4 course dinner, full New Zealand breakfast, lunch, morning and afternoon teas." The home page reassures international readers that the

Lodge "provides all the latest communications technology and services including satellite CNN information direct from the USA" and juxtaposes this with "seclusion from the busy world" in "an inspiring wilderness landscape." The tyranny of distance is a tyranny no more; rather it is a new form of "ecological capital" (Escobar 1996:42). Lilybank Lodge offers an unusual product, the fusion of seeming, but historically linked, opposites—luxury and wilderness, connection and disconnection—and the website states that "the place has changed little in 130 years" except for the accommodation as mountain lodge replaces homestead hub. Only pioneer Captain William Sibbald whose footsteps are to be "followed" is mentioned as part of a cultural heritage to be marketed, and Betty Dick's family and the former station buildings are now invisible.[5] A Dundee sea captain, Sibbald is "legendary" and colorful and dates from an era (1868-1888) that is "one of the most romantic and stirring in Lilybank's early recorded history (Pinney 1971:156; Dick 1964:18). Such a reinvented history is perhaps more readily marketable to international visitors than that of a high-country family embodying habitation and cultural intrusion. Lilybank clearly is not marketing its history; what is marketable are outdoor pursuits in the wilderness: trout fishing, big-game hunting, heli-skiing, mountaineering and deer farming, as well as nature walks and horseback riding; and the serenity of seclusion in a imposing high-end lodge of natural stone and timber. The urban visual ownership of the high country that Inverary runholder John Chapman identified has now been replaced by a different kind of visual ownership in the commodification of seeing—that of international tourists in search of comfort and adventure in an imagined wilderness, a replication of the safari endeavor at the end of the twentieth century (Clifford 1998), a fantasy of urban elites with alienated relationships to land (Cronon 1996:79). Overseas investors have become part of the solution as they rescue the high country economically and displace the runholders.

Recently, some colleagues and I in the Association for Social Anthropology in Oceania worked together to document the diverse ways in which the past is represented in the Pacific. We spoke to a distinctively Pacific historiography, an island historiography that is, as we collectively noted, "ferociously local," strongly geographic in its referents, narrated through stories, and embedded in a politics of self-representation. High-country settler descendants, although players in a colonialist history against which te iwi Maori write, construct their being also in oppositional and strategic ways that have begun to seem distinctively Pacific. In my reflections on changing pakeha self-representations, I hope I have met Roger Keesing's challenge to reveal that "most contemporary humans do not live their lives in bounded worlds, each defined by 'a culture'—if, indeed, humans ever did. The meanings we create together, the texts we write collectively, are evanescent as well as perspectival; the social worlds in which we create them are multiple, complex, open and changing" (1987:175). Our focus must be, he suggests, on "the political processes in which meanings are contested, not simply shared, in which alternative ideologies are negotiated and strategically used." Despite the powerful imagery of social and physical containment characterizing high-country lands, the landscape is similarly permeable, "multiple, complex, open and changing."

My ethnographic research has examined the historically and socioculturally situated ways in which settler-descendant families make themselves at home in a challenging, expansive, and sparsely populated environment. As William Cronon (1993) has argued so convincingly, this kind of particularism of time, place, and landscape demands a focus on the complex, dynamic and diachronic interplay of cultural and environmental systems. Station families resist inclusion as settler descendants in a static, generic, imperialist discourse by acknowledging their changing relationship with land through the generations, and their differences from urban and other rural people. Their discursive agency is a particular expression in Aotearoa/New Zealand of Nicholas Thomas's (1994) notion of "colonialism's culture," and of Arturo Escobar's notion of "ecological culture" (1996:62) that is constitutive of social relations, forces of production, and the idea of nature. Now, as ecotourism and overseas ownership commodify the high country's cultural heritage and landscape, transnational interests and imperatives increasingly define the kinds of landscapes that are at stake for conservation and preservation. In this context and in an arena of shifting land legislation and negotiation of the Conservation estate with the Department of Lands, families articulate endogenous logics of sustainability, which are used locally to resist transnational "sustainability" as the newest form of ecological imperialism. These logics assert that country is an induced landscape, a constantly shifting ecology subject to ongoing transglobal ecological, economic and social processes. Simultaneously their contest for habitation engages collective rhetorics of self making and place making; it is also a contest for pastoral land definition premised upon the imperative of managing a changing ecology in which the authenticity of place is as illusory as the authenticity of culture.

Notes

1. The highly organized social arrangements characterizing the strong-group/strong-grid quadrant of Douglas's typology in *Natural Symbols* exalt society above the self, offer clearly articulated social structures, make symbolic distinctions between the inside and the outside, and offer group accumulation of wealth (as in cathedrals in the Middle Ages). Strong social boundaries emphasize control through ritual, and privilege rationality and regulative mechanisms (Douglas 1982:14). Where grid is strong the value of material things is affirmed.

2. Mountain-land environments invite examination in terms of a processual ecological anthropology that resists earlier neoevolutionist and neofunctional approaches dominating cultural ecology and instead examines the complex interrelation of social and cultural patterns with the environment (Orlove 1980:255). Focusing on the mechanisms of change as well as the mechanisms that link environment and behavior, processual ecological anthropology views culture and ideology "not as epiphenomena but as proximate causes which shape human action" and in this sense foreshadows the emergence of the anthropology of place; it does, however, provide a materialist examination (Orlove 1980:257).

3. See Gisbert Rinschede (1988), "Transhumance in European and American Mountains," for a discussion of transhumance forms that are based not on geographical typologies but rather on cultural bases of classification. New Zealand pastoralism fits his description of temperate-ascending transhumance where seasonal movement of livestock

takes place between a base homestead and summer-range higher-altitude grazing areas; grazing is year-round (1988:98). See also Groetzbach (1988:26) concerning altitudinal zonation. For nonsymbolic analyses, see, for example, Bennett (1969), Clark (1963), Ross (1986), Strickon (1965) and Webb (1936). Argentina and South Africa present other parallels.

4. See <http://www.flockhill.co.nz> (10 June 1998);
<http://nz.com/ SouthIs/GrasmereLodge/index.html>,
<http://nz.com/SouthIs/GrasmereLodge/bthistor.htm >,
<http://nz.com/SouthIs/GrasmereLodge/btmeetin.htm> (22 Aug. 2000);
<http://www.lilybank.co.nz/content.htm>,
<http://www.lilybank.co.nz/content.htm /accom.htm> (14 Sept. 1998).

5. Both Pinney (1971) and Betty Dick (1964:13-27) would dispute the implication of Sibbald's discovery. Dick's historical research lists John Holland Baker, a surveyor, the Studholme Brothers of Waimate, Edward Owen in 1863, and William H. Ostler in 1864 as successively having purchased the lease, but with no evidence of stocking it with sheep, at least according to Julius Von Haast's observations while traveling through Lilybank (1964:17). Sibbald took over the Lilybank runs in 1869.

Glossary

Back country—usually uncultivated, remote grazing land or remote land retired from grazing.

Beat—the area from which a musterer clears sheep, usually on steep hill blocks or in the back country. Musterers are assigned top, middle or bottom beats.

Block—a large area of rural land.

Break or break fence—a portable, usually electric, fence that temporarily subdivides a paddock to ration fodder and control grazing.

Draft—to separate certain animals from a mob.

Drench—forcing an animal to take liquid medicine.

Fan—natural (alluvial) fan-shaped features in Canterbury and Otago resulting from the deposition of shingle from hill creeks in flood. Often tussock-covered or cultivated and containing good land.

Fleece—the wool off the sheep, removed in a single piece.

Freehold—absolute possession of land.

Front country—paddocks and cultivated hill country closer to the homestead.

Greywacke—pre-Cretaceous indurated sandstones that form the underlying rock structure of the high country, especially in Canterbury.

Hieracium—hawkweed that chokes out the native tussock grasses because as an exotic it has no competition.

Hogget—a young sheep not yet a year old.

Homestead—the owner's residence on a sheep or cattle station.

Te iwi Maori—the tribe, the people.

Kowhai—tree on riverbanks and forest edges with yellow spring flowers.

Lucerne—alfalfa, cereal plant with bluish-purple flowers.

Mahinga kai—areas where food is gathered, encompassing fishing, bird, mineral and forestry rights.

Manuka—common New Zealand scrub brush or tree; tea tree.

Matagouri—Wild Irishman, thorny bush, growing in thickets in South Island open country.

Mob—a number of sheep or cattle running together.

Muster—"to collect the sheep together on a block of country, for shearing, drafting, or moving them" Acland (1975:375).

Nor'west—fohn wind that blows from the northwest, especially strong with spring rains.

Number eight—fencing wire.

Packie—person who cares for the packhorses that carry supplies.

Paddock—an enclosed area of land, usually fenced or bounded naturally, and smaller than a block, but larger than a yard (Acland 1975:377).

Pakeha—not Maori, European, usually of Anglo-Celtic descent.

Paradise ducks—brightly colored New Zealand duck.

Preemptive right—a runholder's right to secure his homestead and improvements through a prior right to buy certain areas defined by him (Pinney 1981:6).

Rangatiratanga—chieftainship, tribal authority.

Run—the land area comprising a station, usually under pastoral lease. Traditionally a numbered unit of grazing land acquired from the Crown under pastoral licence or lease. The term also applies to farming sheep, as in "running sheep." Also, shearers divide their days into two-hour "runs."

Runholder—station owner. Used interchangeably with "lessee," "woolgrower," and "farmer," to refer to high-country pastoralists; an antiquated term derived from land units called "runs."

Shelterbelt (or windbreak)—a tree row protecting buildings, stock, or paddocks from the wind.

Shingle—loose, sharp rock or shale, at high altitude or the base of streams and creeks.

Staple—the length and degree of fineness of wool fiber.

Snowfence—a fence confining the sheep to lower areas during the winter.

Stock unit—a conversion ratio equivalent to a ewe, whereby a hogget is 0.6 su, a cow 6.0 su, a calf 3.0 su, and a bull 5.0 su (New Zealand Meat and Wool Board's Economic Service 1985:10).

Tangata whenua—people of a given place; literally, "people of the land." The iwi holding mana whenua, or customary authority, over an identified area.

Toe-toe—in the same genus as South American pampas; "very large endemic grasses up to 6 m high with long leaves, their edges made sharp with silica, which form dense clumps, especially in damp or swampy places" (Fleet 1986: 119).

Tops—or high tops, high summer country.

Turangawaewae—"standing place for the feet," or the rights of the tangata whenua (Kawharu 1989:314).

Tussock grasslands—mid latitude grasslands of bunch-grasses characterizing the eastern half of the South Island, dominated before European contact by perennial bluegrasses and fescues with understory of herbaceous plants and other grasses (Clark 1955).

Two tooth—a young sheep that has cut its first two teeth (18 to 22 months old) and often so designated after its first shearing.

Wether—castrated male sheep.

Woolshed—building in which sheep are shorn adjacent to the station yards.

References

Abu-Lughod, Lila. 1993. *Writing Women's Worlds: Bedouin Stories*. Berkeley: University of California Press.

Acheson, Carole. 1985. Cultural Ambivalence: Ngaio Marsh's New Zealand Detective Fiction. *Journal of Popular Culture* 19:159-174.

Acland, I., G. D. 1975 [1930]. *The Early Canterbury Runs*. Fourth edition, revised by W. H. Scotter. Christchurch: Whitcoulls.

Adams, Jane. 1993. Resistance to "Modernity": Southern Illinois Farm Women and the Cult of Domesticity. *American Ethnologist* 20:89-113.

Allan, Nigel J. R., Gregory W. Knapp, and Christoph Stadel, eds. 1988. *Human Impact on Mountains*. Lanham, MD: Rowman & Littlefield.

Anderson, Grant, ed. 1980. *The Land Our Future: Essays on Land Use and Conservation in New Zealand in Honour of Kenneth Cumberland*. Auckland: Longman Paul.

Anderson, Mona. 1963. *A River Rules My Life*. Wellington: A. H. & A. W. Reed.

———. 1965. *The Good Logs of Algidus*. Wellington: A. H. & A. W. Reed.

Angelo, A. H., and W. R. Atkin. 1977. A Conceptual and Structural Overview of the Matrimonial Property Act 1976. *New Zealand Universities Law Review* 7:237-258.

Ansley, Bruce. 1989a. High Country Boom, *New Zealand Listener* 15 July:16.

———. 1989b. Stock and Station, *New Zealand Listener* 15 July:22.

———. 1994. High Country Sell-Out, *New Zealand Listener* 16-22 July:18-25.

Ardener, Edward. 1987. 'Remote Areas': Some Theoretical Considerations. In *Anthropology at Home*. Anthony Jackson, ed. ASA Monographs, 25. Pp. 38-54. London: Tavistock Publications.

Ardener, Shirley, ed. 1993. *Women and Space: Ground Rules and Social Maps*. Revised edition. Cross-Cultural Perspectives on Women, 5. Oxford: Berg.

Ashcroft, Bill, Gareth Griffiths, and Helen Tiffin. 1989. *The Empire Writes Back: Theory and Practice in Post-Colonial Literatures*. London: Routledge.

Ashdown, Michael, and Diane Lucas. 1987. *Tussock Grasslands: Landscape Values and Vulnerability*. Wellington: New Zealand Environmental Council.

Aspinall, Jerry. 1993. *Farming under Aspiring: An Autobiography*. Alexandra: MacPherson Publishing.

―――. 1996 Cooperative Management of Mountain Lands. In *Mountains of East Asia and the Pacific*. Mary Ralston, Ken Hughey, and Kevin O'Connor, eds. Pp. 172-175. Canterbury, NZ: Centre for Mountain Studies, Lincoln University.

Aubrey, Ben, and Alastair Ensor. 1994. Project FARMER: Towards Farming in the Twenty First Century. January.

Axtell, James. 1985. *The Invasion Within: The Contest of Cultures in Colonial North America*. New York: Oxford University Press.

Baker, Louisa. 1894. *A Daughter of the King*. Chicago: F. Tennyson Neely.

Ball, Murray. 1986. *Footrot Flats: The Dog's ~~Tail~~ Tale*. Lower Hutt, NZ: Magpie Productions.

Barker, Lady (Mary Anne). 1883 [1870]. *Station Life in New Zealand*. London: Macmillan and Company.

Barnes, Trevor J., and James S. Duncan, eds. 1992. Introduction: Writing Worlds. In *Writing Worlds: Discourse, Text and Metaphor in the Representation of Landscape*. Pp. 1-17. London: Routledge.

Barr, Hugh. 1986. Awatere Valley. *Federated Mountain Clubs of New Zealand Bulletin* 88:18-24.

―――. 1994. Pastoral Leases―The Last Great Public Land Carve Up. *Federated Mountain Clubs of New Zealand Bulletin* 118:26-32.

Basso, Keith H. 1988. "Speaking with Names": Language and Landscape Among the Western Apache. *Cultural Anthropology* 3:99-130.

Batteau, Allen W. 1990. *The Invention of Appalachia*. Tucson: University of Arizona Press.

Bedford, Richard, ed. 1979. *New Zealand Rural Society in the 1970s: Some Trends and Issues*. Studies in Rural Change, 1. Christchurch: University of Canterbury.

Behar, Ruth. 1986. *Santa Maria del Monte: The Presence of the Past in a Spanish Village*. Princeton: Princeton University Press.

Belich, James. 1990. Review Article: Hobson's Choice. *New Zealand Journal of History* 24:200-207.

Bell, Jim, and Malcolm Douglas. 1992. Control and Management of Rabbits. In *Guide to Tussock Grassland Farming*. Mike Floate, ed. Pp. 93-98. Mosgiel, NZ: AgResearch, Invermay.

Bender, Barbara. 1993. Introduction: Landscape―Meaning and Action. In *Landscape: Politics and Perspectives*. Barbara Bender, ed. Pp. 1-17. Providence, RI: Berg.

Bennett, John W. 1969. *Northern Plainsmen: Adaptive Strategy and Agrarian Life*. Chicago: Aldine.

Berdoulay, Vincent. 1989. Place, Meaning and Discourse in French Language Geography. In *The Power of Place*. John A. Agnew and James S. Duncan, eds. Pp. 124-139. London: Unwin Hyman.

Berg, Hans. 1973. Sheep Rearing in South Greenland: An Analysis of the Present-day Problems of Adaptation. In *Circumpolar Problems: Habitat,*

Economy and Social Relations in the Arctic. Gösta Berg, ed. Pp. 29-37. Oxford: Pergamon Press.

Bland, Peter. 1979. *Primitives.* Wellington: Wai-te-ata Press.

Booth, Pat. 1988. Learning to Live with the Waitangi Tribunal: The Facts Without Fear. *North and South,* June:75-87.

Boston, Jonathan, and Martin Holland, eds. 1987. *The Fourth Labour Government: Radical Politics in New Zealand.* Auckland: Oxford University Press.

Bourdier, Jean-Paul, and Nezar Alsayyad. 1989. *Dwellings, Settlements, and Tradition: Cross-Cultural Perspectives.* Lanham, MD: University Press of America.

Bowden, M. L. et al. 1983. *The Rakaia River and Catchment: A Resource Survey.* Vol. 1. Christchurch: North Canterbury Catchment Board and Regional Water Board,

Bradley, Tony, and Philip Lowe, eds. 1984. *Locality and Rurality: Economy and Society in Rural Regions.* Norwich: Geo Books.

Bradsen, John. 1994. Legislating for Sustainable Land Management: An Imposition or a Necessity? In *Proceedings of the 1994 New Zealand Conference on Sustainable Land Management.* Pp. 99-104. Canterbury, NZ: Lincoln University, 12-14 April.

Brasch, Charles. 1980. *Indirections.* Wellington: Oxford University Press.

Brinkley, Alan. 1992. The Western Historians: Don't Fence Them In. *New York Times Book Review,* 20 September:1, 22-27.

Brooking, Tom. 1986. "Larkrise to Littledene": The Making of Rural New Zealand Society, 1880s-1939. Manuscript. University of Otago.

Brooks, Frances J. Aaron. 1987. *Conflicts between Commercial Farmers and Exurbanites: Trespass at the Urban Fringe.* Ithaca: Cornell University Press.

Brown, Bob. 1994. Pastoral Futures: The Challenges to Sustaining the Land While Maintaining Livestock Industries and Lifestyles. In *Proceedings of the 1994 New Zealand Conference on Sustainable Land Management.* Pp. 37-40. Canterbury, NZ: Lincoln University, 12-14 April.

Brown, R. J. 1993. Sustainable High Country Farming. In *Grasslands for Our World.* M. J. Baker, ed. Pp. 325-327. Wellington: Scientific and Industrial Research Publisher.

Brush, Stephen B. 1976. Introduction: Cultural Adaptations to Mountain Ecosystems. *Human Ecology* 4(2):125-133.

Burdon, G. L. 1987. *Tall Hills and Tight Lines.* Alexandra, NZ: G. L. Burdon.

Burdon, R. M. 1938. *High Country: The Evolution of a New Zealand Sheep Station.* Auckland: Whitcombe & Tombs.

Butler, Samuel. 1964 [1863]. *A First Year in Canterbury Settlement.* A. C. Brassington and P. B. Maling, eds. Auckland: Blackwood & Janet Paul.

————.1987 [1872]. *Erewhon or Over the Range.* Auckland: Viking Press.

Carrier, James. 1992. Occidentalism: The World Turned Upside-down. *American Ethnologist* 19:195-212.

Carrington, C. E. 1950. *The British Overseas*. Cambridge: Cambridge University Press.

Carsten, Janet, and Stephen Hugh-Jones. 1995. Introduction. In *About the House: Lévi-Strauss and Beyond*. Pp. 1-46. Cambridge: Cambridge University Press.

Carter, Ian. 1986. Recent Developments in Rural Research: An Overview, and the New Zealand Experience. Paper presented to New Zealand Rural Economy and Society Study Group. Canterbury, NZ: Lincoln College, 2 July.

Carter, Paul. 1989. *The Road to Botany Bay: An Exploration of Landscape and History*. Chicago: University of Chicago Press.

Centre for Resource Management 1983. *Pastoral High Country: Proposed Tenure Changes and the Public Interest—a Case Study*. Lincoln Papers in Resource Management, 11. Christchurch: University of Canterbury and Lincoln College.

Chambers, Erve, and Setha M. Low. 1989. Introduction. In *Housing, Culture and Design: A Comparative Perspective*. Setha M. Low and Erve Chambers, eds. Pp. 3-9. Philadelphia: University of Pennsylvania Press.

Chapman, John. 1996. Interaction of Recreational Visitors and Pastoral Residents in the Mid-Canterbury High Country, New Zealand. In *Mountains of East Asia and the Pacific*. M. M. Ralston, F. F. D. Hughey and K. F. O'Connor, eds. Pp. 207-210. Canterbury, NZ: Centre for Mountain Studies, Lincoln University.

Chibnik, Michael, ed. 1987. *Farm Work and Fieldwork*. Ithaca: Cornell University Press.

Clark, Andrew Hill. 1955. The Impact of Exotic Invasion on the Remaining New World Mid-latitude Grasslands. In *Man's Role in Changing the Face of the Earth*. William L. Thomas, Jr. ed. Pp. 737-762. Chicago: University of Chicago Press.

Clark, Manning. 1963. *A Short History of Australia*. New York: Mentor Books.

Classer Registration Committee. n.d. *Classer Registration*. Classer Registration Committee, New Zealand Wool Board, Wellington.

Clendon, Jane. 1988. Protecting Open Space: The Queen Elizabeth National Trust. *Review: Journal of the Tussock Grasslands and Mountain Lands Institute* 44:23-27.

Clifford, James. 1983. On Ethnographic Authority. *Representations* 1(2):118-146.

———. 1986. On Ethnographic Allegory. In *Writing Culture: The Poetics and Politics of Ethnography*. James Clifford and George E. Marcus, eds. Pp. 98-121. Berkeley: University of California Press.

———. 1988. *The Predicament of Culture: Twentieth-Century Ethnography, Literature and Art*. Cambridge: Harvard University Press.

———. 1998. *Routes: Travel and Translation in the Late Twentieth Century*. Cambridge: Harvard University Press.

Cohen, Anthony P. 1982. Belonging: The Experience of Culture. In *Belonging: Identity and Social Organisation in British Rural Cultures*. Institute of

Social and Economic Research. Social and Economic Papers, 11. A. P. Cohen, ed. Pp. 1-17. Newfoundland: Memorial University Press.

———. 1986. Preface. In *Symbolising Boundaries: Identity and Diversity in British Cultures*. A. P. Cohen, ed. Pp. viii-x. Manchester: Manchester University Press.

———. 1987. *Whalsay: Symbol, Segment and Boundary in a Shetland Island Community*. Manchester: Manchester University Press.

Cohen, Anthony P. ed. 1982. *Belonging: Identity and Social Organisation in British Rural Cultures*. Newfoundland: Memorial University Press.

———. 1986. *Symbolising Boundaries: Identity and Diversity in British Cultures*. Manchester: Manchester University Press.

Cole, John W. 1971. *Estate Inheritance in the Italian Alps*. Research Reports, No. 10. Amherst: University of Massachusetts, Department of Anthropology.

———. 1978. Cultural Adaptation and Socio-cultural Integration in Mountain Regions. In *Society and Environment. The Crisis in the Mountains*. David C. Pitt, ed. Papers in Comparative Sociology, 8. Pp. 155-186. Auckland: University of Auckland, Department of Sociology.

Cole, John W., and Eric Wolf. 1974. *The Hidden Frontier: Ecology and Ethnicity in an Alpine Valley*. New York: Academic Press.

Comaroff, John. 1989. Images of Empire, Contests of Conscience: Models of Colonial Domination in South Africa. *American Ethnologist* 16:661-685.

Comaroff, John, and Jean Comaroff. 1992. *Ethnography and the Historical Imagination*. Boulder, CO: Westview.

Conway, Jill Ker. 1989. *The Road from Coorain*. New York: Vintage Books.

Cooper, Frederick, and Ann Stoler. 1989. Introduction: Tensions of Empire: Colonial Control and Visions of Rule. *American Ethnologist* 16:609-621.

Corballis, Richard, and Vernon Small. 1985. New Zealand Cartoon Strips. *Journal of Popular Culture* 19:175-189.

Cowlishaw, Gillian. 1999. *Rednecks, Eggheads and Blackfellas: A Study of Racial Power and Intimacy in Australia*. Ann Arbor: University of Michigan Press.

Crapanzano, Vincent. 1985. *Waiting: The Whites of South Africa*. New York: Random House.

Creed, Gerald, and Barbara Ching. 1997. Recognizing Rusticity: Identity and the Power of Place. In *Knowing Your Place: Rural Identity and Cultural Hierarchy*. B. Ching and G. Creed, eds. Pp. 1-38. New York: Routledge.

Cronon, William. 1983. *Changes in the Land: Indians, Colonists and the Ecology of New England*. New York: Hill & Wang.

———. 1991. *Nature's Metropolis: Chicago and the Great West*. New York: W. W. Norton.

———. 1993. The Uses of Environmental History. *Environmental History Review* 37:2-22.

———. 1996. The Trouble with Wilderness or Getting Back to the Wrong Nature. In *Uncommon Ground: Rethinking the Human Place in Nature*. William Cronon, ed. Pp. 69-90. New York: W. W. Norton.

Crosby, Alfred W. 1986. *Ecological Imperialism: The Biological Expansion of Europe, 900-1900*. Cambridge: Cambridge University Press.

Cumberland, Kenneth. 1981. *Landmarks*. Surrey Hills, N.S.W: Reader's Digest Party Services.

Curnow, Allen. 1997. *Early Days Yet: New and Collected Poems, 1941-1997*. Manchester: Carcanet Press.

Denich, Bette S. 1974. Sex and Power in the Balkans. In *Woman, Culture and Society*. Michelle Z. Rosaldo and Louise Lamphere, eds. Pp. 243-262. Stanford: Stanford University Press.

Dening, Greg. 1988. *History's Anthropology: The Death of William Gooch*. Lanham, MD: University Press of America.

Dick, Betty. 1964. *High Country Family*. Wellington: A. H. & A. W. Reed.

Dominy, Michèle D. 1988. Submission of Evidence on Behalf of the South Island High Country Committee of Federated Farmers to the Waitangi Tribunal Hearings on the Ngai Tahu Trust Claim. Christchurch, December 5, 1988. Wai27. Document P22(e).

————. 1990a. New Zealand's Waitangi Tribunal: Cultural Politics of an Anthropology of the High Country. *Anthropology Today* 6(2):11-15.

————. 1990b. Reply to "Cultural Politics in New Zealand." *Anthropology Today* 6(4):23-24.

————. 1991. Review of *Fear and Temptation*. *Landfall: A New Zealand Quarterly* 179:363-365.

————. 1997a. The Alpine Landscape in Australian Mythologies of Ecology and Nation. In *Knowing Your Place: Rural Identity and Cultural Hierachy*. Barbara Ching and Gerald W. Creed, eds. Pp. 237-265. New York: Routledge.

Donner, William W. 1993. *Kastom* and Modernisation on Sikaiana. In Custom Today. *Anthropological Forum* (Special Issue) 6:541-556.

Douglas, Mary. 1982 [1970]. *Natural Symbols: Explorations in Cosmology*. New York: Pantheon Books.

Douglas, Malcolm, and Bruce Allan. 1992. The Tussock Grasslands. In *Guide to Tussock Grassland Farming*. Mike Floate, ed. Pp. 9-22. Mosgiel, NZ: AgResearch, Invermay.

Douglas, Malcolm, and Fraser McRae. 1992. Future Land Use. In *Guide to Tussock Grassland Farming*. Mike Floate, ed. Pp. 117-123. Mosgiel, NZ: AgResearch, Invermay.

Dowling, Basil. 1973. *The Unreturning Native and Other Poems*. Wellington: Nag's Head Press.

Durkheim, Émile, and Marcel Mauss. 1963 [1903]. *Primitive Classification*. Chicago: University of Chicago Press.

Easton, Brian. 1987. Labour's Economic Strategy. In *The Fourth Labour Government: Radical Politics in New Zealand*. Jonathan Boston and Martin Holland, eds. Pp. 134-150. Auckland: Oxford University Press.

————. 1992. Agriculture in New Zealand's Economy. In *Rural New Zealand— What Next?* L. Tim Wallace and Ralph Lattimore, eds. Pp. 2/1-2/14.

Canterbury, NZ: Lincoln College, Agribusiness and Economics Research Unit.

Eldred-Grigg, Stevan. 1980. *A Southern Gentry: New Zealanders Who Inherited the Earth*. Wellington: A. H. & A. W. Reed.

———. 1982. *A New History of Canterbury*. Dunedin: John McIndoe.

Elworthy, J. H. 1981. Are Pastoral Leases Really Necessary? *Proceedings of the 1981 Hill and High Country Seminar*. Canterbury, NZ: Tussock Grasslands and Mountain Lands Institute, Lincoln College.

Ensor, Alastair. 1994. Aims and Objectives of the Field Workshops. In *Proceedings of the 1994 New Zealand Conference on Sustainable Land Management*. Pp. 79-80. Canterbury, NZ: Lincoln University, 12-14 April.

Ensor, Hamish R. 1987. Problems and Prospects. *Proceedings of the 1987 Hill and High Country Seminar*. Special Publication, 30. Pp. 69-73. Canterbury, NZ: Tussock Grasslands and Mountain Lands Institute, Lincoln College,

———. 1993. *Rangeland Management in the U.S.A.: Implications for New Zealand's Pastoral High Country*. Canterbury, NZ: The Lincoln University Foundation.

Ensor, Peter. 1990. Many Good Years, Some Not So Good: A History of Double Hill Station. Double Hill station and author's files. Manuscript.

Entrikin, Nicholas. 1989. Place, Region and Modernity. In *The Power of Place: Bringing Together Geographical and Sociological Imaginations*. John Agnew and James Duncan, eds. Pp. 30-43. Boston: Unwin Hyman.

Escobar, Arturo. 1996. Constructing Nature: Elements for a Poststructural Political Ecology. In *Liberation Ecologies*. Richard Peet and Michael Watts, eds. Pp. 46-68. New York: Routledge.

Evans, Patrick. 1990. *The Penguin History of New Zealand Literature*. Auckland: Penguin Books.

Evison, Harry C. 1986. *Ngai Tahu Land Rights and the Crown Pastoral Lease Lands in the South Island of New Zealand*. Ka Roimata Whenua Series, 1. 2nd edition. Christchurch: Ngai Tahu Maori Trust Board.

———. ed. 1988. *The Treaty of Waitangi and the Ngai Tahu Claim: A Summary*. Ka Roimata Whenua Series, 2. Christchurch: Ngai Tahu Maori Trust Board.

Fabian, Johannes. 1983. *Time and the Other: How Anthropology Makes Its Object*. New York: Columbia University Press.

Fairburn, Miles. 1975. The Rural Myth and the New Urban Frontier: An Approach to New Zealand Social History, 1870-1940. *New Zealand Journal of History* 9:3-21.

———. 1982. Local Community or Atomized Society? The Social Structure of Nineteenth-Century New Zealand. *New Zealand Journal of History* 16:146-167.

———. 1989 *The Ideal Society and Its Enemies: The Foundation of Modern New Zealand Society, 1850-1900*. Auckland: Auckland University Press.

Fairweather, John R. 1985. White-Settler Colonial Development: Early New Zealand Pastoralism and the Formation of Estates. *Australian and New Zealand Journal of Sociology* 21:237-255.

Federated Mountain Clubs of New Zealand. 1983. *A Record of the F. M. C. Seminar on "The Future of Pastoral Leasehold Lands."* PO Box 1604, Wellington.

Feld, Steven, and Keith H. Basso. 1996. Introduction. In *Senses of Place*. Steven Feld and Keith Basso, eds. Pp. 3-11. Santa Fe: School of American Research.

Ferguson, Denzel, and Nancy Ferguson. 1983. *Sacred Cows at the Public Trough*. Bend, OR: Maverick.

Fisher, R. 1980. The Impact of European Settlement on the Indigenous Peoples of Australia, New Zealand and British Columbia: Some Comparative Dimensions. *Canadian Ethnic Studies* 12(1):1-14.

Fleet, Harriet. 1986. *The Concise Natural History of New Zealand*. Auckland: Heinemann.

Floate, Mike, ed. 1992. *Guide to Tussock Grassland Farming*. Mosgiel, NZ: AgResearch, Invermay.

Foster, Robert J. 1992. Commoditization and the Emergence of *Kastom* as a Cultural Category: A New Ireland Case in Comparative Perspective. *Oceania* 62(4):284-294.

Frake, Charles. 1996. Pleasant Places, Past Times, and Sheltered Identity in Rural East Anglia. In *Senses of Place*. Steven Feld and Keith H. Basso, eds. Pp. 229-257. Santa Fe: School of American Research.

Frame, Janet. 1966. *A State of Siege*. New York: Braziller.

Franklin, S. Harvey. 1978. *Trade, Growth and Anxiety: New Zealand Beyond the Welfare State*. Wellington: Methuen.

Gal, Susan. 1991. Between Speech and Silence: The Problematics of Research on Language and Gender. In *Gender at the Crossroads of Knowledge: Feminist Anthropology in the Postmodern Era*. Micaela di Leonardo, ed. Pp. 175-203. Berkeley: University of California Press.

Gardner, W. J. 1971. *A History of Canterbury*. Vol. 2. Christchurch: Canterbury Centennial Historical and Literary Committee, Whitcombe & Tombs.

————. 1992. *A Pastoral Kingdom Divided: Cheviot, 1889-1894*. Wellington: Bridget Williams Books.

Gee, James P. 1992. Socio-cultural Approaches to Literacy. In *Applied Review of Linguistics* 12:31-48. W. Grabe et al., eds. New York: Cambridge University Press.

Geertz, Clifford. 1996. Afterword. In *Senses of Place*. Steven Feld and Keith H. Basso, eds. Pp. 259-262. Santa Fe: School of American Research.

————. 1998. Deep Hanging Out. *New York Review of Books* 45(16):69-92.

Goldie, Terry. 1989. *Fear and Temptation: The Image of the Indigene in Canadian, Australian and New Zealand Literatures*. Kingston, Canada: McGill-Queen's University Press.

Good, Roger B. 1992a. *Kosciusko Heritage: The Conservation Significance of Kosciusko National Park.* Hurstville, NSW: National Parks and Wildlife Service.

————. 1992b. The Australian Alps. In *Les Alpes Australiennes: Revue de Géographie Alpine* 80(2-3):39-64.

Goody, Jack. 1976. Introduction. In *Family and Inheritance: Rural Society in Western Europe, 1200-1800.* Goody, Jack, J. Thirsk and E. P. Thompson, eds. Pp. 1-9. Cambridge: Cambridge University Press.

Goody, Jack, J. Thirsk, and E. P. Thompson, eds. 1976. *Family and Inheritance: Rural Society in Western Europe, 1200-1800.* Cambridge: Cambridge University Press.

Gordon, Elizabeth, and Tony Deverson. 1985. *New Zealand English: An Introduction to New Zealand Speech and Usage.* Auckland: Heinemann.

Gould, J. D. 1970. The Twilight of the Estates, 1891-1910. *Australian Economic History Review* 10:1-26.

Gowan, Elizabeth. 1985. *Heart of the High Country.* London: Grafton Books.

Graber, Linda H. 1976. *Wilderness as Sacred Space.* Monograph Series, 8. Washington, DC: Association of American Geographers.

Grace, Patricia. 1986. *Potiki.* Auckland: Penguin Books.

Graham, Jeanine. 1981. Settler Society. In *The Oxford History of New Zealand.* W. H. Oliver, ed. Pp. 112-139. Oxford: The Clarendon Press.

Grandin, Temple. 1994. Euthanasia and Slaughter of Livestock. *Journal of the American Veterinary Medicine Association* 204(9):1354-1360.

Gray, Constance, comp. 1970. *Quiet with the Hills: The Life of Alfred Edward Peache of Mount Somers.* Christchurch: Pegasus.

Gregan, J. D. 1983. Letter to the Editor, *New Zealand Times,* 12 October.

Grenier, Philippe. 1992. Introduction. In *Les Alpes Australiennes: Revue de Géographie Alpine* 80(2-3):10-36.

Griffen, Clyde. 1991. Fairburn's New Zealand: From a Vantage Point of North American Studies. *New Zealand Journal of History* 25:98-111.

Groetzbach, Erwin F. 1988. High Mountains as Human Habitat. In *Human Impact on Mountains.* Nigel J. R. Allan, Gregory W. Knapp, and Christoph Stadel, eds. Pp. 24-35. Lanham, MD: Rowman & Littlefield.

Grossmann, Edith Searle. 1910. *The Heart of the Bush.* London: Sands.

Gullestad, Marianne. 1989. Small Facts and Large Issues: The Anthropology of Contemporary Scandinavian Society. *Annual Review of Anthropology* 18:71-93.

Gully, John Sidney, comp. 1984. *New Zealand's Romantic Landscape: Paintings by John Gully.* Wellington: Millwood Press.

Gupta, Akhil, and James Ferguson. 1992. Beyond "Culture": Space, Identity, and the Politics of Difference. *Cultural Anthropology* 7:6-23.

Guthrie-Smith, Herbert. 1999 [1921]. *Tutira: The Story of a New Zealand Sheep Station.* Seattle: University of Washington Press.

Hage, Wayne. 1989. *Storm over Rangelands: Private Rights in Federal Lands.* Bellevue, WA: Free Enterprise Press.

Hall, Peter with Vernon Wright. 1987. *A Shepherd's Year*. Auckland: Reed Methuen.

Hall, Robert R. 1987. Te Kohurau: Continuity and Change in a New Zealand Rural District. Ph.D. Dissertation, Department of Sociology, University of Canterbury.

Hall, R. R., D. C. Thorns, and W. E. Willmott. 1983. *Community Formation and Change: A Study of Rural and Urban Localities in New Zealand*. Working Paper, 4. Christchurch: University of Canterbury, Department of Sociology.

———. 1984. Community, Class and Kinship: Bases for Collective Action within Localities. *Environment and Planning D: Society and Space* 2:201-215.

Hanbury-Tenison, Robin. 1989. *Fragile Eden: A Ride through New Zealand*. Auckland: Century Hutchinson.

Handler, Richard. 1990. Cultural Politics in New Zealand: Responses to Michèle Dominy. *Anthropology Today* 6(3):3-9.

Handler, Richard, and Daniel Segal. 1990. *Jane Austen and the Fiction of Culture*. Tucson: Arizona University Press.

Hanson, F. Allan. 1989. The Making of the Maori: Culture Invention and Its Logic. *American Anthropologist* 91:890-902.

———. 1997. Empirical Anthropology, Postmodernism, and the Invention of Tradition. In *Present is Past: Some Uses of Tradition in Native Societies*. Pp. 195-214. Lanham, MD: University Press of America.

Haraway, Donna. 1989. *Primate Visions: Gender, Race, and Nature in the World of Modern Science*. New York: Routledge.

Harley, J. B. 1992. Deconstructing the Map. In *Writing Worlds: Discourse, Text and Metaphor in the Representation of Landscape*. Trevor J. Barnes and James S. Duncan, eds. Pp. 231-247. London: Routledge.

Harper, Barbara. 1967. *The Kettle on the Fuchsia: The Story of Orari Gorge*. Wellington: A. H. & A. W. Reed.

Hatch, Elvin. 1992. *Respectable Lives: Social Standing in Rural New Zealand*. Berkeley: University of California Press.

Hau'ofa, Epeli. 1993. Our Sea of Islands. In *A New Oceania: Rediscovering Our Sea of Islands*. Eric Waddell, Vijay Naidu, and Epeli Hau'ofa, eds. Pp. 2-16. Suva: University of the South Pacific, School of Social and Economic Development.

Hawke, Gary. 1987. Overview of New Zealand Agriculture. In *Rural New Zealand—What Next?* L. Tim Wallace and Ralph Lattimore, eds. Pp. 1/1-1/11. Canterbury, NZ: Lincoln College, Agribusiness and Economics Research Unit.

Hawkins, D. N. 1957. *Beyond the Waimakariri: A Regional History*. Christchurch: Whitcombe & Tombs.

Hayward, John. 1987a. Environmental Reforms. *Proceedings of the 1987 Hill and High Country Seminar*. Special Publication, 30. Pp. 39-47. Canterbury, NZ: Tussock Grasslands and Mountain Lands Institute, Lincoln College.

————. 1987b. Personal Values in Land and Water Use. In *Rural New Zealand—What Next?* L. Tim Wallace and Ralph Lattimore, eds. Pp. 27/1-27/10. Canterbury, NZ: Lincoln College, Agribusiness and Economics Research Unit.

Henson, David. 1986. *The Management of Pastoral Lands: DOC/Landcorp—an Uneasy Partnership.* Federated Mountain Clubs of New Zealand Bulletin 88:24-25.

Hewitt, Kenneth. 1988. The Study of Mountain Lands and Peoples: A Critical Overview. In *Human Impact on Mountains.* Nigel J. R. Allan, Gregory W. Knapp, and Christoph Stadel, eds. Pp. 6-23. Lanham, MD: Rowman & Littlefield.

High Country Public Lands Campaign. 1995. *Last Chance to Stop High Country Sell-Off.* Pamphlet, May.

Hirsch, Eric. 1995. Landscape: Between Place and Space. In *The Anthropology of Landscape: Perspectives on Place and Space.* Eric Hirsch and Michael O'Hanlon, eds. Pp. 1-30. Oxford: Clarendon Press.

Hirst, John. 1991. Australia, Argentina and Atomization. *New Zealand Journal of History* 25:91-97.

Holcroft, Morgan H. 1940. *The Deepening Stream: Cultural Influences in New Zealand.* Christchurch: Caxton Press.

————. 1943. *The Waiting Hills.* Wellington: Progressive Society.

————. 1990. In Accordance with the Treaty. In *The Village Transformed: Aspects of Change in New Zealand.* Pp. 117-130. Wellington: Victoria University Press.

Hosken, Evelyn. 1964. *Life on a Five Pound Note.* Timaru, NZ: Evelyn Hosken.

Howard, Alan. 1990. Cultural Paradigms, History, and the Search for Identity in Oceania. In *Cultural Identity and Ethnicity in the Pacific.* Jocelyn Linnekin and Lin Poyer, eds. Pp. 259-279. Honolulu: University of Hawai'i Press.

Howe, James. 1981. Fox Hunting as Ritual. *American Ethnologist* 8:278-300.

Hufford, Mary. 1992. Thresholds to an Alternative Realm: Mapping the Chaseworld in New Jersey's Pine Barrens. In *Place Attachment.* Irwin Altman and Setha Low, eds. Pp. 231-52. New York: Plenum Press.

Hulme, Keri. 1986. *The Bone People.* London: Picador Books.

Hutching, Gerard. 1986. Keep Out! High Tension in the High Country. *New Zealand Listener*, 1 March:14-16.

————. 1987. Carving up the Country. *New Zealand Listener*, 20 June:35-38.

Ihimaera, Witi. 1988 [1986]. *The Matriarch.* Auckland: Picador.

Ingold, Tim. 1980. *Hunters, Pastoralists and Ranchers: Reindeer Economies and Their Transformations.* New York: Cambridge University Press.

Isern, Thomas D. 1992. A & P: The Agricultural Historiography of New Zealand. Paper presented at Northern Great Plains History Conference, Fargo, ND.

Jackson, Jean. 1989. Is There a Way to Talk about Making Culture Without Making Enemies? *Dialectical Anthropology* 14:127-143.

288 References

Jackson, MacD. P., and Elizabeth Caffin. 1991. Poetry. In *The Oxford History of New Zealand Literature in English*. Terry Sturm, ed. Pp. 335-445. Auckland: Oxford University Press.

James, Colin. 1986. *The Quiet Revolution: Turbulence and Transition in Contemporary New Zealand*. Wellington: Allen & Unwin/Port Nicholson Press.

Jolly, Margaret. 1992. Custom and the Way of the Land: Past and Present in Vanuatu and Fiji. *Oceania* (Special Issue) 62(4):330-354.

Jolly, Margaret, and Nicholas Thomas, eds. 1992. The Politics of Tradition in the Pacific. *Oceania* (Special Issue) 62(4).

Jones, Lawrence. 1991. The Novel. In *The Oxford History of New Zealand Literature in English*. Terry Sturm, ed. Pp. 105-199. Auckland: Oxford University Press.

Kahn, Miriam. 1990. Stone-Faced Ancestors: The Spatial Anchoring of Myth in Wamira, Papua New Guinea. *Ethnology* 29:51-66.

Kapferer, Bruce. 1988. *Legends of the People, Myths of the State: Violence, Intolerance and Political Culture in Sri Lanka and Australia*. Washington, DC: Smithsonian Institution Press.

Kaplan, Martha. 1989. Meaning, Agency and Colonial History: Navosavakadua and the Tuka Movement in Fiji. *American Ethnologist* 17:3-22.

Kawharu, Ian Hugh. 1989. Introduction. In *Waitangi: Maori and Pakeha Political Perspectives of the Treaty of Waitangi*. Ian Hugh Kawharu, ed. Pp. x-xxiv. Auckland: Oxford University Press.

Keesing, Roger M. 1987. Anthropology as Interpretive Quest. *Current Anthropology* 28:161-176.

———. 1989. Creating the Past: Custom and Identity in the Contemporary Pacific. *The Contemporary Pacific* 1:19-42.

———. 1993. Kastom Re-examined. In Custom Today. Theme Issue. *Anthropological Forum* (Special Issue) 6:587-596.

Kerr, I. G. Chris. 1982. Pastoral Leases. *Aspect*, November:4-5.

———. 1984. Pastoral Leases. *Review: Journal of the Tussock Grasslands and Mountain Lands Institute* 42:25-31.

———. 1987. Land Protection—Some Issues, Some Options. In *Proceedings of the 1987 Hill and High Country Seminar*. Special Publication 30. Pp. 1-8. Canterbury, NZ: Tussock Grasslands and Mountain Lands Institute, Lincoln College.

Knapman, Claudia. 1988. The White Child in Colonial Fiji, 1895-1930. *Journal of Pacific History* 23:206-213.

Kolodny, Annette. 1972. The Unchanging Landscape: The Pastoral Impulse in Simm's Revolutionary War Romances. *Southern Literary Journal* 5(1):46-67.

Lawrence, Denise L., and Setha M. Low. 1990. The Built Environment and Spatial Form. *Annual Review of Anthropology* 19:453-505.

Lawrence, Elizabeth Atwood. 1984. *Rodeo: An Anthropologist Looks at the Wild and the Tame*. Chicago: University of Chicago Press.

Le Roy Ladurie, Emmanuel. 1978. *The Peasants of Languedoc*. Urbana: University of Illinois Press.

Leach, Edmund. 1975. Anthropological Aspects of Language: Animal Categories and Verbal Abuse. In *Reader in Comparative Religion*. William Lessa and Evon Vogt, eds. Pp. 153-166. New York: Harper and Row.

Ledgard, N. J. 1988. The Spread of Introduced Trees in New Zealand's Rangelands: South Island High Country Experience. *Review: Journal of the Tussock Grasslands and Mountain Lands Institute* 44:1-8.

Leopold, Aldo. 1969. The Land Ethic. In *Subversive Science: Essays toward an Ecology of Man*. Paul Shepard and Daniel McKinley, eds. Pp. 402-415. New York: Houghton Mifflin.

Lerner, Bettina. 1990. Letters: The Tasaday. *Anthropology Today* 6(3):21.

Levine, Hal B. 1991. Comment on Hanson's "The Making of the Maori." *American Anthropologist* 93:444-446.

Levine, Stephen. 1990. Cultural Politics in New Zealand: Responses to Michèle Dominy. *Anthropology Today* 6(3):3-9.

Lieber, Michael. Forthcoming. The Sustainable, The Expendable, and the Obsolete. *Pacific Studies* (Special Issue) 22(3).

Lindstrom, Lamont. 1990. *Knowledge and Power in a South Pacific Society*. Washington, DC: Smithsonian Institution Press.

Lindstrom, Lamont, and Geoffrey White. 1993. Introduction: Custom Today. *Anthropological Forum* (Special Issue) 6(4):467-474.

Linnekin, Jocelyn. 1983. Defining Tradition: Variations on Hawaiian Identity. *American Ethnologist* 10:241-252.

————. 1985. *Children of the Land: Exchange and Status in a Hawaiian Community*. New Brunswick, NJ: Rutgers University Press.

————. 1990. The Politics of Culture in the Pacific. In *Cultural Identity and Ethnicity in the Pacific*. Jocelyn Linnekin and Lin Poyer, eds. Pp. 149-174. Honolulu: University of Hawai'i Press.

Linnekin, Jocelyn, and Lin Poyer, eds. 1990. *Cultural Identity and Ethnicity in the Pacific*. Honolulu: University of Hawai'i Press.

Low, Setha M. 1992. Symbolic Ties that Bind: Place Attachment in the Plaza. In *Place Attachment*. Irwin Altman and Setha M. Low, eds. Pp. 165-185. New York: Plenum Press.

Low, Setha M., and Irwin Altman. 1992. Place Attachment: A Conceptual Inquiry. In *Place Attachment*. Irwin Altman and Setha Low, eds. Pp. 1-12. New York: Plenum Press.

Lowenthal, David. 1982. Revisiting Valued Landscape. In *Valued Environments*. John R. Gold and Jacqueline Burgess, eds. Pp. 74-99. London: George Allen & Unwin.

Lutz, Catherine. 1992. *Unnatural Emotions: Everyday Sentiment on a Micronesian Atoll and Their Challenge to Western Theory*. Chicago: University of Chicago Press.

Lutz, Catherine, and Geoffrey M. White. 1986. The Anthropology of Emotions. *Annual Review of Anthropology* 15:405-436.

McAloon, Jim. 1996. The Colonial Wealthy in Canterbury and Otago: No Idle Rich. *New Zealand Journal of History* 30:43-60.

McCaskill, Lance W. 1969. *Molesworth*. Wellington: A. H. & A. W. Reed.

McCay, Bonnie J., and James M. Acheson. 1987. Human Ecology of the Commons. In *The Question of the Commons: The Culture and Ecology of Communal Resources*. Bonnie McCay and James Acheson, eds. Pp. 1-36. Tucson: University of Arizona Press.

MacDonald. n.d. MacDonald Biographical Dictionary. Canterbury Museum Archives.

McEldowney, Dennis. 1991. Publishing, Patronage, Literary Magazines. In *The Oxford History of New Zealand Literature in English*. Terry Sturm, ed. Pp. 543-600. Auckland: Oxford University Press.

McHugh, Ashley George (Judge). 1988. The Role, Structure of the Waitangi Tribunal and General Principles of the Treaty of Waitangi. Address to Annual Conference of Federated Farmers, Wellington, 20 July.

McLeod, David. 1970. *Many a Glorious Morning*. Christchurch: Whitcombe & Tombs.

———. 1972. Hardships. In *Alone in a Mountain World. A High Country Anthology*. David McLeod, ed. Pp. 153-154. Wellington: A. H. & A. W. Reed.

———. 1974. *Kingdom in the Hills: The Story of A Struggle*. Christchurch: Whitcombe & Tombs.

———. 1975. The High-Country Committee: An Early History. *Review: Journal of the Tussock Grasslands and Mountain Lands Institute* 31:72-88.

———. 1980. *Down from the Tussock Ranges*. Christchurch: Whitcoulls.

McNaughton, Howard. 1991. Drama. In *The Oxford History of New Zealand Literature in English*. Terry Sturm, ed. Pp. 271-334. Auckland: Oxford University Press.

McNaughton, Trudie, ed. 1986. *Countless Signs: The New Zealand Landscape in Literature—An Anthology*. Auckland: Reed Methuen.

McPhee, John. 1971. *Encounters with the Archdruid*. New York: Noonday Press/Farrar, Straus & Giroux.

McSweeney, Gerry. 1983. South Island Tussock Grasslands—A Forgotten Habitat. *Forest and Bird* 14(7):50-54.

———. 1994. Current Issues in the Conservation Sector and Opportunities and Challenges for Nature Tourism as a Sustainable Landuse. In *Proceedings of the 1994 New Zealand Conference on Sustainable Land Management*. Pp. 58-62. Canterbury, NZ: Lincoln University, 12-14 April.

McSweeney, Gerry, and Les Molloy. 1984. Tussockland Heritage. *Forest and Bird* 15(4):2-5.

Mahar, Cheleen. n.d. On the Moral Economy of Country Life. Manuscript.

Marcus, George E. 1988. The Constructive Uses of Deconstruction in the Ethnographic Study of Notable American Families. *Anthropological Quarterly* 61:3-16.

———. 1998. *Ethnography Through Thick and Thin*. Princeton: Princeton University Press.

Mark, Alan. 1985. Sanderson Memorial Address. Abridged version. *Forest and Bird* 16(4):30-32.

Marsh, John. 1994. Keynote Address: The Affluent Consumer beyond 2000. In *Proceedings of the 1994 New Zealand Conference on Sustainable Land Management*. Pp. 16-30. Canterbury, NZ: Lincoln University, 12-14 April.

Marsh, Ngaio. 1973 [1945]. *Died in the Wool*. Boston: Little, Brown and Company.

Marshall, Dennis. 1995. See New Zealand Minister of Lands.

Mason, Bruce. 1981. *Blood of the Lamb or Cosi Fan Poche*. Wellington: Price Milburn with Victoria University Press.

Mikaere, Buddy. 1988. *Te Maiharoa and the Promised Land*. Auckland: Heinemann.

Mintz, Sidney W. 1985. *Sweetness and Power: The Place of Sugar in Modern History*. New York: Viking.

Molloy, Brian. 1994. Conservation Values. In *Proceedings of the 1994 New Zealand Conference on Sustainable Land Management*. Pp. 87-88. Canterbury, NZ: Lincoln University, 12-14 April.

Momatiuk, Yva, and John Eastcott. 1978. New Zealand's High Country. *National Geographic* 154(2):246-265.

———. 1987 [1980]. *High Country*. Auckland: Mural Books.

———. 1989. The Runholders. *Equinox: The Magazine of Canadian Discovery* May/June:32-45.

Morris, Jim. 1994. Sustaining the Resource Base—Integrating Production and Conservation Values. In *Proceedings of the 1994 New Zealand Conference on Sustainable Land Management*. Pp. 83-87. Canterbury, NZ: Lincoln University, 12-14 April.

———. 1996a. *Different Worlds: Backcountry Yarns*. Omarama, NZ: Jim Morris, Ben Avon Station.

———. 1996b. Some Ideas on a New Direction in the Quest for Sustainable Use of Mountain Lands. In *Mountains of East Asia and the Pacific*. M. M. Ralston, K. F. D. Hughey and K. F. O'Connor, eds. Pp. 176-178. Canterbury, NZ: Centre for Mountain Studies, Lincoln University.

Mountain Institute, The. 1996. *Report of the Initial Organizing Committee of the Mountain Forum*. Spruce Knob Mountain Center, WV, 21-25 September, 1995.

Mulgan, Richard. 1989. *Maori, Pakeha and Democracy*. Auckland: Oxford University Press.

Murray, Stuart. 1998. *Never a Soul at Home: New Zealand Literary Nationalism and the 1930s*. Wellington: Victoria University Press.

Myers, Fred. 1988. Locating Ethnographic Practice: Romance, Reality, and Politics in the Outback. *American Ethnologist* 15:609-625.

———. 1991 [1986]. *Pintupi Country, Pintupi Self: Sentiment, Place, and Politics among Western Desert Aborigines*. Berkeley: University of California Press.

Nadel-Klein, Janet. 1991. Reweaving the Fringe: Localism, Tradition and Representation in British Ethnography. *American Ethnologist* 18:500-517.

Nell, Mary [Mrs. George Leslie Nell]. 1908-1912 Station Diaries. Double Hill station and author's files. Manuscript.

———. 1960. Notes on the Diaries. Double Hill station and author's files. Manuscript.

Netting, Robert McC. 1981. *Balancing on an Alp: Ecological Change and Continuity in a Swiss Mountain Community.* Cambridge: Cambridge University Press.

———. 1993. *Smallholders, Householders: Farm Families and the Ecology of Intensive, Sustainable Agriculture.* Stanford: Stanford University Press.

Netting, Robert McC., Richard R. Wilk, and Eric J. Arnould. 1984. Introduction. In *Households: Comparative and Historical Studies of the Domestic Group.* Pp. xiii-xxxviii. Berkeley: University of California Press.

Neumann, Roderick P. 1998. *Imposing Wilderness: Struggles over Livelihood and Nature Preservation in Africa.* Berkeley: University of California Press.

Newby, Howard, Colin Bell, David Rose, and Peter Saunders. 1978. *Property, Paternalism and Power: Class and Control in Rural England.* Madison: University of Wisconsin Press.

Newton, Peter. 1947. *Wayleggo.* Wellington: A. H. & A. W. Reed.

———. 1949. *High Country Days.* Wellington: A. H. & A. W. Reed.

New Zealand Association of Social Anthropologists. 1990. Cultural Politics in New Zealand: Responses to Michèle Dominy. *Anthropology Today* 6(3):3-9.

New Zealand Commissioner of Crown Lands. 1994. The Tenure of Crown Pastoral Land: The Issues and Options. Draft copy dated 18 February. Wellington.

New Zealand Conference on Sustainable Land Management. 1994a. *Field Exercise Mount Peel*, Wednesday, 13 April. Lincoln University, Canterbury, NZ.

———. 1994b. *Proceedings of the 1994 New Zealand Conference on Sustainable Land Management.* Canterbury, NZ: Lincoln University, 12-14 April.

New Zealand Department of Conservation. 1990. *Land Evaluation for Nature Conservation: A Scientific Review Compiled for Application in New Zealand*, by Kevin F. O'Connor, F. B. Overmars, and M. M. Ralston. Conservation Sciences Publication, 3. Wellington.

New Zealand Department of Lands and Survey. 1948. *Land Act 1948.* Reprinted as on 1 January 1973 with Amendments to 1984. Wellington.

———. 1979. *Land Amendment Act 1979.* No. 57. Wellington.

———. 1980. *Aerial Photograph.* SN 5688:297. Wellington.

New Zealand Department of Statistics. 1984. *New Zealand Official Yearbook.* 89th ed. Wellington: The Government Printer.

New Zealand Department of Survey and Land Information. 1999a. *New Zealand Terrain Map: Christchurch.* NZMS 262 1:250,000. Sheet 13. Wellington: Terralink.

————. 1999b. *New Zealand Topographical Map: Coleridge.* NZMS 260 1:50,000. K35. Wellington: Terralink.

New Zealand Meat and Wool Boards' Economic Service. 1985. *Sheep and Beef Farm Survey, 1983-1984: Production and Financial Analysis.* Publication No. 1928. Wellington, December.

New Zealand Minister of Lands. 1995. Crown Pastoral Lands: Proposals to Amend the Land Act 1948. February.

New Zealand Ministry for the Environment. 1991. *Resource Management Act 1991. Reprinted on 1 March 1994 with Amendments to 1994.* RS Vol. 32. Wellington.

————. 1995. *Crown Pastoral Land Bill.* No. 86-1. Wellington.

New Zealand Ministry of Agriculture and Fisheries. 1988. Rabbit and Land Management Programme. Various reports and newsletters including the Taylor/Baines study. Christchurch.

New Zealand Mountain Lands Institute. 1989. *Proceedings of the 1989 Hill and High Country Seminar.* B. T. Robertson, ed. Canterbury, NZ: Lincoln University.

New Zealand Rabbit and Land Management Task Force. 1988. *Report to the Right Honourable C. J. Moyle, Minister of Agriculture.* (Amended Impression). Mosgiel, NZ.

New Zealand Waitangi Tribunal. 1988a. *Muriwhenua Fishing Report. Report of the Waitangi Tribunal on the Muriwhenua Fishing Claim.* Wellington: Department of Justice.

————. 1988b *Submission of Evidence in the Matter of the Treaty of Waitangi Act 1975 and in the Matter of a Claim by Henare Rakiihia Tau and Ngai Tahu Trust Board.* Fourteenth hearing at College House, Christchurch, December 5-9, 1988. Wai 27. Documents K and P22(a-e).

————. 1989. *A Report on the Historical Evidence: The Ngai Tahu Claim,* by Alan Ward. Wai 27. Doc T1.

———— . 1991. *Ngai Tahu Claim Report.* 3 vols. Wellington: Brooker and Friend.

New Zealand Wooltesting Authority. n.d. Technical Information Pack. Napier.

Norman, Waerete. 1989. The Muriwhenua Claim. In *Waitangi: Maori and Pakeha Political Perspectives of the Treaty of Waitangi.* Ian Hugh Kawharu, ed. Pp. 180-210. Auckland: Oxford University Press.

Norris, Kathleen. 1993. *Dakota: A Spiritual Geography.* New York: Ticknor & Fields.

Norton, David A. 1991. Conservation of High Country Landscapes. *The Landscape* (winter):15-18.

O'Connor, Kevin F. 1978. Evolution of a New Zealand High Country Pastoral Community. In *Society and Environment: The Crisis in the Mountains.* D. C. Pitt, ed. University of Auckland, Department of Sociology.

————. 1980. The Use of Mountains: A Review of New Zealand Experience. In *The Land Our Future: Essays on Land Use and Conservation in New Zealand in Honour of Kenneth Cumberland.* Grant Anderson, ed. Pp. 193-222. Auckland: Longman Paul.

————. 1987. The Sustainability of Pastoralism. In *Proceedings of the 1987 Hill and High Country Seminar.* Pp. 161-188. Canterbury: New Zealand Mountain Lands Institute, Lincoln University.

————. 1989. The Conservation of Culture and Nature in New Zealand Mountains. In *Proceedings of the 1989 Hill and High Country Seminar.* Pp. 93-119. Canterbury: New Zealand Mountain Lands Institute, Lincoln University.

O'Connor, Kevin F., F. B. Overmars, and M. M. Ralston. 1990. See New Zealand Department of Conservation.

Ogonowska-Coates, Halina. 1987. *Boards, Blades and Barebellies.* Auckland: Benton Ross.

Olssen, Erik. 1981. Towards a New Society. In *The Oxford History of New Zealand.* W. H. Oliver, ed. Pp. 250-278. Oxford: The Clarendon Press.

Orange, Claudia. 1987. *The Treaty of Waitangi.* Wellington: Allen & Unwin.

O'Regan, Tipene. 1989. The Ngai Tahu Claim. In *Waitangi: Maori and Pakeha Perspectives of the Treaty of Waitangi.* Ian Hugh Kawharu, ed. Pp. 234-262. New York: Oxford University Press.

————. 1994. The Maori View of Sustainable Land Management. In *Proceedings of the 1994 New Zealand Conference on Sustainable Land Management.* Pp. 63-66. Canterbury, NZ: Lincoln University, 12-14 April.

Orlove, Benjamin S. 1980. Ecological Anthropology. *Annual Review of Anthropology* 9:235-273.

Orsman, H. W., ed. 1979. *New Zealand Dictionary.* Auckland: Heinemann Educational Books.

O'Sullivan, Vincent. 1997. *Ursula Bethell: Collected Poems.* Wellington: Victoria University Press.

Peace, Adrian. 1993. Environmental Protest, Bureaucratic Closure: the Politics of Discourse in Rural Ireland. In *Environmentalism: The View from Anthropology.* Kay Milton, ed. Pp. 189-204. London: Routledge.

Penz, Hugo. 1988. The Importance, Status and Structure of Almwirtschaft in the Alps. In *Human Impact on Mountains.* Nigel J. R. Allan, Gregory W. Knapp, and Christoph Stadel, eds. Pp. 109-115. Lanham, MD: Rowman & Littlefield.

Phillips, Jock. 1990. Of Verandahs and Fish and Chips and Footie on Saturday Afternoon. *New Zealand Journal of History* 24:118-134.

Pinney, Bernard. 1981. *Early Northern Otago Runs.* Auckland: Collins.

Pinney, Robert. 1971. *Early South Canterbury Runs.* Wellington: A. H. & A. W. Reed.

Pinson, Ann. 1973. The Changing Form of Herding Organization in Rural Iceland. In *Circumpolar Problems: Habitat, Economy and Social Relations in the Arctic.* Gösta Berg, ed. Pp. 57-71. Oxford: Pergamon Press.

Pitt, David C., ed. 1978. *Society and Environment: The Crisis in the Mountains.* Working Papers in Comparative Sociology, 8. Pp. 155-186. Auckland: University of Auckland, Department of Sociology.

Povinelli, Elizabeth. 1993. *Labor's Lot: The Power, History, and Culture of Aboriginal Action.* Chicago: University of Chicago Press.

Pratt, Mary Louise. 1986. Fieldwork in Common Places. In *Writing Culture: The Poetics and Politics of Ethnography*. James Clifford and George E. Marcus, eds. Pp. 27-50. Berkeley: University of California Press.

——. 1992. *Imperial Eyes: Travel Writing and Transculturation*. London: Routledge.

Pred, Allan. 1990. *Making Histories and Constructing Human Geographies*. Boulder, CO: Westview.

Read, Peter. 1997. *Returning to Nothing: The Meaning of Lost Places*. New York: Cambridge University Press.

Relph, Edward. 1991. Review Essay: Postmodern Geography. *The Canadian Geographer* 35(1):98-105.

Rennie, Neil. 1984. *Working Dogs: Breeding, Feeding, Training and Care*. Auckland: Shortland Publications.

Renwick, William L. 1987. "Show Us These Islands and Ourselves . . . Give us a Home in Thought." *New Zealand Journal of History* 21:197-214.

——. 1991. The Undermining of a National Myth: The Treaty of Waitangi, 1970-1990. Paper presented at the Annual Spring Meeting of the American Ethnological Society, Charleston, SC, March.

Rhoades, Robert E., and Stephen I. Thompson. 1975. Adaptive Strategies in Alpine Environments: Beyond Cultural Particularism. *American Ethnologist* 2:535-551.

Riley, Robert B. 1992. Attachment to the Ordinary Landscape. In *Place Attachment*. Irwin Altman and Setha Low, eds. Pp. 13-35. New York: Plenum.

Rinschede, Gisbert. 1988. Transhumance in European and American Mountains. In *Human Impact on Mountains*. Nigel J. R. Allan, Gregory W. Knapp, and Christoph Stadel, eds. Pp. 96-108. Lanham, MD: Rowman & Littlefield.

Ritvo, Harriet. 1987. *The Animal Estate: The English and Other Creatures in the Victorian Age*. Cambridge: Harvard University Press.

Rodman, Margaret. 1992. Empowering Place: Multilocality and Multivocality. *American Anthropologist* 94:640-656.

Rogers, Susan Carol, and Sonya Salamon. 1983. Inheritance and Social Organization among Family Farmers. *American Ethnologist* 10:529-550.

Rosaldo, Renato. 1989. Imperialist Nostalgia. *Representations* 26:107-122.

Rose, Deborah Bird. 1988. Exploring an Aboriginal Land Ethic. *Meinjin* 47(3):378-387.

Ross, P. J., ed. 1986. *Rangelands: A Resource Study Under Siege*. Second International Rangelands Seminar. Canberra: Australian Academy of Science.

Royal Forest and Bird Protection Society. 1984. Tussock Grasslands, Mountainlands and Rivers—60th Jubilee Year November Council Meeting. *Forest and Bird* 15(1).

——. 1995. High Country for Sale. *Conservation News* 91(May):1.

Sahlins, Marshall. 1985. *Islands of History*. Chicago: University of Chicago Press.

————. 1995. *How "Natives" Think, About Captain Cook, For Example.* Chicago: University of Chicago Press.

Salamon, Sonya. 1992. *Prairie Patrimony: Family, Farming and Community in the Midwest.* Chapel Hill: University of North Carolina Press.

Salmond, Jeremy. 1986. *Old New Zealand Houses, 1800-1940.* Auckland: Reed Methuen.

Salzman, Philip Carl. 1991. Post-Modernism and Pastoralism: Cultural Dialectics in Highland Sardinia. Paper presented at the International Congress on "Il Pastoralismo Mediterraneo," Nuoro, November.

Sapir, Edward. 1912. Language and Environment. *American Anthropologist* 14:226-242.

Savage, Deborah. 1986. *A Rumour of Otters.* New York: Collins.

Schwartz, Theodore. 1993. Kastom, Custom, and Culture: Conspicuous Culture and Culture-constructs. In Custom Today. Theme Issue. *Anthropological Forum* (Special Issue) 6(4):515-540.

Scott, D. 1977. South Island High Country: A Review of Work by Grasslands Division DSIR. *Review: Journal of the Tussock Grasslands and Mountain Lands Institute* 34:36-46.

Scotter, W. H. 1965. *A History of Canterbury.* Volume 3: 1876-1950. Christchurch: Canterbury Centennial Historical and Literary Committee.

————. 1972. Ashburton: A History with Records of Town and County. Ashburton Borough and County Councils. Christchurch: Caxton Press.

Scougall, Babette. 1992. Cultural Heritage of the Australian Alps. *Proceedings of the 1991 Symposium.* Canberra: Australian Alps Liaison Committee.

Shadbolt, Maurice. 1986. *Season of the Jew: A Novel.* New York: W. W. Norton.

————. 1990. *Monday's Warriors.* Auckland: Sceptre.

Shadbolt, Maurice, and Brian Brake. 1988. *Reader's Digest Guide to New Zealand.* Sydney: Reader's Digest.

Shanklin, Eugenia. 1976. Pastoral Images and Values in Southwest Donegal. In *The Realm of the Extra-human: Ideas and Actions.* Agehananda Bharati, ed. Pp. 27-42. Chicago: Aldine.

————. 1985. Sustenance and Symbol: Anthropological Studies of Domesticated Animals. *Annual Review of Anthropology* 14:375-403.

Shanklin, Eugenia, and Riva Berleant-Schiller. 1983. Introduction. In *The Keeping of Animals: Adaptation and Social Relations in Livestock Producing Communities.* Riva Berleant-Schiller and Eugenia Shanklin, eds. Pp. ix-xxi. Totowa, NJ: Allanheld.

Shields, Rob. 1991. *Places on the Margin: Alternative Geographies of Modernity.* New York: Routledge.

Shoard, Marion. 1982. The Lure of the Moors. In *Valued Environments.* John R. Gold and Jacqueline Burgess, eds. Pp. 55-73. London: George Allen & Unwin.

Sinclair, Karen. 1992. Maori Literature: Protest and Affirmation. *Pacific Studies* (Special Issue) 15(4):283-309.

Sinclair, Keith. 1959. *A History of New Zealand.* Harmondsworth: Penguin.

————. 1986. *A Destiny Apart: New Zealand's Search for National Identity.* Wellington: Allen & Unwin.

Smith, Henry Nash. 1950. *Virgin Land: The American West as Symbol and Myth.* Cambridge: Harvard University Press.

Somerset, H. C. D. 1974 [1938]. *Littledene: A New Zealand Rural Community.* Educational Research Series, 5. Wellington: New Zealand Council for Educational Research.

South Island High Country Committee of Federated Farmers. 1987. *High Country News.* No. 1. Timaru, NZ.

————. 1992. *Spirit of the High Country: The Search for Wise Land Use.* Timaru, NZ: South Island High Country Committee of Federated Farmers.

————. 1994. *Sustainability in the South Island High Country.* Submission to the Minister of Lands, July.

South Island Working Party on Sustainable Land Management. 1994. *South Island High Country Review.* Final Report [The Martin Report]. April.

Stegner, Wallace. 1994. The Sense of Place. Reprinted in *Hudson Valley Regional Review: A Journal of Regional Studies* 11(2):47-52.

Stewart, Kathleen C. 1996. An Occupied Place. In *Senses of Place.* Steven Feld and Keith Basso, eds. Pp. 137-165. Santa Fe: School of American Research.

Stoler, Ann Laura. 1989. Rethinking Colonial Categories: European Communities in Sumatra and the Boundaries of Rule. *Comparative Studies in Society and History* 31(1):134-161.

Strang, Veronica. 1997. *Uncommon Ground: Cultural Landscapes and Environmental Values.* Oxford: Berg.

Strathern, Marilyn. 1981. *Kinship at the Core: An Anthropology of Elmdon, Essex.* Cambridge: Cambridge University Press.

————. 1982. The Village as an Idea: Constructs of Village-ness in Elmdon, Essex. In *Belonging: Identity and Social Organisation in British Rural Cultures.* Institute of Social and Economic Research. Social and Economic Papers, 11. Anthony Cohen, ed. Pp. 247-277. Newfoundland: Memorial University Press.

————. 1991. *Partial Connections.* ASAO Special Publication, 3. Savage, MD: Rowman & Littlefield.

————. 1992. *After Nature: English Kinship in the Late Twentieth Century.* Cambridge: Cambridge University Press.

Strickon, Arnold. 1965. The Euro-American Ranching Complex. In *Man, Culture and Animals: The Role of Animals in Human Ecological Adjustments.* A. Leeds and A. Vayda, eds. Pp. 229-258. Washington: AAAS.

Strongman, Thelma. 1984. *The Gardens of Canterbury: A History.* Wellington: A. H. & A. W. Reed.

Stuart, Peter. 1971. *Edward Gibbon Wakefield in New Zealand: His Political Career, 1853-4.* Wellington: Price Milburn.

Swaffield, Simon. 1993. Naming the Rose: Observations on "Landscape" Usage and Professional Identity. *Landscape Research* 18(2):58-65.

Temple, Philip. 1979. *Stations: A High Country Novel*. Auckland: Collins.

Thirsk, Joan. 1976. The European Debate on Customs of Inheritance, 1500-1700. In *Family and Inheritance: Rural Society in Western Europe, 1200-1800*. Jack Goody, J. Thirsk and E. P. Thompson, eds. Pp. 177-191. Cambridge: Cambridge University Press.

Thomas, Nicholas. 1991. Against Ethnography. *Cultural Anthropology* 6:306-322.

————. 1992. The Inversion of Tradition. *American Ethnologist* 19:213-232.

————. 1994. *Colonialism's Culture: Anthropology, Travel and Government*. Princeton: Princeton University Press.

Thornton, Geoffrey G. 1986. *The New Zealand Heritage of Farm Buildings*. Auckland: Reed Methuen.

Torgovnick, Marianna. 1990. *Gone Primitive: Savage Intellects, Modern Lives*. Chicago: University of Chicago Press.

Trigger, David S. 1996. Contesting Ideologies of Natural Resource Development in British Columbia, Canada. *Culture* 16(1):55-69.

Turner, Victor. 1974. *Dramas, Fields and Metaphors. Symbolic Action in Human Society*. Ithaca, NY: Cornell University Press.

Tussock Grasslands and Mountain Lands Institute. 1987. *Proceedings of the 1987 Hill and High Country Seminar*. Special Publication, 30. Canterbury, NZ: Lincoln College.

Tyler, Stephen. 1986. Post-Modern Ethnography: From Document of the Occult to Occult Document. In *Writing Culture: The Poetics and Politics of Ethnography*. James Clifford and George E. Marcus, eds. Pp. 122-140. Berkeley: University of California Press.

Urry, James. 1990. The Politics of Anthropology in New Zealand. *Anthropology Today* 6(6):20-21.

Vialles, Noellie. 1994. *Animal to Edible*. New York: Cambridge University Press.

Vowles, Jack. 1987. Liberal Democracy: Pakeha Political Ideology. *New Zealand Journal of History* 21:215-227.

Wall, A. 1975 [1933]. A Sheep Station Glossary. In *The Early Canterbury Runs* by L .G. D. Acland. Christchurch: Whitcoulls.

Ward, Alan. 1989. See New Zealand Waitangi Tribunal.

————. 1990. History and Historians before the Waitangi Tribunal: Some Reflections on the Ngai Tahu Claim. *New Zealand Journal of History* 24:150-167.

Webb, L. C. 1957. The Canterbury Association and Its Settlement. In *A History of Canterbury*, Volume 1: to 1854. James Hight and C. R. Straubel, eds. Pp. 133-233. Canterbury Centennial Association. Christchurch: Whitcombe & Tombs.

Webb, Walter Prescott. 1936. *The Great Plains*. Boston: Houghton Mifflin.

Wedde, Ian, and Harvey McQueen, eds. 1985. *The Penguin Book of New Zealand Verse*. Auckland: Penguin Books.

Weiner, James F. 1991. *The Empty Place: Poetry, Space, and Being among the Foi of Papua New Guinea*. Bloomington: Indiana University Press.

West, Terry L. 1983. Family Herds—Individual Owners: Livestock Ritual and Inheritance Among the Aymara of Bolivia. In *The Keeping of Animals: Adaptation and Social Relations in Livestock Producing Communities.* Riva Berleant-Schiller and Eugenia Shanklin, eds. Pp. 93-106. Totowa, NJ: Allanheld.

White, Richard. 1985. American Environmental History: The Development of a New Historical Field. *Pacific Historical Review* 54:297-335.

———. 1991. *"It's Your Misfortune and None of My Own": A New History of the American West.* Norman: University of Oklahoma Press.

———. 1996. "Are You an Environmentalist or Do You Work for a Living": Work and Nature. In *Uncommon Ground: Rethinking the Human Place in Nature.* William Cronon, ed. Pp. 171-185. New York: W. W. Norton.

Whitehouse, Ian E. 1984. Erosion in the Eastern South Island High Country—A Changing Perspective. *Review: Journal of the Tussock Grasslands and Mountain Lands Institute* 42:3-23.

Wilcox, Leonard. 1985. Introduction to New Zealand Literature and Culture. *Journal of Popular Culture* 19:67-73.

Williams, Mark. 1990. *Leaving the Highway: Six Contemporary New Zealand Novelists.* Auckland: Auckland University Press.

Williams, Raymond. 1973. *The Country and the City.* New York: Oxford University Press.

Willis, Roy G. 1974. *Man and Beast.* London: Hart-Davis, MacGibbon.

Willmott, William E. 1985. Community at Tinui: Hearts and Boundaries. *New Zealand Geographer*, April:15-20.

Woodhouse, A.E. 1950. *New Zealand Farm and Station Verse, 1850-1950.* With an introduction by L. J. Wild. Christchurch: Whitcombe & Tombs.

Woollaston, Philip T. E., M.P. 1987 *DOC—Structure and Function. Proceedings of the 1987 Hill and High Country Seminar.* Special Publication, 30. Pp. 49-56. Canterbury, NZ: Tussock Grasslands and Mountain Lands Institute, Lincoln College.

Worster, Donald. 1977. *Nature's Economy: A History of Ecological Ideas.* Cambridge: Cambridge University Press.

———. 1992. *Under Western Skies: Nature and History in the American West.* New York: Oxford University Press.

Wylie, Jonathan. 1987. *The Faroe Islands: Intepretations of History.* Lexington: University of Kentucky Press.

Wylie, Jonathan, and David Margolin. 1981. *The Ring of Dancers: Images of Faroese Culture.* Philadelphia: University of Pennsylvania Press.

Index

About the Author

Michèle Dominy is professor of anthropology at Bard College, Annandale-on-Hudson, New York.